marcia –
cucina!

ROME

KATIE PARLA

Katie
pw

R

o

m

E

KATIE PARLA

PHOTOGRAPHS BY ED ANDERSON

A CULINARY HISTORY, COOKBOOK, AND
FIELD GUIDE TO THE FLAVORS
THAT BUILT A CITY

CONTENTS

MY ROMAN STORY 8

ABOUT THIS BOOK 11

A HISTORY OF ROME (AND HOW IT EATS) . . . 19

FRIED SNACKS AND STARTERS 70

PASTA AND SOUP 102

FISH, MEAT, AND OFFAL 162

VEGETABLES, SALADS, AND SIDES 208

PIZZA AND BREAD 238

DESSERTS 280

HOW ROME DRINKS 306

#PARLAPICKS: HOW AND WHERE TO EAT AND

             SHOP FOR FOOD IN ROME . . 322

RESOURCES 344

ACKNOWLEDGMENTS 345

INDEX 346

FOR
JOJ

MY ROMAN STORY

I'm Katie Parla, a Rome-based food and beverage writer, culinary guide, cookbook author, and serious eater since long before I had any of those job titles. If you've ever read one of my books, joined one of my food tours, or fallen into a late-night internet hole about Roman pizza (same), chances are we've crossed paths through a shared obsession with this city's singular food culture.

"Obsession" pretty much captures my relationship with the city. I landed in Rome for the first time in March 1996. I was a high school sophomore, deep into my second semester of Latin and reveling in my Junior Classical League membership. My classmates and I were on a breakneck itinerary: a dozen cities in eight days, the kind of whirlwind tour that practically dares you to retain nothing but a blur of gift shops and bus fumes. Rome in the '90s was...not cute. The city was grimy, chaotic, and under construction. Large chunks of the historic center were still dilapidated, including the block around Antico Forno Roscioli, where neighbors raised pigeons for food. Jubilee renovations were underway for the year 2000, which is to say, a decade from completion. Our group, marked by matching backpacks and the unmistakable aura of teenage cluelessness, was a walking invitation for pickpockets.

Needless to say, I loved Rome immediately—every single disorienting second of it—precisely because of its chaos. I decided then and there that I would move to this hectic and contradictory city one day.

When I got back to suburban New Jersey, I signed up for Italian classes at the local community college. I spent my high school summers in art history courses at Rutgers (nerd alert), and in college, I majored in art history, holding down two jobs to fund the future Roman life that I was sure I would lead. After graduating from Yale with a degree in the history of art and a focus on second-century sarcophagi, I packed my bags and moved to Rome, only to be greeted with a reality check. My visa application was denied, and the only job I could find was a sixty-hour-per-week, off-the-books grind that paid only 500 euros a month. It came with an eight-square-meter room, though, so at least I had a place to sleep when I wasn't working or crying.

My next gig was leading small group archaeological tours around Rome for Context Travel, which would set the tone for everything that came next. I was shaping people's experiences of the city, walking them through its layers with the irreverent but informed tone of a Jersey kid who just happened to have a thing for tombs and temples. Around the same time, I started writing about Rome, churning out guidebooks (remember those?) for Rough Guides, Time Out, National Geographic, DK, Fodor's—basically anyone who'd have me (and underpay me). I wrote or updated more than twenty books in that first decade, spending most of my waking hours pounding the pavement through Rome's many neighborhoods and obsessively cataloging every corner of the city.

But the real game-changer came when I enrolled in a master's program in 2007 at Università degli Studi di Roma Tor Vergata in "cultura dell'alimentazione e delle tradizioni enogastronomiche." That mouthful of a degree about Italy's wine and food culture nudged me away from generalist city writing and archaeology tours and toward something that had always been lurking in the background: food. I started pivoting to gastronomic tours and writing about Rome's culinary culture, and the deeper I went, the more infatuated I became with how twenty-first-century Romans were eating, drinking, and navigating their food spaces.

Even though I had started out steeped in the ancient world, I was suddenly more interested in contemporary consumption patterns and the economic and social forces reshaping Rome's food scene in real time. I was documenting a moment—actually, a movement—and I knew it deserved more than a few hundred words in a guidebook. That led to more long-form writing and eventually to cookbooks, which gave me the space to investigate Rome's foodways with the nuance and depth that they demand.

This book, my second non-guidebook about Rome, isn't merely a cookbook, though you will find recipes within these pages. It's a portrait of a city told through its food, a sensory-driven study of how Romans have lived, ruled, worshiped, and eaten across nearly three thousand years. You'll pass through kitchens and ruins, walk through suburban vineyards, and witness modern industrial remnants of slaughterhouses and wholesale markets. Along the way, you will come to understand how power, faith, politics, urbanism, and migration have shaped everything that ends up on the Roman table. Food is the narrative thread, but the real subject is Rome itself: enduring, chaotic, ever-changing, and always hungry.

If 2016's *Tasting Rome* was a snapshot—an accumulation of a decade's worth of reporting on the city for *The New York Times*, *Bon Appétit*, *Food & Wine*, *Saveur*, *Eater*, and others—this book is the deep dive. It's the next chapter, expanding beyond the bounds of neighborhood trattorie and street food stalls to trace the city's culinary story across time and space. There's more here: more recipes, more historical context, more recommendations. But also, more atten-

tion to the social and political realities that shape how and what Romans eat today. After nearly twenty years of living in and obsessing over this city, I felt it was the right moment to bring all of that together and to write something that does justice to the richness, messiness, and complexity of Rome's food culture.

ABOUT THIS BOOK

This isn't a book about "the best" of Rome. It's a book about the real Rome. And I'm here to guide you through it, one bite at a time.

Here's what's inside: The book opens with a deep dive into Rome's culinary past, spanning ancient banquets to contemporary kitchens and providing context that will change the way you see (and taste) the city's most iconic dishes. Then come the recipes, drawn from home cooks, restaurant pros, and food artisans who live and breathe Roman food culture. Each one is introduced with a headnote that explains why it matters and what makes it unmistakably Roman. Scattered throughout are features that go beyond the plate: reflections on the fetishization of the cucina povera, the rise of the city's urban dairy trade, even a look at the company building pizza ovens in Pigneto for local baking legends. At the end, you'll find my essential guides to drinking, eating, and food shopping like a Roman, from the city's best markets, bakeries, and pastry shops to its most beloved trattorie, wine bars, and gelaterie.

Recipe Organization

The chapters are divided by genre and courses to reflect the way we eat in Italy. After spending almost all of my adult life cooking and dining in Rome, I have fully adopted the multicourse daily feast. But to make this book even more fun and practical for those outside Italy, *Rome* is broken up into a thematic approach to (hopefully!) make it equally inviting to home cooks not bound to the traditional five-course meal of antipasto (starter), primo (pasta or soup), secondo (meat or fish), contorno (vegetable side dish), and dolce (dessert). I have also added tips throughout for pairing dishes in different chapters to create a whole meal.

We're kicking things off with Fried Snacks and Starters, running the gamut from street foods to small plates you might encounter at a wine bar. From there, we roll into Pasta and Soup. Because Rome. This chapter is a close look at both the canonical Roman pasta dishes like carbonara (page 107) and gricia (page 128) and the lesser-known but no less beloved ones, like Rigatoni con la Pajata (page 108) and fresh pasta variations you'll want to make from scratch. I'll tell you which shapes to use when it matters (tonnarelli for Cacio e Pepe, always!), but I also give swaps so you can cook with whatever's lurking in the pantry. And if you're ready to get your hands in some flour, I have fresh pasta dough recipes for you, from Gnocchi di Patate (page 122) to Fettuccine (page 134). The chapter wouldn't be complete without acknowledging warming soups like Stracciatella (page 131) and Minestrone (page 144) that sometimes stand in for pasta at the primo course.

The Fish, Meat, and Offal chapter explores Rome's split personality when it comes to protein: part coastal, part carnivorous, and deeply in love with the quinto quarto (the "fifth quarter"), so-called poor cuts and organ meats. There's Saltimbocca alla Romana (page 185) and Pollo alla Cacciatora (page 193), but also plenty for the offal-curious (and the offal-devoted). If you've ever wanted to cook tripe, tongue, or intestines but didn't know where to start, you're in the right place. If that's not your thing, don't worry—there's lamb, beef, and seafood, too.

Vegetables, Salads, and Sides proves that Romans, while they'd never say it out loud, are actually pretty plant-forward. Seasonal, bitter, boldly dressed vegetables are everywhere here: Pomodori a Mezzo (page 234), Carciofi alla Romana (page 229), and Verdure Ripassate in Padella (page 233) wilted in garlic and oil. These dishes cut through the richness and bring balance to the table.

The Pizza and Bread chapter is all about Rome's singular bakery culture. From Pizza Bianca (page 242) and Pizza Rossa (page 244) to Pane Casereccio (page 270), these are the carbs that built a city. Like most Roman baking, these recipes mainly use store-bought yeast and, with one exception, don't require tending to a starter.

Desserts round things out with ricotta, eggs, and seasonal fruit taking center stage. Torta di Ricotta e Visciole (page 287), Maritozzi (page 284), and Pere Cotte (page 293) are simple, satisfying, and deeply rooted in Roman ritual. You'll find everyday dolci alongside holiday standouts.

In the Appendices, there's a full breakdown of the city's drinking culture, from acqua to aperitivo. Last, there are all the #ParlaPicks compiled into a quick guide for your own visit to Rome, from trattorie and pizzerie to the best places to shop for organic produce and artisan cheese.

The Roman Kitchen

TOOLS AND EQUIPMENT

You can cook most Roman dishes pretty much anywhere with whatever gear you've got on hand. Sure, some gadgets make life easier: A Tapù is great for slicing puntarelle (page 227), although a sharp knife and patience work fine; a chitarra turns out consistently shaped Tonnarelli (page 115) better than a knife blade ever will. When baking pizza, specific baking sheets will help you nail the texture, and using a steel (instead of a pizza stone) delivers that professional-grade crust in your home oven. Whenever possible, I suggest easy substitutions for specialty equipment, but honestly, basic kitchen tools usually do the trick. The only thing I really insist on is a digital kitchen scale that measures in grams, crucial for precise pasta, pizza, and bread results. But hey, if you're a completist (or just love kitchen shopping), check out the full tool list that follows. You can snag this stuff online (see Resources, page 344), or better yet, pick them up at my favorite (and appropriately named) shop Kitchen on your next trip to Rome!

- 10- to 12-inch cast iron skillet, for frying
- Instant-read thermometer, for monitoring meat temperatures when roasting and oil temperatures when frying
- Paper towels, for draining fried foods
- Large Dutch oven or other large heavy-bottomed pot with a cover
- Medium and large sauté pans with covers
- Grill pan, for searing
- Roasting pan and rack
- Containers with covers for salting meat and proofing dough
- Small, medium, and large bowls, including a large stainless steel bowl
- Measuring cups and spoons
- Digital kitchen scale
- Potato ricer, for preparing gnocchi
- Chitarra, for cutting perfectly square tonnarelli
- Pasta machine or rolling pin, for making fresh pasta
- Fine-mesh strainer, for draining ricotta
- Food processor or immersion blender
- Tapù, for slicing puntarelle stalks
- Parchment paper, for lining baking sheets
- Baking steel or pizza stone, for baking bread and pizza
- Wire rack, for cooling baked goods
- Two 13 × 18-inch rimmed baking sheets, for pizza
- Stand mixer with dough hook, whisk, and flat beater attachments, for mixing some of the doughs and desserts
- Bench scraper, for shaping dough and cleaning up afterward
- 9-inch pie plate or cake pan and a 9 × 13-inch baking dish

INGREDIENTS

These ingredients form the backbone of Roman cooking, and each comes with a long history and has an indispensable role in the city's culinary identity. You'll find nearly all of them wherever you shop, except for pajata (that's suckling veal intestines), which, trust me, is hard enough to score even in Naples, Florence, or Milan, compelling evidence that it's the most Roman ingredient out there.

Salt

Salt has been crucial to Roman cuisine since antiquity, so much so that the ancient Via Salaria was built specifically to bring it inland from the salt pans near Ostia. The Latin word *sal* even gives us "salary," thanks to soldiers getting a salt-buying stipend called a *salarium*. While they probably weren't literally paid in salt, the connection stuck. Ancient Romans preserved meat and anchovies with salt, laying the groundwork for prosciutto and *garum*. And Romans today remain devoted salt enthusiasts. I use sea salt from Trapani—the coarse kind for salting pasta water, and fine for seasoning food as I prep, cook, and bake.

Black Pepper

Pepper arrived in ancient Rome from the Far East via the spice routes from India and quickly became a high-priced addiction. The historian Pliny even complained about Rome's pepper spending habits, but that didn't stop anyone. Unlike Sicily's cinnamon-and-clove palate, Rome runs on pepper to this day, notably in Cacio e Pepe (page 112), where its bite perfectly pairs with salty Pecorino Romano. Freshly cracked, coarsely ground, or lightly toasted, pepper technique is serious business here. Always use fresh whole peppercorns. I'm partial to the fragrant black Sarawak variety from the brand Maricha sourced from Malaysia. Toasting it compromises the aromatics so I skip that step.

Herbs

Few herbs are more iconic in Roman cooking than mint. But we're not talking just one type. Mentuccia, nepitella, and calamint are often confused, even in Italy, where names and plant varieties vary by region. In Rome, mentuccia typically refers to *Clinopodium nepeta* (also known as *Calamintha nepeta*), a wild herb with a grassy, minty, slightly oregano-like flavor. It's essential in Roman dishes like Carciofi alla Romana, where it's combined with parsley to season artichokes, and often appears in Trippa alla Romana (page 201). Nepitella is a synonym often used outside Lazio, especially in Tuscany, to refer to the same plant. The English term "calamint" usually refers to Clinopodium nepeta as well, though it can also include related species.

Confused yet? To complicate matters, mentuccia and nepitella are sometimes mistranslated as "pennyroyal" in English, but *Mentha pulegium* is a different species, toxic in large doses, and not used in cooking. If you can't find mentuccia, fresh mint is an acceptable substitute.

Parsley also plays a central role in Roman vegetable dishes. Rosemary and sage season lamb roasts, marjoram occasionally appears in soups and braises, and bay leaves are used in grilled liver and stews. Basil is used sparingly (this isn't Naples, after all) and dried oregano is mostly reserved for pizza sauces. With the exception of oregano and sometimes bay, Roman cooking favors fresh herbs added at the right moment to preserve their aroma and complexity.

Garlic

Garlic sparks endless Italian debates. Rome uses it strategically—neither as liberally as the south nor as heavily as in Italian American cooking. Instead, Romans toast it gently in olive oil for Ajo, Ojo, e Peperoncino (page 159), crush it raw into anchovy dressings, or mellow it roasted whole for slow-cooked lamb dishes. Knowing when to hold the garlic—and when to fold it—is the Roman cook's trick. It's your choice whether to togliere l'anima (remove the shoot inside, literally "remove the soul") before cooking with it. In an informal survey, I determined that most Romans do.

Pecorino Romano DOP

Sheep's milk cheese predates Rome's empire, fueling armies with its salty umami punch. Ancient Romans loved it, and Cato the Elder even mentions it in *De agri cultura*. Modern Pecorino Romano is DOP (Denominazione di Origine Protetta) certified, which guarantees that it is produced, processed, and packaged in a specific geographical area using traditional methods. Accordingly, it is made according to strict rules: ewe's milk, rennet, salt, and a minimum aging period of five months for eating, eight for grating. Salty, sharp, and slightly spicy, it defines carbonara, cacio e pepe, and amatriciana. Despite most (97 percent) of Pecorino "Romano" coming from Sardinia these days, it remains Rome's signature cheese. Look for Fulvi brand, one of the few producers still based in Rome.

Parmigiano-Reggiano DOP

Cow's milk Parmigiano-Reggiano may be from near Parma, but it found a home in Roman kitchens, too. Milder and nuttier than Pecorino Romano, it's aged ideally between twenty-four and thirty-six months. Roman cooks often blend it with pecorino to tame the saltiness of pasta dishes, or they grate it into Supplì al Telefono (page 80) and Lasagna della Domenica (page 149).

Ricotta

Technically not cheese but a whey-based dairy product (its name means "re-cooked"), ricotta dates back to when shepherds wasted nothing. It's an everyday staple: spread on bread or used to fill pasta. Roman ricotta, typically made from sheep's milk rather than cow's, also stars in festive sweets like Torta di Ricotta e Visciole (page 287). If you've got a local dairy farm or can track down Caputo Brothers Creamery ricotta, use theirs rather than the bland supermarket brands. In the US, cow's milk ricotta is by far the most common. As long as it's high quality, it makes a fine substitute for its sheep-based counterpart.

Anchovies

Romans have obsessed over anchovies for millennia, from *garum* (the ancient fish sauce, see page 205) to the dressing used for today's puntarelle salads. These salty, umami-packed little fish are often served straight up with bread and butter at wine bars and some trattorie. Quality anchovies from Spain's Cantabrian coast are particularly revered (especially in salads) and are maybe the only foreign product that Romans universally recognize as superior. Regular oil-packed anchovies work fine melted in butter for pasta sauces, but if you're eating the anchovy, uncooked or on its own, reach for the good stuff in extra-virgin olive oil. Anchovies are more about depth than fishiness, vanishing into dishes to enrich and transform without overpowering, making them indispensable to Roman cooks.

Guanciale

Guanciale is the undisputed king of Roman cured meats: fatty, funky, and utterly essential. Unlike pancetta, which is pork belly, guanciale is made from pork jowl, giving it a richer, fattier bite and a deeper flavor. These days, it's the only socially acceptable form of pork for carbonara, amatriciana, and gricia, though Romans love a good argument (see page 57). Cured simply with salt and black pepper, it releases luxurious, porky fat when heated gently in a pan. Mastering guanciale means balancing crispness and moisture. Golden, rendered bits make the difference between an average pasta and a life-affirming one. Sourcing quality guanciale in the US can be tricky. I recommend upstate New York's La Salumina and the Bay Area's Fra' Mani. Or you can substitute pancetta.

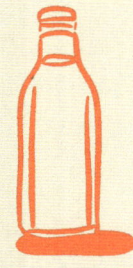

Extra-Virgin Olive Oil

Extra-virgin olive oil might be the defining ingredient of Roman (and Italian) cooking, mainly because lard's PR took a nosedive. Ancient Romans used olive oil for everything: cooking, skincare, religious rituals, even lighting up the lamps in their villas. These days, the area of Sabina, northeast of Rome, produces some of the best stuff around. My pick is Azienda Agricola Fagiolo's Cru di Cures, though

I'm equally obsessed with my friend Joy Kull's La Villana oil from Gradoli in northern Lazio.

In Roman kitchens, extra-virgin olive oil isn't only for cooking—it's a condiment, drizzled generously over vegetables, soups, and grilled meats. Skip the industrially produced junk; a proper Roman oil should taste grassy, peppery, and just a touch bitter.

When frying, I often use extra-virgin olive oil. It's a myth you can't (or shouldn't) fry in it. Frying temperature is below its smoke point. I buy in bulk, so it's not as expensive as it sounds. Otherwise, I fry in neutral oils like canola, sunflower, or grapeseed.

Canned Tomatoes

Italians might seem genetically predisposed to love tomatoes, but the fruit didn't even reach Europe until the sixteenth century; it was initially greeted with suspicion (and a few poison scares). By the eighteenth century, tomatoes had won southern Italy's heart, eventually migrating north and becoming essential in Roman dishes like Amatriciana (page 120), Coda alla Vaccinara (page 169), and countless ragùs. Whole peeled canned tomatoes (pomodori pelati), particularly from Campania, offer the rich, deep flavor essential to these dishes.

But here's the thing: The famed San Marzano DOP tomatoes aren't always worth the hype, especially considering the industry is rife with fraud, sketchy labor practices, and mafia connections. Instead, I stick with producers I've personally vetted, like Gustarosso. And don't sleep on domestic producers like organic Bianco DiNapoli tomatoes from California! Also, steer clear of canned chopped tomatoes; those are usually made from underripe rejects. Whole tomatoes let you spot and toss any questionable bits yourself. I mostly use whole canned tomatoes and crush them by hand, but a few of my pizza recipes call for passata (unseasoned tomato sauce.)

Peperoncino (Chile Pepper)

Like tomatoes, chile peppers came to Italy from the Americas in the sixteenth century. While southern Italy leans heavily on pastes and dried chile flakes, Romans prefer fresh or dried whole peperoncini, little, fiery chiles that provide brief and mild heat to balance fatty, rich dishes. Crushed red pepper flakes are common, too.

Artichokes

In Rome, artichoke fever peaks from January to early May, when the tender Carciofo Romanesco del Lazio floods local markets. This IGP (Indicazione Geografica Protetta) protected variety boasts spineless leaves and a tender, meaty base. Sure, you'll see carciofi romaneschi used loosely in labeling, but the real deal tastes unmistakably Roman, whether braised gently or fried crisp. Unless you're in Rome during artichoke season, you might struggle to perfectly replicate Carciofi alla Romana or Carciofi alla Giudia (page 86)—but hey, it's worth trying. Just look for young, tender artichokes and believe in yourself!

Chicories

Romans have an unmatched love affair with bitter greens, and no veggie holds more sway than cicoria. At the market, cicoria could mean wild or cultivated chicory, basically whatever's bitter and green. Quickly blanched, then sautéed with garlic, olive oil, and chile, cicoria ripassata in padella is Rome's go-to side dish. Puntarelle, the bolted stalks of Catalonian chicory, get shaved thin and tossed with anchovy vinaigrette into Puntarelle alla Romana (page 226), Rome's iconic winter salad. Find them at farmers' markets in the Northeast and Pacific Northwest.

Dried Pasta

Rome is proudly a dried pasta city; fresh pasta is beloved but less practical for feeding the masses. From Rigatoni con la Pajata (page 108) to Spaghetti alla Gricia (page 128), Rome's iconic pastas rely on dried shapes to handle rich, glossy sauces. Buy the highest-quality pasta you can afford. My picks are from Pastificio dei Campi, Faella, Mancini, and Benedetto Cavalieri. Besides proper shopping, the secret is mantecatura, the vigorous tossing of pasta with sauce and starchy pasta water, creating a silky emulsion that transcends the humble ingredients. There's logic behind which shapes pair best with sauces (see page 105), and Romans aren't shy about reminding you.

Eggs

In Roman cooking, eggs are transformative. Take carbonara: Eggs, guanciale fat, and Pecorino Romano emulsify into Rome's iconic creamy sauce, no cream necessary, just the balance of timing and heat control. Egg whites give pasta dough strength; yolks lend rich silkiness. Opt for pasture-raised eggs from hens fed a non-GMO, organic diet when possible. Yolk color reflects the hens' diets: Natural feeds like marigolds or corn yield yolks with vibrant orange hues. But it's worth noting that many industrial producers, both in the US and Europe, feed their hens synthetic additives to influence the color of their egg yolks!

Abbacchio (Suckling Lamb)

Romans eat lamb with reverence. The tradition of abbacchio (young milk-fed lamb) goes back to pre-Christian rituals and remains a centerpiece of Roman feasting, especially at Easter. Unlike the grass-fed lamb found in most of Italy, the milk diet produces tender, subtly sweet meat without gaminess. Befriend a farmer or butcher and snag the youngest lamb you can. True abbacchio is seasonal, fleeting, and unmatched. If that's not in the cards, regular lamb will still get you most of the way there.

Quinto Quarto

Roman meat consumption is built on offal. The city's quinto quarto ("fifth quarter") tradition originated in Testaccio's slaughterhouses, where nobles got prime cuts, leaving butchers with heads, tails, and organs. Rather than sulk, Romans turned scraps into iconic dishes. Trippa alla Romana simmers honeycomb tripe in rich tomato sauce and is finished with Pecorino Romano and minty mentuccia. Coda alla Vaccinara braises oxtail with celery and tomatoes. Rigatoni con la Pajata and Coratella (page 197) are acquired tastes, and worth the effort to seek out. Except for tripe and oxtail, which are easy enough to shop for in the US, sourcing other cuts of offal often requires charm, luck, or a resourceful butcher.

Legumes

Legumes are the backbone of traditional Roman cuisine, the kind of food that kept Romans alive before meat was a daily luxury. Chickpeas, lentils, and beans star in countless soups, stews, and pasta dishes. Pasta e Ceci (page 154) is winter comfort, chickpeas breaking down into a creamy garlic-and-rosemary-infused sauce. Its hearty cousin, Pasta e Fagioli (page 118), layers rich, earthy borlotti beans into fragrant vegetable broth. Lentils take center stage in Pasta e Lenticchie (page 136), a straightforward soup perfect for cold days. Romans favor borlotti beans, those pink-and-white speckled beauties sold already shelled at markets, more than other varieties; borlotti turn nutty and brown when cooked and are generally more common in Rome than cannellini. The recipes here call for dried beans, which deliver deeper flavor and perfect texture. Cooking times will vary depending on how long you soak the beans and how fresh they are.

Vinegar

Roman food can be rich and leave you starving for some acid to brighten things up. You won't always find it, but a few dishes like Abbacchio alla Romana (page 204) and Pollo alla Cacciatora (page 193) offer some tangy relief. Always use high-quality wine vinegar. Save the balsamic for Bolognese, Modenese, and Emilian food.

GENERAL TIPS

Look through any Italian-language cookbook and you'll see it over and over again: *q.b.*, short for *quanto basta*, or "just enough." That's the whole vibe. When I was researching this book, I spent hours in kitchens around Rome watching cooks "measure" in fistfuls, pour wine straight from the bottle into a pot, and eyeball their guanciale quantity. It was useless for me to trail behind with a measuring cup and a scale. So I ate, took notes, and committed the ingredients, methods, and textures to memory, then went home and reverse-engineered the recipes for you.

The recipes in this book were all tested in an American kitchen. Most use volume measurements to keep things approachable. But when it comes to flour—whether you're making pizza, bread, or pasta—we're talking metric. Cups and spoons are cute until your dough is too wet or your loaf collapses. Do yourself a favor and get a digital scale that measures in grams. You can find a decent one for under fifteen dollars, and it might change your life . . . or, at the very least, your pizza.

Seasoning

Salt your water like you mean it. Whether you're cooking pasta, blanching greens, or boiling potatoes, the water should taste like a well-seasoned broth. Go even saltier when boiling fresh pasta—it doesn't hang out in the water long and needs all the help it can get. If you've got the time and fridge space, salt meat the night before. Salting in layers as you cook is essential for building flavor. Trust your instincts and always taste as you cook and before serving. When I say "a heavy pinch," I mean a serious, four-finger pinch of salt.

Prep

Read the headnote and recipe all the way through before you do anything. That's where I tell you if there's an overnight marinade or some other sneaky step.

Pasta Portions and Cook Times

Most of the pasta recipes in this book are portioned at about 100 to 125 grams (3½ to 4½ ounces) per person. If it's the star of the meal, that'll feed four. If you're serving it as a primo before a secondo, it'll stretch to six.

As for doneness: al dente means "to the tooth," but in Rome, you will often find pasta cooked al chiodo, "to the iron nail," less cooked than al dente, with a serious bite. If the pasta seems undercooked to you, trust me, it's intentional.

Baking by Hand

I love mixing dough with my hands. It's the only way to really understand how the dough is changing and how it's coming together. There's something primal and deeply satisfying about it, a little window into how people cooked before stand mixers and sourdough influencers. If you're new to baking, it'll teach you how flour and water behave. If you're a pro, it'll keep you connected to your dough.

A HISTORY OF ROME
(AND HOW IT EATS)

THE IRON AGE
(1200–509 BCE)

Before diving into Rome's history, let's set one guiding principle—one that will repeat for the next twenty-seven centuries: Always be skeptical of what Romans say about themselves. They're master marketers, experts in embellishment. Case in point: the city's own origin story.

Ask any Roman when their city was founded and they'll confidently reply, "Twenty-first of April 753 BCE." That's supposedly when Romulus killed his twin brother, Remus, in a fight over real estate, a suitably dramatic start that tells you how Romans want to be seen: chosen, divine, and ruthless when needed.

Here's the scoop: Romulus and Remus were born in Alba Longa (today's Albano Laziale, about twelve miles southeast of Rome), sons of Rhea Silvia, a Vestal Virgin of Latin tribal origin forced into religious celibacy by a paranoid great-uncle. But naturally, the gods interfered: Mars, the war god, raped her, leading to twins. The babies, inconvenient politically, were tossed into the Tiber after their mom was killed. Of course, they survived, nursed by a she-wolf on a riverbank until local shepherds adopted them.

Still with me? Because it only gets sketchier from here. This whole myth feels crafted by people desperate for legitimacy. By linking themselves to Rhea Silvia, who was a distant descendant of the Trojan hero Aeneas, Romans can then connect their lineage back to the Latin kings, the Trojans, and Aeneas's mom, the goddess

Venus. Pretty fancy pedigree for what were actually swampy, illiterate Iron Age farmers.

There are glaring issues: Alba Longa isn't close to the Tiber, the generational math is dubious, Mars and Venus aren't real, human babies can't survive on wolf's milk, and Romans didn't even tell this story until centuries later. But why let facts ruin a good founding myth?

Ultimately, divine intervention wins out. Just as Venus helped Aeneas reach Italy in the aftermath of the Trojan War, Mars ensured the twins survived—at least until they argued about city planning. Each brother claimed divine bird-omen approval. Romulus spotted more (or better) birds, chose the Palatine Hill as the site to found his city, Remus mocked him, and Romulus killed Remus. Rome was born. Over the next two and a half centuries, Rome was ruled by a series of kings—some legendary, others likely real—who laid the groundwork for many of the city's core institutions, from temples to sewers to civic rituals.

Besides the myths, Iron Age Rome is murky. The archaeological record for 1200–600 BCE is sparse and fragmentary. Much of what we know is inferred from burial patterns, postholes, and material remains on the Palatine and nearby hills, which hosted a modest agrarian settlement—small huts of wattle, daub, and thatch; muddy trails, no grand amphitheaters or marble facades, just simple living spaces doubling as workshops and stalls. That said, early religious structures likely existed, including shrines and wooden temples, precursors to later monumental sanctuaries like the Temple of Jupiter Optimus Maximus on the Capitoline, whose foundations date to the late regal period. And despite the city's humble appearance, major infrastructure was already in motion. The Cloaca Maxima, begun in the sixth century BCE, was a staggering feat of engineering that drained the marshy valley between the hills, making urban life in the Roman Forum possible. It still functions as a sewer today with little maintenance! As modest as Iron Age Rome appears on the surface, these developments hint at a city already thinking ahead socially, politically, and spatially.

The community was tight-knit, governed by clan elders and warrior-aristocrats sharing power. This proto-patrician class oversaw both the land and religion, both of which were inseparable from daily life. Religion was practical, animistic, and full of *numina* (spirits) inhabiting nature. Sacrifices weren't optional; they kept you on the gods' good side, vital in a flood-prone, agrarian society.

Early Roman diets were likely practical and grain-based—we don't know for sure because they weren't writing much back then, much less publishing cookbooks. It's likely that grains such as farro, barley, and millet were boiled into *puls*, a thick porridge as common then as pasta is now. Bread was rare; flatbreads cooked on hot stones were about as fancy as it got.

Legumes must have provided essential protein and could have been seasoned with local herbs like mentuccia and oregano. Seasonal veggies, cultivated or foraged, could have rounded out meals. Olive oil and early wine pressing technology likely arrived via the Etruscans to the north and Greeks to the south, but they were precious ingredients until large-scale cultivation came during the Republic. Later Romans would distance themselves from the Etruscans, despite several early kings having Etruscan heritage. Classic Roman rebranding!

Meals were simple, cooked over open fires in clay pots or metal cauldrons. Utensils were minimal. You ate with hands or basic tools.

So no, Iron Age Romans weren't hosting elaborate banquets or debating the finer points of fish sauce. But even then, their food culture mirrored their environment: resourceful, regional, and ritualistic. As Rome grew from a cluster of huts into an urban center, its cuisine evolved, too, gradually absorbing Mediterranean and eventually global influences.

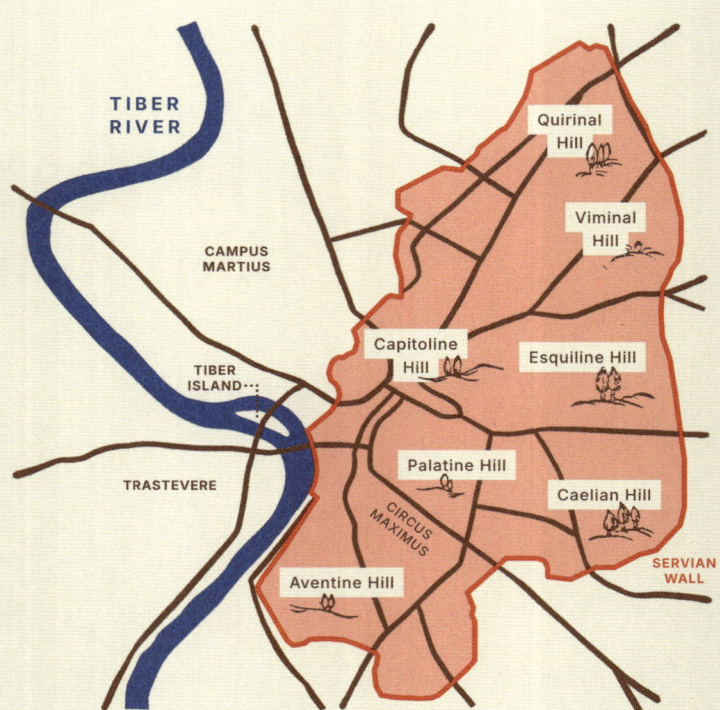

THE ROMAN REPUBLIC
(509–27 BCE)

By the time the Roman Republic got rolling in 509 BCE, Rome had moved past its scrappy hilltop origins. Those rustic Iron Age huts had been replaced by stone houses, paved streets, functioning sewers, and impressive temples springing up on the Capitoline Hill and what became the Forum. Busy livestock and produce markets were booming near the Tiber (see page 22), and Rome was quickly turning into a buzzing city.

Like most ancient societies, Rome ran on conquest and strict hierarchy. At the top sat the patricians—rich landowners claiming divine ancestry—while the plebeians, Rome's working class, farmed, crafted, fought in legions, and pretty much kept the city running. Enslaved people were crucial to daily life, handling everything from grinding grain and cooking meals they rarely tasted to tending vineyards and building the growing city.

Religion infused every aspect of Roman life, including food. The local gods—Jupiter, Juno, Janus, and

Vesta—were soon merged with Greek imports, expanding the pantheon and complicating rituals. Romans regularly provided their gods with grain, wine, and animal sacrifices, with public feasts afterward that blended community bonding and voracious eating.

But divine nourishment didn't guarantee human food security. Rome's explosive growth soon outstripped local grain supplies, leading to dependence on imports, particularly from Sicily after the First Punic War. Disrupted shipments from piracy and warfare caused food shortages and riots, prompting politicians to use *frumentationes* (grain distribution) as populist tools to secure votes and manage unrest.

As for the diet, people ate basics like grains, legumes, vegetables, and occasional meat. Bread, increasingly affordable thanks to improved milling, gained popularity but didn't replace *puls*. The elite enjoyed refined panis *candidus* (white bread), while the masses made do with darker loaves.

Legumes like lentils, chickpeas, grass peas, and favas were, again, nutritional powerhouses. Vegetables such as onions, garlic, cabbages, and turnips were staples, jazzed up with herbs. Olive oil was everywhere: cooking, dressing, fuel, and even skincare.

Dairy, particularly sheep and goat cheese, was essential to the local diet, fueling both civilians and soldiers. The available fruits diversified through contact with the Greeks, both through trade and conquest, adding apples, pears, grapes, and pomegranates. Honey was used to sweeten desserts, as sugar wouldn't appear for another millennium. The wine trade expanded as Rome encroached on and eventually conquered Magna Grecia (Greek territory in southern Italy). Beer? That was for barbarians and Egyptians.

Meat was still a luxury in the Republican era but growing in availability. Pork became dominant in all classes, while mutton and goat were common rural fare; the wealthy feasted on wild game and poultry. Beef was rare; cows were valued for their labor and milk. Fish introduced culinary sophistication with sauces like *garum* (see page 205), a funky staple condiment, while fresh seafood was mainly for coastal elites and villa owners experimenting with fish ponds. Plebians may have enjoyed perch, sturgeon, and eels from the Tiber.

By the second century BCE, villa culture boomed as patricians established massive estates not only in Rome but across Italy, powered by enslaved labor to produce wine, olive oil, and grains. This shift hollowed out the small farmer class and widened wealth gaps—a familiar pattern. Agricultural writers like Cato the Elder and Varro documented this transformation, treating food production as both an economic engine and a source of noble virtue. Their manuals weren't cookbooks, but they reveal a Roman obsession with efficiency, control, and the prestige of self-sufficiency, even if the actual work was done by others.

Republican Rome's food culture expanded as the territory did, each new conquest an opportunity to enrich the capital's table. But as military campaigns stretched farther afield and domestic politics grew more volatile, food became a tool of control. By the Republic's end, Rome was dependent on imported grain, enslaved labor, and political figures who could keep the supply flowing. A pivotal moment in this transformation came in 123 BCE when Gaius Gracchus introduced the first known *lex frumentaria,* a grain law that subsidized monthly grain sales to Roman citizens at a fixed, below-market price. It wasn't a one-off: *leges frumentariae* become a recurring populist tool, later adopted by figures like Publius Clodius Pulcher. But Gracchus' version marked a major shift in how the state engaged with food access, and it came only a decade after his brother Tiberius was killed for attempting agrarian reform.

The final decades of the Republic were marked by political chaos, civil war, and the consolidation of power under Julius Caesar and later, his adopted heir, Octavian, who would become Augustus, Rome's first emperor. Food and supply chains remained central to power. Octavian's defeat of Mark Antony and Cleopatra in 31 BCE was more than a military victory; it secured Egypt's grain fields for Rome, locking in a critical source of food for the capital's growing population. Control of the Egyptian grain supply helped stabilize Rome's breadbasket and strengthen Octavian's claim as the provider and protector of the people. In a city where bread riots were a political liability, securing grain meant solidifying power. The Republic may have died, but Rome's hunger, and its reliance on conquest to feed it, only grew.

A HISTORY OF ROME (AND HOW IT EATS)

FOOD, FAITH, AND FORA: ROME'S ANCIENT WHOLESALE MARKETS

Beneath a busy cobblestone road where buses careen toward crosswalks, two of Rome's earliest and most important food markets once thrived. The Forum Boarium and the Forum Holitorium, now mostly obscured by a wide avenue and monumental buildings commissioned by Mussolini, were the beating heart of early Roman ritual and commerce. Forget the Imperial Fora (see page 36) with their marble propaganda and carefully choreographed statuary. These were older, rougher, and far more essential. They fed the people, supplied the gods, and gave the city its first taste of centralized space.

The Forum Boarium, Rome's cattle market, predates most of what we think of as ancient Rome. Set along a natural ford in the Tiber between the Palatine and Aventine Hills, it was an obvious place for exchange long before Rome was even a city. Herds arrived by land and river, crowding into this low-lying zone near what

would become the Ara Maxima, the Great Altar of Hercules. According to legend, it was here that Hercules, fresh from stealing Geryon's cattle, fought and killed the fire-breathing bandit Cacus. The myth stuck. So did the meat trade.

From at least the sixth century BCE, the Forum Boarium served as Rome's livestock hub, a gritty space filled with animals, traders, sacrificial priests, and probably a whole lot of shit. This was where meat changed hands and where it was transformed into divine currency. Roman religious life revolved around sacrifice, and here, animal butchery was liturgical. Oxen, sheep, goats, and pigs were paraded in, garlanded, and led to temple precincts. With prayers and libations, they were ritually slaughtered. Entrails were inspected for omens. The gods got their cuts: roasted fat and thigh bones, perfumed with incense and wine on open-air altars. The rest was divided up among priests, magistrates, and attendees. It was a blood offering and a communal feast rolled into one. The sacred and the practical, side by side.

Right next door, the Forum Holitorium was a little greener but no less important. Tucked up against the southern edge of the Campus Martius and the lower slopes of the Capitoline Hill, this was where vegetables, legumes, herbs, and grains were sold. The name says it all: *holus*, Latin for "vegetable." If the Forum Boarium dealt in sacrifices, this one was about offerings of a more delicate kind, ritual bundles of leeks and garlic for chthonic deities, garlands for temple altars and sacrificial animals, beans for ancestral rites. Produce markets may not sound dramatic, but they kept the wheels of everyday ritual turning. The gods wanted meat, porridge, pulses, cakes, and wreaths, many of which began their journey here.

And just like its bovine sibling, the Forum Holitorium was replete with sacred architecture. Three Republican-era temples stood there, dedicated to Janus (god of transitions), Juno Sospita (protector in times of war), and Spes (goddess of hope). Their podiums and walls still survive, absorbed into the medieval church of San Nicola in Carcere, where Roman columns now support the facade, the lateral walls, and the nave. Down in the church's burial crypt, the temple podiums reveal their secondary use—workshops, offices, and storerooms that supported forum business.

These spaces didn't disappear with the end of the Republic. They adapted. As the empire expanded and centralized food supply became a state function, new forums and massive horrea (warehouses) emerged. But the fora remained embedded in the ritual geography of the city. The temples kept receiving offerings. The old markets continued to supply food.

Today, the Forum Boarium is best known for a set of arches and its improbably well-preserved temples: the round Temple of Hercules Victor and the rectangular Temple of Portunus. They sit at a bizarre traffic nexus, hemmed in by a Fascist-era road that amputated the site from the river and cut it off from the modern city's flow. Under the pavement of modern Rome, where tour buses idle and the scent of hot brakes wafts through the air, these spaces still pulse with history—messy, layered, and vital.

CALEDONIA

HIBERNIA

BRITANNIA

MAR GERMANICUM

GERMANIA INFERIOR

BELGICA

GERMANIA SUPERIOR

GERMANIA MAGNA

LUGDUNENSIS

NORICUM

PANNONIA SUPERIOR

DACIA

AQUITANIA

RAETIA

PANNONIA INFERIOR

MOI INFE

NARBONENSIS

ITALIA

DALMATIA

MOESIA SUPERIO

Roma

MACEDONI

TARRACONENSIS

SARDINIA ET CORSICA

EPIRUS

O C E A N U S   A T L A N T I C U S

LUSITANIA

SICILIA

BAETICA

AFRICA PROCONSULARIS

MAURETANIA CAESARIENSIS

MARE INTERN

MAURETANIA TINGITANA

CYRENAI ET CRET

GAETULIA

PHAZANIA

THE ROMAN EMPIRE

AT ITS GREATEST EXTENT IN 117 CE

SARMATIA

IBERIA

PONTUS EUXINUS

BITHYNIA ET PONTUS

ARMENIA

ASIA

GALATIA

CAPPADOCIA

LYCIA ET PAMPHYLIA

CILICIA

SYRIA

ASSYRIA

CYPRUS

JUDAEA

REGNUM PARTHICUM

ARABIA PETRAEA

MESOPOTAMIA

AEGYPTUS

ARABIA

OSTIA ANTICA: FROM PORT TO PLATE

Rome may have been the empire's capital, but Ostia Antica kept it fed, at least initially. Founded around the fourth century BCE at the mouth of the Tiber, Ostia was originally Rome's key logistical hub, receiving grain from Sicily and Egypt, *garum* and olive oil from the Iberian Peninsula, and wine from Gaul. Foreign goods were cataloged before getting shipped upriver to supply Rome's markets, bakeries, and taverns.

However, by the first century CE, silting at the Tiber's mouth severely restricted ship access, prompting Emperor Claudius to found a new deepwater port creatively named Portus, near modern-day Fiumicino. Ostia adapted, shifting from a busy maritime port into an essential administrative and logistical center that oversaw the goods arriving through Portus.

Today, Ostia Antica remains one of Italy's most evocative archaeological sites. Its sprawling ruins vividly illustrate not only how food once moved through Rome's imperial arteries, but also how the city evolved to manage and administer these vital supplies over centuries.

Wandering Ostia's basalt streets, you immediately notice how much space was dedicated to storage. The city essentially functioned as a giant pantry, and warehouses appear around nearly every corner. Among the best preserved, the *Horrea Epagathiana et Epaphroditi-ana* housed *dolia* (massive ceramic vessels). These industrial-size jars, holding thousands of liters each, were engineered to preserve staples for local consumption or before their shipment to Rome.

Ostia was more than a logistics hub; it had to feed its own inhabitants, too—a teeming seventy-five thousand by the second century CE. Scattered across the archaeological site are *thermopolia*, which once offered stews, street food, and mulled wine to workers without home kitchens. Marble counters with inset jars testify to quick, hearty meals grabbed by dockhands, haulers, and porters between shifts. At one thermopolium near Ostia's Forum, a menu that survives in the form of a fresco advertises bread, wine, fruit, and sausages, a snapshot of a working class diet.

At the Piazzale delle Corporazioni, a bustling commercial square next to Ostia's theater, the surviving mosaics visually map out Roman food logistics. Outside old shipping offices, black-and-white floor mosaics depict the city's cargo-laden ships and traded goods: sheaves of grain, amphorae, elephants. It's ancient branding. A Roman merchant could scan the floor decoration and quickly locate grain importers, ship builders, cargo handlers, and port services.

Elsewhere, mosaics emphasize the ancient Ostians' appetite and status. Villas and bathhouses are covered in detailed culinary scenes of ducks, squid, and fish that portray food as spectacle. Meanwhile, *insulae* (apartment blocks) reveal how Ostia's everyday Romans ate. Shared ovens suggest families shaped loaves at home but baked communally, highlighting the central role bread played in the community. At the same time, milling complexes in Ostia like the Molino del Silvano, featuring rotary mills, kneading areas, and proofing spaces, underline a sophisticated urban food system, which was industrial yet intimately local.

Though often overshadowed by Pompeii in modern tourism, Ostia Antica uniquely showcases the mechanics of the ancient food supply. Walking through its streets means you're tracing the journey of a Roman meal from port to pantry, finally reaching the worker's plate. Beyond operating as Rome's food storehouse, it was its essential infrastructure in the food system. Its remarkable preservation makes it possible to almost taste the pulse of the city that fed an empire.

THE EMPIRE
(27 BCE–476 CE)

As Rome shifted from republic to empire with Octavian's rise and his assumption of the title Augustus in 27 BCE, its culinary scene blew up, becoming more intricate with every conquest and trade route. By the time the Western Roman Empire officially folded in 476 CE, food had become a spectacle, a deliciously messy combination of politics, identity, and performance stretching from Britain to Mesopotamia.

At the top of Rome's food chain, eating was about flaunting wealth. *Convivia* (banquets) turned into theater: Think roasted peacocks displayed with their feathers painstakingly reattached, dormice stuffed with sausage, and sauces layered with costly imports like black pepper and *garum*. Roman dining was about indulgence and performance. In his gossipy but fascinating *The Lives of the Caesars*, Suetonius describes Nero's revolving dining room in the Domus Aurea, which mimicked the heavens and reportedly rained flower petals and perfume on guests. Domitian, not to be outdone in theatricality, is said to have hosted a black-themed banquet where senators dined in near-darkness beside mock gravestones. So goth! Petronius's biting *Satyricon* skewers these feasts with dishes that literally sprang to life or exploded into live birds, highlighting the absurdity of noble excess.

Elite Roman cuisine also found its way into writing, most famously in the cookbook *De re coquinaria*, attributed to "Apicius." Whether he was a real guy is up for debate; he may have been a wealthy first-century gourmand, a composite of multiple chefs, or a later pseudonym, but the name became synonymous with luxury dining. The surviving text, compiled a few centuries later, captures the opulence of imperial kitchens: recipes for ostrich in date sauce, poached flamingo tongues, and dozens of dishes seasoned with black pepper, laser (an aromatic resin), *garum*, and honey. It's less a manual for everyday cooking than a document of aspiration, spectacle, and the globalization of the Roman palate.

The empire's growth meant that new flavors were flooding Roman markets. Pork ruled common diets, with sausages and cured cuts featured everywhere, from home kitchens to street stalls. For wealthy diners, rare meats like wild boar, venison, and hare symbolized their aristocratic status. The flavor of fish became universally accessible through *garum*, churned out in industrial-scale factories in southern Spain and North Africa. It was a convenient commodity since fresh seafood like mullet, eel, and oysters remained luxury items.

Produce, too, reflected Rome's sprawling empire. Staples like olives, grapes, and figs anchored the Mediterranean diet, while new fruits such as cherries, peaches, apricots, and citrons arrived via trade from Persia and North Africa. Agricultural manuals like Columella's *De re rustica* were essentially lifestyle guides for managing villa orchards, vineyards, and gardens.

Spices were another marker of imperial wealth. Romans were especially enamored of black pepper, which was imported from distant Malaysia by way of southern India. But by the second century CE, cinnamon and ginger from Southeast Asia were arriving via India, too. Pliny the Elder griped loudly about the steep prices of spices in his *Natural History*, but they remained status symbols, appearing in extravagant dishes like *isicia omentata*, ancient Roman burgers spiced and wrapped decadently in caul fat, and exotic birds in cumin-laced sauces.

A HISTORY OF ROME (AND HOW IT EATS)

FROM EMPIRE TO ECCLESIA: EATING THROUGH THE FALL OF ROME

Rome as an empire didn't fall so much as crumble in slow motion, its decline drawn out over centuries like a long, reluctant exhale. Well before the symbolic abdication of Romulus Augustulus in 476 CE, Rome's impressive food-supply system was already failing. At its peak, the city's million residents depended entirely on imported staples, particularly grain from North Africa. The meticulous network of ships, ports, warehouses, and barges was crucial for feeding the capital and maintaining public order.

But disruptions had been mounting for decades. In 410 CE, the Visigoths under Alaric sacked Rome for the first time in eight hundred years, shocking the empire and shaking its foundations. Fun fact: when Alaric arrived in Rome, he demanded three thousand pounds of black pepper as ransom to lift his siege. The Romans obliged but he went back on the deal.

By the late fourth century CE, the Roman Empire had formally split into two administrations: a Western Empire governed from Ravenna and an Eastern (Byzantine) Empire governed from Constantinople. Egypt, once Rome's most reliable grain source, remained under Eastern Roman control, but was increasingly inaccessible to the West as administrative and logistical networks fractured. In 439 CE, the Vandals captured Carthage in modern-day Tunisia, cutting off a critical supply line and halting regular shipments of grain, olive oil, and *garum*. Just over a decade later, in 455 CE, the Vandals struck again, sacking Rome itself, looting the city over the course of two weeks, and damaging the aqueducts that supplied water for irrigation and mills. Each invasion chipped away at the complex bureaucratic machinery that once kept the empire running. By the time of the Gothic Wars in the mid-sixth century, when Totila and the Ostrogoths laid repeated siege to Rome, the city had entered a sharp decline. Its population plunged to mere tens of thousands by the time the Goth invaders withdrew due to sickness and starvation, clustering in neighborhoods near the Tiber.

The loss of the grain dole represented not only a logistical collapse but a profound cultural shift. Imported spices vanished, regional specialties disappeared, and local, seasonal ingredients became the norm. The sophisticated culinary traditions tied to imperial Rome became fragmented and replaced by practical, modest eating habits driven by necessity. The elite likely maintained some semblance of formal dining, but ordinary Romans faced significant scarcity from the fifth century CE onward.

Into this void stepped the church. As imperial institutions collapsed, ecclesiastical authorities emerged as Rome's new administrators. By the sixth century CE, popes were actively involved in managing logistics and infrastructure to feed the city's impoverished residents. Along with bishops, the popes of late antiquity repurposed ancient granaries, temples, and marketplaces into charitable food distributions.

Outside Rome, the church bestowed land on allies in exchange for food and tribute. Peasants traded labor for protection, sustenance, and spiritual guidance, reshaping the countryside into isolated agricultural communities. Meanwhile, Rome's urban residents transformed the Roman Forum and Circus Maximus into farms and vineyards, setting the tone for the next twelve centuries to come.

Wine was everywhere. Romans typically watered theirs down, sometimes adding honey, herbs, or spices, not because it was weak, but because drinking it straight was considered uncivilized. Plus, additives like pine resin contributed to the wine's longevity while others masked off flavors. Falernian wine from Campania was the Barolo of the era—expensive, age-worthy, and praised by cultural commentators—but vineyards thrived throughout Italy, Gaul, and Hispania. *Popinae* (taverns) kept the working classes lubricated with cheap pours, while elite diners sipped resin-perfumed, aged vintages from delicate glassware and silver cups.

Everyday Romans ate simpler fare. Cereals continued to dominate the plebeian diet. Grain was so essential to urban stability that the state distributed it through the *annona*, a grain distribution system formalized by Augustus. Legumes like chickpeas and lentils continued to be crucial protein sources, and *De re coquinaria* even acknowledges their use in humbler dishes, alongside vegetables like onions, garlic, cabbage, and turnips.

For ordinary Romans crammed into crowded *insulae*, cooking at home wasn't always an option. Enter the *thermopolium*— ancient Rome's answer to a fast-food joint. These street-facing establishments served ready-to-eat meals like *puls*, lentil stew, sausages, and bread, often kept warm in large terra-cotta jars called *dolia*, which were set into masonry *mensae* (counters) that opened directly onto the sidewalk. It was the ultimate convenience food: hot, hearty, and accessible to anyone with a few coins or something to barter.

With a population soaring past one million by the second century, Rome sucked in resources from every corner of the empire to feed its residents. Grain shipments arrived from Egypt, olive oil from North Africa and Hispania, *garum* from southern Gaul, and wine from Campania. Massive warehouses lined the Tiber at modern-day Testaccio, and bustling markets like the Forum Boarium (cattle market, see page 22) at the base of the Palatine Hill teemed with activity. Political power hinged on controlling these supply lines, and leaders knew that hungry citizens meant trouble.

Beyond Rome, local food customs in the imperial territories evolved but resisted total Romanization. In Britain and Gaul, Mediterranean imports like wine and olive oil mingled with native cereals, dairy, and game. Egypt layered Roman viticulture onto its established beer scene, while North Africa's prolific olive groves and grain fields became economic cornerstones. The impact of this trade is still visible in Rome's landscape—Monte dei Cocci (see page 91), a hill of broken amphorae in Testaccio, stands as a monument to the empire's import industry.

By the time Rome's western empire crumbled, one of its most enduring legacies was a culinary map etched across three continents. You can still trace its lines in the olive groves of Tunisia and Andalusia, in the vineyard terraces of Gaul and Vesuvius, and in the spice routes that passed through Alexandria and Antioch. Rome expanded its reach not only through roads and legions, but through flavor. Every conquest brought new ingredients, techniques, and appetites into the fold. The result was a food culture that was never static, always absorbing, adapting, and asserting itself bite by bite.

SEASONING AN EMPIRE: ROME'S SPICE BAZAAR

Just off the Roman Forum's Via Sacra, behind what's left of the Basilica of Maxentius, sits one of ancient Rome's lesser-known but wildly important commercial buildings: the *Horrea Piperataria*, the black pepper warehouses. Built in the second century CE, this brick-and-concrete structure was the spice cabinet of the empire. We're talking the most elite imports: black pepper from Southeast Asia, cardamom and cinnamon from Sri Lanka, and other goods so valuable and aromatic they needed to be housed like treasure. Which they basically were.

And they weren't hidden in some dusty port district or shoved out by the city walls. They were in the Forum, steps from a monument the Romans called "the navel of the city" (and, therefore, the world). The spice trade was essential and prestigious. If you were rich in Rome, you weren't seasoning your food with local herbs alone. You were reaching for stuff that had crossed oceans and deserts to land on your table.

The *horrea* themselves were practical and a little bit genius. Their vaulted rooms were built to keep out heat and light, perfect for preserving goods that would spoil or lose potency if they weren't handled right. These weren't modest storerooms; they were purpose-built, high-security facilities for small, expensive, fragrant things that fueled patrician tastes and imperial medicine cabinets.

The supply chain behind all this was *intense*. Spices left India's Malabar Coast and Sri Lanka, rode the monsoon winds across the Arabian Sea, landed in Red Sea ports like Berenice Troglodytica and Myos Hormos, then were hauled over desert roads to the Nile, floated to Alexandria, and shipped to Portus. From there they came upriver to Rome. It was a long and treacherous journey that relied on wind patterns, maritime knowledge, and a whole lot of middlemen. Red Sea inscriptions even mention Tamil-speaking merchants from southern India, proof that Rome's spice game was international, multilingual, and very lucrative.

The *Horrea Piperataria* did brisk business until the third century CE, when Rome's city center started shifting from a hub of commerce to a stage for imperial decline. When Maxentius built his enormous basilica in 308 CE, he didn't bother knocking down the warehouses. He just built over them. The northern vaults of the spice storage complex got folded right into the foundation. The trade didn't disappear overnight; it got literally buried under unrealized political ambition. Within four years of the basilica's construction, Maxentius would drown in battle in the Tiber River, ceding his power to Constantine.

Today, when visitors stroll through what's left of the basilica, they're mostly looking up, taking in the scale of what Maxentius left behind. But look down— or better, imagine below—and you'll find the ghost of a different kind of empire: one built on global trade, sharp flavors, and the Roman obsession with controlling both territory and taste.

ANGLO-SAXON KINGDOMS
CELTIC LANDS
FRANKISH KINGDOM
BURGUNDIAN KINGDOM
SLAVIC PEOPLES
LOMBARDS
OSTROGOTHIC EMPIRE
EASTERN ROMAN (BYZANTINE) EMPIRE
VISIGOTHIC KINGDOM
VANDAL KINGDOM

MIDDLE AGES: A CITY BETWEEN RUINS AND RESURRECTION
(476–1420 CE)

When the Western Roman Empire collapsed in 476 CE, Rome didn't suddenly fall silent. The emperors were gone, but life carried on—messy, improvised, and increasingly local. Germanic kings Odoacer and then Theodoric ruled from Ravenna, leaving Rome with fading senatorial families and rising popes who stepped into the power vacuum. The papacy, once mainly spiritual, became deeply political. While imperial authority fizzled, the pope was the one organizing grain shipments and patching roads.

Under Theodoric, some Roman institutions like baths, aqueducts, and roads still functioned, and despite being a nontrinitarian Arian Christian, Theodoric tolerated Rome's trinity-forward Nicene brand of Christianity. But everything unraveled during the Byzantine-Gothic Wars. When Emperor Justinian of Byzantium tried to reclaim Italy, Rome suffered immensely. Invasion after invasion left the city starved, besieged, and gutted. By the late sixth century CE, it was a shell of itself, its population a fraction of its imperial height, likely no more than twenty or thirty

thousand. The aqueducts were shattered. The markets struggled. People scavenged stone from the Forum to cobble together hovels inside crumbling monuments.

After the Gothic Wars, as Byzantium's grip on Italy weakened, the Lombards (the German conquerors of Italy) invaded in 568 CE, seizing much of the north and center of the peninsula and further destabilizing eastern control. Rome's survival depended more and more on the church. Pope Gregory the Great (590–604 CE) went beyond his role as a spiritual leader—he ran the city like a mayor. He set up grain imports from Sicily, distributed food from church-run deaconries (see page 33), and launched a kind of early-medieval welfare system. These deaconries, scattered around the city, offered bread, oil, wine, and general care for the poor, not unlike early models of the soup kitchen–hospital hybrid.

By the reign of Gregory, Rome had become a rural city. Vast swaths of land within the ancient walls were given over to farming. The Aventine, Caelian, and even Palatine Hills—once the beating heart of imperial power—reverted to countryside, dotted with vegetable gardens, grazing pastures, and the odd monastery. Vines and fig trees crept into collapsed *insulae*. Goats grazed among the ruins of temples. The food supply depended heavily on subsistence agriculture, monastic production, and the occasional organized grain import when the pope had enough pull with foreign powers.

Still, Rome was never fully abandoned. Pilgrims came to venerate relics and tombs. Tiber-side neighborhoods like Trastevere remained active, home to artisans, dockworkers, and religious communities. The fish

DIACONIAE: SERVANTS OF THE CITY

In early-medieval Rome, the church was more than a spiritual authority. It became a hub for public services once provided by the imperial administration. A clear illustration of this transformation was the *diaconia*, a church-affiliated institution dedicated to organizing and distributing charitable aid. These establishments served as spiritual successors to the *stationes annonae* (imperial-era grain distribution depots), continuing the essential function of feeding Rome's population in times of need.

Several prominent *diaconiae* highlight how Christian charity took root within key ancient Roman sites. For instance, Santi Cosma e Damiano (built 527 CE) was established directly in the heart of the Roman Forum, cobbling together the so-called Temple of Romulus and a part of the Temple of Peace, literally integrating Christian charitable activities within Rome's former political and civic center. Similarly, San Giorgio in Velabro (built 625–638 CE) was strategically positioned near the Forum Boarium, Rome's ancient cattle market (see page 22), illustrating a tangible link between the area's long-standing commercial activity and its new ecclesiastical charitable role.

Churches like Santa Maria in Cosmedin (begun 772 CE), also near the Forum Boarium, and Sant'Angelo in Pescheria (circa 770 CE), adjacent to the medieval fish market, reinforced this continuity, embedding Christian charity within Rome's historic infrastructure for feeding the populace.

By the eighth and ninth centuries, *diaconiae* operated like early welfare centers. Some may have preserved aspects of Roman hygiene culture, including access to water and occasional bathing facilities, as part of restoring dignity through service.

The word *diaconia* (or the Greek-derived *diakonia*) speaks volumes. At its root is *diakonos*, Greek for "servant," and it appears throughout the New Testament, especially in the Acts of the Apostles, in reference to acts of service. In early Christian communities, deacons were both assistants to bishops and frontline social workers. They served food, distributed alms, and cared for widows and orphans. It was a theological, liturgical, and profoundly practical role.

If you're walking through Rome today and happen upon a church with the word *diaconia* in its history, pause and consider: It was more than a place of worship. It was once a lifeline. A place where service, both real and practical, was offered to those who needed it most. And in that way, these spaces are some of the most enduring legacies of early Christian urban culture, where faith was something you lived and leaned on in times of need.

market thrived beneath the shadow of the Portico d'Ottavia (see page 187). In the Campus Martius, daily life unfolded among the ruins: improvised markets, bakeries, and street vendors hugging the bones of the old empire.

By the late medieval period, instability was the norm. The ninth century saw Saracen raids, often launched from Muslim-held Sicily. In 1084, Norman troops entered Rome to rescue Pope Gregory VII from imperial siege, but managed to loot and burn much of the city in the process. Papal elections were often violent. In 1309, the papacy abandoned Rome entirely, moving to Avignon, France, in what became a seventy-year exile. During this time, Rome collapsed even further. Without the papal court and its economic engine, the city emptied out. Powerful families like the Colonna, Orsini, Savelli, and Annibaldi waged open warfare in the streets for control of neighborhoods. Church properties fell into disrepair. The food supply became more precarious. Without consistent governance, maintaining granaries, roads, or even mills was nearly impossible.

Saint Birgitta of Sweden, one of the most vivid chroniclers of Rome's decline, visited the city in the fourteenth century and found it in spiritual and physical ruin. Her writings describe a once-sacred capital consumed by filth, corruption, and vice. City life was defined by crumbling churches, lawless streets, and clergy more interested in power than piety. This was Rome's rock bottom and recovery was just around the corner.

The popes returned to Rome in fits and starts, and in 1420 Pope Martin V reestablished the city as the papal seat for good. He got to work rebuilding infrastructure, repairing roads, restoring aqueducts, and restabilizing the food supply through more regular imports and market regulation. His reign marked the beginning of the city's long climb out of its medieval funk and into Renaissance rebirth.

Medieval Rome wasn't glorious. It was unstable, fragmented, often half empty. But it was lived-in. It was a city of contradiction: pilgrims walking barefoot past ruined temples, barons waging turf wars beneath ancient arches, farmers tending cabbages in what had been marble-clad piazzas. Through famine and feast, exile and return, Rome endured. Not as the capital of an empire but as a city clinging to its sanctity, improvising survival in the shadow of its own ruins.

RENAISSANCE ROME
(1420–1527)

While Florence, Siena, and Venice were witnessing (and spearheading) the beginning of the Renaissance in the fourteenth century, Rome was still in the throes of the Middle Ages. After nearly a century of neglect during the papacy's Avignon exile, the city lacked any sort of stability needed for a rebirth of culture. The place was in tatters: plague-scarred, depopulated, and overrun by squabbling noble families.

But in 1420, Pope Martin V returned from France, parked himself at Rome's cathedral at the Lateran, and began the long and expensive process of turning a chaotic husk into a proper capital again. If medieval Rome was a faded relic of its imperial past—its aqueducts busted, its temples turned into goat pens—Martin V wanted to make sure the city clawed its way out of the rubble and reclaimed its place at the center of the world. But Renaissance Rome wasn't born in a day; it was dragged back to life, brick by brick and banquet by banquet.

One of Martin V's top priorities was repairing infrastructure, including churches, bridges, and palaces, as well as Rome's essential food technologies: aqueducts, mills, and public fountains. Aqueduct repair had more at stake than aesthetics—it was about bread. Literally. Flour mills powered by water wheels depended on that flow in order to keep producing grain for the city's daily loaves. Rome's reliance on imported grain remained strong, but fixing the local system was key to food security.

The revival of Rome included the strategic relocation and regulation of its marketplaces, reflecting an ambition to create a more orderly, "civilized" city. Piazza Navona, built atop the ancient Stadium of Domitian, emerged in the late fifteenth century as a central open-air market after Pope Sixtus IV moved the city's primary commercial activities there. Vendors and vignarole (women who grew and sold produce from suburban plots) regularly brought vegetables, grains, and livestock to this humming piazza.

Campo de' Fiori, today beloved for its flower stalls and classy joints like the Drunken Ship, had a different role in the late Middle Ages and early Renaissance. Originally a grassy meadow, it was paved in 1456 by Pope Callixtus III, transforming it into a bustling commercial hub notable for its twice-weekly livestock market and regular public executions and book burnings. Surrounding streets filled with inns and artisan shops named for local trades, from tailors (giubbonari) to crossbow makers (balestrari). Only much later, in 1869, did Campo de' Fiori inherit Piazza Navona's daily market traditions, with guild-specific areas for butchers, fishmongers, greengrocers, and cheesemongers. The market thrived until the early twenty-first century when the boom of vacation rentals shifted the neighborhood's demographics, contributing to its sad decline.

Daily life for most Renaissance Romans involved modest, seasonal fare: chickpeas, lentils, onions, cabbage, and bread baked in communal ovens. Meals were simple but flavored with garlic and wild herbs. Street food culture thrived around pilgrimage routes and market days.

But in the palaces of noble families, things were different. Banquets were used as political theater, just as they had been in ancient Rome's golden years. Wealthy families like the Colonna and Orsini outdid each other in spectacle, hiring celebrated chefs (often from Naples or Florence) to stage elaborate meals with dozens of courses, each more ornate than the last. They served pheasant, sometimes redressed in its own plumage, and game birds in gilded pastry coffins. Trionfi (sugar sculptures) depicted mythological scenes and allegories, towering over diners as centerpieces. These were edible status symbols: sweet, expensive, and fleeting.

The papal kitchen was no slouch either. Under Sixtus IV and especially Leo X, the Vatican became one of the city's most important centers of culinary innovation. The papal pantry was stocked with proto-Parmigiano-Reggiano from Emilia, salted cod from Norway, and spices from Venice's trade routes. Agostino Chigi, a powerful banker and Leo X's favorite host, threw feasts in his Trastevere villa (now known as the Villa Farnesina, see page 231), where guests dined off silver plates that, according to legend, were tossed into the Tiber afterward—a practice both performative and not altogether impractical, since servants would collect them with nets downstream and reuse the plates.

A typical upper-class Renaissance banquet often started with preserved fruits or almonds, followed by pasta and meat dishes like roasted kid, veal, or occasionally, game such as pheasant. Sauces leaned toward acidity and complexity, incorporating vinegar, dried fruits, wine, and spices—an inheritance from medieval cooking traditions. Pasta dishes, such as tortelli filled

A HISTORY OF ROME (AND HOW IT EATS)

Despite their name, the Imperial Fora, a set of public spaces between the Colosseum and modern day Piazza Venezia, really got their start before the empire was established. In 46 BCE, during Rome's Late Republic, Julius Caesar—never one to shy away from grandeur—constructed his own forum beside the older Republican one. This kicked off more than a century and a half of monumental building, with four emperors adding their own piazza: Augustus built a forum crowned with the Temple of Mars Ultor; Vespasian created the misleadingly named "Temple of Peace" (it was essentially a war trophy museum); Domitian began, and Nerva completed, a narrow connecting forum that served as a transitional corridor between earlier complexes. And in the second century CE, Trajan constructed what was the largest and most ambitious forum to date.

Trajan's Forum was especially audacious, requiring the excavation and removal of volcanic stone from the Quirinal Hill—a huge engineering feat. The vast plaza featured the Basilica Ulpia and the spiral-carved Column of Trajan, celebrating military victories. On the exposed hillside, the Romans built Trajan's Markets, a multilevel complex with offices, archives, and some storefronts, including food spaces, integrated directly into the slope. Though dubbed "markets," the complex functioned more like an office building than a shopping mall.

But the era of imperial splendor didn't last forever. By the sixth century CE, the Fora were in total disrepair, ravaged by earthquakes and invasions, stripped for building materials, and gradually repurposed for farming and shelter. Marble piazzas became gardens and vegetable patches. Chickens roamed among fallen columns; vines covered once-grand porticoes. These symbols of Roman power transformed into practical agricultural spaces.

Trajan's Markets survived largely due to their sturdy construction. By the twelfth century, the upper levels became a noble fortress for the Conti family, including gardens for food. Over time, these ancient buildings were further repurposed. People farmed there, built modest homes against ancient walls, and raised animals. It wouldn't be the last time the area was a farm—during the Second World War, the avenue that slices through the Fora today was the home of vast victory gardens.

Today, the Imperial Fora and Trajan's Markets are museums, but their deeper significance lies in their survival. These sites vividly illustrate Rome's resilience: the city's capacity to adapt, decay, and reinvent itself. Long after empire, Rome continued living among its ruins, a testament to its creative spirit. From marble and military might to gardens, fortresses, and cloisters, the Fora embody the city's ever-evolving history. Rome, after all, always finds a way.

with herbs or pastelli stuffed with spiced meat blends, frequently featured at papal tables. Fish was essential, especially considering the over one hundred fifty fasting days required by the liturgical calendar. Salt cod and eel became Lenten staples, inspiring chefs to create elaborate dishes molded into shapes or encased in pastry.

The introduction of the printing press in the mid-fifteenth century spurred the publication of cookbooks and culinary theories. Bartolomeo Sacchi (1421–1481), better known as Platina, served as Vatican librarian under Pope Sixtus IV and authored *De honesta voluptate et valetudine (On Honest Pleasure and Good Health)*. Debuting in 1474, it was among Europe's earliest printed cookbooks. Platina combined medical theory, moral instruction, and practical recipes, many of which were adapted from Maestro Martino da Como (1430–date unknown), a renowned chef employed by cardinals. Recipes such as hare with sour cherries, saffron-marjoram meatballs, and rosewater-sweetened fried dough illustrate a cuisine balanced between medicinal advice and indulgent pleasure.

At the dawn of the sixteenth century, while Bramante was constructing the new Saint Peter's Basilica, Michelangelo was decorating the Sistine Chapel ceiling, and Raphael was adorning the papal apartments and the Villa Farnesina, the culinary arts also flourished. Just as the ideas of perspective and proportion were dominating conversations about painting and architecture among elite Romans, their chefs experimented extensively with spices from distant lands. Medieval favorites like clove, cinnamon, and nutmeg persisted, but Renaissance humanists revisited ancient Roman texts, notably Apicius's *De re coquinaria*, to influence culinary methods and menus; Platina was the first edition's editor. This rediscovery marked a true culinary Renaissance.

And then came the crash. The damage caused by Martin Luther's Reformation in 1517 and the Sack of Rome in 1527 devastated the city. During the invasion, the Holy Roman Emperor's imperial troops pillaged churches, looted palaces, and slaughtered thousands. Artists and chefs alike fled the city. Bread prices soared, meat vanished from the markets, and the banquet halls went dark. The High Renaissance was over, and when things picked up again, the city had shifted to simpler, more austere tastes in many things, including cuisine—matching the spirit of decline that fell over the city.

THE COUNTER-REFORMATION
(1527–1700)

Rome in the early sixteenth century was feeling itself. The Renaissance had flooded the city with beauty: frescoed walls, gilded ceilings, and papal feasts that made Nero's dinner parties look tame. But all that grandeur was doomed to collapse. The papacy had become a nepotistic, bloated bureaucracy with a taste for excess and a PR problem by the name of Martin Luther. So when the Catholic Holy Roman Emperor Charles V's army (the one sworn to protect the pope) sacked the city in 1527, it was more than a military failure; it was a full-on humiliation.

Pope Clement VII, a Medici with a knack for indecision, had tried to hedge his bets between rivals Charles V, Holy Roman Emperor and King of Spain, and Francis I of France. That gamble backfired. Charles V's unpaid, mutinous, and majority Lutheran Protestant troops stormed the city and turned Rome into a vision of hell. The Swiss Guards died almost to the man. The pope fled to Castel Sant'Angelo, watching the horror unfold from

A HISTORY OF ROME (AND HOW IT EATS)

THE GUILDS THAT SHAPED THE ROMAN TABLE

In Renaissance Rome, arti (food guilds) were power brokers. These organizations, which first emerged in the middle ages, shaped the city's food economy, protected professional prestige, and, in many cases, embedded themselves in its religious and architectural fabric. Their influence still lingers in Roman culinary culture today, even if their names have long since faded from street signs and shop windows.

Each trade had its own guild: The fornari (bakers), beccai (butchers), vermicellari (pasta makers), pizzicaroli (grocers), and vinai (wine sellers) were just a few of the major players. Together, they formed a kind of culinary bureaucracy, responsible for regulating everything from pricing to quality control to who could sell what, where, and when. If a baker sold underweight bread or cut the dough with filler, he could be fined, publicly shamed, or kicked out of the guild, effectively banned from doing business in Rome.

The fornari were especially scrutinized, given the centrality of bread in the Roman diet. They had to follow precise weight and purity regulations. The beccai, too, had strict protocols around slaughter and hygiene, especially important in a city where meat was consumed in both sacred and secular settings—and where the pope himself might be your customer.

The guilds were also cultural institutions. Many sponsored chapels or even entire churches. Santa Maria dell'Orto in Trastevere was built and funded by Rome's food guilds. Inside, each trade had its own space, complete with iconography. The vinai, naturally, were responsible for ensuring the sacramental chalices were filled—and for stocking the city's osterie. The vermicellari, experts in dried pasta, helped make pasta a year-round staple, rather than a food for special occasions.

Education and professional training were central, too. Young apprentices learned by shadowing master artisans, inheriting skills and recipes passed down through generations. Guilds not only upheld high standards but also allowed for measured innovation, ensuring that Rome's culinary traditions evolved without losing their roots. Behind the scenes of papal feasts, public banquets, and bustling market days was a guild-led infrastructure that kept the city fed and its foodways thriving. The guilds' enduring legacy reminds us that Rome's food culture has always relied on both mastery and community, a truth that any thoughtful guide to the city's cuisine must honor.

behind its fortified walls. It marked the end of Rome's golden age of the Renaissance, and nothing would ever be the same.

In time, the makeover began. The Counter-Reformation wasn't a single event, but a decades-long reckoning. The church, staring down Protestantism, started tightening its belt and its moral code. And because this was Rome, that meant doctrine as well as urban planning, architecture, aqueducts, and a its deeply choreographed relationship between penance and pageantry.

If the Renaissance had turned the papal court into a feast, the Counter-Reformation tried to add a vegetable course. Meat, long the cornerstone of elite dining, became a moral liability, especially with new fasting rules and stricter definitions of spiritual discipline. But Rome being Rome, no one was about to stop throwing banquets. So the solution? Fish. And not any old fish.

Elite Roman tables groaned under the weight of sculpted sturgeon, glazed lampreys, and aspic-locked allegories built from seafood. It was penitential performance art. These dishes signaled religious observance (no meat!) while flaunting wealth through imported spices and the kind of workforce it took to mold marzipan into saints. Sugar, pouring in from the Americas, became a sign of both devotion and domination. It coated nuts, preserved citrus, and bound together towering trionfi, elaborate sugar sculptures that told guests your soul was pure but your wallet was deep.

The makeover extended from the dinner table to the streets. Rome, still scarred from the 1527 sack, had to be reimagined as the capital of a global faith. That meant cleaning up in every sense. Enter Pope Paul III. Elected in 1534, he was Rome's comeback pope. A savvy mix of reformer and dynastic schemer, he understood that saving the church required both spiritual realignment and strategic politics. He convened the Council of Trent, a series of meetings of bishops tasked with defining doctrine and reforming corrupt practices. But let's not canonize him just yet. Paul was also a world-class nepotist, handing out duchies like party favors to his next of kin. He carved out Parma and Piacenza for his son (yeah, you read that right) and he appointed his grandsons as cardinals when they were still teenagers. Cool!

Still, Paul knew that optics mattered. He brought Michelangelo back into the Vatican fold, overseeing his completion of *The Last Judgment* in the Sistine Chapel and directing his redesign of the Capitoline Hill. Antonio da Sangallo the Younger was called in to reinforce the city's walls and to fortify Castel Sant'Angelo. Rome was rearming itself, physically and spiritually.

Years later, after Paul III served as Rome's cautious restorer, Pius V became its righteous executioner. A Dominican friar with zero patience for moral gray areas, he cracked down on everything from concubinage to clowning (yes, court jesters were banished). His vision for papal Rome moved away from extravagant processions and social gatherings in grand palaces. Instead, it centered on discipline, moral reform, and authority. The Inquisition, which had been inconsistently enforced by earlier popes, now functioned with alarming precision. Blasphemers were jailed. Prostitutes were exiled. Even the cardinals were expected to live in Rome and act like they meant it. Under him, the Roman Inquisition gained teeth. Public morality didn't stop at the pulpit—it was policed.

One of the ugliest chapters of the Counter-Reformation unfolded in the Jewish quarter (see page 40). In 1555, Pope Paul IV issued a papal bull forcing the city's Jewish residents into a walled ghetto near the Portico d'Ottavia. They were locked in at night, made to wear yellow identifiers (hats for men, veils for women), and cut off from most professions. More than a policy, the rules enforced upon the Ghetto were about a performance of power, an assertion of Catholic dominance in brick, mortar, and social control.

That same pope, hated so fiercely by Romans that they toppled his statue and torched the Inquisition's headquarters after his death, had no problem making enemies. He believed in a purified Rome, even if it meant ruling through fear. But in retaliation, the Ghetto cooked. Carciofi alla Giudia (deep fried artichokes, page 86) came to define the Roman spring. Concia (vinegar-dressed zucchini, page 85), Filetti di Baccalà (salt cod fillets, page 78) and stracotto (braised beef) were part coping mechanisms, part culinary resistance.

Fast-forward to Sixtus V, the pope who made the Counter-Reformation's ethos literal in Rome's stone and skyline. His short but ferocious reign (1585–1590) was a blitz of reform and construction. Nicknamed the Iron Pope, he cleaned up the streets—sometimes with lethal

A HISTORY OF ROME (AND HOW IT EATS)

ROME'S GHETTO: FORCED PROXIMITY AND PERSEVERANCE

Rome's Jewish community is one of the oldest in Europe, possibly the oldest continuous Jewish settlement on the Continent, predating Christianity itself. Jews arrived in town well before the birth of Christ, likely around 161 BCE, as diplomats, merchants, and travelers, migrating voluntarily along trade routes. They settled in Trastevere, living generally as a tolerated minority under the Roman Republic and, later, the empire. The free Jews were joined in the Trastevere neighborhood by prisoners of war and slaves from the first centuries BCE and CE, many ultimately freed during the empire.

While the ancient Roman authorities weren't exactly known for religious tolerance, Jews in Rome were largely permitted to practice their religion, observe the Sabbath, and maintain their dietary laws. As long as they paid taxes and didn't stir up trouble, they were mostly left alone. But that tentative equilibrium never guaranteed safety or dignity. Rome's Jews existed in a liminal space—considered both insiders and outsiders, Roman and foreign, always vulnerable to the whims of political shifts and papal moods.

By the Middle Ages, the treatment of the Jewish community had shifted, largely due to Christian perceptions, and a period of marginalization set in. Things took a darker, more systematized turn in the sixteenth century, when what had long been informal discrimination became official policy.

By the time the Ghetto was formally established in 1555, Rome's Jewish population was diverse and deeply rooted and it wasn't monolithic. During the Inquisition, Jews fled cities like Seville and Toledo following the Alhambra Decree of 1492, which expelled them from Spain. In the early sixteenth century, another influx followed when the Kingdom of Naples expelled Jews from southern Italian cities like Trani, Bari, and Palermo. Many of these displaced families also found their way to Rome.

These newcomers brought their own customs, rabbinical scholarship, and culinary traditions. Southern Italian Jews brought eggplants and artichokes, while the Sephardic refugees from Iberia brought along recipes marked by spices, rice, and almonds. These were not trivial differences. Jewish Rome became a patchwork of distinct identities and practices, which coexisted—but not always peacefully. When space was scarce and resources limited, communal tensions simmered beneath the surface.

The tipping point came in 1555, under Pope Paul IV, one of the harshest and most fanatically anti-Jewish pontiffs in church history. He issued the infamous bull *Cum nimis absurdum* on July 14 of that year, a document whose name translates as "Since it is completely absurd," and continues, "and inappropriate that the Jews, who through their own guilt were condemned by God to eternal slavery, should enjoy the favor and protection of Christian society, and should even live among us; for instead of showing gratitude for the kindness shown to them they respond with insult." The bull goes on to cite the Jews' supposed insolence and refusal to convert, and used these claims as justification for a sweeping set of restrictions.

Chief among them: the mandatory establishment of a ghetto. Rome's Jews were ordered to leave their homes throughout the city and relocate to a small, flood-prone section near the Tiber, squeezed between the Portico d'Ottavia, Piazza Mattei, and the Isola Tiberina. This was not a ghetto in the abstract sense—it was a walled-in, physically segregated neighborhood. Gates locked at dusk and reopened at dawn, always under papal police supervision. The area became known simply as *il Ghetto*, borrowing a term from Venice's Jewish quarter.

Paul IV's law ordered Jews to wear distinguishing markers (a yellow hat for men, a yellow veil or kerchief for women), banned them from owning property, forbade them from practicing medicine on Christians, and disqualified them from most professions except ragpicking, moneylending, and selling secondhand goods. The Jewish community was now legally second-class, by design and by decree.

Over the next three centuries, the Ghetto became both a prison and a paradox—a place of deep suffering and profound cultural endurance. Despite being physically cramped (seven acres for thousands of people), socially restricted, and economically deprived, the Roman Jewish community survived within its limits.

The conditions in the Ghetto were grim, and at its peak there were some four thousand mouths to feed with few resources. And yet, out of this constriction came a cuisine of astonishing creativity. With pork forbidden and resources tight, Roman Jews leaned into offcuts, preserved fish, bitter greens, and deep fat frying. The result was a series of dishes that would eventually define the city's broader food culture.

Vegetables were fried in oil and repurposed into satisfying fritters. One of the most iconic dishes to emerge from this period is Carciofi alla Giudia, flattened like sunbursts, crisped to gold. The dish was, and still is, made by trimming the outer leaves, poaching in oil to cook it through, then frying once again at a higher temperature to crisp it up. It's a culinary flex: turning poverty into pleasure.

Many other fried specialties emerged from the neighborhood. So did Filetti di Baccalà, Concia, and Fiori di Zucca (page 74). Liver and onions, a humble Ghetto staple, became a Roman home-cooking classic. Even desserts like Torta di Ricotta (ricotta cake, page 287), almond pastries, and Pizza Ebraica (a dense, fruit-studded sweet bread, page 283) emerged from this tight-knit, resourceful community.

There's no direct documentation of papal laws banning specific Jewish food practices per se (Rome was more interested in controlling Jews than in what they put on the table), but the economic and social restrictions imposed by the Ghetto laws naturally affected food availability. The inability to own land, for example, meant Jews had no control over agriculture and had to rely on what was available at market, often the discards or lower-quality produce.

Roman Jewish staples were survival foods—flavorful, fast, deeply rooted in Jewish dietary law—and they weren't eaten just within the Ghetto walls. Over time, they migrated into Roman street culture and onto Catholic tables and even modern pizzeria menus; I challenge you to find a Roman pizza spot that doesn't serve cod fillets. The irony is hard to ignore: A community isolated by religious edict became one of the city's most influential tastemakers.

Despite the oppressive conditions, the community held on to religious rituals, educational structures, and spiritual leadership. Rabbis and scholars continued to teach, to write, to translate sacred texts. Community institutions pooled resources to care for the poor, the sick, the orphaned. Even the daily humiliations, like attending compulsory conversion sermons held in churches on Shabbat, were met with quiet resistance.

The Ghetto walls stood for more than three hundred years, with one notable interruption. During the Napoleonic occupation in the early nineteenth century, the French dismantled the walls and granted Roman Jews full civil rights. But when the papacy regained control, those freedoms were revoked once again and the walls were rebuilt. It wasn't until 1870, when the Papal States fell and the new Italian nation-state annexed Rome that the Ghetto was fully abolished. With unification came emancipation: Jews were granted full citizenship, allowed to live freely, own property, and no longer subject to church rule. The physical walls came down. The social and psychological ones took much longer.

Today, Rome's Jewish Ghetto is a bustling cultural and culinary hub. Tourists flock to the kosher restaurants and bakeries, many unaware that the cobbled streets they tread were once a carceral zone teeming with improvised street food stalls. Roman Jewish cuisine, la cucina ebraica romanesca, is a testament to what happens when a community is pushed to the margins and responds not with assimilation but with resilient, flavorful endurance.

A HISTORY OF ROME (AND HOW IT EATS)

force—and made sure that no one, not even cardinals or nobles, was above the law. He taxed heavily but spent smartly, restoring ancient aqueducts, paving roads, and laying down the blueprint of modern Rome. He wanted pilgrims to move through the city like blood through arteries, flowing from basilica to basilica without getting lost in medieval alleys. So he built straight roads, raised obelisks as spiritual signposts, and redeveloped desolate hills like the Esquiline and Quirinal. Rome was no longer a labyrinthine relic. Under Sixtus V, it became a city of purpose.

His most important tool was water. Rome doesn't work without it. Physically, the fountains have to flow. Spiritually, the city has to baptize, cleanse, and hydrate its pilgrims. Sixtus V knew that. In a grand act of urban hygiene and spiritual branding, he commissioned the Acqua Felice, a new aqueduct that revived parts of ancient Roman infrastructure and brought fresh water to the city's northeastern hills, naming it after his given name, Felice Peretti. You can still see it today running through Mandrione, Tor Pignattara, and Porta Maggiore. Water flowed into working-class neighborhoods, bakeries, markets, and kitchens, where it developed dough, boiled beans, and filled carafes on tavern tables.

Not everyone had access to eel towers and candied citrus. For most Romans, food was a matter of ingenuity and grind. Bread, beans, wild greens, and salt cod were the building blocks of everyday meals. In the now-destroyed Piazza Montanara, wedged between Teatro di Marcello and the Capitoline Hill, vendors hawked produce, cheese, and dry goods in one of the city's the rough roughest and most vibrant social spaces.

By the time the seventeenth century rolled around, Rome had been transformed—again. It wasn't the open-air art studio of Raphael's time anymore. It was a disciplined, designed, and spiritual capital. Churches boomed with Baroque drama. Streets pointed pilgrims like compass needles. Obelisks, fountains, and facades all worked in harmony to proclaim Catholic dominance. But under that choreography, life pulsed with familiar chaos. Romans haggled over bread prices, sipped wine in dodgy taverns, and cursed tax collectors between rounds. The church may have reclaimed its authority, but it didn't erase Rome's essence. Because in the end, this city is always both sacred and profane. It feeds on contradiction and always finds a way to eat well, even while repenting.

The aesthetic of Counter-Reformation Rome crystallized in the Baroque: dramatic, didactic, and overwhelming by design. Architecture became a sensory strategy, engineered to assert Catholic truth through marble, light, and scale. Early architects like Vignola laid the groundwork, while Bernini and Borromini expanded the vision into a theatrical language of power and ecstasy. Every block of marble, gilded cornice, and sculpted plaster coffer cried out: *The church is back—and we've still got it, baby!* This full-on assault of the senses wasn't subtle evangelism. It was a declaration of victory over the Protestants. It's a nice message but pretty far from the truth.

Much of the grandeur that defined papal Rome in this era was bankrolled by Catholic empires, especially Spain and Portugal, whose colonial conquests in the Americas fed both the Church's coffers and its vision. As missionaries spread the Catholic faith abroad, silver flowed back to Europe, underwriting monumental projects and institutions in Rome. At the same time, ships returning from the so-called New World carried ingredients like tomatoes, potatoes, and squash that would gradually take root in Roman kitchens. These foods, now so deeply entwined with Roman identity, arrived through the same networks of conquest and conversion that financed the Church's spectacular revival. The result was a Rome remade: spiritually militant, artistically dazzling, and, unknowingly, on the cusp of a culinary revolution.

Bartolomeo Scappi (1500–1577), personal chef to multiple popes and the literal author of Counter-Reformation cooking, published his monumental *Opera dell'arte del cucinare* in 1570. It was a 1,200-recipe manual for how to perform power, piety, and sophistication through food. Lavishly illustrated and meticulously organized, the *Opera* reads like a Renaissance tasting menu spliced with court protocol, a text as much about managing cooks and provisioning pantries as it is about preparing veal tongues or stewing snails.

Scappi wrote in the vernacular Italian rather than Latin, making his techniques accessible to the rising class of literate culinary professionals working in noble and ecclesiastical households. This was revolutionary: by putting elite kitchen knowledge in the hands of laymen, Scappi quietly democratized culinary excellence, even as he documented its most rarefied forms.

Rome in the 1570s was a city under intense scrutiny. The Inquisition policed belief. Urban renewal campaigns whitewashed sacred spaces. Facades were simplified to emphasize spiritual clarity. But behind convent walls and palazzo kitchens, excess thrived. Food offered a rare zone of sanctioned indulgence, so long as it bowed, at least outwardly, to Church rules. Scappi cooked in this paradox: for a Church that preached temperance but demanded spectacular fish feasts on Fridays, and for cardinals who ruled over penitent congregations while ordering sculptural desserts.

He understood the power of performance. The *Opera* offers instructions on what to serve and how to stage meals that thrilled guests and reinforced social hierarchy. Among the most memorable dishes are digestible illusions: pies that released live birds when cut open (a showpiece famously referenced by Scappi and later popularized in *Sing a Song of Sixpence*), and sugar sculptures shaped into allegories, saints, and even entire architectural scenes. These were edible sermons, performed during banquets to mirror the Church's own blend of spectacle and symbolism.

Even fasting days, which technically forbade meat, were reimagined as occasions for opulent seafood spreads. Scappi's chapters on *magro* cuisine (meals prepared for lean days) include detailed recipes for fried frogs, stuffed eels, and lamprey molded to resemble roasts. Far from restraining creativity, fasting laws became frameworks for culinary ingenuity.

One of his more striking fixations is *poppe di vacca* (cow's udders), prepared boiled, braised, fried, or layered into cinnamon-scented pies. In Renaissance Rome, such cuts weren't stigmatized. Offal in general was prized for texture and intensity of flavor. Scappi's treatment of these ingredients reveals a palate fluent in contradictions: sweet and salty, rich and lean, humble and theatrical.

The *Opera* codified what elite Roman food could be at a moment when the Catholic Church was reasserting its authority through dogma, discipline, and grandeur. It helped canonize the idea that orthodoxy could be delicious, that repentance didn't preclude indulgence, and that a meal could serve as both a statement of faith and a demonstration of dominance.

His legacy still lingers in the Roman kitchen. Today's trattorie might not serve pies of cow udder or gilded lampreys, but they carry forward Scappi's love of offal, bold contrasts, and the theatricality of the table. Rome's relationship with food remains what it was in Scappi's time: a negotiation between rules and appetite, simplicity and excess. Even when Rome repents, it eats well—and heartily.

THE EIGHTEENTH CENTURY AND GRAND TOUR ROME
(1700–1798)

The Sack of Rome and the Reformation wreaked havoc on the papacy, weakening the institution on the global stage. And the Counter-Reformation may have been too little, too late for restoring the dignity and authority of the popes. But the institution wasn't down for the count. Indeed, during these otherwise austere times, the papal kingdom, called the Papal States, reached one of

its largest expanses yet. In the eighteenth century, the states fanned out across the Italian peninsula, through Lazio and Umbria all the way up to Emilia and Romagna, with papal outposts as far-flung as Benevento in the south and the Comtat Venaissin in modern-day France. This ecclesiastical territory was at once a political map and a system that shaped urban life, visual culture, and what Romans put on their plates. When not wielding spiritual power, the Catholic Church set the rhythm of the day, the calendar, and the kitchen.

Rome in the 1700s was at once sacred and decadent. Still wrapped in the glow of religious authority, it had also become a playground for Grand Tourists— young nobles from across Europe, arriving in powdered wigs and silk stockings, eager to soak in antiquities, admire towering ruins, and, let's be honest, indulge in a little Roman excess. The city had been experiencing a makeover.

The Baroque, a politically affiliated art movement, was giving way to Rococo, over-the-top ornamentation for art's sake. In 1732, Nicola Salvi broke ground on the Trevi Fountain, a marble fantasy where Neptune watches over Tritons and sea horses in a surging pool. A few years later, vineyards on the Pincian Hill were torn up and the Spanish Steps were laid out in their place like a theater set, a stage for Roman society to strut and flirt and for rural peasants to try to hook a Roman. Among the noble destinations was the luxe Antico Caffè Greco, established in 1760 and still a popular haunt considered the epitome of old-world elegance.

Just as the city dazzled with its architecture and salons, it began to position itself as a cultural capital. The Capitoline Museums opened in 1734 in the hill's matching Renaissance palaces, making Rome the first place in Europe where you could stroll into a museum because you wanted to and not because your pedigree entitled you to access. The Pio-Clementine Museum of the Vatican followed in 1771, opening its collection to the public.

Meanwhile, Piranesi's etchings made the city's ruins seem even more epic than they already were. These romanticized prints circulated through Europe, seducing future visitors with impossible arches and crumbling temples between which farmers tilled and livestock grazed. But if you looked past the colonnades and cupolas, you'd see that Rome was, as always, a working city with a hungry population to feed. Markets buzzed with life, especially in Piazza Montanara, which by then had been providing food to the hungry masses for four centuries.

Roman poet Giuseppe Gioacchino Belli sheds light on the recipes that would have been enjoyed at this time: peas with dill, simmered lentils, sausages, and tripe stews. Predictably, wine flowed freely, transported from Frascati and Marino in the Castelli Romani to Rome's taverns, refreshing laborers and cardinals alike. The osterie and fraschette (rustic taverns) of the time were focused on drinking; bringing your own food was common, but proprietors began to prepare simple dishes in improvised kitchens in this era as well.

The culinary divide between classes was sharp. Nobles and prelates dined in private palazzi, waited on by cooks trained in French technique but working with local ingredients. Their tables featured filled pastas and elaborate timballi—layered pasta pies swaddled in pastry, often stuffed with minced meats, béchamel, and black truffles from northern Lazio. Their sweet tables groaned with citrus-scented marzipan and Jordan almonds from Sulmona, along with sugar-syrup-soaked pastries inspired by Naples.

By contrast, Rome's working class leaned into humble, hearty food rooted in necessity and tradition. Chickpeas simmered with rosemary. Bitter greens braised with garlic and oil. Stews were stretched with bread. Nothing went to waste. Beyond marking the holy days, the church calendar mapped out what you could eat and when. During Lent, fish from the Tiber or salted cod from Norway remained staples for the rich. For the poor, Fridays meant beans or beans.

By the century's end, political winds were shifting. Napoleon's ambitions and the reverberations of the French Revolution reached Rome's gates. The Papal States—once seemingly eternal—started to unravel.

NAPOLEON IN ROME: LOOT, LAYERS, AND MILLEFOGLIE
(1798–1814)

Napoleon isn't usually the first name that comes up in conversations about Roman food culture—or Roman history, for that matter. His name conjures images of French conquest, gilded coronations, and exile on remote islands, not so much the Italian capital. But between 1798 and 1814, Napoleon's forces occupied Rome twice, and his rule over the city, though short-lived, left behind traces that are still visible today, not only in archives and museums but also, weirdly enough, in pastry cases.

When French troops entered Rome in 1798, they did more than depose Pope Pius VI and declare a Roman Republic modeled after their own revolutionary ideals. They also upended centuries of papal governance, dismantling the Inquisition, dissolving religious orders, and secularizing the city's institutions. After a temporary papal restoration in 1800, Napoleon returned in 1808, formally annexed Rome into the French Empire the following year, and envisioned the city as an imperial capital in its own right, his spiritual second city after Paris. He introduced the Napoleonic Code, scrapped canon law, and imposed sweeping administrative and legal reforms. He fancied himself a modern Augustus, aggressively excavating and restoring imperial monuments to further the comparison.

In classic imperial style, Napoleon treated Rome like both a trophy room and fixer-upper. He ordered massive quantities of art seized from churches and aristocratic collections, including works from the Borghese family, whose patriarch, Camillo Borghese, conveniently became Napoleon's brother-in-law. In 1807, under heavy political pressure, Camillo sold over five hundred ancient sculptures and antiquities to France, many of which still reside in the Louvre today.

Ironically, Antonio Canova, the neoclassical sculptor whom Napoleon admired, was later sent by the restored papacy to recover looted artworks after Napoleon's defeat. But before that, Canova famously sculpted Pauline Bonaparte, Napoleon's sister and Camillo Borghese's wife, as a seminude Venus Victrix, reclining on a marble couch holding an apple. That sculpture remains in the Galleria Borghese, one of the most provocative and iconic examples of neoclassical art in Rome.

Napoleon also invested in urban improvements and excavation. The Roman Forum, the Forum of Trajan, and the Colosseum, long buried under sediment and medieval debris, became targets for orchestrated digs under French supervision. These efforts, while politically symbolic, also marked the beginning of systematic archaeological practice in the city, including mapping and cataloging. Today's archival standards and topographical studies owe much to these early Napoleonic bureaucrats, whose flair for filing and categorizing helped professionalize Rome's archaeological record.

But life under French occupation wasn't all cartography and cultural theft. Rome's economy tanked. Monasteries—major providers of charity—were dissolved. With no one distributing free loaves or soup, famine hit hard. Food riots broke out, especially in working-class districts as grain prices soared. The cost of a loaf of bread could wipe out a family's weekly earnings. Police reports from the period detail bread thefts, riots at mills, and angry petitions to French authorities. Perhaps only the Ghetto residents fared better under French rule, as the revolutionaries dismantled the walls, abolished discriminatory laws, and briefly granted Jews full civil rights, effectively sweeping away centuries of papal segregation in the name of liberty and equality.

Still, not all of Napoleon's influence was catastrophic. In fact, some of it reshaped Rome's food and beverage culture in ways that still ripple through the city today. The French didn't mess with olive oil (they weren't that audacious), but they did bring with them a heightened appreciation for pastry. While Rome had its own sweet traditions, especially in Jewish bakeries—ricotta cakes, almond biscotti, and honey-drenched fried matzoh—the French flair for laminated doughs made an impression. Millefoglie (a Roman adaptation of the mille-feuille) became a staple, its crackly pastry and silky crema pasticcera a subtle nod to France, filtered through a Roman sensibility.

You'll still find millefoglie in pastry shops all over the city, as well as on trattoria dessert menus. It's a dessert that straddles the border between French refinement and Roman indulgence—rich, a little messy, but undeniably delicious. And while Napoleon never sipped an espresso at Sant'Eustachio or strolled through Campo de' Fiori with a maritozzo in hand, his imprint on Roman life lingers in ways both subtle and enduring.

Napoleonic rule collapsed in 1814. The pope returned. French rule evaporated. But the systems, institutions, and pastries they left behind remained. Like many chapters in Roman history, Napoleon's was disruptive, oppressive, and surprisingly generative. The French came for power, prestige, and art and left behind a reorganized city, an archaeological legacy, and perhaps even a better dessert menu.

REPUBLIC TO RISORGIMENTO

(1815–1922)

When most people think about the Risorgimento (the unification of Italy), Rome often takes center stage in the imagination. But the truth is, by the time the Italian tricolor flew over Porta Pia in 1870, most of the peninsula had already been stitched together under Piedmont's House of Savoy and its king Vittorio Emanuele II. Rome, ruled by the pope as a theocratic monarchy for the better part of eleven hundred years, had been the holdout. And getting it finally into the fold of the unifying nation was anything but straightforward.

Let's rewind a bit. In 1849, a Roman Republic was declared—not to be confused with the earlier French-backed republic imposed by Napoleon in 1798. It was an ambitious but short-lived homegrown experiment in secular republicanism. After Pope Pius IX fled the city during political unrest in late 1848, a constituent assembly of elected Roman citizens convened. On February 9, 1849, they formally abolished the Papal States and proclaimed the Republic. Governance fell to a triumvirate: Giuseppe Mazzini, the philosophical heart of Italian unification; Carlo Armellini, a moderate jurist; and Aurelio Saffi, a young republican firebrand. Together, they tried to build a modern, democratic state.

But the dream didn't last. Mazzini and Giuseppe Garibaldi, the Republic's muscle, held out on the Janiculum Hill above Trastevere, defending the city from French troops sent by Napoleon III to restore papal rule. Their ideals were high, their barricades improvised. The defense collapsed by July of that year. Garibaldi escaped with his life; Mazzini left with his ideals intact.

Rome was once again under the pope's control.

As the Risorgimento picked up steam in the 1860s, Garibaldi led the flashier campaigns, famously landing in Sicily in 1860 with around a thousand volunteers, the Mille, while Count Camillo Cavour, the prime minister of Piedmont-Sardinia, played diplomatic chess behind the scenes. Officially, Cavour disavowed Garibaldi's rogue mission; unofficially, he armed it and made sure the British navy looked the other way as the volunteers crossed the Strait of Messina. Garibaldi took Sicily, then Naples, ousting the Bourbon monarchy in the south. The Kingdom of Italy was proclaimed in 1861, but Rome was conspicuously missing.

France still protected the Papal States with troops, and neither Cavour nor King Victor Emmanuel II wanted to provoke France's Napoleon III. When the Austro-Prussian War erupted in 1866, Italy opportunistically joined Prussia. They got Venice and its surroundings out of it, even though their army was, frankly, a mess. That left only Rome and the surrounding Lazio region as holdouts.

The moment came in 1870, when France pulled its troops from Rome to fight Prussia. With the pope suddenly unprotected, Italian forces seized the opportunity. On September 20, 1870, Italian troops breached the third-century Aurelian Walls at Porta Pia after a brief cannonade. Papal forces offered token resistance before surrendering. Rome was annexed with minimal bloodshed, ending papal temporal rule.

A plebiscite followed—hardly a neutral affair—but the vote to join the Kingdom of Italy passed by a suspiciously overwhelming margin: more than 133,000 in favor, fewer than 1,500 against. Rome officially became the Italian capital in 1871. Pope Pius IX, refusing to recognize the Italian state's authority, declared himself a "prisoner in the Vatican," launching a nearly sixty-year standoff between church and state during which the popes remained in political limbo until Mussolini and Pius XI signed the Lateran Treaty of 1929, officially es-

A HISTORY OF ROME (AND HOW IT EATS)

PORTO FLUVIALE: ROME'S INDUSTRIAL UNDERBELLY

Rome has never quite known what to do with the Tiber. Unlike the Seine in Paris or the Arno in Florence—rivers that have long played starring roles in their cities' self-mythology—the Tiber has always been cast in a more complicated light. Sure, its waters nourished the earliest settlements and brought grain from Etruria and wine from Latium into the city during the Republic. But it also flooded with spectacular fury, drowning whole neighborhoods and spreading disease in its wake. By the late nineteenth century, after yet another catastrophic deluge, the state had had enough. Engineers encased the river in muraglioni (massive embankments) that turned it into essentially a moat, simultaneously protecting the city but also severing its relationship to the water that had shaped it.

In the process, Rome lost its historic river ports—Ripa Grande in Trastevere and Ripetta near Piazza del Popolo—both active for centuries and central to river trade and transport. They were dismantled during the embankment works, erasing not just infrastructure but a vital connection between the city and its river.

That severance was both physical and symbolic. But at the turn of the twentieth century, a newly unified Italy was keen to rebrand Rome not as a city of ruins, relics, and religious authority, but as a proper modern capital. Cue the industrial makeover.

In 1907, work began on Porto Fluviale, a river port meant to tether the city once again to the Tiber as a working artery for moving coal, grain, and other essentials. The port's location in Ostiense wasn't accidental. The area was sparsely populated, and largely unburdened by ancient ruins. In other words, perfect for planners who wanted to pave, pour concrete, and get shit done. The neighborhood rapidly filled with infrastructure: train tracks, warehouses, factories, and silos. These weren't the grand civic projects of Mussolini's showy Fascist era—they were practical, muscular structures built to haul, store, and sort the stuff a city needed to run. The area was gritty, unglamorous, and oddly beautiful.

Those massive grain silos, currently crumbling due south of the Garbatella overpass, once stored wheat from Puglia and Sicily. The flour ended up in everything from everyday pane casereccio to the more indulgent maritozzi. Coal, imported from Sardegna and offloaded from barges on the Tiber, fired ovens and boilers across

the city. You don't get warm winter minestrone in Monteverde or baked pasta al forno in San Giovanni without a supply chain, and for a few brief decades, Porto Fluviale was the city's beating industrial heart.

A short walk away, the Centrale Montemartini, completed in 1912, turned all that coal into electricity, powering the city's tramlines and factories. Today, the old power station houses one of Rome's most quietly extraordinary museums, a trove of classical sculptures from the Capitoline Museums set against art nouveau machinery and massive, black turbines. Marble deities stands poised beside a hulking generator, their flowing drapery contrasting with steel bolts and pistons in a surreal juxtaposition only Rome could pull off.

Then there were the Mercati Generali (see page 237), inaugurated in 1914, which brought the foodways of the port full circle. The covered wholesale markets pulsed with life every morning as buyers and sellers moved crates of chicory plucked from nearby fields, cheese from suburban hills, and fish from the coast. This was where food retailers and produce vendors struck their deals. Before Eataly (see page 68) put prosciutto and Parmigiano behind glass in air-conditioned displays down the street, this was the true food hub of Rome. The markets were shuttered in the early 2000s and have stood largely defunct since, awaiting redevelopment projects that have been stalled, restarted, and reimagined more times than I can count.

A few blocks away, the ex-Caserma del Porto Fluviale, once military barracks, is now a grassroots multicultural housing project, featuring apartments for scores of families, community kitchens, artist studios, spaces for mutual aid projects, and a secondhand market. As much as the grain silos and markets showcase Rome's industrial past, the ex-Caserma embodies its countercultural spirit.

The Porto Fluviale district might not have fulfilled its original dream of industrial dominance, but it has—slowly, messily, wonderfully—become a neighborhood that mirrors the city's complexity: layered, contradictory, and ready for reinvention.

tablishing the papal sovereignty of the Holy See.

While the Vatican became increasingly self-contained, the city surrounding it was transforming from papal city-state to modern capital. Roads were widened, administrative buildings were erected, and new middle-class neighborhoods were developed, like Piazza Vittorio and Prati.

For the next few decades, Rome underwent a seismic cultural and political shift. With the Savoy monarchy came a wave of northern aristocrats, bureaucrats, and civil servants from Turin, Milan, Bologna, and beyond, each bringing along their dialects, manners, and kitchens, too. The capital filled with northerners who had grown up on butter, risotto, and Alpine cheeses. Rome's famously offal-forward menus of braised tripe and simmered oxtails must have seemed hopelessly rustic to the new elite.

The café culture of the city took on a northern polish. Rome had its intellectual hangouts—Caffè Greco on Via dei Condotti was already a magnet for artists and exiled romantics—but the new arrivals brought with them a taste for coffee and northern European–style pastry culture. Antico Caffè della Pace near Piazza Navona and Caffè Aragno on Via del Corso became favored haunts for northern transplants who liked their coffee with a side of diplomatic gossip and a proper slice of Sacher torte. If anything, the northern presence only made Romans double down on their food identity.

Victor Emmanuel II, the Savoy king who brought Italy under a single flag, was buried in the Pantheon in 1878. The gesture was symbolic, placing the architect of national unity in the context of Rome's imperial grandeur. The massive monument to his legacy, the Altare della Patria, wouldn't be completed until decades later, an enormous white marble ziggurat that looks like it crash-landed from a neoclassical spaceship. It still divides opinion—some Romans call it the "typewriter," others the "dentures"—but its message is clear: The unification of Italy is permanent, whether you like it or not.

The idea of a unified Italy might have taken root politically, but in the kitchens of Rome, things were far less settled. National cuisine? That was a fantasy still decades away from coalescing, and arguably is still unfixed today.

FASCISM AND FOOD: ROME ON RATIONS
(1922–1943)

Long before Mussolini stormed the stage, Italy's political and social systems were already simmering. The late nineteenth and early twentieth centuries were marked by economic instability, rural poverty, and a deeply uneven distribution of wealth and land, especially in the south.

Italy may have been mostly unified in 1861, with Rome becoming the capital in 1871, but by the time the twentieth century rolled around, it was clear that unification was still mostly theoretical. Regionalism thrived, the monarchy floundered, and parliamentary governments collapsed with numbing regularity. The First World War only deepened the crisis. Postwar disillusionment, inflation, and labor unrest created fertile ground for a movement that promised order, strength, and national pride. Enter Fascism.

By the time Benito Mussolini came to power in 1922, bolstered by his infamous March on Rome, Italy was exhausted. It was ready, or at least susceptible, to being sold a myth of rebirth. Mussolini's vision of the new Italian citizen was militarized, disciplined, and completely devoted to the state. That devotion extended all the way to the dinner table.

Food was both a symbol and a strategy. In a throwback to the Empire, Mussolini and his regime understood that controlling the stomach was a direct path to controlling the citizen. The Fascist obsession with autarchia, or economic self-sufficiency, went beyond asserting Italy's independence from foreign powers. It aimed to prove that the nation could nourish itself, body and soul, without outside interference. In reality, of course, this was fantasy.

Rome, like most of the country, had never been able to feed itself. Even at the height of the Empire, the city depended on grain shipments from its provinces in Sicily and North Africa. That reliance never really went away. In the early twentieth century, Italy was still importing huge amounts of wheat, mainly from the US, Russia, and Argentina. But in 1925, Mussolini launched La Battaglia del Grano (the Battle for Grain) a national campaign to supercharge domestic wheat production and wean Italy off foreign imports. It was agriculture as performance art, and wheat was cast as the hero. Mussolini played the part with theatrical zeal, famously posing bare-chested in wheat fields, swinging a scythe under the summer sun, an image designed to link his personal virility to the fertility of the land and the strength of the nation.

To further support this transformation, the regime undertook massive public works projects known as the bonifiche integrali, or land reclamations, draining marshlands like the Agro Pontino south of Rome. These areas were converted into wheat fields and dotted with newly constructed Fascist towns like Littoria (now Latina), meant to embody both agricultural rebirth and Fascist modernity.

Farmers were strong-armed into planting wheat on every available patch of land, whether it made sense or not. Olive groves were ripped out. Diversified farms became monocultures. And while yields did rise in parts of the Po Valley in the north, the results were ecologically and economically catastrophic elsewhere, especially in Lazio and Sicily. Italy's already fragile soil was depleted, legumes and vegetables disappeared from fields and markets, and systems of rotation fell by the wayside.

Meanwhile, rice was promoted through the Ente Nazionale Risi, a national board created to boost domestic production. Fascist dietary doctrine expanded to include new patriotic foods: rice, barley-based coffee substitutes, and so-called "pane di Stato" (state bread made with darker, whole-grain flours that represented both nutritional austerity and national resilience). Refined white bread and foreign luxury goods like butter and sugar were discouraged or stigmatized as bourgeois or unpatriotic.

Through a web of bureaucracies and agencies, many headquartered in rationalist buildings that still line the city, the Fascist state sought to reshape every part of Italy's food system. The Ente Nazionale del Grano controlled wheat prices and stockpiles. The regime didn't stop at wheat, though. The Ente Nazionale Dopolavoro organized leisure activities and workplace meals that doubled as vehicles for ideological indoctrination. The Ente Nazionale del Vino promoted Italian wine as a patriotic beverage. What you drank said as much about your politics as it did your taste.

In Rome, this transformation left a physical mark. The Esposizione Universale di Roma (EUR) district—originally conceived for a never-realized 1942 World's Fair that was supposed to showcase Italy's Fascist might—was designed with massive food pavilions and agricultural exhibits in mind. Back in central Rome, Palazzo dell'Agricoltura on Via XX Settembre, built to house the Ministry of Agriculture, looms like a stone sentinel to the regime's agricultural ambitions. Down in Ostiense, the Mercati Generali (see page 237) were expanded to bring Rome's chaotic food supply under state control. And although the Testaccio slaughterhouse predates Mussolini, it was retooled for the regime to suit Fascist ideas of hygiene, efficiency, and authority.

Fascist food propaganda was relentless. Posters of Il Duce urged Italians to eat pasta made with national grain. Slogans like Chi mangia italiano aiuta l'Italia ("Those who eat Italian help Italy") tied patriotism directly to the pantry. Even coffee came under fire at

A HISTORY OF ROME (AND HOW IT EATS)

Born into comfort and privilege in 1881, Ada Boni came of age in a Roman household that teetered between the old aristocratic order and the modern bourgeois ideal. Her family's home near Piazza del Popolo sat at the intersection of old Baroque Rome and the emerging modern city, a metaphor that would later echo in her food writing. Unlike many culinary figures of her era, Boni wasn't raised in a rural kitchen or trained in professional brigades. She grew up in salons and drawing rooms, where her earliest experiments with cooking took place using toy stoves and miniature pots. Her passion, however, was real. At just ten years old, she was preparing meals, perhaps inspired by her uncle Adolfo, a chef and the founder of the culinary periodical *Il Messaggero della Cucina*. It would be a lifelong obsession.

While Italy's most famous (and IMO most boring) cookbook author, Pellegrino Artusi, looked to the past, compiling a nostalgic, unifying vision of the Italian table after the Risorgimento, Boni turned her focus toward the present and future. She wasn't interested in aristocratic banquet fare or culinary nationalism in the abstract. Her concern was practical: how to teach Roman housewives, especially those entering marriage and adulthood in the rapidly modernizing early twentieth century, to cook well, economically, and with pride.

In 1915, just as the First World War was reshaping Europe's social and political landscape, Boni launched *Preziosa*, a magazine aimed squarely at middle-class Roman women. It wasn't purely a lifestyle publication; it was a manual for modern womanhood. Through advice on etiquette, budgeting, housekeeping, and cooking, *Preziosa* proposed that running a home was not only a moral duty but an art. At a time when domestic labor was rarely acknowledged as intellectual work, Boni framed it as both noble and essential. Her recipes were meticulously tested, her guidance clear and replicable. For young women navigating the expectations of marriage, motherhood, and modest urban life, *Preziosa* was a lifeline and Ada Boni was their compass.

Her legacy, however, would be cemented with the 1929 publication of *Il talismano della felicità* (*The Talisman of Happiness*), a cookbook so comprehensive and influential that it became the default culinary reference for generations of Italians. This was no pamphlet or promotional booklet; it was a full-blown culinary encyclopedia, sprawling in scope and domestic in spirit. In its first edition, *Il talismano* contained over 880 recipes spanning Italy's regional cooking traditions, with references to her native Roman canon: abbacchio, coda, trippa, carciofi, and gnocchi alla romana.

But what set Boni apart wasn't the breadth of her content; it was her method. She codified recipes that had previously lived in the oral traditions of working-class kitchens. She wrote for the home cook, not the chef, and provided step-by-step instructions in accessible language. Her work professionalized domestic cooking in a way that aligned with the spirit of her time: orderly, rule-driven, modern.

Ada Boni

IL TALISMANO DELLA FELICITÀ

Editore Colombo

And this is where Boni's legacy becomes more complicated. By the late 1920s, Italy was a Fascist state, and Mussolini's regime had begun its campaign to reshape Italian life culturally, economically, and gastronomically. Food became a battleground for propaganda. The state promoted autarky (self-sufficiency) and valorized rural simplicity while demonizing foreign ingredients and cosmopolitanism. Women were encouraged to leave factory jobs and return to the home, where their primary function, in the regime's view, was to bear children and cook for the family. In this climate, Ada Boni's work centered on domesticity, culinary structure, and national unity through food dovetailed neatly, perhaps too neatly, with Fascist ideals.

There is no evidence that Boni was explicitly political, or that she collaborated directly with the regime. But her writing and publishing thrived in an atmosphere that rewarded exactly the kind of culinary nationalism and gender essentialism she practiced. *Il talismano*'s emphasis on Italian ingredients and recipes, its valorization of thrift and self-sufficiency, and its central premise that a well-fed family is the foundation of a happy marriage and, by extension, a stable society fit cleanly into the moral and ideological scaffolding of Fascist domestic policy.

That's not to say Boni was merely a tool of propaganda. In many ways, she was subversive. Her authority as a female writer and editor at a time when few women held such positions speaks to her autonomy and intellect. She created a platform for other women to take pride in their work, and she shaped a national conversation about what it meant to cook well, live well, and eat as an Italian, not just as a Roman. If her vision of womanhood aligned with state rhetoric, it also carved out space for women to develop their own expertise and confidence in the kitchen, something that had long been dismissed as either drudgery or instinct.

Boni continued to write and publish long after the war ended and the regime collapsed. In the 1950s and '60s, she expanded her body of work with more specialized books, including *La cucina romana*, a love letter to the capital's traditional foodways. While *Il talismano* had taken a national view, *La cucina romana* zeroed in on the dishes at risk of disappearing in the postwar rush toward modernization. It was preservationist, passionate, and deeply informed—one of the earliest serious attempts to document Roman food on its own terms.

In her final years, Boni devoted time to charitable work and even brought her voice to the radio, where she hosted a weekly program with RAI, guiding a new generation of cooks through Italy's gastronomic heritage. When she died in 1973 at the age of ninety-two, she left behind a legacy of structured, intelligent food writing that changed how Italians, especially women, related to their kitchens.

Ada Boni didn't shape Roman cuisine by clinging to nostalgia. She brought order to it. Through clarity and structure, she captured the city's food traditions and elevated home cooking with discipline and precision. Her recipes endure because they work, and because they reflect a methodical, thoughtful approach to feeding a household. Boni's legacy isn't wrapped in flair or spectacle. It endures in the quiet confidence she instilled in generations of cooks who saw the kitchen as a place for agency, creativity, and cultural continuity.

times. Imports were expensive and unreliable, so the regime pushed barley-based caffè d'orzo as a home-grown alternative. It tasted like roasted regret, but it was patriotic.

Food-themed sagre (festivals), agricultural competitions, and rural pageantry further celebrated the peasant ideal. The Fascist regime wanted Italians to perform food patriotism through ritual and display. Fascist ideology promoted a vision of meatless masculinity, casting the strong, frugal peasant body as the physical ideal of the new Italy. The regime publicly framed meat as bourgeois excess, asserting that true patriots thrived on grain, legumes, and olive oil. Of course, Mussolini himself enjoyed rich meals and kept a well-stocked pantry.

Women were tasked with turning scarcity into strength. Fascist ideology cast them as nutritional patriots, responsible for making and feeding future soldiers and embodying sacrifice in the home. Propaganda celebrated the figure of the tireless, fertile, disciplined housewife, whose frugality was framed as a feminine virtue. Fascist magazines promoted "heroic housewifery," encouraging efficient meal planning, clever substitutions, and creative uses of leftovers as acts of national service. In this vision, women's domestic labor upheld the regime's ideals, and even a pot of soup became a tool of social engineering.

Still, despite all the grandstanding, Mussolini never succeeded in achieving autarky. By the time World War II engulfed the country, rationing was in full swing. People lined up for bread, traded cigarettes for butter, and grew what they could in all corners of the city, including Via dei Fori Imperiali, the avenue leading to the Colosseum, still called Via dell'Impero at the time.

By 1943, provisioning in Rome under the Fascist regime had largely collapsed, leaving the city gripped by severe food shortages and widespread hunger. Citizens could barely rely on ration cards to access basic goods like bread, pasta, and oil, but official supplies were meager and often replaced with poor-quality substitutes. As the war intensified and supply chains broke down, especially after Mussolini's fall in July 1943 and the brutal German occupation that followed, Romans increasingly turned to the black market and bartered with farmers in the countryside to survive.

The rationing system, once a tool of state control, had become ineffective, fueling public discontent and further eroding faith in the regime.

Today, the physical legacies of this era remain. The Fascist facades still stand, many of them repurposed but unmistakable. Some of the regime's food institutions morphed into modern agricultural agencies. But the centralized, coercive vision of Italian cuisine that Fascism tried to enforce never really stuck. Instead, Italy's postwar culinary identity went in the opposite direction, celebrating regional diversity, hyperlocal ingredients, and recipes that resist standardization.

POSTWAR ROME
(1944–1955)

By the time Rome was liberated by the Allies in June 1944, the city was physically intact compared to the bomb-flattened landscapes of other European capitals. But the scars ran deep. Rome had survived Nazi occupation, food shortages, and economic collapse. Its ancient streets were lined with rubble, not from bombs but from bad governance and the collapse of a regime that had promised glory and delivered misery. And while the Colosseum still stood, the Roman people were exhaust-

Rome has always been a magnet for the movement of people, goods, empires, and ideas. That's been true since ancient times, when North African merchants unloaded amphorae of *garum* along the Tiber, and it's still true today, though the cargo looks more like spice blends and tef (an ancient grain) than fish sauce. Nowhere is this more visible than in the city's East African communities, particularly Ethiopian and Eritrean, whose presence is deeply intertwined with Italy's imperial endeavors in the Horn of Africa—a colonial past that Italy has never fully reckoned with.

Italy's attempts to build an empire began late—at least compared to its European neighbors—and were driven as much by national insecurity as ambition. Eritrea was formally colonized in 1890; Italian Somaliland was consolidated by 1908. Ethiopia, fiercely independent and never technically colonized, held out until Mussolini invaded in 1935, deploying mustard gas and aerial bombings to crush resistance. The occupation lasted just five years, from 1936 to 1941, but its legacy lingers—in collective memory and in the lives of people who were forcibly entangled across continents.

Some Italians stayed on in Eritrea and Ethiopia even after the fall of the Fascist regime, working in agriculture and construction, running pasta factories, or trying to hold on to some fragment of their imperial dream. Others came home with wives and children of mixed heritage, weaving East African traditions into Roman households—quietly, often invisibly. Meanwhile, Rome itself, the symbolic capital of a short-lived African empire, became a natural destination for migrants from the Horn of Africa in the decades that followed.

In the 1980s and '90s, a new wave of East Africans, fleeing famine, war, and political upheaval, settled in the city's eastern quadrants, especially along the Prenestina. That corridor is now dotted with family-run restaurants, cultural centers, and corner shops stocked with tej (a honey wine), berbere (the essential spice blend), and sacks of green coffee beans destined for long, fragrant roasting.

It's in these places you'll find injera, the spongy, fermented tef-based flatbread that anchors nearly every East African meal, and zighinì, a long-cooked meat stew infused with warmth, depth, and heat. Zighinì has become something of a Roman Eritrean calling card. You'll spot it heaped on injera at homey restaurants like Mrgda and Enqutatash off the Via Prenestina or, if you're wandering through Testaccio or Trastevere, folded into a trapizzino (a soft wedge of pizza bianca that acts like an edible cone, page 256). It's a Roman street food concept, sure, but the fillings range far and wide, and zighinì has more than earned its spot on the roster.

That slow braise of meat and spices fits right in with Roman culinary tradition, which reveres long simmers and gutsy flavors. And while you might not find zighinì on trattoria menus, East African food is far more present in Rome than most visitors (or even locals) realize. It's in the storefront kitchens of immigrant matriarchs and second-generation chefs. It's in the cross-cultural families who blend tagliatelle with t'ibs (spiced stewed meat). It's in the sound of a traditional buna ceremony (coffee prepared with reverence and shared in community), the fragrance drifting through apartment blocks built during the economic boom, now home to communities whose roots trace back to Addis and Asmara.

ed, malnourished, and scrambling to rebuild a daily life that no longer resembled what it had been even five years earlier.

Amid the physical and emotional ruins, Rome became the backdrop for a new kind of storytelling. In 1945, Roma Città Aperta, Roberto Rossellini's groundbreaking neorealist film, captured the trauma and resistance of the Nazi occupation. Shot in the devastated streets of the city, the film offered a raw, unvarnished portrayal of recent events and helped define a new cinematic era born from the wreckage of war.

When the Allies arrived, they brought relief—but also their own kind of chaos. American soldiers became a near-ubiquitous presence in postliberation Rome, and with them came something utterly foreign to most Italians: the K ration. Designed by physiologist and Mediterranean diet advocate Ancel Keys, the K ration was a compact, calorie-dense meal kit designed for US troops in combat. It was meant to be temporary sustenance and was followed by B rations once troops were stationed in Italy after the war. For many Romans, these became an object of fascination and, often, a means of survival. Each B ration contained three meals—breakfast, lunch, and dinner—packed in a cardboard box with items like canned meat, dehydrated eggs, powdered drinks, biscuits, and chocolate. To a malnourished Roman family, a single ration was a miracle in wax paper. Soldiers traded them for favors or goodwill, sometimes for wine, sometimes for companionship, and often simply out of generosity.

The barter economy between locals and Allied troops flourished in the months following liberation. Roman kids lingered near military trucks hoping for handouts. Women waited near field kitchens with pots, hoping to scoop up leftovers. American rations were currency, social glue, a way to connect in the ruins. The irony was hard to miss: Italy had spent two decades under Fascist rule being told to drink charred barley instead of coffee and to eat national grain instead of foreign imports, all in the name of self-sufficiency. Now, it was living off tinned meat from Minnesota and chocolate bars made in Pennsylvania.

Despite all this, Rome didn't spiral. It limped, but it moved forward. The city's population, ever adaptive, turned survival into a form of resistance. Empty buildings were squatted, informal cafeterias popped up in social clubs, and Roman ingenuity reasserted itself in kitchens and markets. In Trastevere, women cooked for Allied officers using whatever they could get from the black market or through contacts in the countryside. Recipes got creative, teasing permutations of bread, pasta, potatoes, and legumes into hearty stews.

The rebuilding effort was slow. The economy didn't bounce back immediately, and many Romans continued to rely on UN relief programs and American aid into the 1950s. It's not a coincidence that the UN's Food and Agriculture Organization (FAO, see page 58) was headquartered in Rome from 1951. But help arrived in a big way with the Marshall Plan. Starting in 1948, American aid flowed into Italy in the form of cash, commodities, and agricultural products. Wheat, sugar, and milk powder arrived by the shipload, and propaganda posters in Rome declared this new abundance: *Il pane americano è qui* ("American bread is here"). The posters were part relief, part reminder: This was no longer Mussolini's Italy. A new political order was taking shape, one that looked to the West rather than Fascist fantasies of imperial glory.

In the meantime, Allied troops remained in Rome, leaving their mark on both geopolitics and local culture. American jazz wafted from radios. Soldiers drove demand in osterie and cafés, especially in the areas they were based, Monte Mario and EUR, mainly.

When fresh food returned to markets, when rationing finally ended, Romans returned to what they knew best: cooking seasonally, cooking simply, and stretching ingredients into miracles. Rome didn't come out of the war unscathed, but it emerged with its soul intact. If anything, the deprivation and desperation of the postwar period clarified how much food meant in the Roman imagination: sustenance, community, memory, and pride. The ruins were still there, of course, a cacophony of broken aqueducts and crumbling palazzi. But so was the aroma of pasta e ceci, simmering on a stove somewhere, reminding everyone that they had survived.

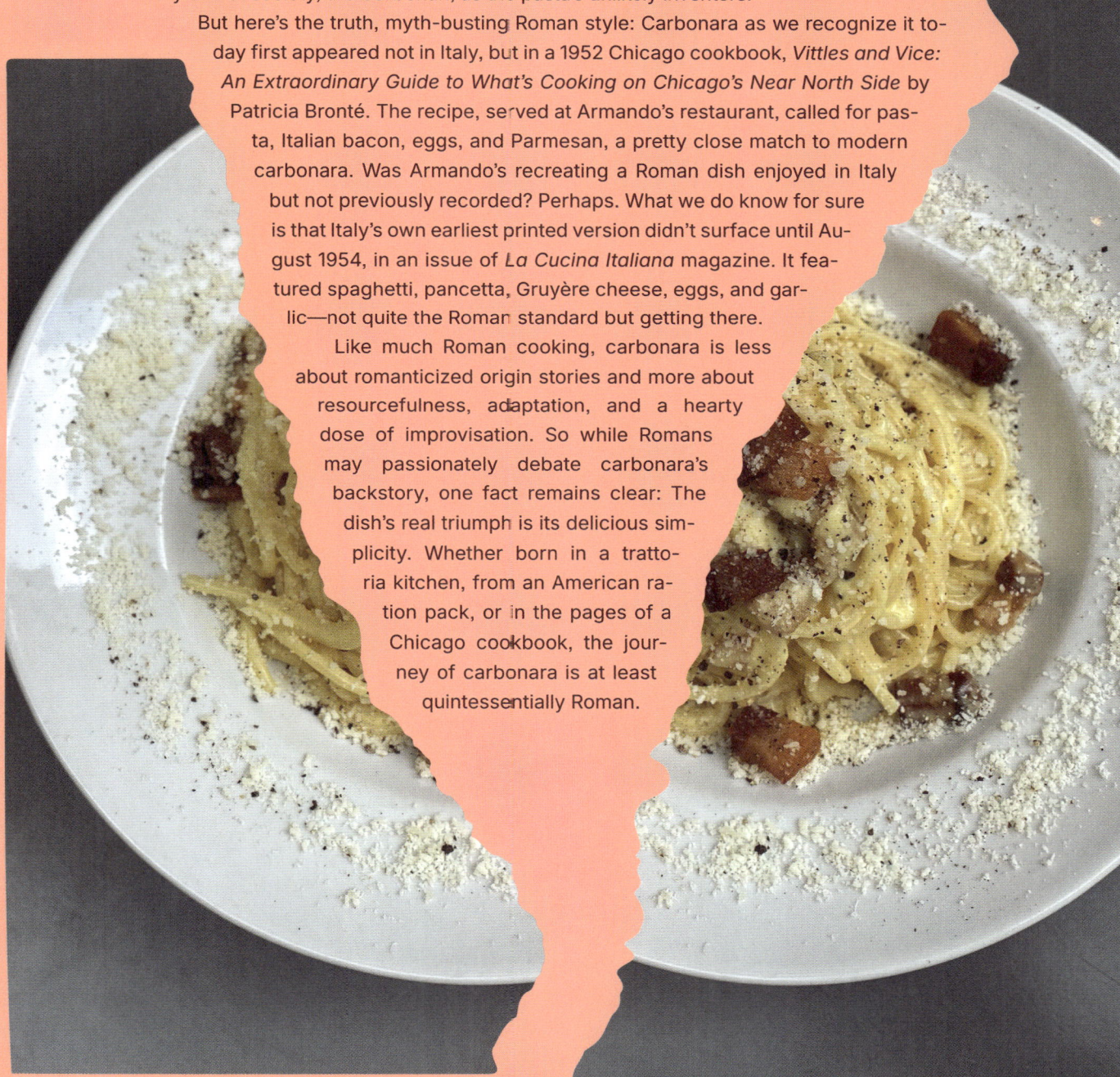

CARBONARA CRACKED!

Romans hotly contest the origins of carbonara (page 107), the city's most famous dish. One popular tale links carbonara to carbonai (charcoal makers) claiming the dish was named after these soot-covered laborers. Then there's the enduring World War II legend, suggesting that American GIs stationed in Rome tossed their rations of powdered eggs and bacon together with pasta, accidentally creating a classic. Even Naples stakes a claim, pointing to its nineteenth-century secret society, the Carbonari, as the pasta's unlikely inventors.

But here's the truth, myth-busting Roman style: Carbonara as we recognize it today first appeared not in Italy, but in a 1952 Chicago cookbook, *Vittles and Vice: An Extraordinary Guide to What's Cooking on Chicago's Near North Side* by Patricia Brontë. The recipe, served at Armando's restaurant, called for pasta, Italian bacon, eggs, and Parmesan, a pretty close match to modern carbonara. Was Armando's recreating a Roman dish enjoyed in Italy but not previously recorded? Perhaps. What we do know for sure is that Italy's own earliest printed version didn't surface until August 1954, in an issue of *La Cucina Italiana* magazine. It featured spaghetti, pancetta, Gruyère cheese, eggs, and garlic—not quite the Roman standard but getting there.

Like much Roman cooking, carbonara is less about romanticized origin stories and more about resourcefulness, adaptation, and a hearty dose of improvisation. So while Romans may passionately debate carbonara's backstory, one fact remains clear: The dish's real triumph is its delicious simplicity. Whether born in a trattoria kitchen, from an American ration pack, or in the pages of a Chicago cookbook, the journey of carbonara is at least quintessentially Roman.

FROM EMPIRE TO EMPATHY: ROME AS A CAPITAL OF FOOD AID

Rome has no shortage of grand, imposing buildings with complex histories, but few carry the same literal and symbolic weight as the headquarters of the Food and Agriculture Organization of the United Nations (FAO). Set on the edge of the Baths of Caracalla, the massive compound is a paradox: a relic of Fascist-era architecture now serving as the beating heart of global food security efforts. It's a place where ancient, Fascist, and contemporary Rome collide, all under the banner of feeding the world.

The building itself has a loaded past. It was originally commissioned by Mussolini in the 1930s as the Ministero dell'Africa Italiana, a government department meant to administer Italy's colonial holdings in Ethiopia, Eritrea, and Somalia. Taking a move from Augustus's handbook, the Duce even erected an obelisk from Aksum in front of it (it was sent back to the Ethiopian city in 2003). Like much of the EUR district, the FAO headquarters was designed to showcase Fascist grandeur, its blocky rationalist style emphasizing strength, order, and permanence. But before it could fulfill its intended purpose, the tides of history shifted. Italy lost its colonial empire in World War II, and by 1951, the building was repurposed to house the FAO, marking a radical departure from its original imperialist intent. Instead of controlling foreign land and resources, it would now be dedicated to ending hunger and improving agricultural sustainability worldwide.

Rome, with its deep ties to agricultural history, was a fitting choice for FAO headquarters. From the grain shipments that fed the Roman Empire to the papal estates that supplied food to the Vatican, the city has always been linked to the logistics of feeding people. And in the modern era, it has become a global hub for food policy. The FAO works on everything from combating desertification in Africa to developing sustainable fishing practices, with a focus on eradicating hunger and ensuring food security. It also plays a critical role in responding to global crises. When famine strikes, when natural disasters disrupt food supply chains, when war forces mass displacement, the FAO mobilizes expertise, resources, and aid to prevent starvation and long-term agricultural collapse.

But the FAO isn't the only food-focused organization operating in Rome. The city is also home to the World Food Programme (WFP), the UN's frontline agency for emergency food aid, and the International Fund for Agricultural Development (IFAD), which finances projects in some of the world's poorest regions. Together, these three institutions make Rome an unlikely capital of global food governance, a place where policymakers, scientists, and economists work to address some of the most pressing food challenges of our time.

The FAO's presence in Rome also has local implications. The organization employs thousands of people from around the world, injecting a distinctly international energy into an otherwise deeply traditional city. Walk through the Viale Aventino, the neighborhood's main thoroughfare, at lunchtime and you'll hear snippets of conversations in a half-dozen languages as FAO employees spill out into nearby restaurants and cafés. Their presence has also contributed to a microeconomy of businesses catering to Rome's expat population in Aventino and its close neighbors—restaurants with Greek, Malaysian, and Japanese menus that lean more global than Roman, and bars where English is as common as Italian.

Yet for all its prestige, FAO remains somewhat disconnected from the daily food culture of Rome. While the organization tackles food security on a global scale, Rome itself still struggles with local food challenges: rising costs for restaurants and markets, threats to small-scale agriculture in Lazio, and an increasing reliance on industrially produced food. It's a strange contradiction—the city that hosts the world's leading food organizations is also a place where its own historic markets and producers are under pressure from economic and political forces.

Despite these tensions and criticisms, Rome's role as a global food hub is undeniable. The building that houses the FAO headquarters may have started as a monument to Fascist ambition, but today, it represents something entirely different: a city at the center of the fight against hunger, working—imperfectly, but persistently—to ensure that food remains a universal right, not a privilege.

MID-CENTURY ROME
(THE 1950S TO MID-1960S)

By the late 1950s, Rome had shaken off the postwar hangover. Romans collectively agreed to suppress the trauma of Fascism, hunger, and loss. (A reckoning for the Fascist sins of the past? No, grazie!) There were less painful things to focus on: The economy was taking off, and the capital was the epicenter of a cultural and culinary glow-up in anticipation of the 1960 Olympic Games.

The so-called miracolo economico (economic miracle), a period of rapid and prolonged growth, transformed the city. Suddenly, industry was booming, factories were churning, FIAT was putting cars on the road faster than anyone could count, and a new Roman middle class was beginning to emerge. That surge of prosperity pulled thousands of people from regions like Sardegna, Abruzzo, and Calabria into Rome in search of work. Whole families packed up their lives and came north. With them came new dialects, new customs, and, most importantly, new flavors.

All this migration changed the way the city ate. Roman food wasn't strictly Roman anymore; it was increasingly peppered with Apennine and southern influences. And as more and more people had a few extra lire in their pockets, they started going out to eat. Not to the fancy ristoranti that their grandparents might have scorned as extravagant, but to casual osterie and trattorie, where you could get a decent plate of pasta or roasted meat without blowing your paycheck. More than meals, they were declarations of socio-economic success. If you weren't scraping by anymore, you could afford to have someone else cook for you.

Enter the supermarket. It may not sound sexy, but this was a radical idea in a city where food shopping had always meant chatting up your butcher, baker, and fruttivendolo six days a week. Now you could wheel a cart around fluorescent-lit aisles, buy milk in a carton, and pick up imported canned goods, American cereals, and frozen peas. Sure, a lot of people still swore by their neighborhood market (and honestly, thank god) but the shift toward mass consumption had begun, and there was no turning back.

This whole era hit its peak with the *Dolce Vita* years—the late '50s and early '60s—when Rome was both a city and a lifestyle brand. Federico Fellini captured it on-screen, but the real show was happening nightly on the Via Veneto. American movie stars, jet-setters, Italian paparazzi (a word literally born from this moment), and glitterati poured into Rome like it was Cannes, Vegas, and New York rolled into one.

Audrey Hepburn and Gregory Peck may have immortalized the city in *Roman Holiday* a few years earlier, but now it was Liz Taylor, Richard Burton, Ava Gardner, and Frank Sinatra downing fettuccine Alfredo at Alfredo alla Scrofa. There were flashbulbs and furs, liveried waiters, and a whole lot of cacio e pepe being eaten by people who couldn't pronounce it. Rome was glitzy and a little gaudy, but after the gray years of the war, it was a dazzling Technicolor dream.

At the same time, a very different version of Rome was being projected in black and white. Neorealist filmmakers like Roberto Rossellini and Vittorio De Sica turned their lenses toward everyday life in the city's working-class neighborhoods. Their films portrayed bombed-out buildings, food shortages, and the moral complexity of survival in a society still reeling from war. This wasn't the Rome of aperitivi and paparazzi, but one where poverty and resilience shaped the rhythm of daily

THE SALT MONOPOLY: A BRIEF HISTORY OF STATE-CONTROLLED SEASONING

In Rome, salt has been a form of currency, a driver of conflict, and the basis for one of the country's longest-standing state monopolies. For centuries, the production and sale of salt were tightly controlled by governments, from medieval popes to the post-unification Italian state. And while today it's something you can grab for less than a euro per kilo at the supermarket, salt's story in Italy is anything but bland.

By the late Middle Ages, the Church and various city-states had realized that controlling salt meant controlling people's access to preservation and flavor and, by extension, their wallets. In the Papal States, salt was heavily taxed and strictly distributed. Smuggling was common, especially in border zones like Romagna and southern Lazio. Entire economies emerged around evading or enforcing salt law.

When the Kingdom of Italy was unified in 1861, it inherited a patchwork of local policies and folded them into a national salt monopoly. From then until the 1970s, salt could only be produced, imported, and sold under the supervision of the Italian state. You had to be licensed as an authorized reseller of both salt and tobacco. These businesses were marked by the familiar "Sali e Tabacchi" signage still visible across Italy today.

Under the monopoly, salt came in standard blue boxes and was sold at fixed prices. In many parts of the country, especially the south, the state discouraged or outright banned artisanal salt harvesting, even in regions like Sicily and Sardegna, where salt had been collected for millennia. This created a paradox: Italy, surrounded by salt flats and saltwater, was importing industrial salt from abroad while local traditions were being erased or pushed underground.

The monopoly began to crumble in the 1970s, when Italy started deregulating the salt trade. But it wasn't until 1994 that the European Union formally ended the last vestiges of the state's monopoly, opening the market to private producers. That paved the way for a revival of historic saltworks like Trapani and Mozia in Sicily and a new wave of artisanal producers reclaiming traditional harvesting methods.

life. Together, these contrasting visions of the city, one saturated in glamour, the other stripped bare, captured the emotional and cultural tension of the era.

And yet, even as luxury flooded the capital, the soul of Roman food stayed grounded. This is the moment in which the trattoria (see page 63) emerged, eclipsing the osteria as the iconic Roman eatery. The male-dominated, heavy-drinking scene at osterie didn't exactly vanish, but it had stiff competition in the more inclusive trattoria that welcomed women and families.

The postwar boom went beyond economic stats and industrial output. It was about what landed on people's tables and how it made them feel. It was about the dignity of being able to feed your family meat, the thrill of a supermarket haul, the pride of feeding your kids store-bought yogurt instead of watered-down milk. But the boom wasn't universal and many Romans and Italian migrants dwelling in the city still faced with hardship. Rome's food culture, like the city itself, was evolving. And if it occasionally got caught in the flash of a paparazzo's camera, so be it. It had earned its close-up, though not everyone had a seat at the table.

TOWARDS A MODERN ROME
(1960–2000)

The 1960s and '70s in Rome were tense. Pasolini's Accattone (1961) portrayed the moral and economic desperation in the borgate, Rome's marginalized postwar periphery. It served as a cinematic counterpoint to the myth of national progress, revealing how uneven and exclusionary the so-called economic miracle had been.

By the late '60s, the city, like the rest of Italy, was in the grip of what came to be called the Anni di Piombo (the Years of Lead), a time of political violence and assassinations during which a heavy fear seeped into everyday life. Far-left groups like the Red Brigades were kidnapping politicians and murdering magistrates. Far-right extremists carried out bombings and were often aided or shielded by elements within the state.

Daily life in the city got weird. People avoided crowded places. Trattorie were quieter at night. You didn't linger over a plate of pasta without checking who was sitting around you. There was a creeping paranoia that maybe the kid with the flyer or the guy with the bulky jacket wasn't a regular student or an ordinary citizen. But in true Roman fashion, people carried on. You still went to the market, still cooked Sunday lunch. The world may have been unstable, but la cucina romana remained a source of identity and comfort.

Meanwhile, behind the scenes, Rome was changing—again! By the '80s, the political violence began to wane, and Italy found itself at the threshold of a new era. Rome entered the decade with a cautious optimism. The economy was stabilizing, and there was a sense that things might get better. Families who had once pinched lire to make ends meet now had a little extra to spend. Women were becoming increasingly part of the workforce, more people were going to university, and television was shaping culture like never before.

And all this had a ripple effect on food. The '80s were the beginning of what we might call Rome's real reckoning with globalization and consumer culture. First, McDonald's showed up near the Spanish Steps in 1986 (see page 191), and locals freaked out. It wasn't only a matter of disliking the food, but what it represented: Americanization, industrialization, the slow erasure of profoundly rooted food traditions. The postwar gleam of American generosity and the admiration that accompanied it had officially faded. That same year, the Slow Food movement gained momentum with their protests in Rome, not far from where tourists were ordering Big Macs with Coke. The idea wasn't literally about eating slowly—it was about preserving something deeply Italian. Gambero Rosso (see page 64) was founded in a similar spirit later in the year as well.

OSTERIA TO TRATTORIA: TRANSITIONS IN ROMAN DINING OUT

One of the most common questions I get on food tours is "What's the difference between an osteria, a trattoria, and a ristorante?" To visitors, these words can feel interchangeable. After all, in North America, they'd all be just plain "restaurants." But in Rome, each term has historical roots that say a lot about how locals have eaten, drank, and socialized over the centuries. Understanding these distinctions is more than semantics: they're a window into Roman life.

Let's start with the osteria (sometimes spelled *hostaria*). In the old days, osterie were glorified, tavern-like drinking dens. Their main function wasn't to feed you—it was to pour you inexpensive local wine. That's it. They were boisterous and smoky, full of men playing cards, gossiping, arguing politics, and whiling away the hours. The point was more about conviviality than cuisine. Food was an afterthought, if it was offered at all—maybe some olives, a boiled egg, or a slab of pecorino if you were lucky. More often, you'd bring your own food from home or buy a snack from a street vendor on your way in. The vibe was no-frills, borderline chaotic, and deeply communal, all with a steady chorus of romanesco dialect echoing off the walls.

The transformation from osteria to trattoria didn't happen overnight. Many of the trattorie that claim roots before the 1950s were almost certainly born as osterie. After World War II, as Italy entered its "economic miracle" phase, urban migration and rising incomes changed how people dined. Romans, especially the expanding middle class, began eating out more frequently. In response, osterie started adding simple, homestyle dishes to their offerings.

This shift gave birth to the trattoria: still casual, still affordable, but now reliably feeding you a full meal, from antipasto to dolce, built around regional traditions. Trattorie became spaces for families, not just men, and their menus reflected the cucina romana that the city was starting to be prouder of than ever: bucatini all'amatriciana, trippa alla romana, abbacchio a scottadito. These weren't fancy dishes, but they were rooted in tradition and made with local ingredients, often drawn from Rome's surrounding countryside. In a rapidly modernizing society, trattorie became cultural anchors, preserving recipes and also ways of cooking and eating that might have otherwise faded into obscurity.

Then there's the ristorante. Historically, that term implied a more formal, polished affair, with printed menus, professional service, and a chef in the kitchen (as opposed to a mom-and-pop operation). Restaurants were more likely to adopt trends, lean into nouvelle cuisine, or cater to international tastes. They weren't necessarily better, just different and more exclusive. In fact, the line between trattoria and ristorante started to blur in the 1980s and '90s, especially in tourist-heavy areas, where even a fine dining spot might slap *hosteria* onto their sign to conjure nostalgia.

Today, these distinctions are less rigid. You might find a place calling itself an osteria that serves a tasting menu, or a trattoria with ristorante prices. But knowing the roots helps decode what kind of experience you might be walking into and what kind of story that venue is choosing to tell about itself and the city's past.

A HISTORY OF ROME (AND HOW IT EATS)

FROM MANIFESTO TO MONEYMAKER: THE RISE OF GAMBERO ROSSO

Long before Gambero Rosso was a sprawling culinary media empire synonymous with three-fork ratings, wine scores, and global events, it was a scrappy insert tucked inside *il manifesto*, Italy's leftist daily. Launched in Rome in 1986 as a lean eight pages, the insert carried a revolutionary idea: Food and wine weren't merely bourgeois indulgences: they were culture. Pleasure wasn't antithetical to politics; it was fundamental to life itself. Today, you'll spot the brand's signature sticker in the windows of establishments they recommend, a quiet nod to an institution that began as a countercultural voice and grew into a powerful tastemaker.

The late Stefano Bonilli, a former *il manifesto* journalist, was behind this radical vision. Together with graphic designer Piergiorgio Maoloni, whose bold layouts shaped the publication's visual identity, Bonilli created a fresh approach to food journalism, one blending critical commentary, cultural insight, and celebration of Italy's culinary richness. Naming it Gambero Rosso (a nod to the tavern in Pinocchio where deceit and allure intertwined) signaled clearly that food was storytelling as much as sustenance.

By the late '80s, Gambero Rosso had outgrown its cult-zine status, blossoming into a publishing powerhouse. In 1987, Bonilli joined forces with the burgeoning Slow Food movement, cofounding Vini d'Italia, which quickly became Italy's definitive wine guide, arguably surpassing Michelin's influence. Edited by Daniele Cernilli and Slow Food pioneer Carlo Petrini, it started to reshape how Italians judged wine.

In 1990, Gambero Rosso introduced the Ristoranti d'Italia guide, rating restaurants with forks instead of stars, acknowledging that greatness didn't always involve white linen or formal attire. Over time, it embraced trattorie, wine bars, street food stalls, and pizzerias, becoming Italy's most democratic dining authority.

In 1999, Gambero Rosso leaped into television, launching Italy's first dedicated food and wine channel. Long before chefs dominated global TV and streaming platforms changed media forever, Gambero Rosso set the standard, eventually migrating to Sky Italia and broadcasting in HD by 2012.

Then came Rome's original Città del Gusto in 2002—a sprawling culinary campus overlooking the Tiber, featuring cooking schools, TV studios, tasting theaters, a wine bar, an osteria, and a pizzeria. Built without public funding, it quickly became the template for gastronomic education across Italy, with campuses opening throughout the country from Naples to Torino. More than culinary schools, these were incubators shaping Italy's next generation of chefs, sommeliers, and food communicators.

Yet success wasn't frictionless. In 2008, Bonilli was forced out, eventually winning a court battle against the company he founded. Undeterred, Gambero Rosso expanded, embracing digital apps and global events like the Tre Bicchieri wine awards and the Top Italian Wines Roadshow, touring more than thirty cities annually.

From its radical roots to today's gourmet empire, Gambero Rosso has left an indelible mark on how middle-class Romans and Italians perceive wine and restaurants today. It wasn't always this way. For much of the twentieth century, serious discussions about wine and dining were confined to elite circles, niche knowledge passed among sommeliers, critics, and the upper classes. Gambero Rosso helped blow that wide open. By reframing food and wine as culture, not class, it democratized access to information and taste. Its guides, TV programs, and cooking schools gave ordinary Italians the tools and the language to talk about wine pairings, regional specialties, and restaurant quality with authority. What had once been the preserve of fine dining became part of everyday life. In this way, Gambero Rosso went beyond reporting on Italy's food culture, it helped create a new one.

That tension between tradition and progress defined the decade. On one hand, you had supermarkets offering convenience, uniformity, and products from all over the world. On the other, you had a renewed appreciation for regional products and home cooking. You started to see a push to document and preserve Rome's culinary identity—books and shows about Roman food, chefs reclaiming old recipes and giving them new life in trattorias that were suddenly being written up in foreign travel guides.

Of course, Rome has always been porous, always adapting. There's fortunately no such thing as a perfectly preserved culinary tradition here. But in the 1980s, the stakes suddenly felt higher. The influx of international influences like fast food, frozen products, and imported ingredients coincided with a growing awareness that some things were worth protecting. Recipes like Coda alla Vaccinara (page 169) or Trippa alla Romana (page 201) came to embody Rome's collective memory.

By the end of the '80s, Roman food wasn't only about survival anymore, or even just tradition. It was about pride. The city had emerged from a very dark period, and though things were far from perfect—corruption, inequality, and political dysfunction persisted—there was a desire to root the future in something meaningful. Food, as always, was the foundation.

CONTEMPORARY ROME
(2000–PRESENT)

By the turn of the twenty-first century, Rome had settled into the rhythms of a modern European capital, but its food culture was far from settled. The economic boom of the postwar decades had long since faded, and the last great wave of internal migration from southern Italy was mostly complete. Rome's culinary identity, once defined by that influx of regional traditions, began shifting in new directions, shaped by changing work patterns, economic crises, immigration, gentrification, and evolving tastes.

As more Roman women entered the workforce in the 1990s and first decade of the 2000s, and as work days grew longer and more erratic for everyone, the daily ritual of shopping at the market and cooking a full meal became increasingly rare. Convenience gained ground. Supermarkets, which had been relatively scarce in Rome until the late twentieth century, rapidly expanded. By the early 2000s, the city had one of the highest per capita concentrations of supermarkets in Europe, comparable to the United States. For a growing number of residents, the daily food shop had been replaced by the weekly car trip to a hypermarket or a late-night run to a twenty-four-hour Todis.

This shift in shopping habits didn't just change what people bought; it also affected how and what they cooked. The postwar staples of Roman home cooking like minestra and offal-based secondi began to appear less frequently on home tables. The younger generation, raised on frozen food and a faster pace of life, turned increasingly to delivery, takeaway, and premade meals. And as incomes stagnated in the aftermath of the 2008 global financial crisis, dining out became more occasional, more selective. Restaurants had to respond or close.

Some did close, especially those midrange family trattorias that had once formed the backbone of Roman dining. Others adapted. What emerged in their place was a new genre: the neo-trattoria. These pared-down, chef-driven restaurants maintained a deep respect for Roman culinary tradition, but they approached it with a fresh eye. Many were opened by chefs who had trained in Michelin kitchens or culinary schools in northern Italy and abroad. They returned to Rome with technique, restraint, and a desire to reframe local food in a modern context. Dishes like Pasta e Ceci (page 154) and Coratella (page 197) remained staples, but now they were plated with precision, made with top-tier ingredients, and served in minimalist dining rooms with curated wine lists heavy on natural bottles from Italy and France.

Street food (see page 334) also underwent a transformation during this time, propelled by both economic necessity and creative rethinking. Stefano Callegari's 2008 invention of the trapizzino (page 256), a handheld triangle of pizza bianca filled with classic Roman stews, reimagined leftovers as high-concept fast food. Other vendors followed suit, elevating supplì from basic rice balls to expressions of culinary experimentation, filled with ingredients like truffle, pumpkin, or oxtail. Pizza al taglio, too, evolved from quick lunch to high art. Pizzaioli like Gabriele Bonci, of Pizzarium and Panificio Bonci fame, pioneered long-fermented doughs made from stone-milled wheats, topped with hyperseasonal, often organic produce. What had once been the food of schoolchildren and office workers became a showcase for serious baking technique and ingredient sourcing.

This revival of bread-making spilled into Rome's bakery culture. A wave of small, independent bakeries like Triticum and Lievito emerged across the city, turning out naturally leavened loaves made with heritage grains. It was a quiet revolution in a country where industrial white bread had long dominated. Artisanal baking came to represent not just a return to tradition but a rejection of the mass-produced.

Coffee culture (see page 308) began to change as well. For decades, the Roman bar experience had remained virtually unchanged: Stand at the counter, shoot back an espresso, maybe grab a cornetto. But in the 2010s, third-wave coffee culture began to take root. Cafés like Faro introduced Romans to single-origin beans, pour-over brewing, and oat milk flat whites. They didn't replace the classic bars, but they gave Romans, especially younger ones, a new kind of space: one that encouraged lingering, working, and drinking coffee slowly.

Meanwhile, Rome's cocktail scene (see page 319), practically nonexistent outside swanky hotel bars, exploded. The Jerry Thomas Project, a speakeasy-style bar that opened in 2010, helped jump-start the city's craft mixology movement. Soon, cocktail bars were cropping up across Monti, Trastevere, Pigneto, and Prati. The rise of cocktails paralleled the shift toward aperitivo culture, where the pairing of drinks and food after work became more curated, often influenced by international trends and local reinterpretation.

Immigration, long a part of Roman life, continued to reshape the city's foodways. While systemic racism and economic marginalization often kept immigrant chefs and food workers on the fringes of culinary visibility, the flavors of Bangladesh, Peru, North and East Africa, and the Philippines became increasingly present in the city's diet, especially in multicultural neighborhoods like Tor Pignattara, Esquilino, and Centocelle. Some Roman chefs began incorporating these influences into their menus, while others, often second-generation immigrants, opened their own places, merging Roman techniques with family traditions.

Through all this, Rome remained a city in flux, economically precarious, socially stratified, and deeply attached to its past. But its food never stopped evolving. Even as tourists sought "authentic" carbonara in trattorias, Romans themselves were eating poke bowls for lunch, ordering sushi on Saturday nights, and slamming smashburgers at hipster joints. Taste shifted with age, income, trend cycles, and Instagram.

The visual economy of food had an outsize impact, too. Rome's food scene went from being locally anchored to globally visible. Social media drove interest in Roman food but also standardized it in some ways. Suddenly, carbonara had to look a certain way. Maritozzi had to ooze cream for the camera. Supplì had to stretch like a mozzarella commercial. Some cooks leaned into that aesthetic, while others rejected it outright, focusing instead on flavor, ethics, and sustainability.

Today, contemporary Roman food is defined less by a singular set of dishes than by an attitude: one that reveres tradition but resists dogma. It is found in neighborhood trattorias serving unflashy but deeply satisfying plates; in natural wine bars with no written menu; in Libyan Jewish bakeries, Egyptian-run pizzerias, and bakeries reviving heritage grains. It thrives in aperitivo spreads and pastry counters, delivery apps and fermentation labs. It is diverse, contradictory, and constantly changing, just like Rome. In short, the Roman table is still being set.

EATALY AND MERCATO CENTRALE: THE MALL-IFICATION OF FOOD CULTURE

In twenty-first-century Rome, two major food spaces have significantly reshaped how Romans experience food outside traditional marketplaces: Eataly, opened in 2012, and Mercato Centrale, launched in 2016. Both are strategically housed in repurposed railway spaces: Eataly in the vast Ostiense terminal and Mercato Centrale within Termini. These locations were deliberate, exploiting high foot traffic and convenience, yet their polished veneers often emphasize marketing and curated aesthetics more than culinary authenticity.

Eataly, founded in Piedmont in 2007 by Italian businessman Oscar Farinetti, ultimately arrived in Rome as an ambitious culinary megastore, blending big-box grocery shopping with casual dining. You might think Romans would be skeptical of such places, remaining fiercely loyal to neighborhood alimentari and local markets. Nah. Supermarkets are the norm for shopping. No one blinked. This success reveals how Italian food identity, long promoted under the "Made in Italy" brand, can blur the line between genuine tradition and skillful marketing. On four expansive floors, Eataly offers meticulously arranged aisles of incredible small-batch olive oils, high-quality pastas, and artisan wines, right alongside inferior industrial counterparts, conflating the high quality of one with the other. It's a problem.

Mercato Centrale shares similar strategic positioning, leveraging the busy crossroads of Rome's main train station. Founded by Italian entrepreneur Umberto Montano, Mercato Centrale transformed a former fascist-era bar-restaurant and later piano store into a sleek, vibrant market hall. It debuted with popular vendors such as pizza megastar Gabriele Bonci's Panificio, butcher Roberto Liberati's eponymous Bottega Liberati, and pizza innovator Stefano Callegari's Trapizzino. Only the latter survives in the Mercato, the other stalls having become a veritable revolving door as vendors get enticed to open, then can't make it work financially. This fact has done nothing to dampen the high energy of the place, which churns out pizzas, steaks, and smashburgers while guests order drinks via an app. To say it lacks the chaotic charm and genuine soul of traditional markets like Testaccio would be an understatement. And yet, I don't hate Mercato Centrale. In fact, I include it on my Esquilino tour—mostly for Trapizzino but also for the conversation it permits about the reality of consumption in Rome and how it conflicts with romantic stereotypes.

Both spaces reflect broader European trends where modern food markets are increasingly becoming stylish, commercial destinations rather than purely functional urban amenities. They offer controlled environments and a sanitized, accessible version of Rome's food culture ideal for contemporary consumer habits. Eataly and Mercato Centrale successfully cater to modern Romans, expats, tourists, and food professionals looking for convenience and variety. For now, however, they do not replace Rome's historical food traditions but rather coexist alongside them.

A HISTORY OF ROME (AND HOW IT EATS)

FRIED SNACKS AND STARTERS

POLPETTE DI BOLLITO

FRIED
    BRAISED-BEEF
MEATBALLS

Makes 12 polpette

1 pound beef shin or chuck,
    connective tissue
    removed
1 cup dry white wine
2 carrots
2 celery stalks
1 medium yellow onion
10 whole black peppercorns
1 medium potato, boiled
    until tender, peeled, and
    roughly chopped
Grated zest of 1 lemon
½ cup finely grated Pecorino
    Romano
1 tablespoon finely chopped
    fresh flat-leaf parsley
Sea salt and freshly ground
    black pepper
4 large eggs
1 cup all-purpose flour
1½ cups breadcrumbs or
    panko
Neutral oil, for frying
2 lemons, cut into wedges,
    for serving

Romans never have been shy about putting leftovers to good use, especially when they involve meat that's already been simmered to tender perfection. Polpette di bollito are a thrifty byproduct of allesso di bollito, a slowly braised cut of beef similar to brisket. Once the broth has done its work, the leftover meat is shredded, bound with egg and breadcrumbs, and fried into golden spheres or patties that are crisp on the outside and soft and savory within. The polpette are usually served hot, as an antipasto or snack, perhaps with a wedge of lemon or a dab of salsa verde to cut through the richness. Taking a page from Mara Esposito's book at Mordi e Vai in the Testaccio Market, I add lemon zest to my polpette for flavor and aroma.

Place the beef in a large pot. Cover with cold water and bring to a boil over high heat, skimming off any foam that rises to the top. Once the foam has subsided, add the wine, carrots, celery, onion, and peppercorns and return to a boil, then reduce to a simmer over low heat until the beef is fork-tender, 2 to 3 hours. Set aside to cool in the liquid.

When cool enough to handle, transfer the beef to a cutting board; strain and reserve the broth for another dish. Chop or shred the beef into small pieces. Transfer to a large bowl and add the potato, lemon zest, Pecorino Romano, and parsley. Mix well with your hands and season with salt and pepper until the mixture tastes well seasoned. Mix in 2 of the eggs.

Set up your breading station: Pour the flour into a shallow bowl. Beat the remaining 2 eggs in a medium bowl. Pour the breadcrumbs into another shallow bowl. Season the flour, eggs, and breadcrumbs with salt.

Form the beef mixture into 3-inch patties, about ½ inch thick. Dredge each one first in the flour, shaking off the excess, then dip in the egg, allowing the excess to drip off, and finally coat in the breadcrumbs. Set the patties aside on a plate.

Line a platter or baking sheet with paper towels.

Heat 2 inches of oil to 350°F in a medium frying pan or cast-iron skillet. Fry the meatballs in batches, taking care not to overcrowd the pan, until golden brown, 4 to 5 minutes. Turn midway through to ensure even browning.

Remove the polpette with a slotted spoon and drain on the paper towels. Sprinkle with salt and serve hot with lemon wedges on the side.

FIORI DI ZUCCA

FRIED SQUASH BLOSSOMS STUFFED WITH MOZZARELLA AND ANCHOVIES

Serves 6

¾ cup very cold lager or sparkling water

1½ cups all-purpose flour

½ teaspoon baking soda

Sea salt

Neutral oil, for frying

6 ounces fresh mozzarella, cut into 12 equal pieces and squeezed dry

12 oil-packed anchovy fillets, drained

12 squash blossoms, stamens removed

Of all the things in Rome I am guaranteed to burn my mouth on, this fried staple is at the top of the list. Fiori di zucca are served at some trattorie and at one hundred percent of pizzerias, alongside other classics like Filetti di Baccalà (page 78), olive ascolane (meat-filled fried olives in the style of Le Marche), and Supplì (page 80). The softly fried outer layer and delicate flower give way to molten mozzarella and salted anchovy within. You'll find fiori di zucca year-round, as some sort of zucchini or squash is always in season in central Italy, but they are especially popular in the summer, when they are sold in bunches at markets, and they rarely surpass the outrageously low price of €1.50 for six.

Tip: Always start with the liquid in the bowl, then gradually add the flour to minimize lumps.

Line a platter or baking sheet with paper towels.

Whisk together the lager, flour, baking soda, and a heavy pinch of salt in a medium bowl until the batter is smooth and lump-free. Set over an ice bath to keep it very cold.

Heat 2 inches of oil to 350°F in a medium frying pan or cast-iron skillet.

Gently tuck a piece of mozzarella and an anchovy fillet inside each squash blossom, taking care not to tear the delicate petals. One at a time, grasp the tips of the flowers, dip them into the batter, and coat them evenly, letting any excess drip off while making sure the tips stay sealed. Lower them into the hot oil and fry in batches, turning once, until golden and crisp, 2 to 3 minutes.

Remove the flowers with a slotted spoon and drain on paper towels. Sprinkle with salt and serve immediately.

FRITTATA AI CARCIOFI

ARTICHOKE
OMELET

A frittata is the ultimate fridge clean-out meal, but don't let that fool you into thinking it's some sad, last-resort dish. In Rome, it's a staple, whether packed into a panino for a quick lunch, sliced into neat wedges for an antipasto spread, or eaten straight from the pan when no one's watching. The beauty of a frittata is its adaptability: a handful of greens past their prime, a nub of pecorino, some leftover roasted potatoes—nothing goes to waste. The key is patience. Cook it low and slow, resisting the urge to poke at it, until the edges crisp up and the center just sets. No flipping theatrics required. And if you're eating it in a ciabatta on the sidewalk in front of Forno Campo de' Fiori at lunchtime? Congratulations, you've officially mastered Rome.

Makes 1 frittata, serving 4 to 6

¼ cup extra-virgin olive oil
1 garlic clove, smashed
3 tender young globe
   artichokes, cleaned and
   trimmed (see Tip), then
   cut into eighths
Sea salt
8 large eggs
Freshly ground black pepper

Preheat the oven to 325°F.

Heat the olive oil in a medium ovenproof pan over low heat. When the oil begins to shimmer, add the garlic and cook just until it starts to take on color, about 5 minutes. Remove and discard the garlic. Add the artichokes to the pan and season with a heavy pinch of salt. Increase the heat to medium and continue to cook, stirring, for 5 minutes. Cover, reduce the heat to medium-low, and cook until tender, 20 to 25 minutes. Stir every few minutes.

Meanwhile, whisk the eggs in a large bowl with salt and pepper.

Add the eggs to the pan, stirring a few times, moving from the edge of the pan toward the middle. Once the eggs begin to set around the edge of the pan 1½ to 2 minutes, turn off the heat. Transfer the pan to the oven and bake until the top of the frittata starts to brown and the edges pull away from the sides of the pan, 8 to 10 minutes.

Set aside to cool slightly. To unmold, run a heatproof spatula around the edges of the frittata. Slide it onto a serving plate. Serve at room temperature, sliced into wedges or as a sandwich filling.

Tip: Fill a large bowl with cold water, squeeze in the juice of 1 lemon, and toss in one of the spent halves. To prep the artichokes, snap off the tough outer leaves near the base, continuing to peel them away until you reach the pale, tender inner ones. With a sharp knife held at an angle, trim the top of the artichoke to remove any remaining tough bits. Rub the cut surfaces with the second lemon half to keep them from browning. Use a paring knife to carefully strip away the dark green outer layer around the base. Trim the stem, leaving about 3 inches attached, and peel the tough exterior until you reach its pale center. Drop everything into the lemon water to prevent discoloration.

CLEANING AND TRIMMING ARTICHOKES

FILETTI DI BACCALÀ

BATTERED
FRIED COD
FILLETS

Serves 6

¾ cup very cold lager or
   sparkling water
1½ cups all-purpose flour
½ teaspoon baking soda
Sea salt
1½ pounds salt cod fillets,
   soaked (see Tip), rinsed,
   patted dry, and cut into 12
   equal pieces
Neutral oil, for frying
2 lemons, cut into wedges,
   for serving

Rome may not be a seaside city, but that hasn't stopped its residents from developing a serious taste for fried fish. Filetti di baccalà (plump fillets of imported salt cod dipped in a batter and fried until golden) are a cornerstone of the city's fritti culture. These crisp, tender slabs originated in the Jewish Ghetto and have become a fixture at pizzerias. They're especially popular on meatless Fridays and Christmas Eve, when religious observance calls for fish, not flesh. Salt cod's appeal in Rome goes way back: It's inexpensive, easy to store, and once properly soaked, it's a blank canvas for flavor. The quintessential place to try one is at Dar Filettaro di Santa Barbara near Campo de' Fiori, where the fillets are massive, slightly greasy (OK, disconcertingly greasy), and absolutely worth it for the full time-capsule experience transporting you back to the 1960s. Eat the cod hot, preferably standing on the cobblestones outside, with a cold beer in hand to wash it all down. Then, when you want a properly fried one without the excess grease, visit A Rota in Tor Pignattara or Trattoria da Cesare al Casaletto in the Gianicolense district.

Tip: To desalinate the cod, soak it in plenty of water for at least 24 hours, changing the water at least three times, until both the water and the fish lose their saltiness.

Line a platter or baking sheet with paper towels.

Whisk together the lager, flour, baking soda, and a heavy pinch of salt in a medium bowl until the batter is smooth and lump-free. Set over an ice bath to keep it very cold.

Heat 2 inches of oil to 350°F in a medium frying pan or cast-iron skillet.

Working in batches, dip the fillets into the batter, letting the excess drip off, then lower them carefully into the hot oil. Fry, turning once, until they are golden and crisp, about 5 minutes total.

Remove the cod with a slotted spoon or tongs and drain on paper towels. Sprinkle with salt and serve immediately with lemon wedges on the side and cold, cheap beer on the table.

SUPPLÌ AL TELEFONO

FRIED
CHEESE-FILLED
RICE
CROQUETTES

There are a few places in town that are truly worth the hype of their fried rice croquettes. Supplì in Trastevere is one of them. This place delivers consistency and affordability—at two euros a piece—with each oblong supplì that fulfills the promise of a mozzarella pull, hence the name *al telefono*, a nod to old-school phone cords. Their secret is frying in small batches so that they're always serving piping-hot croquettes, unlike other spots that might fry all their snacks at noon and dole them out for the rest of the day, only to result in congealed centers. My own supplì recipe is a mashup of the versions from Supplì, Arcangelo Dandini (owner of Supplizio), and Ada Boni (the godmother of Roman cooking, see page 52), all of whose recipes use meat. You can keep it vegetarian by omitting the meat and substituting vegetable broth for beef broth.

Line a platter or baking sheet with parchment paper.

Heat the olive oil in a medium pan over low heat. When the oil begins to shimmer, add the carrot, celery, onion, and a heavy pinch of salt and cook until the vegetables are very soft, about 20 minutes. Increase the heat to medium and add the ground beef. Break up the meat with a spoon and cook until lightly browned, about 8 minutes, then add the rice and stir to coat. Continue stirring until the rice is lightly toasted, about 2 minutes, then add the wine and increase the heat to high. Stir until the alcohol aroma dissipates, about 1 minute, then add 2 cups of the broth. Cook, stirring occasionally, until the broth has been absorbed, about 5 minutes. Add the tomatoes and cook, stirring occasionally, until the liquid has been absorbed, 3 minutes more. Add the remaining broth ½ cup at a time, stirring occasionally, waiting until the rice has absorbed the broth each time before adding more. The rice is ready when it is al dente, 15 to 17 minutes total. You may not need all the broth.

Makes 10 supplì

2 tablespoons extra-virgin
   olive oil
1 carrot, finely chopped
1 celery stalk, finely chopped
½ medium yellow onion,
   finely chopped
Sea salt
3 ounces ground beef
1¼ cups Arborio rice
½ cup dry white wine
5 cups beef broth, warmed
1 (14-ounce) can whole
   peeled tomatoes, crushed
   by hand and warmed
1 cup finely grated
   Parmigiano-Reggiano
Freshly ground black pepper
1 cup all-purpose flour
2 large eggs
1 cup breadcrumbs or panko
Neutral oil, for frying
4 ounces low-moisture
   mozzarella, cut into 10
   equal pieces

Remove the pan from the heat and stir in the Parmigiano-Reggiano. Season with salt and pepper. Spread the rice over the prepared platter and refrigerate until cool, about 1 hour.

Meanwhile, set up your breading station: Pour the flour into a shallow bowl. Beat the eggs in a medium bowl. Pour the breadcrumbs into another shallow bowl. Season the flour, eggs, and breadcrumbs with salt.

Remove the platter from the refrigerator and shape the rice into ten equal balls; each should be the shape and size of a goose egg. Working with one ball at a time, hold it in your palm and make a depression in the center. Place a piece of mozzarella in the depression and close the rice around the mozzarella.

Dredge each supplì first in the flour, shaking off the excess, then dip in the egg, allowing the excess to drip off, and then coat in the breadcrumbs. Set the supplì aside on a plate.

Line a platter or baking sheet with paper towels.

Heat 2 inches of oil to 350°F in a medium frying pan or cast-iron skillet. Fry the supplì in batches, turning to cook evenly, until deep golden brown, 6 to 7 minutes.

Remove the supplì with a slotted spoon and drain on the paper towels. Sprinkle with salt and allow to cool for 5 minutes before serving. You'll be tempted to try one sooner, but let me tell you: Molten mozzarella will ruin your day and your soft palate.

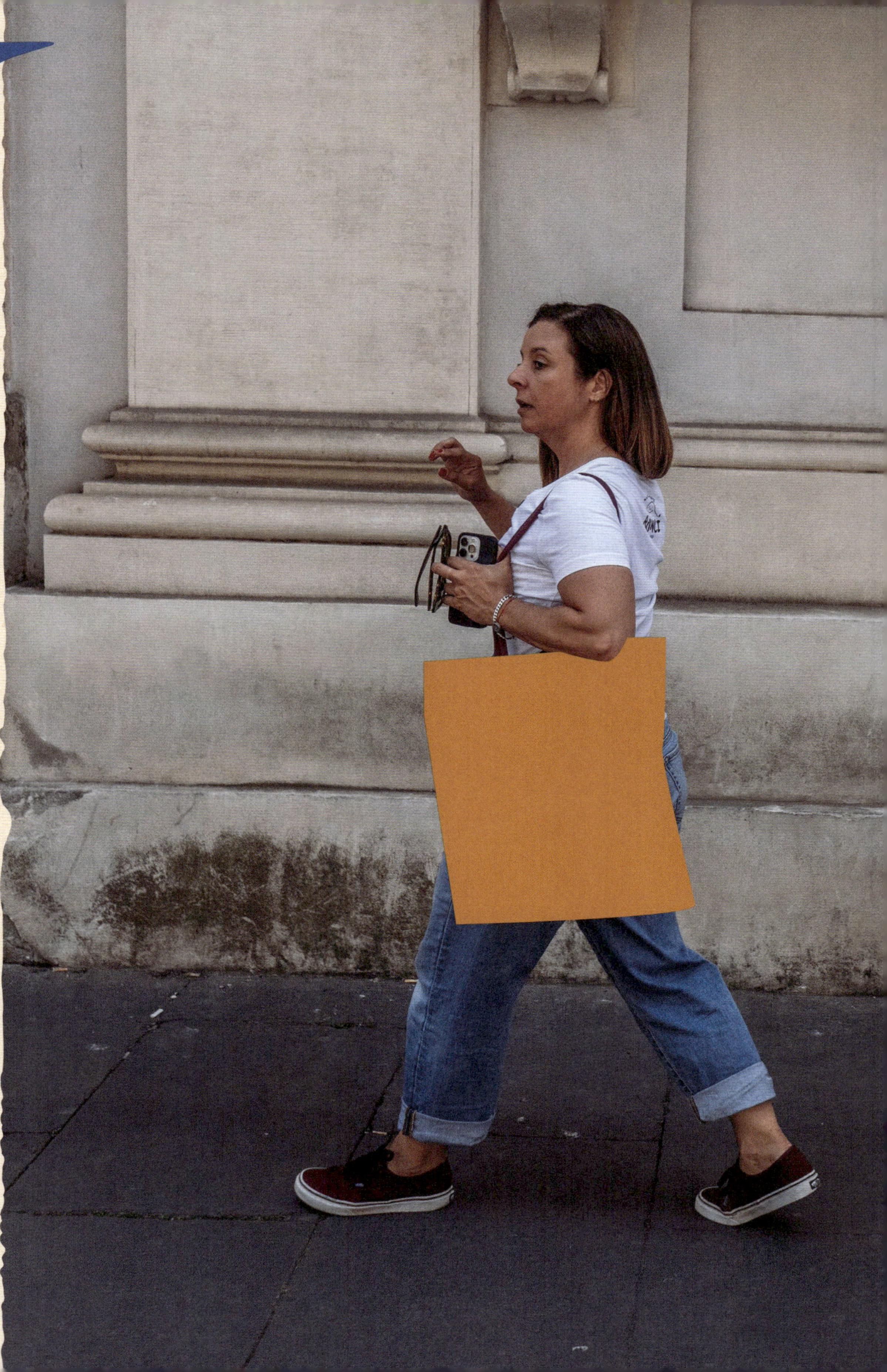

CONCIA

FRIED MARINATED ZUCCHINI

If fried artichokes are the famous stars of Rome's Jewish kitchen, concia (fried zucchini soaked in a punchy, garlicky marinade) is its best-kept secret. Zucchini slices are fried until deeply golden, then hit with vinegar, garlic, and mint (or sometimes parsley), transforming humble summer squash into something addictive. It's classic Roman-Jewish cooking: simple ingredients, smart technique, big flavor. Concia is best at room temperature, after it's had time to marinate, and it shines with good bread or as part of a larger spread. In Rome, we use zucchine romanesche, the pale green, ridged kind, and we're not shy about frying them unti they're browned beyond recognition. Grow your own or use conventional zucchini instead.

Serves 4 to 6

6 medium zucchini, cut into ¼-inch-thick rounds

Sea salt

2 garlic cloves, roughly chopped

2 tablespoons fresh mint leaves, torn

⅔ cup white wine vinegar

Extra-virgin olive oil, for frying

Sliced toasted bread, for serving

Toss the zucchini in a colander with a few heavy pinches of salt to draw out the moisture and set over the sink to drain for 30 minutes. Rinse and pat dry.

Line a platter or baking sheet with paper towels.

Combine the garlic, mint, and vinegar in a casserole dish and set aside.

Heat ½ inch of olive oil to 350°F in a medium frying pan or cast-iron skillet. Fry the zucchini in batches until golden brown, 5 to 7 minutes, adding more oil as needed.

Remove the zucchini with a slotted spoon and drain on the paper towels. Season with salt.

Add the zucchini and mint to the vinegar mixture and toss to coat. Cover and transfer to the refrigerator to marinate for at least 2 hours or overnight.

Bring to room temperature, then serve with toast, as a sandwich filling, or on it's own.

CARCIOFI ALLA GIUDIA

TWICE-FRIED
JEWISH-STYLE
ARTICHOKES

Serves 6

Neutral oil, for frying
6 tender young globe
   artichokes, cleaned and
   trimmed (see Tip on page
   75)
Sea salt

It's hard to imagine Roman cuisine without artichokes, but for centuries they were deeply tied to the city's Jewish community, which was forced to live in a cramped, flood-prone slum known as the Ghetto (see page 40). It was there, in improvised kitchens and at makeshift fry stations, that carciofi alla giudia (Jewish-style fried artichokes) were born. The dish likely dates back to the arrival of Sephardic Jews fleeing the Inquisition; they brought with them culinary traditions rooted in eastern ingredients, like artichokes. For a long time, artichokes were dismissed by Catholic Romans for their Jewish associations, but today they're a defining feature of the Roman table.

This recipe calls for young globe artichokes, the kind you can eat whole after some trimming. The outer leaves crisp like chips, the heart softens, and the whole thing takes on a bronzed, almost sculptural beauty. You'll need a fair amount of oil—and some patience—but the payoff is pure Roman history you can eat with your hands. No sauce needed.

Line a platter or baking sheet with paper towels.

Pour enough oil to submerge the artichokes in a deep pan or Dutch oven and heat to 275°F. Gently fry the artichokes until the heart is fork-tender, about 20 minutes. Transfer to the paper towel–lined plate and set aside to cool.

When cool enough to handle, use your thumbs to fan out the artichoke leaves, exposing the heart. Use a melon baller or spoon to scoop out any spiny choke.

Heat the oil to 350°F and, working in batches, fry the artichokes until the leaves are crispy, about 3 minutes. Replace the paper towels. Remove the artichokes with a slotted spoon or tongs and drain on paper towels. Sprinkle with salt and serve immediately.

MOZZA-RELLA IN CARROZZA

FRIED MOZZARELLA AND ANCHOVY SANDWICHES

Serves 4

8 slices Pullman loaf or sandwich bread, crusts removed

7 ounces low-moisture mozzarella, cut in ¼-inch-thick slices (see Tip)

8 oil-packed anchovy fillets, drained and patted dry

Flaky sea salt and freshly ground black pepper

2 large eggs

½ cup whole milk

¾ teaspoon sea salt

1 cup fine breadcrumbs

Neutral oil, for frying

I can't eat one of these molten, deep-fried, white-bread sandwiches without thinking that Rome would give the Minnesota State Fair a run for its money. Mozzarella in carrozza (literally "mozzarella in a carriage") is what happens when you take slices of soft white bread, stuff them with cheese and anchovy, then dip the whole thing in batter or breadcrumbs (I prefer the crunch of the latter) before frying until crisp and golden. It's Roman comfort food at its most indulgent, often served at rosticcerie and friggitorie as part of the city's glorious fritti lineup. The dish has its roots in Campania, where it was devised as a way to use up stale bread and aging mozzarella, but Romans have fully claimed it as their own. It's best eaten hot, when the mozzarella stretches with every bite and the crust still crunches audibly.

Tip: Use very dry mozzarella that is nothing fancy; a juicy high-quality cheese actually ruins the experience.

Start by assembling the sandwiches. Lay out four slices of bread and place the slices of mozzarella on top, leaving a bit of space around the edges so things don't get too messy when frying. Place two anchovy fillets centered over the mozzarella. Give the cheese a light sprinkle of flaky salt and pepper, then seal everything up with the remaining bread slices, pressing down around the edges so they hold together.

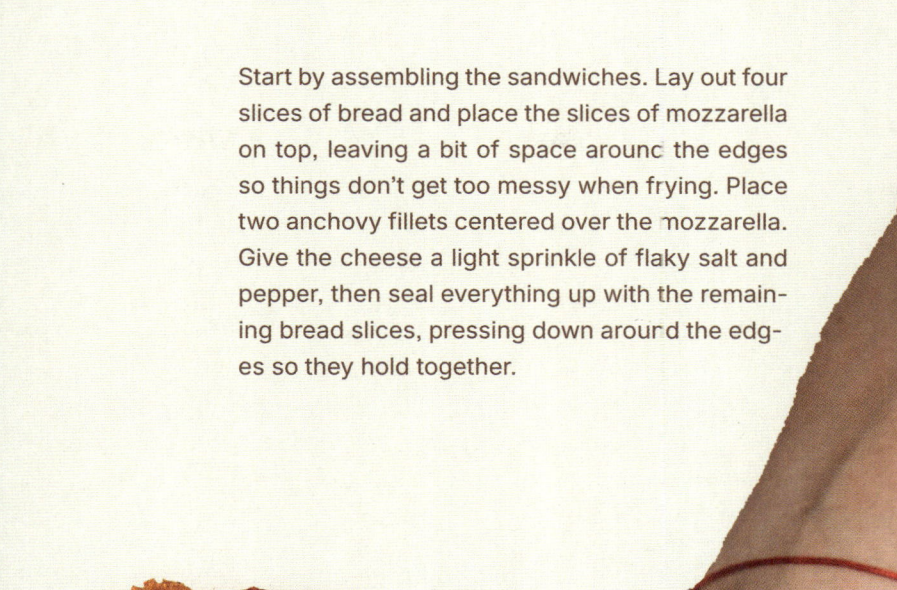

Set up your breading station: Whisk together the eggs, milk, and a ½ teaspoon of the salt in a shallow bowl. Pour the breadcrumbs into another shallow bowl and season with the remaining ¼ teaspoon salt.

Dip the sandwiches into the egg mixture, turning to make sure they're fully coated and letting any excess drip off. Then, roll them in the breadcrumbs, pressing gently to make sure they stick on all sides. If you want extra crunch, go for a double dip—back into the egg, then into the breadcrumbs again.

Line a platter or baking sheet with paper towels.

Heat 2 inches of oil to 325°F in a medium frying pan or cast-iron skillet. Fry the sandwiches in batches, turning once to ensure even browning, until deep golden brown, 4 to 5 minutes total.

Remove the sandwiches with a slotted spoon or tongs and drain on paper towels. Allow to cool for a few minutes before serving. Cut each sandwich on the diagonal, and serve hot.

UOVA SODE

HARD-
 BOILED
EGGS

Is this really a recipe? Debatable. Does it deserve a full page? Absolutely. That's how Roman these objectively overcooked (in a great way!) hard-boiled eggs are. There's no room for on-trend jammy yolks in this town. Once a staple of the city's wine bars, eggs were boiled at home by the owner and brought in to help guests "absorb" the booze—turns out a little protein and fat actually do help. You can still spot them at a few old-school haunts. At Il Goccetto, they're halved and topped with a dab of anchovy sauce (but not enough to hide the telltale gray ring around the yolk). My favorite version is at Il Vinaietto near Largo Argentina, where they sit in a tower on the bar next to rice-stuffed salt shakers. Peel, season, and let the sulfurous funk fill the room.

Makes 6 eggs

6 large eggs
Sea salt

Place the eggs in a medium pot with water to cover. Bring to a boil over high heat, reduce to a simmer over low heat, and cook until your kitchen smells of eggy sulfur, about 12 minutes. Remove from the heat and let cool in the pot. Serve at room temperature, peeled and sprinkled with salt before (or during) a night of heavy drinking.

MONTE DEI COCCI: THE WORLD'S COOLEST LANDFIL

If you've wandered through Testaccio, you've probably noticed the lopsided hill rising up behind the trattorie and more than a few auto body shops. That's Monte dei Cocci, or Monte Testaccio, and it's not a natural formation. It's a trash heap. A two-thousand-year-old, half-mile circumference, 120-foot-high mound made entirely of broken amphorae, tens of millions of clay jugs that once held olive oil shipped to Rome from across the empire.

Back when Rome ran on imports, this neighborhood was the site of the city's river port. Olive oil came in mainly from what's now Spain and Tunisia. Wine amphorae could be reused. Olive oil amphorae? Not so much. The porous clay soaked up oil, went rancid, and couldn't be cleaned. So the Romans smashed the amphorae and stacked the shards in an orderly landfill. Layer upon layer, century after century. Lime was sprinkled between the fragments to control the smell and keep pests away. Over time, this well-organized dump became a man-made hill and a monument to infrastructure and appetite.

Monte Testaccio sat mostly ignored through the Middle Ages. No one knew quite what to do with it. But it didn't go to waste. In the tenth century, it hosted religious processions. By the fifteenth, it had become the centerpiece of Carnival festivities: Think Roman Mardi Gras chaos, horses, and plenty of wine. During the Renaissance, it got a second life in the food world. Its clay-packed interior stayed cool year-round, perfect for carving out wine caves. Osterie and wine merchants set up shop in its belly, aging their barrels in ancient trash. In the twentieth century, the hill pivoted again, this time to nightlife. Locals turned those wine caves into taverns and, later, clubs. DJs, discos, and dancing, all set to a backdrop of terra-cotta shards. Some of those same caves are still in use today, their damp stone walls a direct link between Testaccio's Roman past and its food-loving present, now home to a Peruvian chicken spot, a butcher, trattorie serving offal-centric classics, and even a cheese cave.

Archaeologists started taking Monte Testaccio seriously in the nineteenth century. Heinrich Dressel's amphora typologies, especially the chubby Dressel 20 jars from Baetica (southern Spain), mapped the city's olive oil supply chain in amazing detail. Later scholars, like Emanuele Greco and José Remesal Rodríguez, expanded on that work, tracing how shifts in amphora shapes reflected changes in trade and imperial policy. It's rare to find a site so intact, so specific, and so revealing about how a trade network really worked.

Today, Monte Testaccio is fenced off, but you can still see its slopes from the street—or on a private visit with me—crumbly, layered, and unmistakably ceramic. The rest is obscured by hundreds of species of plants that flourish on the hill, a new life for a rather impressive trash heap.

FRIED SNACKS AND STARTERS

LUMACHE ALLA ROMANA

SNAILS
IN
TOMATO
SAUCE

In the Italian south, the June 24 feast of Saint John the Baptist means heading into the woods to harvest green walnuts for nocino. For Romans, it spells snails cooked in a slightly spicy tomato sauce. Snails need to be purged before being eaten, so if you happen to be hunting your own, get started no later than June 21. Substitute high-quality canned snails if you don't have a local wild source. And if you don't intend to track down either, order a plate at Al Moro near the Trevi Fountain, one of the few places this disappearing dish is reliably served in season.

Place the snails in a large pot with water to cover. Stir in the vinegar. Bring to a boil over low heat. Gently simmer for 10 minutes, then drain and rinse.

Serves 4 to 6

2 pounds purged rigatelle or *Helix aspersa* snails with shells, rinsed

1 tablespoon white wine vinegar

1 tablespoon extra-virgin olive oil, plus more for serving

1 garlic clove, smashed

½ teaspoon crushed red pepper flakes

3 oil-packed anchovy fillets, drained

½ cup dry white wine

1 (14-ounce) can whole peeled tomatoes, crushed by hand

Leaves from 1 sprig mentuccia or mint

Sea salt

Heat the olive oil in a large saucepan over low heat. When the oil begins to shimmer, add the garlic, red pepper flakes, and anchovies and cook until fragrant, about 1 minute. Stir in the snails, increase the heat to high, and add the wine. Cook until the alcohol aroma dissipates, about 1 minute, then add the tomatoes and mentuccia. Season with salt and cook until the sauce has thickened and the snails are tender, 1½ to 2 hours. Add water if the sauce starts to become thick and pasty.

Serve the snails drizzled with olive oil and a side of toothpicks to liberate them from their shells. And of course plenty of napkins.

VITELLO TONNATO

VEAL WITH TUNA SAUCE

Vitello tonnato is a summer dish from the northern Italian region of Piedmont, but I dare you to find a wine bar in Rome that doesn't also serve it in the summer. Some pizza-by-the-slice joints like Pizzarium have even gotten in on the action, serving the dish as a topping or filling for pizza sandwiches. Though the literal translation of the dish is "tuna'd veal," an alternative theory suggests that the name derives from the French word *tanné*, meaning "tanned." In this context, *tonné* or *tonnato* would refer to a preservation method, an interpretation that aligns with historical recipes where veal was treated to resemble preserved tuna, rather than being served with actual tuna. Either way, these days, the sauce that gets spooned over the thin veal slices features oil-packed tuna mixed with hard-boiled eggs, anchovies, capers, and lemon juice. My version excludes mayonnaise, a late twentieth-century addition to the historic recipe.

Serves 4

1 pound veal fillet, cleaned and trimmed of any silver skin

5 tablespoons extra-virgin olive oil

Sea salt and freshly ground black pepper

2 large eggs, hard-boiled and peeled

5 ounces good-quality tuna in oil, drained

3 oil-packed anchovy fillets, drained

1 tablespoon salted capers, rinsed

2 tablespoons fresh lemon juice

Rub the veal with 1 tablespoon of the olive oil, then season it generously with salt and pepper. Heat a large pan over medium-high heat and sear the veal until it develops a golden crust all over, about 4 minutes total. Reduce the heat to medium-low and continue cooking, flipping occasionally, until and instant-read thermometer reaches 135 to 145°F and the meat is medium-rare, about 2 minutes per side. Transfer the veal to a plate and let it rest for 10 minutes, then chill in the refrigerator, about 2 hours.

Meanwhile, combine the hard-boiled eggs, the tuna, anchovies, capers, remaining 4 tablespoons of the olive oil, and 1 tablespoon of the lemon juice in a food processor and blend until creamy. Season with salt and pepper. Taste and add the remaining lemon juice as needed, blending to incorporate. Refrigerate until ready to serve.

Once chilled, slice the veal thinly against the grain and arrange the pieces on a platter, overlapping slightly. Spoon the tonnato sauce over and serve.

MATTON- ELLE DI LASAGNA

FRIED LASAGNA BRICKS

Makes 12 mattonelle

Lasagna della Domenica
    (page 149), at room
    temperature
1 cup all-purpose flour
3 large eggs
3 cups panko or breadcrumbs
Sea salt
Neutral oil, for frying

In Rome, Supplì al Telefono (page 80) are the OG fried carbs. But in recent years, Roman street food spots, especially pizza-by-the-slice joints, and inventive home cooks have begun riffing on the format, pushing boundaries while staying rooted in tradition. Enter fried lasagna: a caloric, handheld twist that reimagines Sunday's baked pasta as a crunchy, golden brick (mattonella). Layers of pasta, ragù, and béchamel are chilled, cut into squares, breaded, and deep-fried until crisp. The recipe below is for a whole tray, but it can easily be modified to fry whatever leftovers you've got. Just make sure the lasagna isn't fridge cold when you start frying.

Slice the lasagna into 12 pieces of equal size.

Set up your breading station: Pour the flour into a shallow bowl. Beat the eggs and ¼ cup of water in a medium bowl. Pour the panko into another shallow bowl. Season the flour, egg mixture, and panko with salt.

Dredge each piece of lasagna first in the flour, shaking off the excess, then dip in the egg, allowing the excess to drip off, and finally coat in the panko. Set aside on a plate.

Line a platter or baking sheet with paper towels.

Heat 2 inches of oil to 350°F in a medium frying pan or cast-iron skillet. Fry the lasagna in batches, taking care not to overcrowd the pan, until golden brown, 4 to 5 minutes. Turn midway through to ensure even browning.

Remove the lasagna with a slotted spoon and drain on paper towels. Sprinkle with salt and serve warm.

SUPPLÌ ALLA CARBONARA
Fried Spaghetti alla Carbonara

If Mattonelle di Lasagna are doses of Sunday comfort, then these fried carbonara parcels are Rome's most indulgent snack. Inspired by the egg-shaped structure of supplì but with strands of spaghetti instead of rice, this variation delivers all the richness of carbonara in a crispy, burnished shell. Use the carbonara recipe on page 107, but scale back the pasta to 12 ounces to keep the sauce-to-carb ratio extra creamy and cohesive.

Makes 9 supplì

Spaghetti alla Carbonara
1 cup all-purpose flour
2 large eggs
3 cups panko or breadcrumbs
Sea salt
Neutral oil, for frying

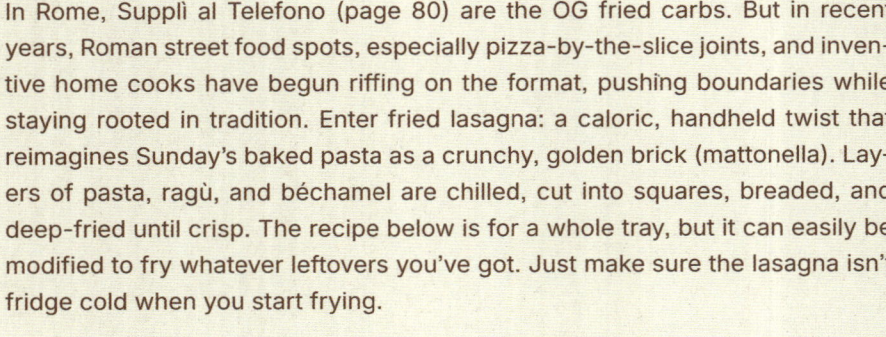

Cool the carbonara in a 9-inch square baking dish, then cover it with plastic wrap and refrigerate until firm, 3 to 4 hours.

Slice the carbonara into 9 equal pieces. Use your hands to shape each portion into an egg-shaped parcel. Set aside on a plate, then transfer to the refrigerator to chill, 20 to 30 minutes.

Follow the recipe and instructions above for setting up a breading station, dredging, and heating the oil.

Fry the supplì in batches, turning to cook evenly, until deep golden brown, 6 to 7 minutes.

Remove the supplì with a slotted spoon and drain on paper towels. Sprinkle with salt and serve immediately.

PROSCIUTTO E FICHI

FIGS
   AND
PROSCIUTTO

Serves 4

8 ounces thinly sliced
   prosciutto crudo (about 16
   slices)
8 ripe figs, peeled and halved

In the psychosis-inducing heat of a Roman summer, few things offer as much relief as prosciutto e fichi. This classic pairing, served at wine bars or trattorie as an antipasto, balances the salty delicacy of cured ham with the lush sweetness of ripe figs, which are unceremoniously plated without garnish in August and September, when figs are in season. Look for figs so jammy and ripe that they are nearly bursting open.

Distribute the prosciutto slices evenly among four plates. Lay the fig halves over the prosciutto. Serve.

Tip: To make this combo portable, cut Pizza Bianca (page 242) into four (4-inch squares. Slice open, keeping it hinged. Squish 2 figs into the crumb of each pizza square. Drape over the prosciutto, dividing evenly. Close the sandwich and devour.

ZOZZONI AND BORGHETTI: THE SACRED RITUAL OF STADIUM SNACKING

Anyone who's ever attended a Roman wedding knows that the claim "You can't have a bad meal in Rome" is a straight-up lie. Terrible catering monopolies have cornered that market, pumping out factory-made mediocrity for huge profit. Shockingly, these same culprits run the food at the Stadio Olimpico, where VIP lounges serve up troughs of terrible dishes to Rome's richest fans, who happen to have awful taste.

For everyone else, the pregame meal is provided by the city's rough-and-ready kiosks, affectionately dubbed *zozzoni* (literally "very filthy things"), or by the camion bars, grim food trucks selling dry porchetta sandwiches, bottles of Ceres beer, Bacardi Breezers, and shots of Borghetti, Rome's cult coffee liqueur. It's definitely not fancy, and it's barely good, but at least it's honest.

There's no elegant way to eat a sandwich from a zozzone, and that's the entire point. You grab something dripping in mayo and oil, scarfing it down before making your way to the entry turnstiles with a few plastic containers of Borghetti in your pocket to fuel you through ninety tense minutes inside the stadium.

Getting to the Olimpico is half the experience: squeezing into crowded trams echoing with chants, or crossing Ponte Duca d'Aosta amid waves of giallorosso-clad fans (Lazio merda). As you approach the stadium, grilled meat and greasy fries scent the air, mingling with the smoke from the stadium's flares in team colors. The zozzoni and camion bars are already hard at work fueling the faithful.

After a win, you might stick around for another drink or greasy sandwich. The only viable option after a loss is heading straight home for mom's spaghetti.

PARMIGIANA DI MELANZANE

EGGPLANT
PARMIGIANA

Eggplant parm is a beloved summer dish, traditionally served as a starter or a main when eggplants are at their peak. In Roman trattorie and homes, it appears on the table when gardens and markets are overflowing with glossy purple eggplants, fried (but not breaded), layered with tomato and cheese, then baked until tender and bubbling. Parmigiana is also a staple of tavole calde, lunchtime cafeterias that serve homemade meals to workers, students, and locals on the go. You'll find it tucked between lasagna and roast chicken at bakery counters and rosticcerie, too, sold in foil trays, ready to be reheated or eaten at room temperature. Whether enjoyed hot or cold, plated or packed up, this dish is a deeply satisfying expression of Rome's love for simple ingredients and layered flavor.

Serves 6

4 medium eggplant or 2 large
globe eggplant (about 3
pounds total), stemmed
and cut crosswise into
⅛-inch thick slices
Sea salt
1 cup extra-virgin olive oil
1 (14-ounce) can whole
peeled tomatoes, crushed
by hand
½ cup basil leaves, torn
12 ounces scamorza or
mozzarella, cut into
¼-inch cubes (about 2
cups)
¾ cup finely grated
Parmigiano-Reggiano

Place the eggplant in a colander, sprinkle with salt, then set aside to drain for an hour. Rinse and pat dry.

Preheat the oven to 350°F.

Line a platter or baking sheet with paper towels.

Heat ½ cup of the olive oil in a large skillet over medium heat. When the oil begins to shimmer, add the eggplant, working in batches so as not to crowd the pan. Fry the eggplant until golden on both sides, about 3 minutes per side. Use the remaining ½ cup olive oil for later batches as needed. Drain on the paper towels and sprinkle both sides with salt.

Spoon some of the tomatoes over the bottom of a large casserole, then top with a layer of eggplant. Add another layer of tomato, then a layer of basil. Top the basil with a layer of scamorza and sprinkle with some Parmigiano-Reggiano. Repeat until all the ingredients have been used, ending with the Parmigiano-Reggiano.

Cover with aluminum foil and bake until the eggplant is very tender and the cheese is melted, about 30 minutes. Remove the foil, raise the heat to 400°F, and bake for 5 to 10 minutes more (or broil for 1 minute more) to brown the cheese. Remove from the oven and set aside to cool for at least 20 minutes before slicing and serving. The cooled eggplant parm will keep in the refrigerator, covered, for up to 4 days.

PARMIGIANA DI ZUCCHINE:

Wanna switch it up? You can give zucchini the parmigiana treatment. Just substitute 6 large zucchini for the eggplant and cut into ⅛-inch slices lengthwise. Salt in advance, then pat dry before frying and follow instructions for assembly and baking above.

PASTA
AND SOUP

THE ROMAN PASTA PANTHEON

There's a lot of passionate debate outside Italy about whether fresh pasta is "better" than dried pasta. Like most Italians, I would argue that it depends on the shape, the maker, and the chosen condimento. Romans enjoy both fresh and dried pasta shapes, each traditionally paired with specific sauces. Mixing and matching pasta and sauces isn't really a Roman thing—we stick closely (often rightly) to ideal combinations that maximize flavor, texture, and sauce cling.

Fresh Pastas

Tonnarelli
Tonnarelli are square-cut strands of egg pasta that are either extruded or made using a chitarra, a wire-strung, wooden pasta tool. The toothsome texture of tonnarelli makes it perfect for Cacio e Pepe (page 112), standing up to the bold flavors of the sauce, which cling to the long strand.

Fettuccine
These long, flat egg noodles are Roman weekend favorites, traditionally served with rigaglie di pollo (page 139) or simply tossed with butter and Parmigiano-Reggiano (page 160). Rome's version is thicker than its northern counterpart.

Gnocchi di Patate
These soft potato dumplings are a Roman institution, famously served on Thursdays (the city's culinary calendar calls for "giovedì gnocchi"). Typically, you'll find them paired with a straightforward tomato sauce, sometimes enriched with meat.

Gnocchi all'Amatriciana (page 120) is the definition of luxury.

Ravioli
Not strictly Roman, but you'll often find these ricotta-filled pasta pillows dressed in a simple tomato sauce at local trattorie.

Lasagna
In Rome, lasagna (page 149) tends to appear during celebratory meals like Easter and Christmas.

Dried Pastas

Spaghetti and Spaghettoni
Classic spaghetti and its thicker cousin, spaghettoni, are staples for unctuous Roman sauces like Carbonara (page 107) or Ajo, Ojo, e Peperoncino (page 159).

Bucatini
This hollow, thick spaghetti is traditionally served with amatriciana sauce. Its hole helps it cook quickly but creates a twirling dilemma: Properly al dente bucatini can be tough to handle, while easier-to-twirl bucatini tends to be overcooked. Personally, I find it inferior—fight me!

Rigatoni
Already familiar to many, rigatoni are large ridged tubes ideal for hearty meat sauces like sugo di coda (page 132). The ridges capture sauce exceptionally well, ensuring each bite is deeply flavorful.

Mezze Maniche
Literally meaning "short sleeves," these half-size rigatoni tubes are beloved for sauces like amatriciana. Their compact shape and ridged texture ensure maximum sauce absorption and a satisfying chew.

Bombolotti
Often used interchangeably with mezze maniche, these shorter, ridged rigatoni tubes are girthier and offer an extra-chewy bite. They're excellent with fatty, guanciale-based sauces like carbonara or gricia (page 128).

Cannolicchi
Small, short, rigid pasta tubes, cannolicchi are used in hearty soups like Pasta e Ceci (page 154). Their compact shape and hollow center are perfect for capturing thickened broth.

SPAGHETTI ALLA CARBONARA

SPAGHETTI
WITH EGG,
GUANCIALE,
AND PECORINO

Serves 4 to 6

8 ounces guanciale, cut into
    approximately ¾-inch
    cubes
6 large egg yolks
1½ cups finely grated
    Pecorino Romano, plus
    more for serving
2 teaspoons freshly ground
    Sarawak black pepper,
    plus more for serving
Sea salt
1 pound spaghetti

If you ever want to see a Roman absolutely lose their mind, read aloud the ingredients from the carbonara recipe in the 1956 edition of Ada Boni's (see page 52) landmark cookbook *Il Talismano della Felicità*: pancetta, butter, onion, white wine, eggs, Parmigiano-Reggiano, parsley, and black pepper. While her condiemnto captures the basic structure—eggs, cheese, and cured pork—the details would spark a full-blown identity crisis in today's Rome. These days, there's a sacred canon: guanciale (pancetta only in emergencies), Pecorino Romano (don't even think about Parmigiano-Reggiano), black pepper, eggs (mostly yolks), and dried pasta—spaghetti or rigatoni only. No alliums, no herbs, no vino. Capito?

Despite its now-orthodox formula, carbonara is a relatively recent addition to the Roman canon. In postwar Italy, recipes were fluid, ingredients varied by availability, and everyone's nonna made it a little differently—often scrambled. Believe it or not, some Roman grandmothers never made the dish at all. It wasn't until the late twentieth century that carbonara was codified, becoming a symbol of the city itself.

In Rome, the purity of carbonara is generally protected, while outside, even in other parts of Italy, it's gone rogue. Peas, cream, bacon, and even tofu have made appearances in various chefs' interpretations. And while most Romans will scoff at these versions, the evolution of carbonara reminds us that even the most sacred dishes have a history of change. Even within Rome's walls, some long-standing deviations exist: in the Jewish Ghetto, kosher kitchens adapt the dish with carne secca (cured beef) in place of guanciale and omit the cheese; and at Al Moro, their carbonara-adjacent cult classic, spaghetti alla Moro, calls for smoked pancetta and dried chile flakes. What matters most is using great ingredients and mastering the technique: silky, not scrambled eggs, crisp guanciale, and a salty, peppery punch. Inspired by versions at Baccano, Salumeria Roscioli, Santo Palato, and Pipero, I use the double boiler method so the eggs take on a creamy, zabaione-like consistency.

Heat the guanciale in a large pan over medium-low heat. Cook, stirring occasionally, until golden brown and crisp, about 10 minutes. Remove from the heat and set aside. Transfer the guanciale to a paper towel-lined plate and let the fat completely cool in the pan.

Whisk together the eggs, Pecorino Romano, pepper, and cooled guanciale fat in a large stainless steel bowl.

Bring a large pot of water to a rolling boil over high heat. Add salt until the water tastes like a seasoned soup. Add the pasta and cook until al dente.

While the pasta cooks, set the bowl with the egg mixture on top of the pot of water, taking care to avoid direct contact between the bowl and the water. Whisk continually until it thickens and coats the back of a spoon.

When the pasta is al dente, use tongs to transfer the pasta to the egg mixture and toss vigorously to emulsify. Fold in the reserved guanciale and serve with more Pecorino Romano and pepper freshly ground on top.

RIGATONI CON LA PAJATA

RIGATONI
WITH
SUCKLING VEAL
INTESTINES

If you've spent any time in Rome and haven't tried rigatoni con la pajata, you need to reconsider your life choices. This dish—pasta tossed with the tender, milk-filled intestines of unweaned veal slow-cooked in tomato sauce—speaks volumes of the Roman penchant to use every part of the animal. In this case, the veal intestines are tied into rings bound with mesenteric fat (the layer of fat surrounding the intestines) and simmered in tomato sauce, each one bursting with creamy sweetness. In Rome, pajata tossed with rigatoni is more common, but you can also find pajata in umido, a pasta-free version served as a secondo. If you are able to find pajata in the US, I need to know your source. It's tough to track down even outside Rome, so consider cooking it on your next trip to the Italian capital, or at least try it at a trattoria!

Serves 4 to 6

1 pound pajata
2 tablespoons extra-virgin
    olive oil
½ medium white onion, finely
    chopped
Sea salt and freshly ground
    black pepper
½ cup dry white wine
1 (14-ounce) can whole
    peeled tomatoes, crushed
    by hand
¾ cup finely grated Pecorino
    Romano
1 pound rigatoni

Prepare the pajata by gently pulling off the exterior mesenteric fat from the intestine exterior, taking care not to spill the curdled milk within. Cut the fat membrane into 3-inch pieces. Lay the intestines out on your work surface and cut into 5-inch segments. Carefully tie the ends of each segment together with the membrane to form a ring.

Heat the olive oil in a large pan over low heat. When the oil begins to shimmer, add the onion. Season with a heavy pinch of salt and cook until very soft, about 20 minutes. Add the pajata rings to the pan and season with salt and pepper. Increase the heat to medium and cook, gently shaking the pan to prevent the casings from sticking, until lightly browned, about 3 minutes per side. Add the wine and cook until the alcohol aroma dissipates, about 1 minute, then add the tomatoes and ½ cup of water. Bring to a simmer, reduce the heat to low, and cook, partially covered, until the pajata casings are tender and the tomato sauce has reduced, about 1 hour.

Remove the pan from the heat and gently stir in ½ cup of the Pecorino Romano. Break open one of the pajata rings and incorporate the filling into the sauce, discarding the casing.

Meanwhile, bring a large pot of water to a rolling boil over high heat. Add salt until the water tastes like a seasoned soup. Add the rigatoni and cook until al dente. Use a spider to transfer the rigatoni to the pan and swirl the sauce and pasta together. Add pasta cooking water as needed to loosen the sauce. Serve with the remaining Pecorino Romano sprinkled on top.

FRESH PASTA SHAPES

While Piedmontese pasta makers might boast about doughs packed with forty yolks per kilo—we get it, you're rich!—Rome takes a more pragmatic approach. This is a city where pasta tradition leans humble and efficient, not decadent and baroque. Roman egg pasta dough usually calls for just one yolk or one whole egg per 100 grams of flour. It's a formula built on frugality and function, and it works.

Eggs, of course, aren't unique to Roman pasta. They're fundamental across much of Italy, but they're used differently here. In Emilia-Romagna, for example, yolk-rich doughs create silky ribbons of tagliatelle or delicate pouches of tortellini. Rome's fresh pastas are sturdier. Think Tonnarelli (page 115) with their squared-off edges, built to withstand a clingy shower of cacio e pepe. Or Fettuccine (page 134), a Sunday favorite cut from hand-rolled sheets. By contrast, Gnocchi di Patate (page 122), when done well, are pillowy and ethereal, earning their place at the Roman table each and every Thursday.

The egg yolks themselves tell a story. In some Roman homes and pastifici (fresh pasta shops), you'll find doughs tinged pale yellow; in others, a deeper marigold hue. That spectrum has everything to do with what the hens ate: grain makes for lighter yolks, while carotenoid-rich diets (think corn, grass, and marigolds) produce eggs that practically glow. Some farms supplement the grain-based feed to fake the deep orange hue of a natural diet.

Roman doughs may not have the over-the-top richness of their northern cousins, but they're resilient, satisfying, and built to carry the bold, savory, and peppery sauces that Romans love. In the recipes that follow, we'll make these doughs from scratch—rolled by hand, or by machine—and shape them into the fresh pasta classics that help define Rome's daily and festive tables alike.

ALL ABOUT THAT FLOUR

If you've spent any time in an Italian supermarket staring at bags of flour, you've probably been confronted by an overwhelming array of numbers—00, 0, 1, 2—and wondered what they all mean. And if you've ever tried to recreate Italian pasta at home and ended up with a stiff, uncooperative dough, chances are the flour was to blame. Let's unpack it.

Italian Flour 101

The numbers on Italian flours refer to how finely the wheat has been milled and how much of the bran and germ have been left in. Tipo 00 is the finest grind, with virtually all the bran and germ sifted out. It's soft, powdery, and the most refined. Like all-purpose flour, it's all endosperm (the starchy, carbohydrate-rich interior of the wheat kernel), but it's milled more finely. Tipo 0 has slightly more of the grain's bran and germ present in its outer layers, while 1 and 2 are coarser and increasingly whole grain. For pasta, I reach for 0, hence the darker color of my dough in the tonnarelli-making spread (see page 116), but you'll have an easier time finding 00. Subbing all-purpose flour for either one is just fine.

Elasticity

Pasta dough for Roman pasta shapes needs to be elastic, which means it should stretch willingly without tearing. The goal is a dough you can roll into long sheets without a fight. This comes from using the right flour and the right technique.

Semola and Semolina—Not the Same Thing

In Italy, semola di grano duro rimacinata refers to durum wheat flour that's been double-milled into a fine powder. This is the stuff of southern pasta dreams—think orecchiette, cavatelli, and all the bronze-cut dried shapes. Don't confuse it with the gritty semola also made from durum wheat, which has a much coarser grind. In the US, semolina is closest in texture to Italy's semola, while semola di grano duro rimacinata is sometimes labeled "fancy durum," or simply durum flour.

A Note on Protein Content

Protein is always listed on Italian flour bags: the ingredients list mentions how many grams per 100 grams of flour. That's your percentage. Look for something around 11 to 12 percent for making pasta dough. Generally, higher-protein flours make tougher doughs that are harder to roll out and shape. Lower protein means tenderness and workability—the sweet spot for pasta. Bear in mind that using whole eggs means you're introducing a little extra protein to the dough in the form of the albumen.

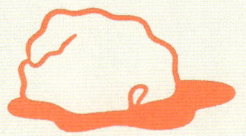

Bottom Line

Whatever flour you use, treat it right: Weigh it, rest your dough to allow the flour to hydrate and the gluten to develop, and knead with intention to build strength. The flour is the foundation, and you want that foundation to be rock solid—or rather, supple and silky, and willing to be coaxed into your desired shape.

TONNA-RELLI CACIO E PEPE

PASTA
　　WITH PECORINO
　　　　ROMANO
　　AND
　　　　BLACK PEPPER

Serves 4 to 6

Sea salt
Fresh Tonnarelli (recipe
　　follows) or 1 pound store-
　　bought spaghetti
1½ cups finely grated
　　Pecorino Romano, plus
　　more for serving
½ cup finely grated
　　Parmigiano-Reggiano (or
　　more Pecorino Romano)
2 teaspoons freshly ground
　　Sarawak black pepper,
　　plus more for serving

Cacio e pepe *is* your grocery list: Pecorino Romano and black pepper. Think of it as mac and cheese's cooler, better-smelling Roman cousin. In nineteenth- and early twentieth-century Rome, before trattorias dotted every block, taverns served as local hangouts where people brought their own food and drank with lifespan-threatening enthusiasm. To keep the crowd going, tavern keepers would whip up this quick, cheap, and carb-loaded snack.

It sounds simple, but getting that silky, creamy texture is notoriously tricky. The internet myth about mixing cheese with hot pasta water is a lie—it causes the cheese to "break," making a clumpy mess. Instead, finely grate your Pecorino Romano on the punched holes of a box grater and mix it with cold or room-temperature water to form a paste. Some chefs take it even further: At Cesare al Casaletto, Leonardo Vignoli uses ice to make his emulsion, keeping the cheese from breaking while delivering maximum creaminess.

In Rome, there's only one acceptable pasta shape for this dish: tonnarelli. Most dining establishments use extruded noodles, but if you're going homemade, reach for a chitarra. I break down the process for homemade tonnarelli in the following pages. If, as I do, you're using the very salty Fulvi brand of Pecorino Romano (available in the US), cut the savoriness with a bit of Parmigiano-Reggiano, as chef Nabil Hadj Hassen does at Baccano. With other brands of pecorino, you can replace the Parm with more Pecorino Romano. I reach for Sarawak pepper when making cacio e pepe. This fragrant Malaysian variety brings complex aromas to the dish. If you can't track it down, just be sure to use very fresh black pepper.

Bring a large pot of water to a rolling boil over high heat. Add salt until the water tastes like a seasoned soup. Add the tonnarelli and cook until they float and have lost their raw flavor, about 3 minutes. Before the pasta is done cooking, scoop out 1 cup of pasta cooking water and set it aside to cool.

Meanwhile, combine the Pecorino Romano, Parmigiano-Reggiano, pepper, and ¼ cup of cold water in a large bowl. Mix to form a paste.

When the pasta is cooked, turn off the heat and use tongs to transfer it to the bowl with the cheese mixture. Pour in ¼ cup of the reserved cooled pasta cooking water. Toss vigorously, adjusting with more pasta cooking water a tablespoon at a time as necessary to obtain a creamy sauce that completely coats the pasta, about 2 minutes.

Plate and sprinkle each portion with some more Pecorino Romano and black pepper. Serve immediately.

recipe continues on next page ▶

GNOCCHI FRITTI CACIO E PEPE
Fried Potato Gnocchi on a Pool of Cacio e Pepe Sauce

This modern-day classic, a creative merging of traditional Roman flavors, is served as a sharable antipasto at Trattoria da Cesare al Casaletto in Rome's Gianicolense district.

Serves 6 to 8

Extra-virgin olive oil, for frying
Fresh Gnocchi di Patate (page 122) or 1 pound
    store-bought gnocchi
Sea salt
1½ cups finely grated Pecorino Romano
2 teaspoons freshly ground Sarawak black
    pepper, plus more as needed

Line a platter or baking sheet with paper towels.

Heat 1 inch of olive oil to 350°F in a large frying pan or cast-iron skillet. Fry the gnocchi in batches until golden brown, 3 to 4 minutes, then use a spider to transfer them to paper towels to drain. Season with salt.

Meanwhile, whisk together the Pecorino Romano, pepper, and ½ cup of cold water in a small saucepan. Cook over low heat, stirring constantly, until the sauce is just warmed, 3 to 4 minutes. Take care not to overheat the mixture or the cheese will break. Spoon the sauce over a plate and serve with the fried gnocchi on top. Serve immediately.

FRESH TONNARELLI

Tonnarelli are Rome's answer to spaghetti, but with more bite and a rustic edge. Traditionally, they're made from flour and eggs, square in cross-section, and have a pleasantly firm, almost chewy texture that holds up beautifully to bold sauces. They're rolled and cut on a chitarra, a wooden frame strung with taut metal wires that slices the sheet of dough into perfectly uniform strands. This technique connects tonnarelli to spaghetti alla chitarra, an Abruzzese specialty—which makes total sense given the long history of migration from Abruzzo to Rome. Even today, you'll meet plenty of Roman cooks and bakers with roots east of the Apennines.

While you can make tonnarelli by hand, hardly anyone does in Rome. Most people buy them from pasta shops or the supermarket, where they're always extruded. Even small pastifici skip the traditional rolling and cutting method in favor of machines that deliver consistent results with less labor.

There's no single dough formula for tonnarelli. Some versions are made with whole eggs, others with egg whites only; others use water. Whole eggs bring both protein and fat to the dough—the whites help build structure, while the yolks lend richness and a supple texture. Then there's the flour. Some doughs use all 00, while others mix in semolina for extra bite and backbone. The proportions of moisture and flour—and whether the pasta is rolled or extruded—ultimately shape the noodle's personality, from toothsome and smooth to compact and rough.

Whatever the dough, tonnarelli are the ideal vehicle for rich, clingy sauces like cacio e pepe.

Tip: If rolling the pasta with a machine, cut the dough into 4 to 6 equal pieces, forming each into a tight ball, then press into a flat disk using flattened fingertips. Starting with one piece, while keeping the rest covered, pass the dough through the machine on the widest setting twice. Continue passing the dough through the settings of your pasta machine until it is ⅛ inch thick. Lightly flour the pasta sheet with semolina and roll into a loose tube. Use a sharp knife to cut the pasta into ⅛-inch-thick strands. Unfurl the pasta, form the strands into a nest, and set aside on a surface lightly dusted with semolina. Alternatively, pass through a pasta cutter set at ⅛-inch thickness. Repeat with the remaining dough.

Makes 480 grams of dough, serving 4 to 6

200 grams 0 or 00 flour, plus more for dusting
100 grams semolina or semola di grano duro rimacinata, plus more for dusting
½ teaspoon sea salt
180 grams (about 3 large) eggs

Mix the 0 and semolina flours and the salt in a medium bowl and use your fingers or a spoon to form a well in the center. Crack the eggs into the well and gently beat them together with a fork. Working from the inside of the well to the edges, slowly incorporate the flour into the eggs until a shaggy dough forms.

Turn the dough out onto your work surface and knead until it is supple and glossy, 7 to 8 minutes. Form into a tight ball, cover tightly with plastic wrap, and set aside to hydrate the flour for 30 minutes and up to 2 hours.

Lightly dust your work surface with 0 flour. Unwrap the dough and, working with 80 to 100 grams at a time and keeping the rest covered, use a rolling pin to roll the dough into a sheet measuring 5 × 12 inches and ⅛ inch thick. Roll with smooth, fluid movements, working from the center outward, and turning the dough 90 degrees every 3 to 4 rolls until you reach the desired size. The pasta should be the thickness of the space between the chitarra strings. Lay the dough over the strings of your chitarra and roll over the sheet with a rolling pin or dowel in firm, decisive movements. The pasta strands will fall into the well beneath the strings. Collect them, form them into a nest, and set aside on a surface lightly dusted with semolina. Repeat with the remaining dough.

The dough will keep, refrigerated and tightly wrapped in plastic, for up to 2 days. Do not freeze. Before rolling, bring the dough to room temperature, about 1 hour.

FRESH TONNARELLI MAKING

PASTA E FAGIOLI

PASTA
AND
BEANS

Serves 6

1 (½-ounce) slice lardo
   (cured fatback) or
   guanciale, finely chopped,
   or 2 tablespoons extra-
   virgin olive oil
1 carrot, finely chopped
1 celery stalk, finely chopped
1 medium yellow onion, finely
   chopped
1 tablespoon tomato paste
1 pound dried borlotti beans,
   soaked overnight and
   drained (see Tip)
1 sprig rosemary
8 ounces cannolicchi, ditalini,
   or Fresh Maltagliati (see
   Tip on page 134)
Sea salt and freshly ground
   black pepper
Extra-virgin olive oil, for
   serving

Pasta e fagioli might be found all over Italy, but the Roman version hits different. It's a humble dish rooted in poverty, and when done right, it eats like a rich,
slow-cooked stew. The flavor starts with battuto, here, a mix of lardo or guanciale, carrot, celery, and onion cooked down until meltingly soft and deeply
aromatic. Borlotti beans bring body and creaminess, and the pasta—tiny cannolicchi (the Roman name for ditalini pasta) or scraps of fresh maltagliati—gets
cooked right in the pot, soaking up every bit of savory broth. A touch of tomato
paste adds depth without hijacking the earthy vibe.

Heat the lardo, carrot, celery, and onion in a large pot over low heat and
cook, stirring occasionally, until the vegetables are very soft, about 20
minutes. Increase the heat to medium-high, add the tomato paste, and
cook until brick red, about 2 minutes. Add the beans with enough water
to cover by a few inches. Bring to a rolling boil, then reduce to a simmer.
Cook, partially covered, until the beans are very soft, 45 minutes to 1½
hours. Add hot water if the beans begin to dry out.

Add the rosemary and pasta and cook until the pasta is al dente. Remove
and discard the rosemary. Season with salt and pepper and drizzle with
olive oil. Serve immediately.

Tip: Soak the beans in a large bowl with plenty of water. Discard any beans that
float or look damaged. Drain and rinse. You don't have to soak the beans but they
will cook faster if you do. Budget 2 to 2½ hours for unsoaked beans. Overall cooking times depend on how fresh the dried beans are.

GNOCCHI ALL'AMATRICIANA

POTATO GNOCCHI WITH TOMATO, GUANCIALE, AND PECORINO ROMANO

Serves 4 to 6

8 ounces guanciale, cut into ¾-inch cubes
1 (14-ounce) can whole peeled tomatoes, crushed by hand
Sea salt
1½ cups finely grated Pecorino Romano
Freshly ground black pepper
Fresh Gnocchi di Patate (recipe follows) or 1 pound store-bought gnocchi

Amatriciana—or matriciana, depending on whom you ask—is one of Rome's most beloved and controversial pasta dishes, sparking endless debates over its origin, name, and ingredients. Many point to the town of Amatrice in northern Lazio as its birthplace, and indeed, the city hall there has a version of the recipe officially registered. But urban Romans claim it as their own, some dropping the initial "*a*" and tracing the name not to the town, but to *matrici*, stamps once seared into cured pork products. What likely started as a tomato-sauced evolution of gricia has now become a symbol of Roman culinary identity.

The arguments don't stop at the name. Purists insist on guanciale, San Marzano tomatoes, and Pecorino Romano, while others claim pancetta is just fine, the heat can come from black pepper or peperoncino, and to some onions and garlic are welcome. Though in 2015, Michelin-starred chef Carlo Cracco stirred the pot by adding garlic to his version, prompting a national outcry that people are still talking about a decade later. The pasta shape is up for grabs, too—bucatini was classic, but rigatoni mezze maniche, and bombolotti have robbed the long noodle of its place (I'm not mad about it; bucatini is the world's worst shape). I like to serve amatriciana with potato gnocchi, which is pure luxury, but mezze maniche and bombolotti work great and offer the possibility of catching a guanciale chunk in their tubular architecture.

Tip: Stir in a tablespoon of good-quality wine vinegar as chefs like Sarah Cicolini of Santo Palato and Nabil Hadj Hassen of Baccano do to lighten up the unctuous sauce.

Heat the guanciale in a large pan over medium-low heat. Cook, stirring occasionally, until golden brown and crisp, about 10 minutes. Remove from the heat and set aside. Transfer the guanciale to a paper towel-lined plate.

Carefully add the tomatoes to the pan, season with a heavy pinch of salt, and cook until the sauce has reduced and the tomatoes have lost their raw flavor, about 15 minutes. Stir in the reserved guanciale. Remove from the heat and stir in 1 cup of the Pecorino Romano and pepper.

While the sauce is cooking, bring a large pot of water to a rolling boil over high heat. Add salt until the water tastes like a seasoned soup. Add the gnocchi and cook until they float and have lost their raw flavor, 3 to 4 minutes. Use a spider to transfer the gnocchi to the pan and mix gently to coat. Serve immediately, sprinkled with the remaining Pecorino Romano, and black pepper.

FRESH GNOCCHI DI PATATE

Potato Gnocchi

It's a myth that Romans don't love rules—they're obsessed with them, at least when it comes to food. Case in point: giovedì gnocchi. Thursday is gnocchi day, and everyone knows it. But not all gnocchi are created equal. These days, gnocchi di patate are often dense, gummy, and sticky, the result of industrial production and shortcuts. Even small neighborhood pastifici tend to rely on dehydrated potato flakes and mediocre flour, which produce a pasty texture and rob gnocchi of their signature lightness. I'll never forget having to cancel a TV shoot at a pastificio in Testaccio when we turned up to film their gnocchi production, only to find they had poured a massive bag of potato flakes into the mixer with hot water. Not exactly what the crew and I had in mind.

If, like me, you're after soft, pillowy dumplings that practically dissolve on your tongue, you're going to have to make them yourself. Roman lore says the secret to ethereal gnocchi lies in using dry, starchy potatoes grown at high altitudes, ideally from Avezzano, in Abruzzo's Marsica plateau. If those aren't available, seek out old, yellow-fleshed potatoes with low moisture content and dense texture. And whatever you do, skip the food processor. A ricer keeps the potatoes fluffy and helps preserve that delicate, tender bite that defines good gnocchi.

Once you've nailed the texture, don't drown them in sauce. A gentle coating is all they need—try amatriciana, the rich tomato sauce from involtini (page 194), Ragù (page 137), or oxtail sauce (page 132). Feeling extravagant? Fry the gnocchi until golden and crisp, then serve them over a pool of cacio e pepe sauce (page 114).

Fun fact: *Gnocca* is Roman slang for a hot chick and her lady parts!

Makes about 1 pound of gnocchi, serving 4 to 6

1 pound dry, floury potatoes, such as russets
¾ cup all-purpose flour, plus more for dusting
1 teaspoon sea salt

Place the potatoes in a large pot and cover them with cold water. Bring to a rolling boil over high heat, then cook until the potatoes are fork-tender, about 40 minutes. Drain and set aside to cool slightly. Peel the potatoes, pass them through a ricer onto a dry work surface, and allow them to cool further, letting the escaping steam dry them out a bit more.

Sprinkle the flour and salt evenly over the potatoes. Gently mix by hand, gradually incorporating the flour until a dough forms. Knead gently, just until the dough comes together. Set the dough aside to rest at room temperature, covered, for about 30 minutes.

On a lightly floured surface, shape a fistful of dough into a rope about 1 inch in diameter. Using a knife, cut the rope crosswise into ¾-inch pieces. Set the gnocchi aside on a lightly floured surface, spacing them apart to prevent sticking. Repeat with the remaining dough. Let them dry out slightly, uncovered, for 20 to 30 minutes before cooking.

It's best to cook gnocchi the day they are made, rather than to store them in the refrigerator. To freeze, lay the gnocchi on a baking sheet in a single layer. Once solid, transfer to a freezer bag and store up to 1 month.

Just across from the Circus Maximus on Via dei Cerchi, there's a building that looks like any other old municipal structure. In fact, today it houses the city's Dipartimento Sviluppo Economico e Attività Produttive (Department of Economic Development and Productive Activities). But in the late nineteenth century, it was the beating heart of Rome's pasta industry: the Pantanella factory, the city's first large-scale pasta operation.

Its founder, Michelangelo Pantanella, arrived in Rome from Arpino in southern Lazio in 1848 with little more than ambition and a new marriage. He started out selling polenta cakes near the Colosseum and on the Campidoglio, later reinvesting profits from a grain windfall into a bakery on Via della Fontanella. He eventually set his sights on something bigger: a steam-powered bakery and pasta plant at the Circus Maximus, an area that at the time was practically the suburbs.

By 1878, construction had begun. Archaeological officials opposed the project, but Pantanella compromised, setting the building back from the Circus proper, and got the go-ahead. Later, archeologists discovered ancient ruins beneath the factory, including a sanctuary dedicated to the eastern god Mithras.

Pantanella rose quickly, becoming one of the city's wealthiest entrepreneurs and a leader in the national millers' association. But by the 1890s, his independence was under pressure from the Banco di Roma–backed Molini e Magazzini Generali di Roma. The two firms dominated Rome's grain trade, and the tension came to a head in 1892, when a fire gutted Pantanella's factory. The damage, paired with the collapse of the Banca Romana—Pantanella's main creditor—left him vulnerable. His debts were absorbed by his rivals, and a merger followed. He lost control of his company and died five years later.

Production moved to a new facility near Porta Maggiore in 1929 and eventually shuttered in the 1970s. Today it is a condo complex, complete with a bingo hall. Meanwhile, the Via dei Cerchi building was briefly home to city museums before becoming a government office building and costume and set warehouse for the Teatro dell'Opera, functions it still serves today.

Plans to restore the building are underway, but the story of Pantanella remains a window into a lesser-known part of Rome's food history, when city residents were eating fresh pasta that they made at home and also dried pasta manufactured right in their backyard.

MINESTRA DI BROCCOLI E ARZILLA

ROMANESCO
AND
SKATE SOUP

Serves 6

1½ pounds skinless, bone-in
   skate fillets
4 sprigs fresh, flat-leaf
   parsley
1 celery stalk, roughly
   chopped
1 carrot, roughly chopped
1 medium yellow onion,
   halved
10 whole black peppercorns
2 tablespoons extra-virgin
   olive oil
1 garlic clove, smashed
1 (2-pound) head romanesco,
   roughly chopped
¼ cup tomato sauce
   (passata)
Sea salt
6 ounces spaghetti, broken
   into 3-inch pieces
Freshly ground black pepper

This is the dish that proves Romans are more devoted to culinary tradition than they are to religion. Even the most secular families tend to avoid meat on Fridays, especially in winter, when minestra di broccoli e arzilla makes its way to the table. It's a brothy, warming soup that blends broccolo romanesco (that fractal, chartreuse cousin of cauliflower), skate, and broken spaghetti (sometimes breaking pasta *is* allowed) into something far greater than the sum of its parts. The fish is simmered into a delicate broth that's later enriched with tomato and a hit of chile. If your fishmonger doesn't have skate, go with monkfish or another firm white fish. If you can't find romanesco, cauliflower will do in a pinch, but it won't look nearly as dramatic.

Combine the skate, parsley, celery, carrot, onion, peppercorns, and 6 cups of water in a large pot over high heat. Bring to a rolling boil, reduce the heat to low, and simmer, skimming off any foam that rises to the top, until the skate flesh falls away from the bone easily, about 30 minutes.

Use a slotted spoon to transfer the skate to a bowl. Once cool enough to handle, pick the meat and discard the bones and any cartilage. Pour the broth through a fine-mesh strainer into a bowl and add enough water to make 6 cups total. Discard the aromatics.

Wipe the pot clean. Add the olive oil and garlic and cook over low heat until the garlic just starts to take on color, about 5 minutes. Add the romanesco and ¼ cup of water and cook until tender, 15 to 20 minutes. Add the skate, the broth, and the tomato sauce, season with salt, increase the heat to high, and bring to a rolling boil. Add the spaghetti and cook until al dente. Season with salt and pepper. Serve immediately.

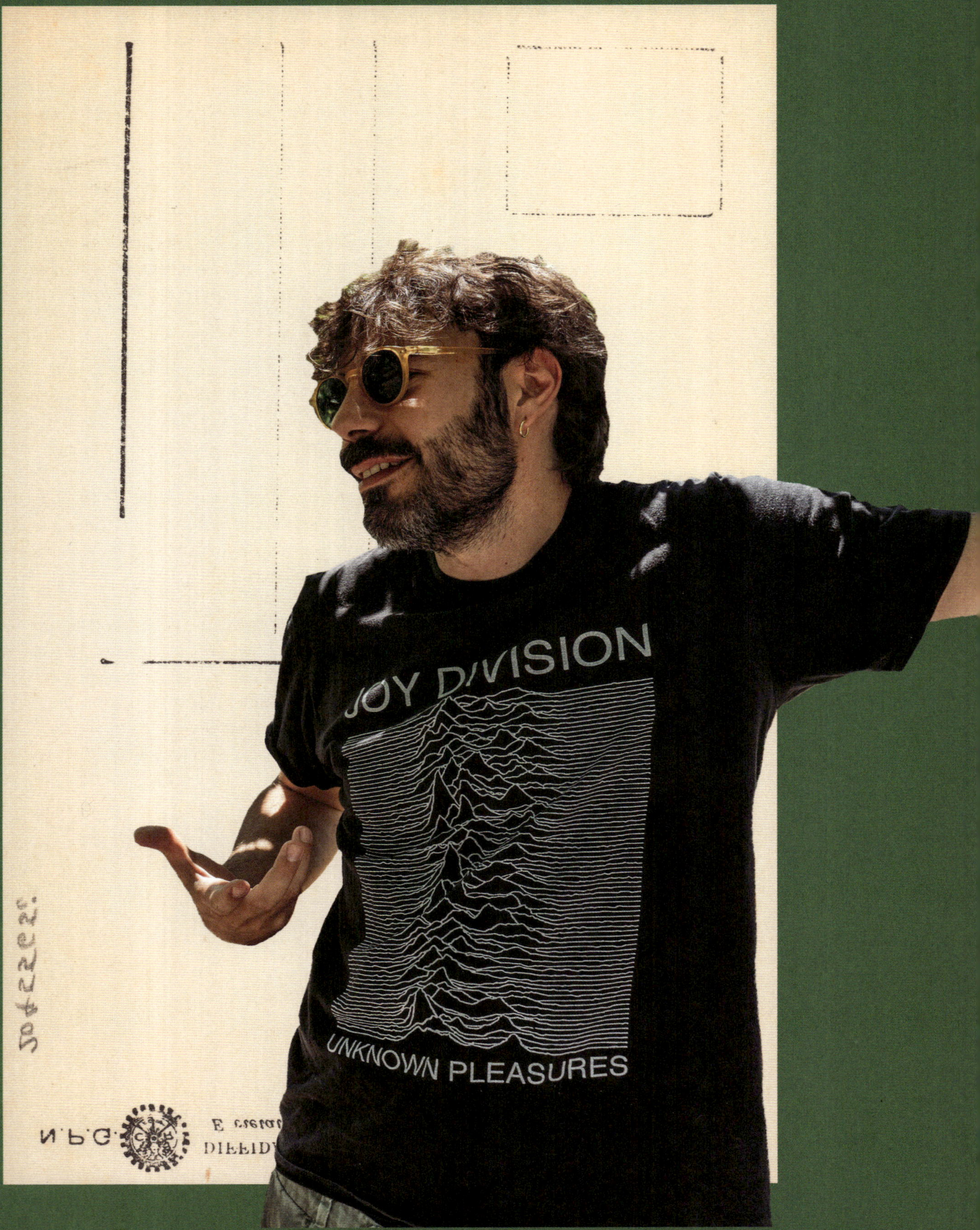
JOY DIVISION
UNKNOWN PLEASURES

SPAGHET-TI ALLA GRICIA

SPAGHETTI WITH
BLACK PEPPER,
GUANCIALE,
AND PECORINO

Serves 4 to 6

8 ounces guanciale, cut into
¾-inch cubes
Sea salt
1 pound spaghetti
1½ teaspoons freshly ground
Sarawak black pepper,
plus more for serving
1 cup finely grated Pecorino
Romano

Several years back, I attempted a campaign to make gricia a household name. I like carbonara and everything, but it hardly deserves the entire Roman pasta spotlight. My efforts were a spectacular failure. I can't even get people to say it right: GREE-chah.

Like all great Roman pastas, gricia depends on technique rather than elaborate ingredients. The guanciale must be cooked just right—rendered enough to impart its fat to the sauce without withering away. The Pecorino Romano, ideally sourced from the countryside around Rome (Fulvi is my choice), should be grated fine enough to melt seamlessly into the starchy pasta water, forming a glossy sauce that clings to every piece of rigatoni, inside and out. Black pepper, cracked fresh, should be applied with a generous hand, reinforcing the dish's bold, unembellished character. In an era where even classic Roman trattorie feel the pressure to modernize, gricia remains a relic of a time when food was defined by its ingredients rather than its Instagram potential.

Heat the guanciale in a large pan over medium-low heat. Cook, stirring occasionally, until golden brown and crisp, about 10 minutes. Remove from the heat and set aside to cool.

While the guanciale cooks, bring a large pot of water to a rolling boil over high heat. Add salt until the water tastes like a seasoned soup. Add the pasta and cook until very al dente.

Add ½ cup of the pasta cooking water to the pan with the cooled guanciale. Use tongs to transfer the pasta to the pan and set it over high heat. Cook, mixing vigorously, until the pasta is al dente. Add more pasta cooking water as needed to keep the sauce silky and not dry.

Remove from the heat and stir in the pepper and ¾ cup of the Pecorino Romano. Serve immediately with the remaining Pecorino Romano and additional pepper freshly ground on top.

MEZZE MANICHE ALLA GRICIA CON ZUCCHINE
Half-Rigatoni with Guanciale, Pecorino Romano, Black Pepper and Zucchini

This is classic gricia with a zucchini boost—a practical way I use up the summer surplus from my garden. The base stays true: guanciale, Pecorino Romano, and black pepper bound by starchy pasta water. The zucchini adds a soft, vegetal note that lightens the dish without changing its character. But don't confuse this twist with gricia di zucchine, a vegetarian version that swaps in zucchini for guanciale. That's a different dish entirely...good, maybe, but *not* gricia.

Follow the recipe above, swapping spaghetti for 1 pound of mezze maniche or rigatoni. While the pasta cooks, cook ¾ cup of grated zucchini in the rendered guanciale fat over medium heat, just until tender, about 3 minutes. Then continue as directed: Finish the pasta in the pan with a splash of starchy water, then toss off the heat with Pecorino and pepper to form a creamy emulsion.

STRACCIATELLA

ROMAN
EGG DROP
SOUP

This brothy, comforting soup is a staple of home cooking in Rome, often served as a light first course when something warm and soothing is in order. You can find it at select trattorie, too, like at my go-tos Armando al Pantheon and Al Moro. Its name, *stracciatella*, comes from *stracce*, "rags," a nod to the wispy strands of egg that form when the mixture is poured into hot broth. The technique is simple, but the texture can be dialed up or down depending on how vigorously you stir; gentle movement yields silky ribbons, while more enthusiastic whisking creates a finer scramble. With good broth, fresh parsley, and a hit of Parmigiano-Reggiano, this humble soup is a master class in simplicity.

Bring the broth to a rolling boil in a large stockpot over medium-high heat. Reduce the heat to low so the broth is gently simmering and add salt until it tastes like a seasoned soup.

Meanwhile, beat together the eggs, Parmigiano-Reggiano, lemon juice, and parsley in a medium bowl. Season with salt. Transfer to a measuring cup with a spout or a small pitcher.

While stirring the broth in a circular motion with a whisk or a fork, drizzle in the egg mixture from a height of about six inches, forming ribbons of cooked egg. Turn off the heat and stir gently for 1 minute. Serve immediately.

Serves 4 to 6

6 cups beef or chicken broth

Sea salt

4 large eggs, at room temperature

¼ cup finely grated Parmigiano-Reggiano

1 tablespoon fresh lemon juice

2 tablespoons finely chopped fresh flat-leaf parsley

FETTUCCINE AL SUGO DI CODA

FETTUCCINE
WITH
OXTAIL SAUCE

Serves 4 to 6

2½ pounds oxtails, trimmed
and separated

Sea salt and freshly ground
black pepper

3 tablespoons good-quality
lard or extra-virgin olive
oil

½ cup dry white wine

1½ (28-ounce) cans whole
peeled tomatoes, crushed
by hand

5 celery stalks, outer fibres
removed (see Tip), then
roughly chopped

Fresh Fettuccine (recipe
follows) or 1 pound store-
bought fettuccine

¼ cup coarsely grated
Pecorino Romano

In Rome, this deeply flavored tomato sauce is a by-product of Coda alla Vacci-nara (page 169), a slow-braised oxtail dish. Traditionally, you'd serve the oxtails themselves as the main course and stretch the sauce across a first course of pasta, often fettuccine, rigatoni, or mezze maniche. This recipe is a meatier version than the classic. Rather than just using leftover sauce, this one uses all the meat from the oxtail, discarding the bones. It's a meat-forward sugo that sticks to your ribs and coats the pasta just right. Season the oxtail segments the night before you intend to cook.

Season the oxtail segments with salt and pepper. Transfer to a covered container and refrigerate overnight.

The next day, remove the oxtail from the refrigerator and pat dry with paper towels. Heat the lard in a large heavy-bottomed pot over medium-high heat until shimmering. Add the oxtail segments and cook, turning as needed, until browned all over, about 15 minutes.

Add the wine, scraping up any browned bits from the bottom of the pot, and cook just until the alcohol aroma dissipates, about 1 minute. Add the tomatoes, season with salt and pepper, and bring the sauce to a boil. Reduce the heat to low, cover, and simmer, moving the oxtail segments every 30 minutes or so, until the meat is falling off the bone, 3 to 4 hours, adding water as necessary if the sauce reduces too much. Add the celery about 1 hour before the oxtails are done.

Remove from the heat, then use a slotted spoon to transfer the oxtails to a plate and let cool slightly. Once cool enough to handle, pick the meat off the bones (don't you dare discard them before sucking out the marrow from those little holes) and return the meat to the pot with the sauce.

Bring a large pot of water to a boil over high heat. Add salt until the water tastes like a seasoned soup. Cook the pasta until it floats and loses its raw flavor, about 3 minutes, then use tongs to transfer the pasta to a large bowl, add 2 to 3 cups of sauce, and toss gently to coat. Plate the pasta, sprinkle with the Pecorino Romano, and serve.

Reserve any leftover sauce for another day; it can be stored in an airtight container in the refrigerator for up to 3 days or in the freezer for up to 3 months.

Tip: Peel away and discard the stringy outer fibers from the celery with a paring knife or vegetable peeler.

FRESH FETTUCCINE

There are two schools of thought when it comes to fettuccine in Rome. The first, and by far the most common, is the thick, toothsome variety you'll find in classic trattorie, typically paired with rigaglie di pollo (page 139), sugo di involtini (page 194), or sugo di coda (previous page). These fettuccine are a far cry from the translucent, almost silky sheets of pasta you find in Emilia-Romagna. Roman-style fettuccine are at least twice as thick, and twice as filling.

Then there's the outlier: the paper-thin fettuccine served at the dueling Alfredo restaurants in central Rome. Both lay claim to the invention of fettuccine Alfredo (page 160), and both serve delicate and thin noodles that are more Emilian in style than Roman.

The classic egg-based pasta dough in Italy calls for one egg per 100 grams of flour. Whether you use the whole egg or just the yolk depends on who's doing the kneading. Personally, I like the texture that comes from using the whole egg. There's a certain bite and spring from the whites that I love. Plus, every time I separate eggs I tell myself I'll use the leftover whites for something virtuous or meringue-y like Montblanc (page 290), and I never do. So in the spirit of texture and reducing waste, I'm a whole-egg kinda lady.

Tips: If rolling the pasta with a machine, cut the dough into 4 to 6 equal pieces. Form each into a tight ball, then press into a flat disk. Starting with one piece and keeping the others covered, pass the dough through the machine on the widest setting twice. Continue passing the dough through the settings of your pasta machine until it is ⅟₁₆-inch thick. Lightly flour the pasta sheet with semolina and roll into a loose tube. Use a sharp knife to cut the pasta into ¼-inch-thick strands. Unfurl the pasta, form the strands into a nest, and set aside on a lightly floured surface. Alternatively, pass the sheets through the fettuccine cutting setting on your machine. Repeat with the remaining dough.

To make Tagliolini (page 143), follow the recipe here, then use a sharp knife to cut the pasta into ⅛-inch-thick strands.

Fresh Maltagliati are misshapen pieces of pasta made from scraps of fresh dough—why waste those? It's a common shape used in soups like Pasta e Ceci (page 154). Use a sharp knife to cut the pasta scraps into irregular pieces about the size of a postage stamp. No need to be precise here.

Makes 480 grams of dough, serving 4 to 6

300 grams 0 or 00 flour, plus more for dusting
½ teaspoon sea salt
180 grams (about 3 large) eggs

Pour the flour and salt into a medium bowl and use your fingers or a spoon to form a well in the center. Crack the eggs into the well and gently beat them together with a fork. Working from the inside of the well to the edges, slowly incorporate the flour into the eggs until a shaggy dough forms. Turn the dough out onto your work surface and knead until it is supple and glossy, about 10 minutes. Form into 2 tight balls, cover tightly with plastic wrap, and set aside to hydrate the flour for 30 minutes.

Lightly dust your work surface with flour. Unwrap one dough ball, place it on your work surface, and flatten it into a uniform disk. Position your rolling pin at 9:00 and 3:00 o'clock and with firm, even pressure, roll away from you. Rotate the dough 90 degrees every 3 to 4 rolls. As you roll, your dough disk will get larger, so to make rolling easier, allow the bottom half to hang over your work surface. When ready to turn, fold the dough over your rolling pin and use it to turn the dough a quarter turn. Repeat until you have rolled the dough to a thickness of ⅟₁₆ inch.

Use a sharp knife to cut the pasta sheet in half. Cut the sheet into a rectangle, setting the curved parts aside to use as maltagliati (see Tips). Lightly flour the dough and roll into a loose tube. Use a sharp knife to slice the pasta into ¼-inch-wide fettuccine. Unfurl the pasta, then form the strands into a nest, and set aside on a lightly floured surface. Repeat with the remaining dough.

The dough will keep, refrigerated and tightly wrapped in plastic, for up to 2 days. Do not freeze. Before rolling, bring the dough to room temperature, about 1 hour.

SERRANDE: CLOSED FOR BUSINESS, OPEN TO INTERPRETATION

You'll find a very particular kind of art in Rome, and it's not displayed in museums or hanging over church altars. It's on the metal serrande, the roll-down shutters

that guard the city's shops when they're closed. These painted metal canvases are a category all their own, commissioned by proprietors who want to give their storefronts a little flair. Yet they inevitably end up with something just a little off: a hamburger with a mustache and the word *pizza* written underneath, a plate of carbonara against an inexplicable backdrop of palm trees, a butcher's happy pig giving a thumbs-up to its own impending fate. These are not artistic masterpieces, but they are unmistakably Roman.

There is something deeply endearing about these works. They are earnest, often unintentional tributes to the things that keep Rome running: coffee, bread, a butcher with a meat cleaver. They are declarations of purpose—this is what we do here, in case you had any doubts—but also reminders that the city is lived in, that commerce here is not faceless or corporate. These aren't chain stores with sleek branding. They are butchers who want a giant, disembodied steak on their shutter and tabacco vendors that insist on a portrait of a horse smoking a cigarette for reasons only they understand.

The painted serrande of Rome are like the city itself: imperfect, quirky, and a little bit haunting.

PASTA E LENTICCHIE

PASTA
WITH
LENTILS

Serves 6

2 tablespoons extra-virgin
   olive oil, plus more for
   serving
1 carrot, finely chopped
1 celery stalk, finely chopped
½ medium yellow onion,
   finely chopped
Sea salt
1 pound dried brown lentils (I
   like lenticchie di Onano)
12 ounces cannolicchi or
   Fresh Maltagliati (see Tip
   on page 134)
Freshly ground black pepper

Lentils have been sustaining Italians for millennia, from the ancient Etruscans who cultivated them on the hills around modern-day Lazio to medieval monks who swore by legumes as a path to piety. Lentils were cheap, filling, and virtuous, practically the holy trinity of Roman austerity. The lentils simmer until they create a starchy, earthy broth, the kind that clings to cannolicchi or maltagliati. My favorite place to eat this is at da Corrado in the Testaccio Market. Corrado serves it in the winter, drizzled with olive oil so fragrant you can smell it three aisles away.

Heat the olive oil in a large pot over low heat. When the oil begins to shimmer, add the carrot, celery, onion, and a heavy pinch of salt and cook until the vegetables are very soft, stirring occasionally, about 25 minutes.

Add the lentils along with water to cover by a few inches. Bring to a boil over high heat, then reduce the heat to low and cook, covered, until the lentils are cooked through, 25 to 30 minutes. Add the cannolicchi to the pot, increase the heat to high, and cook until the pasta is al dente, or if using fresh pasta, cook until it has lost its raw flavor. Season with salt and pepper and serve drizzled with olive oil.

GNOCCHI AL RAGÙ

GNOCCHI
WITH
MEAT SAUCE

As we have repeatedly established, Thursdays are gnocchi day in Rome, and if you've ever had a proper bowl of these potato dumplings in the Italian capital, you'll understand why. They are dressed with heavy meat sauces—ragù, oxtail sauce, meat-roll sauce—that conspire with the gnocchi to fill your stomach and get you thinking you won't need to eat another thing until the weekend. That's fortunate because Fridays were traditionally lean days in Rome, meaning Catholics had to abstain from meat, so Thursdays were all about filling your belly to stave off the next day's hunger. Whether you're observant or not, this recipe lets you do just that.

Serves 4 to 6

2 tablespoons extra-virgin
    olive oil
1 carrot, finely chopped
1 celery stalk, finely chopped
½ medium white onion, finely
    chopped
Sea salt
8 ounces ground beef
½ cup dry red wine
1 (14-ounce) can whole
    peeled tomatoes, crushed
    by hand
Fresh Gnocchi di Patate
    (page 122) or 1 pound
    store-bought gnocchi
¼ cup finely grated
    Parmigiano-Reggiano

Heat the olive oil in a medium pot over low heat. When the oil begins to shimmer, add the carrot, celery, onion, and a heavy pinch of salt and cook until the vegetables are very soft, 15 to 20 minutes. Add the ground beef, increase the heat to medium-high, and cook until well browned, 8 to 10 minutes. Add the wine, scraping the bottom of the pot, and cook until the liquid reduces by half, 2 to 3 minutes. Add the tomatoes, bring to a rolling boil, then reduce the heat to low and simmer until the tomatoes have lost their raw flavor, 20 to 25 minutes.

Bring a large pot of water to a rolling boil. Add salt until the water tastes like a seasoned soup. Gently add the gnocchi and cook until they float and have lost their raw flavor, 3 to 4 minutes. Use a spider or large slotted spoon to transfer the gnocchi to the pot with the sauce. Swirl and mix gently to coat, then serve immediately sprinkled with the Parmigiano-Reggiano.

Tip: You can make the ragù a couple of days ahead of time, especially convenient if you're making gnocchi from scratch.

FETTUCCINE CON LE RIGAGLIE DI POLLO

FETTUCCINE
WITH
CHICKEN
INNARDS

This is one of my absolute favorite Roman dishes, a masterful harmony of textures. At its best, it's an opera of offal: toothsome ribbons of fettuccine (thicker here in Rome than anywhere else in Italy) tangled up with tender hearts and livers and springy gizzards. The trick is giving each part of the bird the attention it needs—hearts seared, livers gently cooked, gizzards simmered low and slow—so they all land on the plate perfectly cooked, not a second overdone.

Armando al Pantheon serves my platonic ideal of this dish, and I've converted more than a few offal skeptics into devotees over steaming bowls of the trattoria's version. It's both the gateway dish and comfort food, rich with flavor and soul, and a dish that proves (yet again) that Roman cuisine knows exactly how to make the most of every part of the animal.

Serves 4 to 6

Sea salt

6 ounces chicken gizzards, cleaned (see Tip)

2 tablespoons extra-virgin olive oil

1 carrot, finely chopped

1 celery stalk, finely chopped

1 medium yellow onion, finely chopped

6 ounces chicken hearts, cleaned (see Tip) and chopped

1 cup dry white wine

1 (14-ounce) can whole peeled tomatoes, crushed by hand

6 ounces chicken livers, cleaned (see Tip) and chopped

Fresh Fettuccine (page 134) or 1 pound store-bought fettuccine

½ cup grated Pecorino Romano (optional)

Bring a medium pot of water to a gentle simmer over low heat. Add salt until the water tastes like a seasoned soup, then add the gizzards and simmer until tender, 1½ to 2 hours. Drain the gizzards and, when cool enough to handle, chop into ¼-inch pieces.

Heat the olive oil in a large pan over low heat. When the oil begins to shimmer, add the carrot, celery, onion, and a heavy pinch of salt and cook until the vegetables are very soft, about 20 minutes. Add the chicken hearts and cook until browned all over, 5 to 6 minutes. Add the wine and cook until the liquid has reduced by half, 4 to 5 minutes. Add the tomatoes, season with salt, and cook until concentrated, 30 minutes, then add the livers and gizzards. Cook until the livers are just cooked through, about 3 minutes.

Meanwhile, bring a large pot of water to a rolling boil over high heat. Add salt until the water tastes like a seasoned soup. Cook the fettuccine until they float and have lost their raw flavor, about 3 minutes. Use tongs to transfer the fettuccine to the pan, tossing gently to coat. Season with salt and serve immediately with the chunky sauce spooned over the top and sprinkled with the Pecorino Romano, if desired.

Tips: To clean chicken gizzards, slice them in half lengthwise and remove any yellowish membrane or grit inside. Trim off any tough silver skin or excess fat. Rinse thoroughly under cold water, scrubbing gently if needed.

To clean chicken hearts, slice off the top portion to remove the valve and any tough connective tissue. Trim away excess fat around the base, then halve the hearts lengthwise and rinse well.

To clean chicken livers, gently separate any lobes that are stuck together and trim off visible green or yellowish bits. Remove any white connective tissue or veins with a small knife. Rinse briefly under cold water, then pat dry thoroughly.

PASTA CON BROCCOLI

PASTA

WITH

ROMANESCO

Broccolo romanesco (or in Rome, simply *broccolo*) is a striking vegetable with a bright green fractal pattern. It's been cultivated in Italy since at least the sixteenth century, particularly in Rome and the Lazio region, where it remains a staple of local cuisine. Milder and sweeter than broccoli, with a slightly nutty flavor and firm, cauliflower-like texture, it is often steamed or sautéed with olive oil, garlic, and salt, allowing its natural taste to shine. Here, that classic side dish becomes the pasta condiment.

Serves 4 to 6

Sea salt
1 (2-pound) head romanesco, stalks and leaves roughly chopped and florets separated into equal pieces
¼ cup extra-virgin olive oil
1 garlic clove, smashed
1 peperoncino (whole dried chile pepper) or ¼ teaspoon crushed red pepper flakes
Freshly ground black pepper
1 pound Fresh Fettuccine (page 134) or rigatoni
½ cup finely grated Pecorino Romano

Fill a large pot with water and bring to a rolling boil. Add salt until the water tastes like a seasoned soup. Add the romanesco and blanch until tender fork-tender, 8 to 9 minutes. Use a spider or a slotted spoon to transfer the romanesco to a medium bowl, reserving the blanching water.

Heat the olive oil, garlic, and peperoncino in a large pan over low heat. When the garlic just starts to take on color, about 5 minutes, add the romanesco and season with salt and pepper. Increase the heat to medium and cook, adding reserved blanching water to the pan ¼ cup at a time to keep everything nice and juicy and steamy, until the romanesco is super soft and falling apart, about 15 minutes.

Meanwhile, return the pot with the blanching water to a rolling boil over high heat. Add the fettuccine and cook until it floats and has lost its raw flavor, about 3 minutes. If using dried pasta, cook until al dente. Use a spider or slotted spoon to transfer to the pan with the romanesco, adding pasta cooking water as needed to loosen the sauce. Remove the pan from the heat and stir in the Pecorino Romano. Serve immediately. Watch out for the garlic.

TAGLIOLINI AI FUNGHI PORCINI

**TAGLIOLINI
WITH PORCINI
MUSHROOMS**

Serves 4 to 6

Sea salt
3 tablespoons extra-virgin
    olive oil
1 tablespoon unsalted butter
1 garlic clove, smashed
10 ounces fresh porcini
    mushrooms, cleaned and
    sliced, or 1 ounce dried
    porcini (see Tip)
Fresh Tagliolini (see Tip on
    page 134) or 1 pound
    store-bought tagliolini or
    tagliatelle
Freshly ground black pepper
A few sprigs fresh flat-leaf
    parsley, roughly chopped

Not so long ago, foragers used to make the rounds in Rome, their satchels emitting the earthy aroma of mushrooms plucked from Apennine forests in Lazio, Molise, and Abruzzo. A few of them are still out there, but proper porcini are increasingly hard to come by, a by-product of climate change and a frugal public unwilling to pay for them. In season, you can find perfect porcini sliced and gently cooked in garlic-infused oil at Piatto Romano in Testaccio, the texture nearly matching the toothiness of the tagliolini they are served with.

A fresh porcino is firm, with a perfectly fused stem. Neither should bear blemishes or holes, the telltale signs of worm infestation. If you can get your hands on fresh porcini, cook them the day you buy them. If you're using dried, go for high-quality ones from Italy or the Balkans; they should smell like the forest, not like old cardboard.

Tip: Soak dried porcini in a medium bowl with warm water for 30 minutes to rehydrate. Once softened, remove and roughly chop the mushrooms. Don't toss the soaking liquid. Strain it through a fine sieve or coffee filter to remove grit, then use it to deepen this dish, as well as sauces, risotto, or stews.

Bring a large pot of water to a rolling boil. Add salt until the water tastes like a seasoned soup.

Meanwhile, heat the olive oil and butter in a large pan over medium-low heat. Add the garlic and cook until fragrant but not browned, about 1 minute.

Add the porcini and a heavy pinch of salt. Cook, stirring occasionally, until the mushrooms release their liquid and begin to brown, 8 to 10 minutes. If using dried porcini, add a few spoonfuls of their strained soaking liquid to intensify the flavor.

Cook the tagliolini until they have lost their raw flavor, 2 to 3 minutes. Use tongs to transfer them to the pan and add ¼ cup of pasta cooking water.

Mix well and add more pasta cooking water as needed to achieve a creamy sauce. Season with salt and pepper, stir in the parsley, and serve immediately.

MINESTRONE

BROTHY
VEGETABLE
SOUP

Roman minestrone is the cure for fiber deprivation, a common ailment in the Italian capital. This soup is a market-driven, fruttivendolo-assisted miracle that tastes like whatever's in season and is simmered for just long enough. Unlike the starchy, bread-thickened soups of the north, this version is all about brothy goodness and vegetal variety—maybe fennel in the fall, zucchini in the summer, a little kale or cabbage when the temperature drops. Around Rome, market vendors pre-bag mixes labeled *minestrone*, usually a mystery medley of chopped produce that you can just dump in a pot and forget about for an hour. Strictly vegan, this soup nods to the lean meals of religious fasting days, but it doesn't feel like a sacrifice. A potato adds flavor and a little extra sustenance.

Serves 4 to 6

2 tablespoons extra-virgin olive oil, plus more for serving

½ medium yellow onion, finely chopped

1 medium Yukon Gold potato, peeled and roughly chopped

1 cup (1-inch) cauliflower or romanesco florets

3 cups Tuscan kale, ribs and stems removed, then roughly chopped

3 medium carrots, roughly chopped

½ medium fennel bulb and stalks, roughly chopped

1 tablespoon sea salt, plus more as needed

Freshly ground black pepper

Heat the olive oil in a large pot over low heat. When the oil begins to shimmer, add the onion and cook until it is soft and translucent, 10 to 15 minutes. Add the potato, cauliflower, kale, carrots, and fennel to the pot along with 6 cups of water. Season with the salt. Bring to a simmer over high heat, then reduce to medium-low and cook, partially covered, until the vegetables are nearly falling apart, about 50 minutes. Season with pepper and more salt, if needed. Serve drizzled with olive oil.

CANNELLONI DI CARNE

MEAT-FILLED
FRESH PASTA
TUBES

Cannelloni aren't exactly a dish you whip up after work on a weeknight. They are part of a quintessential pranzo della domenica (Sunday lunch), requiring multiple steps while guaranteeing supreme comfort. The filling isn't weighed down with ricotta or drowned in tomato sauce. It's a tight, savory mix of ground beef and béchamel, rolled into fresh egg pasta and baked just until the edges bubble and the top goes golden. There are lighter and quicker ways to feed a crowd. But none as satisfying as this.

Makes 10 to 12 cannelloni, serving 4 to 6

For the pasta:
160 grams 0 or 00 flour, plus more for dusting
100 grams (about 2 large) eggs

For the filling and topping:
¼ cup plus 2 tablespoons extra-virgin olive oil, plus more for greasing
1 small onion, finely chopped
Sea salt
9 ounces finely ground beef
1½ cups finely grated Parmigiano-Reggiano, plus more for dusting
6 tablespoons Besciamella (recipe follows)
1 garlic clove, smashed
1 (14-ounce) can whole peeled tomatoes, crushed by hand
2 to 3 fresh basil leaves, torn

Make the pasta: Pour the flour into a large bowl and use your fingers or a spoon to form a large well in the center. Crack the eggs into the well and gently beat them together with a fork. Working from the inside of the well to the edges, slowly incorporate the flour into the eggs until a shaggy dough forms.

Turn the dough out onto your work surface and knead until it is supple and glossy, 7 to 8 minutes. Form into a tight ball, cover tightly with plastic wrap, and set aside to hydrate the flour for 30 minutes and up to 2 hours.

Unwrap the dough and halve, keeping the piece you're not yet working with covered. Gently press the dough into a rough rectangle using flattened fingertips. Dust lightly with flour, then pass the pressed dough through your pasta machine's widest setting. Fold the dough in thirds like a letter. Rotate it 90 degrees and run it through the wide setting again. Repeat this folding and rolling process twice more to smooth and align the gluten network. Begin reducing the roller setting one notch at a time. Run the dough through each setting once (no more folding) and lightly dust with flour as needed to prevent sticking. Support the sheet with your hands as it lengthens. Pass the sheet through the machine until it reaches the second-thinnest setting. Set aside on a lightly floured work surface. Cut the pasta into pieces, each about 5 inches long. Set aside on a floured tray and cover loosely with a clean kitchen towel. Repeat with the second piece of dough. Let the pasta sheets cure, uncovered, for 30 minutes before cooking.

Make the filling and toppings: Heat ¼ cup of the olive oil in a large pan over low heat. Add the onion and a heavy pinch of salt. Cook until the onion is soft and translucent, about 15 minutes. Add the beef and another pinch of salt. Increase the heat to medium and cook until browned all over, 10 to 12 minutes. Remove from the heat and stir in 1 cup of the Parmigiano-Reggiano and 3 tablespoons of the béchamel. Set aside to cool.

recipe continues on next page ▶

Heat the remaining 2 tablespoons olive oil and the garlic in a second large pan over low heat and cook just until the garlic starts to take on color, about 5 minutes. Add the tomatoes and a heavy pinch of salt. Simmer gently until the tomatoes have lost their raw flavor, about 15 minutes. Stir in the basil and set aside to cool.

Preheat the oven to 350°F. Lightly oil a 9 ×13-inch baking dish.

Bring a large pot of water to a rolling boil. Add salt until the water tastes like a seasoned soup. Working in batches, blanch the pasta sheets for 30 seconds. Use a spider to transfer the pasta to a clean kitchen towel and set aside to cool.

Spoon the beef filling lengthwise down the center of each pasta sheet and roll into semi-tight tubes. Place seam-side down in the prepared baking dish. Top with the tomato sauce, then spoon over the remaining 3 table-spoons béchamel. Dust with the remaining ½ cup Parmigiano-Reggiano.

Bake, covered with foil, for 20 minutes. Uncover and cook until the cannelloni are bubbling and browned at the edges, 20 to 25 minutes more. Set aside to rest for 10 to 15 minutes before serving.

BESCIAMELLA
Béchamel

Makes 1½ cups

2 tablespoons unsalted butter
⅓ cup 00 flour, sifted
¼ teaspoon freshly grated nutmeg
2 cups whole milk
Sea salt

Melt the butter in a medium saucepan over low heat. Slowly rain in the flour and nutmeg, whisking continuously. Cook until the flour smells toasted and nutty, 4 to 5 minutes. Slowly whisk in the milk, 4 minutes. Bring to a simmer and cook, whisking frequently, until thickened, about 10 minutes. Season with salt and set aside.

LASAGNA DELLA DOMENICA

SUNDAY
LASAGNA

Makes one 9 × 13-inch lasagna, serving 6 to 8

300 grams 00 flour, plus
   more for dusting
½ teaspoon sea salt, plus
   more for salting the water
180 grams (about 3 large)
   eggs
Ragù di Carne (recipe
   follows)
Besciamella (opposite page)
1⅓ cups finely grated
   Parmigiano-Reggiano

In Rome, lasagna is stripped of the pageantry you find in its northern cousin from Bologna. There's no pork, no veal, no pancetta or nutmeg, just a straight-forward beef ragù, slow-simmered until tender and rich. The béchamel is classic but unfussy, and the pasta egg-based and rolled into wide sheets that hold the layers together without fuss. This is the kind of dish that shows up at Sunday lunch and leaves a big impression. And while it asks you to prep three separate elements, the rhythm is meditative, the process grounding. When I make lasagna, I prefer to roll out the pasta with a rolling pin, rather than with a pasta machine, since the width of the pasta rolled through the machine is a couple of inches too narrow for the baking dish. Rolling by hand lets me cut a single sheet the size of the baking dish, rather than cobbling together smaller pieces for each layer.

Combine the flour and salt in a large bowl and use your fingers or a spoon to form a large well in the center. Crack the eggs into the well and gently beat them together with a fork. Working from the inside of the well to the edges, slowly incorporate the flour into the eggs until a shaggy dough forms.

Turn the dough out onto your work surface and knead until it is supple and glossy, 7 to 8 minutes. Form into a tight ball, cover tightly with plastic wrap, and set aside to hydrate the flour for 30 minutes and up to 2 hours.

Lightly dust your work surface. Unwrap the dough and, working with around 110 grams at a time while keeping the rest covered, gently press the dough into a rough rectangle using flattened fingertips. Dust the top of the dough with flour and begin rolling from the center outward in smooth, fluid movements, turning the dough 90 degrees every 3 to 4 rolls to maintain an even shape. Use light, steady pressure and add flour as needed to prevent sticking. Keep rolling until the sheet is smooth, elastic, and thin enough to faintly see your hand through it when held up to the light. Using a sharp knife, cut the dough into an approximately 10 ×14-inch sheet. Set aside on a lightly floured work surface. Repeat with the remaining dough. Set aside any pasta scraps for Maltagliati (see Tip on page 134). Let the pasta sheets cure, uncovered, for 30 minutes before cooking.

Meanwhile, preheat the oven to 375°F. Lightly oil a 9 ×13-inch baking dish.

Line two baking sheets with clean kitchen towels. Bring a large pot of water to a rolling boil. Add salt until the water tastes like a seasoned soup. Working in batches, blanch the pasta for 30 seconds. Use a spider to transfer the pasta to the kitchen towels and set aside to cool.

recipe continues on next page ▶

Spoon ⅔ cup of ragù into the prepared baking dish, distributing it evenly. Spread ⅓ cup of the béchamel over the ragù, distributing it evenly.

Place one pasta sheet over the sauce and béchamel layer. Spread about ⅔ cup of ragù over the pasta, followed by ⅓ cup of béchamel, distributing it evenly. Dust with about ⅓ cup of Parmigiano-Reggiano. Repeat the pasta, ragù, béchamel, and Parmigiano-Reggiano layering three more times.

Cover the baking dish with aluminum foil and bake for 30 minutes. Remove the foil and bake until the pasta is cooked through and the edges are crispy and browned, about 30 minutes more. Set the lasagna aside to rest for at least 30 minutes before slicing and serving.

The cooked lasagna will keep in the refrigerator for up to 3 days, or in the freezer for up to 3 months. Reserve any leftovers for Mattonelle di Lasagna (page 96).

RAGÙ DI CARNE
Roman Meat Sauce

Makes about 3 cups

2 tablespoons extra-virgin olive oil
1 carrot, finely chopped
1 celery stalk, finely chopped
1 small yellow onion, finely chopped
Sea salt
8 ounces ground beef
Freshly ground black pepper
½ cup dry white wine
1 (14-ounce) can whole peeled tomatoes,
   crushed by hand

Heat the olive oil, celery, carrot, and onion in a large pan over low heat. Season with a heavy pinch of salt and cook until the vegetables are very soft, about 25 minutes.

Add the ground beef, increase the heat to medium-high, season with salt and pepper, and cook until browned all over, 8 to 10 minutes. Add the wine and cook just until the alcohol aroma dissipates, about 1 minute. Add the tomatoes, bring to a boil, then reduce the heat to low and simmer, covered, until the flavors have married, about 20 minutes.

SPAGHETTONI BURRO E ALICI

SPAGHETTONI
    WITH BUTTER AND
SALTED
    ANCHOVIES

The deeply Roman combo of anchovies and butter shows up at natural wine bars across the city, slathered on toast and washed down with skin-contact, Malvasia or Passerina. But it really reaches the next level when melted to coat spaghettoni, thick-cut pasta that holds on to every glossy drop. There's no cheese, no herbs, no showing off—just the savory depth of good anchovies (get the Cantabrian ones in olive oil, or gently rinse salted anchovies) and butter doing what they do best.

Bring a large pot of water to a rolling boil over high heat. Add salt until the water tastes like a seasoned soup. Add the spaghettoni and cook until very al dente.

Meanwhile, gently melt the butter in a large pan over low heat, taking care not to brown. Add the anchovy fillets to the pan and let them melt into the butter, stirring frequently. Use tongs to transfer the pasta to the pan along with ½ cup of the pasta cooking water. Increase the heat to medium-high and stir vigorously to emulsify. Add more water as needed to finish cooking the pasta until it is al dente. Serve immediately.

Serves 4 to 6

Sea salt
1 pound spaghettoni
2 sticks (8 ounces) unsalted
    butter
12 to 14 oil-packed
    Cantabrian anchovy
    fillets, drained

PASTA E CECI

PASTA WITH CHICKPEAS

Serves 6

¼ cup extra-virgin olive oil,
  plus more for serving
1 garlic clove, finely chopped
  (see Tip)
1 carrot, finely chopped
1 celery stalk, finely chopped
½ medium yellow onion,
  finely chopped
Sea salt and freshly ground
  black pepper
6 fresh sage leaves, finely
  chopped
Leaves from 2 rosemary
  sprigs, roughly chopped
1 pound dried chickpeas,
  soaked overnight and
  drained (see Tip on page
  118)
12 ounces cannolicchi, or
  Fresh Maltagliati (see Tip
  on page 134)

Tip: Chop the garlic with a pinch of salt. It helps to release the garlic juices and prevents it from sticking to the knife.

Romans have been cooking with chickpeas since before the Colosseum saw its first gladiator spill blood in the arena. Horace wrote about *lagana e cicer* (sheets of pasta with chickpeas) in his *Satires*, and Martial hyped their aphrodisiac qualities (I'll buy it). Pliny the Elder even documented the popularity of chickpeas in taverns, where they were roasted and salted to keep customers drinking. Pasta e ceci is a descendant of those ancient staples and remains one of Rome's most comforting one-pot meals. I soak my chickpeas overnight so they cook faster and more evenly. If you prefer not to, budget an additional hour or so to cook them. Overall cooking time can vary widely based on the age of the chickpeas.

Heat the oil in a large pot over low heat. When the oil begins to shimmer, add the garlic, celery, carrot, onion, and a heavy pinch of salt and cook until the vegetables are very soft, 15 to 20 minutes.

Add the sage and rosemary and cook until fragrant, about 30 seconds. Add the chickpeas along with 3 quarts of water. Bring to a boil over high heat, then reduce the heat to low and cook, covered, until the chickpeas are cooked through and nearly falling apart, 2 to 2½ hours. Add the cannolicchi to the pot and cook until al dente, or if using fresh pasta, cook until it has lost its raw flavor. Season with salt and pepper and serve drizzled with olive oil.

Roman hardware stores are magic. Not the sleek, sterile DIY chains of the sub-urbs, but the dimly lit, overstuffed ferramente wedged between bars and bakeries on cobbled side streets. These are palaces of utility, labyrinths of brass fittings and mis-matched screws, where the air smells like sawdust, rubber gaskets, and industrial-strength adhesive. The aisles—if you can call them that—are a study in organized chaos, lined with precarious stacks of plastic bins that contain everything and nothing at the same time.

Here, the old-school proprietors have seen it all. Need a key duplicated for a lock that hasn't been manufactured since the 1990 World Cup? They'll find a way. Looking for an odd-ly specific washer for a faucet no plumber will touch? There's a box of them somewhere, buried behind a stash of replace-ment moka pot funnels. If you ask for a certain size of screw, expect to be quizzed about its exact application before they wordlessly disappear into the back and return with exactly what you need . . . or something close enough.

But let's be honest: The real treasure in these spaces isn't the hardware, it's the kitchen section where the everyday meets the esoteric, where culinary dreams are realized in aluminum, wood, and steel. Here is where you find a chitarra for mak-ing tonnarelli, a sturdy wire-and-wood puntarelle cutter, a box grater with holes so sharp it could double as a medieval tor-ture device. There are pasta rollers older than you, citrus juic-ers heavy enough to crack a countertop, and gas stove ring reducers in at least a dozen different sizes. Every time I go in looking for one thing, I leave with three others I never knew I needed but now cannot imagine living without.

In a city where hyperspecialized shops are dying out, the ferramenta holds its ground, resistant to modern convenience. It is a bastion of the analog world, where planned obsolescence holds no sway and the clerks keep their inventory in their heads rather than on a digital screen. Rome may be eternal, but its hardware stores feel immortal.

RAVIOLI CACIO E PEPE

**RAVIOLI FILLED
WITH RICOTTA,
PECORINO ROMANO,
AND BLACK PEPPER**

**Makes 30 to 40 ravioli,
serving 6 to 8**

For the pasta:
300 grams 00 flour, plus
    more for dusting
180 grams (about 3 large)
    eggs
Semolina, for dusting

For the filling:
2 cups whole-milk ricotta,
    well-drained (see Tip on
    page 287)
1 large egg
1 cup finely grated Pecorino
    Romano
1 teaspoon freshly ground
    black pepper
Sea salt

For the final dish:
Sea salt
¼ cup extra-virgin olive oil
2 tablespoons unsalted
    butter
¼ cup finely grated Pecorino
    Romano
Freshly ground black pepper

Cacio e pepe is one of Rome's holy pastas, but that hardly means it's sacred. Innovators have been repackaging the Pecorino Romano and black pepper combo for well over a decade now. Stefano Callegari was the first to innovate, serving cacio e pepe pizza at his numerous pizzerie. A dozen years ago, Gabriele Bonci used the duo to flavor supplì. The classic still reigns but a handful of trattorie and wine bars serve ravioli cacio e pepe, and more often than not, they are made by Mauro Secondi, a veteran fresh pasta maker, in his laboratorio in Torre Maura in Rome's eastern periphery. In a subtle marriage of flavors, sheets of tender pasta cradle a ricotta filling seasoned with salty pecorino and piquant pepper. It's best to dress the ravioli simply, just a drizzle of olive oil and a hint of butter, cheese, and pepper, and you've got a modern riff that still feels deeply Roman.

Make the pasta: Pour the flour into a large bowl and use your fingers or a spoon to form a large well in the center. Crack the eggs into the well and gently beat them together with a fork. Working from the inside of the well to the edges, slowly incorporate the flour into the eggs until a shaggy dough forms.

Turn the dough out onto a clean, dry work surface and knead energetically until it is supple and glossy, 7 to 8 minutes. Form into a tight ball, cover tightly with plastic wrap, and set aside to rest for 30 minutes and up to 2 hours.

Make the filling: Pour the ricotta into a fine-mesh strainer set over a bowl to allow any excess liquid to drain off, about 30 minutes. Combine the ricotta, egg, Pecorino Romano, pepper, and a heavy pinch of salt in a medium bowl. Transfer to a pastry bag or zip-top plastic bag and set aside in the refrigerator.

Roll the pasta: Unwrap the dough and halve, keeping the piece you're not yet working with covered. Gently press the first piece of dough into a rough rectangle. Dust lightly with flour, then pass the pressed dough through your pasta machine's widest setting. Fold the dough in thirds like a letter. Rotate it 90 degrees and run it through the wide setting again. Repeat this folding and rolling process twice more to smooth and align the gluten network. Begin reducing the roller setting one notch at a time. Run the dough through each setting once (no more folding) and lightly dust with flour as needed to prevent sticking. Support the sheet with your hands as it lengthens. Pass the sheet through the machine until it reaches the second-thinnest setting. Set aside on a lightly floured work surface and halve crosswise. Repeat with the remaining dough. Do not flour the top of the dough.

Assemble: Cut a corner of the zip-top bag off, if using. Lay out one piece of dough horizontally on your work surface and pipe about 2 teaspoons of the filling, starting 1 inch from the top corner of the dough and spacing the filling 1½ inches apart. Gently cover the filling with a second dough sheet, so the unfloured side is in contact with the filling and bottom pasta sheet. Press around the filling to create closed parcels. Use a ravioli cutter to separate the ravioli into squares. Repeat with the remaining dough and filling.

Set aside in a single layer on a semolina-dusted tray. The ravioli will keep for up to 1 day, uncovered, in the refrigerator.

Prepare the final dish: Bring a large pot of water to a rolling boil over high heat. Add salt until the water tastes like a seasoned soup. Add the ravioli and cook until they float and have lost their raw flavor, 3 to 4 minutes.

Meanwhile, heat the olive oil and butter in a large pan over low heat. Mix until well combined. Use a spider to transfer the ravioli to the pan. Add ¼ cup of pasta cooking water, increase the heat to medium, and gently swirl the pan to coat the ravioli and emulsify the sauce, about 1 minute.

Serve dusted with the Pecorino Romano and pepper.

AJO, OJO, E PEPERONCINO

SPAGHETTI WITH GARLIC, OIL, AND CHILE

This is the world's greatest drunk food: garlicky, unctuous, and with a little bit of heat. Bonus: It tastes great when you're sober, too! According to a popular myth, it was invented by a woman who had been too busy with her lover to cook a proper dinner for her husband. In a panic, she tossed together garlic, oil, and chile flakes to distract him with bold flavors and satisfying richness. Whether or not that tale holds water, the dish has stuck around for good reason. It's what we cook in Rome after a night out drinking. While some versions call for adding pasta water to create an emulsion, I prefer to drain the pasta completely so the spicy, garlic-infused oil remains front and center. I don't use parsley in my version, but they do at Armando al Pantheon, and it adds a nice herbal note. Add it if you like, but don't even think about cheese.

Serves 4 to 6

Sea salt

1 pound spaghetti

⅓ cup extra-virgin olive oil

3 garlic cloves, smashed

3 peperoncini (whole dried red chile peppers) or ¾ teaspoon crushed red pepper flakes

1 tablespoon roughly chopped fresh flat-leaf parsley (optional)

Bring a large pot of water to a rolling boil over high heat. Add salt until the water tastes like a seasoned soup. Add the spaghetti and cook until al dente.

Meanwhile, heat the olive oil, garlic, and peperoncini in a large pan over low heat. Cook just until the garlic starts to take on color, about 5 minutes. Remove from the heat and set aside.

Drain the pasta in a colander, transfer to the pan, and toss to coat. Stir in the parsley, if using. Serve immediately with 2 liters of water on the side if you're hoping to combat a hangover.

FETTUCCINE BURRO E PARMIGIANO

FETTUCCINE
ALFREDO

Serves 4 to 6

Sea salt
2 sticks (8 ounces) unsalted
butter
Fresh Fettuccine (page 134)
or 1 pound store-bought
fresh fettuccine
3 cups finely grated
Parmigiano-Reggiano

When Alfredo Di Lelio whipped up a buttery pasta dish in 1908 to coax his wife to eat post-childbirth, he couldn't have imagined he was creating an international sensation. What started as a richer spin on pasta in bianco (Italy's go-to comfort food for the unwell) morphed into fettuccine Alfredo, thanks to Di Lelio's and his descendants' masterful marketing and Hollywood royalty. Famously, Mary Pickford and Douglas Fairbanks fell for it on their Roman honeymoon and brought word back to LA. Despite its stateside reputation as a cream-laden gut bomb, the original Italian form is absurdly simple: just pasta, Parmigiano-Reggiano, and a dangerous amount of butter, all emulsified tableside into a glossy sauce. No cream, no garlic, and for damn sure no chicken or shrimp.

Today, two rival Alfredo restaurants in central Rome, Il Vero Alfredo and Alfredo alla Scrofa, claim to be the dish's Roman birthplace, each touting original recipes and century-old photos as proof. Both have ridden a fresh wave of popularity on TikTok, where creamy pasta twirls and old school dining rooms rack up millions of views. But beyond the glitz and social media fanfare, these spots are more legacy attractions than culinary standouts. If your trip to Rome isn't guided by a "doing it for the 'gram" mantra, you'll find far more satisfying pasta experiences elsewhere, where tradition isn't theatrically staged, but genuinely lived.

Bring a large pot of water to a rolling boil over high heat. Add salt until the water tastes like a seasoned soup.

Meanwhile, melt the butter in a large, deep pan over low heat, 1 to 2 minutes, taking care not to brown. Remove from the heat.

Add the fettuccine to the boiling water and cook until they float and lose their raw flavor, about 3 minutes. Use tongs to transfer the pasta to the pan with the butter, along with ½ cup of the pasta cooking water, and toss gently to coat. Stir in the Parmigiano-Reggiano, tossing gently from the bottom until the sauce is velvety and creamy, about 2 minutes. Season with salt as needed. Serve immediately.

Please enjoy this image of Sylvester Stallone being hand-fed fettuccine at Il Vero Alfredo.

FISH, MEAT, AND 'OFFAL'

PICCHIAPÒ

MEAT BRAISED
IN SPICY
TOMATO SAUCE

Serves 4 to 6

1 pound beef chuck or shin
Sea salt
1 cup dry red wine
2 carrots, halved
2 celery stalks, halved
2 medium yellow onions,
    halved
10 whole black peppercorns
2 whole cloves
2 tablespoons extra-virgin
    olive oil
1 peperoncino (whole dried
    red chile pepper) or ½
    teaspoon crushed red
    pepper flakes
1 (14-ounce) can whole
    peeled tomatoes, crushed
    by hand

Picchiapò is Roman thrift and flavor rolled into one frugal, saucy dish. Born out of the tradition of reusing stewed beef—often leftover allesso di bollito—picchiapò turns what might be a bland remnant into something bold and craveable. It's made by simmering shredded meat in a tomato and onion sauce that's sweet, spicy, and just messy enough to demand a napkin pressed against the chest. These days, picchiapò is often prepared from scratch rather than crafted from leftovers. My favorite version is at Trattoria da Cesare al Casaletto, where there are hunks of meat rather than pulpy strands. For more flavorful beef, season the meat with salt 4 hours and up to 24 hours before cooking.

Season the beef with salt. Transfer to a covered container and refrigerate for 4 hours or overnight.

Place the beef in a large pot with water to cover. Bring to a boil over high heat, then reduce the heat to low and simmer gently, skimming off any foam that rises to the top, about 30 minutes. Add the wine, carrots, celery, one of the onions, the peppercorns, and the cloves and continue to simmer until the beef is fork-tender, 2 to 3 hours. Set the meat aside to cool in the cooking liquid. Once cool, cut it into 2-inch pieces. Strain the broth and reserve it for another dish.

Finely chop the remaining onion. Heat the olive oil and onion in a large pan over low heat. Season with a heavy pinch of salt and cook until very soft, about 20 minutes. Add the peperoncino and cook until fragrant, about 30 seconds. Add the tomatoes, season with salt, and cook until they have lost their raw flavor, 25 to 30 minutes. Transfer the beef to the pan, then cook for 15 minutes more to allow the sauce to come together and to infuse the meat with flavor.

Serve immediately or cover and refrigerate to serve the next day, after the flavors have intensified. Warm before serving.

ABBACCHIO PANATO

FRIED
LAMB CHOPS

Serves 4

1¾ pounds (about 8) milk-fed
    lamb rib chops
Sea salt and freshly ground
    black pepper
2 large eggs
½ cup finely grated Pecorino
    Romano
1 cup breadcrumbs
Neutral oil, for frying
2 lemons, cut into wedges,
    for serving

In Rome, spring belongs to abbacchi, young milk-fed lambs slaughtered before they transition to a grass-based diet. The meat is tender, pale, and subtly sweet, and it shows up everywhere in season: drenched in egg sauce in Abbacchio Brodettato (page 188), roasted in Abbacchio alla Romana (page 204), grilled in Abbacchio a Scottadito (page 180), or braised in vinegar and wine for abbacchio alla cacciatora. It's so common in spring that we have to get creative with how we cook it. One of my favorite versions is breaded and fried until crisp and golden, which locks in all that juiciness. A squeeze of lemon cuts through the richness, and a hit of pecorino in the breading amps up the umami.

Use a meat mallet to gently flatten each chop to an even ½-inch thickness, taking care not to break the bone. Season both sides generously with salt and pepper.

Set up your breading station: Beat the eggs with the Pecorino Romano in a shallow bowl. Spread the breadcrumbs on a separate plate. Season the egg mixture and breadcrumbs with salt and pepper.

Dip each chop into the egg mixture, letting the excess drip off, then press into the breadcrumbs, coating well on both sides. Set aside on a plate for 10 to 15 minutes to help the coating adhere.

Line a platter or baking sheet with paper towels.

Heat ½ inch of oil to 350°F in a large frying pan or cast-iron skillet. Fry the chops in batches, taking care not to overcrowd the pan, until deep golden and cooked through, 3 to 4 minutes per side. Transfer to paper towels to drain.

Serve hot with lemon wedges and a punchy bitter green salad like Puntarelle alla Romana (page 226) on the side.

CODA ALLA VACCINARA

BRAISED OXTAIL

Coda alla vaccinara is one of Rome's defining comfort foods, a slow-braised oxtail dish that includes or omits pine nuts, raisins, and cocoa powder, depending on the cook. Its roots allegedly lie in the Field of Mars, the area of Rome's center where bovine butchers from the vaccinari guild once processed cattle and developed recipes to make the most of what little they kept for themselves. Simmered low and slow in a tomato sauce with plenty of celery, the oxtail releases its fat, creating a deep and unctuous condimento, which is perfect for dressing pasta (see page 132). This is one of those dishes that begs to be eaten with your hands, ideally while wearing a patterned, darkly colored shirt. For best results, season the oxtail overnight.

Serves 4 to 6

4 pounds oxtail, trimmed and separated
Sea salt and freshly ground black pepper
2 tablespoons lard or extra-virgin olive oil
1 cup dry white wine
1½ (28-ounce) cans whole peeled tomatoes, crushed by hand
4 celery stalks, fibrous outer bits stripped, (see Tip on page 132), cut into 3-inch pieces
¼ cup raisins (optional)
¼ cup pine nuts, toasted (optional)
1 tablespoon unsweetened cocoa powder, or 70% dark chocolate shavings (optional)

Season the oxtail segments with salt and pepper. Transfer to a covered container and refrigerate overnight.

The next day, remove the oxtail from the refrigerator and pat dry with paper towels.

recipe continues on next page ▶

FISH, MEAT, AND OFFAL

Heat the lard in a large heavy-bottomed pot over medium-high heat until shimmering. Add the oxtail segments and cook, turning as needed, until browned all over, about 15 minutes.

Add the wine, scraping up any browned bits from the bottom of the pot, and cook just until the alcohol aroma dissipates, about 1 minute. Add the tomatoes, season with salt and pepper, and bring the sauce to a boil. Reduce the heat to low, cover, and simmer, moving the oxtail segments every 30 minutes or so, until the meat is falling off the bone, 3 to 4 hours, adding water as necessary if the sauce reduces too much. Add the celery about 1 hour before the oxtails are done.

Toward the end of cooking, add the raisins, pine nuts, and cocoa, if using, mixing well. Simmer until the flavors are married.

Remove from the heat and allow the oxtail to rest for at least 1 hour, ideally overnight in the refrigerator. Warm before serving. Reserve any leftover sauce for dressing pasta for up to 4 days in the refrigerator.

GAROFOLATO

BEEF
SIMMERED
WITH TOMATO
AND CLOVES

This long-braised meat dish, rich in cloves (called chiodi di garofano in Italian), is among Rome's many disappearing dishes. Once a staple, garofolato is now served in only a few institutions. I visited one of them, Checchino dal 1887 in Testaccio, when I was covering Rome's vanishing classics for Saveur magazine. Chef Elio Mariani told me it was once a staple among noble servants, who would pinch a few spices from their noble bosses to enrich their beefy stews. Unlikely, considering most Roman peasants ate close to no meat until the mid-twentieth century, a fact that places this recipe firmly in middle-class territory.

Serves 4 to 6

1 (2-pound) beef eye of
    round, tied with kitchen
    twine (ask your butcher to
    do this)
Sea salt and freshly ground
    black pepper
2 tablespoons extra-virgin
    olive oil
1 garlic clove, smashed
1 celery stalk, finely chopped
1 carrot, finely chopped
½ medium yellow onion,
    finely chopped
1 cup dry red wine
1 (14-ounce) can whole
    peeled tomatoes, crushed
    by hand
10 whole cloves

Preheat the oven to 250°F.

Season the beef all over with salt and pepper.

Heat a large, ovensafe Dutch oven over medium-high heat. Add the meat to the pan, reduce the heat to medium-low, and cook until golden brown on all sides, about 10 minutes. Transfer the meat to a plate and return the pan to medium-low heat.

Heat the olive oil until shimmering, then add the garlic, celery, carrot, and onion and cook, stirring, until very soft and caramelized, 25 to 30 minutes. Pour in the wine and cook, scraping the bottom of the pot, until the liquid reduces by half, 4 to 5 minutes. Add the tomatoes and cloves, season with salt and pepper, and bring the sauce to a simmer. Return the meat to the pot. Remove from the heat, cover the pot, and transfer to the oven, turning every 45 minutes until the beef is very tender, 3 to 3½ hours.

Remove from the oven and allow the meat to cool in the sauce for 1 hour. Transfer the beef to a cutting board and cut into ¼-inch-thick slices. Plate, spooning over the sauce, and serve. Watch out for cloves!

SEPPIE CON PISELLI IN UMIDO

CUTTLEFISH
AND
PEA STEW

Relatively landlocked and historically wary of the sea, Rome has never fully embraced seafood the way coastal cities like Naples or Venice have. Romans treated fish as a luxury—something for fasting days or splurges. But cuttlefish was a rare exception. It was cheap, abundant in the nearby Tyrrhenian, and sturdy enough to withstand a long simmer. In seppie con piselli, it's stewed with peas, wine, and tomato, enough to round things out without stealing the spotlight. This is humble, homey food, best eaten with lots of bread for doing a scarpetta. And don't dare be fancy and use fresh peas. The frozen ones do the trick. I'm talking Pisellini Primavera Findus (IYKYK).

Serves 4 to 6

¼ cup extra-virgin olive oil, plus more for serving
1 medium yellow onion, finely chopped
Sea salt
½ peperoncino (whole dried red chile pepper) or ¼ teaspoon crushed red pepper flakes
1 tablespoon chopped fresh flat-leaf parsley
2 pounds cuttlefish, cleaned, tentacles separated, and body cut into strips
½ cup dry white wine
1 (14-ounce) can whole peeled tomatoes, crushed by hand
1 pound frozen peas

Heat the olive oil, onion, and a heavy pinch of salt in a large pan over low heat. Cook, stirring occasionally, just until the onion softens and turns translucent, 15 to 20 minutes. Add the peperoncino and parsley and cook until fragrant, about 30 seconds.

Increase the heat to medium-high, add the cuttlefish, and cook until they have released their moisture, 2 to 3 minutes. Add the wine and cook until the liquid reduces by half, 4 to 5 minutes. Add the tomatoes and peas. Season with salt, reduce the heat to medium-low, and simmer gently, partially covered, until the cuttlefish are very tender, about 30 minutes.

Season with salt and serve drizzled with olive oil.

LINGUA IN SALSA VERDE

TONGUE WITH PARSLEY-GARLIC SAUCE

Boiled meat might not get the glory elsewhere, but in Rome, it's always had a seat at the table, especially when it comes to tongue. Lingua in salsa verde takes this humble quinto quarto cut and transforms it with a blast of sharp, herbaceous flavor. The salsa verde here isn't the breadcrumb-thickened Pied-montese version: it's a leaner, punchier Roman take, with parsley, capers, an-chovies, and vinegar pulling more than their weight. Tongue, still a staple at the city's butcher stalls, becomes silky and tender after a long simmer, and when sliced and drenched in this sauce, it's anything but boring. This is old-school Roman home cooking: simple, thrifty, and absolutely not afraid of offal. Just be sure you start a day ahead: The tongue needs a good salting before it hits the pot.

Serves 4 to 6

1 (2-pound) beef tongue
Sea salt
1 carrot, halved
1 celery stalk, halved
1 yellow onion, halved
1 bay leaf
10 whole black peppercorns
1 cup dry white wine
Leaves from 2 bunches
    flat-leaf parsley, finely
    chopped
½ garlic clove
3 oil-packed anchovy
    fillets, drained and finely
    chopped
2 tablespoons salted capers,
    rinsed and finely chopped
2 tablespoons white wine
    vinegar, plus more as
    needed
3 tablespoons extra-virgin
    olive oil

Season the tongue with plenty of salt. Transfer to a covered container and refrigerate overnight.

Remove the tongue from the refrigerator and place it in a large pot with cold water to cover. Bring to a boil over high heat, then reduce the heat to low and keep at a gentle simmer, skimming off any foam that rises to the top. Once the foam subsides, about 30 minutes, add the carrot, cel-ery, onion, bay leaf, peppercorns, and wine and continue simmering until the tongue is very tender and the outer skin peels away easily, 2½ to 3½ hours. Remove from the heat and set aside to cool in the cooking liquid.

Meanwhile, make the salsa verde: Combine the parsley, garlic, ancho-vies, capers, vinegar, olive oil, and a heavy pinch of salt in a medium bowl. Add more vinegar as needed to achieve a balanced flavor.

Remove the tongue from the pot. Peel off and discard the skin and trim away any gristly bits or glands from the underside. Slice the tongue crosswise into ¼-inch-thick slices. Serve with the sauce slathered on top.

ABBACCHIO A SCOTTADITO

GRILLED
      LAMB CHOPS

Abbacchio a scottadito, a classic of Roman cuisine, features succulent suckling lamb chops so irresistible they're traditionally eaten scorching hot, often leading to singed fingers—hence the name *scottadito*, meaning "burned finger." In Rome, *abbacchio* refers to tender, milk-fed lamb prized for its delicate flavor and tenderness. While true abbacchio is a Roman specialty, elsewhere, it's best to seek out the most tender lamb chops available.

Heat a grill pan over medium-high heat. Season the lamb chops all over with salt and pepper and drizzle with the olive oil. Grill until the lamb is medium-rare, 2 to 3 minutes per side.

Drizzle the lamb with more olive oil and season with Maldon salt. Serve immediately, with lemon wedges on the side.

Serves 6

2 racks of lamb, cut into 8
    chops per rack
Sea salt and freshly ground
    black pepper
2 tablespoons extra-virgin
    olive oil, plus more for
    serving
Maldon salt, for seving
1 lemon, cut into wedges, for
    serving

BACCALÀ ALLA ROMANA

SALT COD WITH TOMATO, ONIONS, PINE NUTS, AND RAISINS

Serves 4

1¼ pounds salt cod, soaked (see Tip on page 78), rinsed, skin and bones removed, and cut into 2-inch pieces

3 tablespoons extra-virgin olive oil, plus more for serving

½ medium yellow onion, roughly chopped

Sea salt

1 (14-ounce) can whole peeled tomatoes, crushed by hand

2 tablespoons raisins, soaked in warm water for 10 minutes and drained

2 tablespoons pine nuts, toasted (see Tip)

Freshly ground black pepper

1 tablespoon good-quality white wine vinegar

Fresh basil leaves, for garnish

Cod with pine nuts, raisins, and onions is a classic of Roman Jewish cuisine, but its origin story begins far from the Tiber. In the Lofoten Islands of Norway, Viking-era fishermen perfected the art of air-drying cod in frigid winds, a method that centuries later caught the attention of Venetian nobleman Pietro Querini, who was shipwrecked there in 1432. Querini and his crew were taken in by local fishermen and introduced to stockfish, or unsalted dried cod. He returned to Venice with a written account praising both the hospitality and the preserved fish, helping lay the groundwork for future trade between Norway and Italy. As preservation methods evolved, Italy embraced both stockfish and salt cod (baccalà), especially inland and during Catholic fasting days. Though the fish is Nordic, Romans made it their own, seasoning it with Mediterranean staples—the pine nuts and raisins are reminiscent of Jewish cooking, brought to the city by refugees fleeing the Inquisition—and turning a northern product into a deeply local tradition.

Pat the fish dry with a kitchen towel.

Heat the olive oil, onion, and a heavy pinch of salt in a large pan over low heat and cook until the onions soften, 20 minutes.

Stir in the tomatoes, raisins, and pine nuts. Season with pepper. Simmer, uncovered, until the sauce thickens and loses its raw flavor, about 15 minutes.

Gently place the baccalà pieces in the sauce. Cover and cook until the fish is tender and flakes easily with a fork, 30 to 40 minutes. Turn the fish once halfway through, taking care not to break it apart. Gently stir in the vinegar. Season with salt as needed.

Serve warm with the sauce spooned over and finish with a drizzle of olive oil. Garnish with basil.

Tip: Heat a dry pan over medium heat, add the pine nuts in a single layer and toast them, stirring frequently, until fragrant and golden, 3 to 5 minutes.

Walk through the ex-Mattatoio in Testaccio today and you'll find contemporary art installations, architecture students sketching under the industrial porticoes, and the occasional pop-up food market. But not so long ago, this complex—anchored at the foot of Monte dei Cocci (see page 91), the ancient mound of discarded amphorae shards—was the visceral center of Rome's meat trade.

Testaccio's slaughterhouse opened in 1891, a monument to industrial efficiency with just enough architectural flair to feel civic. Designed by Gioacchino Ersoch, the complex was Rome's answer to a rapidly growing population and its voracious appetite. Cattle and other livestock arrived by train, were processed in pavilions, and dispatched to feed the capital. But Testaccio did more than slaughter. It shaped the city's culinary identity. The meat and offal cuts were shipped to noble and middle-class kitchens and butcher shops to become the anchor dishes of the cucina romana.

By the 1970s, Rome had outgrown the slaughterhouse's central location. Urban expansion and public health regulations pushed meat processing to the periphery, and in 1975, operations shifted to Viale Palmiro Togliatti, in the far-flung eastern district of Tor Sapienza. Where the old slaughterhouse had atmosphere and grit, the new Centro Carne di Roma had sprawl: two hundred thirty thousand square meters (around 2.5 million square feet) of pragmatic concrete, divided into zones for halal and kosher processing, poultry, aging rooms, and cold storage. It wasn't pretty, but it worked.

These days, this utilitarian fortress is under threat. Management is in constant flux. And even more destabilizing than bureaucracy is the creeping dominance of vertically integrated supermarket chains. These corporate juggernauts have absorbed every link in the food chain—from breeding to butchering to packaging—cutting out wholesalers, slaughterhouses, and, most tragically, independent butchers. Neighborhood macellerie are struggling to compete with shrink-wrapped, loss-leader pork chops and boneless chicken breasts. And the knowledge that was once passed down in Rome's meat shops—the kind with individual butchers who knew a customer's stew required a certain cut from the shoulder, not the loin—is quietly disappearing.

Ironically, Centro Carne di Roma now serves the very supermarket systems that threaten its existence. While it was built to support a diverse, independent meat economy, more and more of its output goes straight to corporate distribution hubs.

But Romans, ever stubborn, are resisting. Some butchers, like Bottega Liberati in the Don Bosco district, have carved out niches, focusing on traceable meat, whole-animal butchery, and products with a story. There's a growing appetite for traditional cuts and preparations, especially those associated with Rome's rich offal traditions. Meanwhile, the transformation of the old Testaccio slaughterhouse into a vibrant cultural hub reminds us that food infrastructure, even when no longer used for its original purpose, still shapes the city.

SALTIMBOCCA ALLA ROMANA

VEAL CUTLET WITH PROSCIUTTO AND SAGE

Saltimbocca alla romana is one of those emblematic dishes that embodies Rome's confident minimalism. Meaning "jump in the mouth," saltimbocca lives up to its promise, with tender slices of veal layered with salty prosciutto and herbaceous sage. The whole thing gets a quick bath in butter and white wine—simple and effective. This dish doesn't need tweaking, and it definitely doesn't need cheese (seriously, don't do it). What it does need is heat: Serve it straight from the pan with its buttery juices.

Tip: Take care not to overcrowd the pan. If necessary, cook in three or even four batches, adding more butter and olive oil as needed.

Serves 6

1½ pounds veal cutlets, pounded to a ¼-inch thickness and cut into fifteen 3-inch-long pieces

Sea salt and freshly ground black pepper

7 slices prosciutto

15 large fresh sage leaves

¼ cup all-purpose flour

2 tablespoons unsalted butter, plus more as needed

2 tablespoons extra-virgin olive oil, plus more as needed

½ cup dry white wine

Lightly season the veal with salt and pepper.

Place a piece of prosciutto, followed by a sage leaf, on top of each piece of veal, cutting the prosciutto as needed to cover about half of the veal's surface area. Secure the prosciutto and sage to the veal with a toothpick inserted at an angle through the center, ensuring it goes through all three layers.

Pour the flour into a shallow bowl. Season with salt and pepper and dredge the underside (veal side only) in the flour, shaking off any excess.

Heat 1 tablespoon each of the butter and olive oil in a large pan over medium-high heat until foaming. Add a single layer of the cutlets, prosciutto-side down, to the pan, and cook until lightly browned, about 1½ minutes. Turn and cook for 30 seconds more. Set aside on a plate. Add the remaining butter and olive oil to the pan and repeat with the remaining cutlets, setting them all aside on a plate. Add the wine, reduce the heat to medium and cook until the sauce thickens, 2 to 3 minutes.

Serve immediately with the sauce drizzled on top.

FISH, MEAT, AND OFFAL

STRACCETTI CON LE ZUCCHINE

ROMAN-STYLE BEEF STRIPS WITH ZUCCHINI

Straccetti di manzo is Roman summer cooking at its simplest and most satisfying. It's named after the thin, rag-like slices of beef (*straccetti* literally translates to "little rags"). The quick-cooking method reflects the pace of Rome itself, a city where even the busiest workday can accommodate a seasonal lunch, even on a hot day. Plus, straccetti cook so fast, you don't need to spend much time at the stove. Romans usually favor leaner cuts like eye of round, briefly seared. Serve this immediately, ideally alongside a crusty chunk of bread for mopping up the juices, and you'll see why this classic remains essential in Roman home kitchens and cafeterias.

Heat the olive oil in a large pan over low heat. Add the shallots and a heavy pinch of salt and cook until translucent, about 5 minutes. Add the zucchini, season with salt, increase the heat to medium, and cook until tender, about 12 minutes. Add the beef strips in an even layer and season with salt and pepper. Let the meat brown without stirring it, about 1 minute. Stir and continue to cook until the meat is evenly browned.

Serve immediately.

Serves 6

2 tablespoons extra-virgin olive oil

2 shallots, thinly sliced

Sea salt

2 zucchine romanesche or conventional zucchini, cut into ¼-inch-thick rounds

2 pounds thinly sliced eye of round or sirloin, cut into 1-inch strips

Freshly ground black pepper

THE FISHY PAST OF
THE PORTICO D'OTTAVIA

Rome isn't a seaside town. It's about thirteen miles from the coast as the crow flies, and considerably more if you follow the winding path of the Tiber River. That distance, trivial today, was formidable until the mid-twentieth century. Before widespread refrigeration and postwar infrastructure projects connected the city to its coastline, Romans relied on what was local and preserved. That meant freshwater species from the Tiber—eel, catfish, perch, carp, the occasional sturgeon—and pantry staples like salted anchovies from Campania and preserved cod imported from the cold waters of Scandinavia. So while twirling spaghetti alle vongole in Trastevere might feel deeply Roman, seafood has a surprisingly shallow history in the city.

But what the city lacked in coastal access, it made up for in ingenuity and bureaucracy. Nowhere was that more visible than at the Portico d'Ottavia in the Sant'Angelo district, where ancient stone and medieval commerce collided. Rebuilt by Augustus in the first century BCE and dedicated to his sister Octavia, the Portico was once a showpiece of imperial grandeur. It enclosed temples to Juno and Jupiter, a library, and gathering spaces, all designed to telegraph Rome's cultural supremacy. But like much of the empire, the

structure eventually fell into disuse and decay. That is, until fish gave it a second life.

By the twelfth century CE, the Portico and the area around it had morphed into the Pescheria, Rome's official fish market. Its proximity to the river made it a logical choice, and the shade of awnings anchored to its columns offered some measure of relief from the Roman sun. The market operated there for centuries, and if the ruins could talk, they'd tell stories of piety and power. The city implemented one of the most Roman systems of taxation you can imagine visible in the form of a Latin inscription on one of the brick pillars: *Capita piscium, qui longiores erunt quam hie lapis, dato rectoribus, usque ad primas pinnas.* (The heads of fish that are longer than this stone must be given to the city magistrates, up to the first fins.) It was a culinary tithe and a practical reminder of who ran the show. The rest of the fish could be sold to the public, but those heads and collars went straight to city hall.

By the sixteenth century, the Portico d'Ottavia sat at the edge of another transformation: the establishment of the Jewish Ghetto (see page 40). When Pope Paul IV confined Rome's Jewish population to this flood-prone wedge along the Tiber, the Portico became the unofficial threshold between the Christian city and the segregated Jewish quarter. The fish market was one of the few spaces where both communities mingled daily. Kosher laws permitted the consumption of certain fish, and today, the signature dishes of the cucina ebraica include Baccalà alla Romana (page 182) and aliciotti con l'indivia. Born out of necessity, these dishes evolved into icons.

The fish market lasted until the late nineteenth century, when urban redevelopment pushed the fish trade to Via di San Teodoro near the Circus Maximus (now the location of the weekend Campagna Amica farmers' market), as civic restoration efforts sought to "clean up" Rome's historical center. But the Portico remains, flanked by restaurants, echoing with stories. Its columns bear witness to centuries of adaptation from civic structure to fish-stall backdrop and stand as a reminder that, in Rome, ruins tell stories about what people ate, what they sold, and how a city survives through power, and through food.

FISH, MEAT, AND OFFAL

ABBACCHIO BRODETTATO

**EASTER LAMB
IN EGGY SAUCE**

Rome doesn't need an excuse to eat lamb, but abbacchio brodettato—a dish of tender braised suckling lamb cloaked in an egg-thickened sauce—feels particularly tied to Easter, when lamb is the star of the table and eggs symbolize resurrection. The name comes from *brodo*, meaning "broth," but what makes this dish stand out is the finish: egg yolks and lemon juice whisked into the cooking liquid, creating a silky, golden sauce that clings to the meat. It's among Rome's many disappearing dishes and few trattorie serve it, though Sora Lella on the Tiber Island has it when suckling lambs are in season, and Santo Palato serves it around Easter. Season the lamb with salt 24 hours in advance.

Serves 4 to 6

3½ pounds bone-in lamb
   shoulder or shank, salted
   in advance and cut into
   2-inch pieces
Sea salt
All-purpose flour, for
   dredging
2 tablespoons extra-virgin
   olive oil
1 garlic clove, smashed
3 slices fatty prosciutto,
   diced
1 cup dry white wine
6 cups lamb or vegetable
   broth, warmed
4 large egg yolks
3 tablespoons fresh lemon
   juice (from 1 lemon)
1 tablespoon roughly
   chopped fresh flat-leaf
   parsley
1 tablespoon roughly
   chopped fresh marjoram
Freshly ground black pepper

Season the lamb with salt. Transfer to a covered container and refrigerate overnight.

The next day, remove the lamb from the refrigerator about 90 minutes before you intend to cook and pat dry with paper towels.

Pour the flour into a shallow bowl and season with salt.

Heat the olive oil in a large pot over medium heat. Dredge the lamb in the flour, shaking off any excess, and add it to the pan. Cook until browned on all sides, 4 to 5 minutes. Remove from the pan and set aside on a plate.

Add the garlic and prosciutto and cook just until the garlic starts to take on color, about 5 minutes. Add the wine, scraping up any browned bits from the bottom of the pan. Once the alcohol aroma dissipates, about 1 minute, return the meat to the pan. Add enough broth so that the lamb is about halfway submerged and simmer, partially covered, until fork-tender, and falling off the bone, 2½ to 3 hours. Add more broth to the pot as needed to keep the lamb partially submerged. Remove from the heat.

Just before serving, whisk together the egg yolks, lemon juice, parsley, and marjoram in a small bowl. Temper the egg mixture by pouring in a few ounces of the very warm broth. Add the tempered egg mixture to the pot and return to low heat, stirring, taking care not to scramble the eggs (tempering should reduce this risk). Remove the pot from the heat. Season with salt and pepper and serve immediately.

FEGATELLI DI MAIALE

GRILLED
      PORK LIVER

Once a familiar sight at the winter pig slaughter, fegatelli are a rustic preparation that transforms fresh pork liver into something deeply savory and aromatic. Fresh bay leaves are tucked under a lacy sheet of caul fat, which both secures the herb and bastes the liver as it cooks. If you're not keen on cooking liver, I insist you at least try it next time you're in Rome, at Trattoria da Cesare al Casaletto.

Place the caul fat in a medium bowl with warm water to cover. Pour in the vinegar and set aside for 30 minutes.

Season the liver all over with salt and pepper.

Drain the caul fat, pat it dry, and lay it out on a clean, dry work surface. Place a bay leaf in the center of each piece, followed by the liver and another bay leaf. Wrap the fat around the liver. Pat the outside dry with a paper towel.

Heat an oiled grill pan or skillet over high heat. Grill the liver just until it is just cooked through, 2 to 3 minutes per side. The liver should still be rosy in the center.

Remove from the heat and allow the parcels to rest for 3 minutes, then serve, discarding the bay leaves, with lemon wedges on the side.

Serves 4

5 ounces caul fat, cut into 4 pieces of about 4 × 4 inches each

2 tablespoons white wine vinegar

1 pound pork liver, cut into 4 pieces

Sea salt and freshly ground black pepper

8 fresh bay leaves

Extra-virgin olive oil, for greasing

1 lemon, cut into wedges, for serving

THE BIG MAC EMPIRE

Rome has been resisting foreign invaders for over two thousand years, but in 1986, the city met a new kind of adversary: McDonald's. When the fast-food giant opened its first Roman location near the base of the Spanish Steps, the reaction was swift and furious. Locals protested the "Americanization" of their city's culinary and cultural identity. Italian food activist and journalist Carlo Petrini helped organize demonstrations, and the uproar around the golden arches helped inspire what would become the global Slow Food movement. That first Big Mac on Piazza di Spagna ignited a whole new way of thinking about tradition and food sovereignty.

The Spanish Steps McDonald's is still there today, just as cavernous and pastel-hued as ever. It seats eight hundred people and has adapted to local tastes, offering Italian pastries and numerous espresso drinks at the McCafé counter. While tourists inevitably flock to the location, McDonald's Italy reports that most customers in Rome are locals—students, families, commuters, and workers grabbing something predictable, fast, and air-conditioned.

Since that first opening, McDonald's has spread throughout Rome, now boasting over fifty locations, many of which adapt to the city's ancient landscape. At the Termini Station location, you can eat your McCrunchy Chicken and fries next to the Servian Wall, the fourth-century BCE defensive fortification that once encircled ancient Rome. Then there's the location in Frattocchie near Ciampino Airport that incorporates a subterranean archaeological site and museum directly beneath the dining room. Through a glass panel in the floor, visitors can peer down at a second-century CE pavement and funeral monuments, complete with human remains.

Before McDonald's took over the city, Italians had their own homegrown fast-food chain: Burghy. Founded in Milan in the early 1980s and owned by the Cremonini family, Burghy slung burgers and fries across Italy before being bought out by McDonald's in 1996. The Cremoninis didn't exit the game, though. They pivoted to food supply and became the primary meat distributor for McDonald's in Italy, effectively feeding the beast they once tried to compete with.

In 2023, McDonald's opened its newest Roman branch just a few steps from the Mercato di Testaccio. Not a protester in sight. What helped ease McDonald's transition from foreign invader to domestic convenience were its high-profile collaborations with Italian culinary royalty. In 2011, the late Gualtiero Marchesi, arguably Italy's most revered chef, designed two burgers for the chain, one of which came topped with pancetta, grilled eggplant, and balsamic vinegar. It scandalized food purists but subtly signaled that eating McDonald's didn't necessarily mean turning your back on Italian food culture. Two years later, the brand entered its first of many partnerships with restaurateur and TV host Joe Bastianich, whose My Selection menus blend Italian and American influences.

Rome, of course, persists. The Gran Crispy McBacon is unlikely to edge out supplì or pizza by the slice anytime soon. But its presence is a reminder that convenience always wins. Whether you see it as cultural erosion or just another quirky layer in the city's culinary collage, McDonald's is part of the landscape now, wedged between ruins and monuments, feeding Romans who live, work, and snack in a city that never stops changing.

FISH, MEAT, AND OFFAL

POLLO ALLA CACCIATORA

TANGY
CHICKEN STEW

Pollo alla cacciatora, or "hunter's chicken," is a staple of central Italian home cooking, though its form varies widely from region to region—and even more so across the Atlantic. I grew up eating the Italian American version in New Jersey, where tomato sauce, mushrooms, peas, and more often made their way into the pot. But when I moved to Italy, I discovered that the Roman and southern styles lean more herby and acidic, relying on white wine and white wine vinegar instead of tomatoes to brighten the dish.

My version takes inspiration from Stefano Callegari's at Trapizzino, which, in turn, is influenced by his mother Luana's recipe. I skip the breasts and use only dark meat so everything stays tender and juicy. Plus, the dish only gets better after a night in the fridge. Season the chicken with salt at least a few hours and up to 12 hours before you intend to cook it.

Serves 4 to 6

3 pounds bone-in chicken
  legs and thighs, separated
Sea salt
¼ cup extra-virgin olive oil
2 garlic cloves, smashed
Leaves from 1 sprig
  rosemary, roughly
  chopped
Leaves from 1 sprig sage,
  roughly chopped
¾ cup dry white wine
2 cups chicken broth,
  vegetable broth, or water,
  plus more as needed
¼ cup white wine vinegar

Season the chicken with salt. Transfer to a covered container and refrigerate for at least a few hours and up to 12 hours.

Remove the chicken from the refrigerator 90 minutes before you intend to cook.

Heat the olive oil in a large pan over low heat. When the oil begins to shimmer, add the garlic and cook just until it begins to take on color, about 5 minutes. Add the chicken, skin-side down, increase the heat to medium, and cook until browned on all sides, 10 to 12 minutes. Add the rosemary and sage and cook until fragrant, 30 seconds. Add the wine, increase the heat to high, and cook just until the alcohol aroma dissipates, about 1 minute. Add the broth and bring to a simmer.

Reduce the heat to low and cook, partially covered, checking at the 30-minute mark to be sure there is enough broth in the pan. Add more as needed to keep the chicken partially submerged. Cook until the chicken is super tender and easily releases from the bone, about 1 hour. Add the vinegar about 10 minutes before the chicken is ready. If at this point the sauce is really juicy, leave the pan uncovered, increase the heat to medium-high, and cook until the liquid thickens. Season with salt and pepper. Serve directly from the pan (and eat with your hands).

INVOLTINI ALLA ROMANA

MEAT ROLLS FILLED WITH PROSCIUTTO, CELERY, AND CARROT

The beauty of these involtini (thin slices of beef rolled around a simple filling of prosciutto, carrot, and celery and gently braised in tomato sauce) is that they are a one-pot, two-meal dish. As the meat rolls cook, they impart their flavor to the tomato sauce, which can then be used to dress pasta, ideally rigatoni or gnocchi (page 122). If you want a lot of extra sauce, double the quantity of tomatoes.

Lightly season the beef all over with salt and pepper. Place a slice of prosciutto over each beef slice. Arrange the carrot and celery at one end of each slice of beef, distributing it evenly. Starting from the end with the vegetables, roll the beef to form a medium-tight involtino. Secure each roll by inserting a toothpick flush with the meat to keep it closed.

Heat the garlic and olive oil in a large pan over low heat. Cook just until the garlic starts to take on color, about 5 minutes. Add the involtini and brown them on all sides, about 5 minutes total. Add the wine, increase the heat to medium-high, and cook until the alcohol aroma dissipates, about 1 minute, then stir in the tomatoes and basil. The meat should be about halfway covered by the tomato sauce. If not, add water as needed. Cover and cook over low heat until the meat is fork-tender, 1½ hours to 2 hours, checking occasionally to ensure the meat is at least halfway submerged and adding water as necessary. Season with salt and pepper.

Serve immediately or, even better, the next day, warmed.

Serves 4

1½ pounds top round or sirloin, cut into eight ¼-inch-thick slices

Sea salt and freshly ground black pepper

8 thin slices prosciutto

1 carrot, cut into thin sticks

1 celery stalk, cut into thin sticks

1 garlic clove, smashed

2 tablespoons extra-virgin olive oil

½ cup dry white wine

1 (14-ounce) can whole peeled tomatoes, crushed by hand

5 or 6 fresh basil leaves

CORATELLA

LAMB HEART,
        LUNGS, AND
LIVER STEW

Serves 4

2 tablespoons extra-virgin
    olive oil
1 medium white onion,
    roughly chopped
Sea salt
1½ pounds lamb coratella
    (lungs, heart, and liver),
    cleaned and cut into
    ½-inch pieces (see Tip)
¼ cup dry white wine
Freshly ground black pepper

Zampetti (lamb trotters) and testine (heads) might have gone out of fashion, but coratella, the sautéed heart, lungs, liver, and sometimes trachea of young lamb, is still going strong. Traditionally served at Easter and in lambing seasons, coratella is a staple of the cucina romana that turns humble offal into something rich and celebratory. The key is timing. Each organ has a different texture: Lungs need a head start to tenderize, the heart wants a moderate cook, and liver should go in last to stay soft and velvety. Everything is sautéed slowly with onions and deglazed with dry white wine. My version is inspired by Piatto Romano's onion-forward preparation.

Tip: The USDA prohibits the sale of animal lungs for human consumption. But don't be discouraged! You can still make a delicious, modified coratella using heart and liver, or by subbing in sweetbreads or kidneys for texture contrast.

Heat the olive oil, onion, and a heavy pinch of salt in a large pan over low heat. Cook until the onion is soft and translucent, about 15 minutes. Increase the heat to medium and add the lungs. Cook, stirring occasionally, until they begin to brown and release some liquid, about 10 minutes.

Add the heart and cook for 3 minutes more, then add the wine and cook just until the alcohol aroma dissipates, about 1 minute. Add the liver, season with salt and pepper, and cook just until it's cooked through but still tender, 2 to 3 minutes more. Serve immediately.

POR-CHETTA

ROASTED
PORK

Serves 12 to 16

6 to 8 pounds boneless pork
loin with the belly still
attached, skin-on

6 garlic cloves, mashed to a
paste

3 tablespoons fresh
rosemary, finely chopped

2 tablespoons fresh thyme
leaves, finely chopped

1 teaspoon fennel pollen or
ground fennel seeds

1 tablespoon coarsely ground
black pepper

2 tablespoons sea salt, plus
more for seasoning skin

2 tablespoons extra-virgin
olive oil

Pizza Bianca (page 242) or
crusty bread, for serving
(optional)

Porchetta is tied with mortadella as one of Rome's most beloved sandwich fillings. Unlike mortadella, which is brought down from Bologna, porchetta comes from pork artisans in the Apennines and Roman suburbs like the Castelli Romani. While the official Porchetta di Ariccia IGP (Indicazione Geografica Protetta) has its roots just outside the city, much of what's sold under that name in Rome's markets and alimentari is underseasoned and overcooked. Even worse, the IGP certification only requires that the pork be seasoned and roasted in the area, while the meat can come from who knows where. If you would like to have the real deal, skip Ariccia altogether and high-tail it for Norcino Bernabei in the small town of Marino—or hope that Vitaliano Bernabei has delivered his porchetta, made from Italian pigs, to Panificio Bonci in Rome on the day you happen to be visiting.

Making porchetta at home is well worth it, especially if you can source a boneless pork loin with the belly still attached. You'll probably have to special order it, so let your butcher know you're making porchetta. Ask them to butterfly the loin for easier seasoning and to score the skin for easier rolling (and crisping). The meat dry brines overnight, then slow-roasts with little fuss. Just make sure the whole thing fits in your oven before you get started. If you can't find a single belly-loin cut, use individual pieces of boneless loin and skin-on pork belly (two and four pounds, respectively), and roll together instead.

On a clean, dry work surface, use a very sharp knife or box cutter to score the pork skin in a diamond pattern, taking care not to cut into the fat layer beneath the skin.

Mix together the garlic, rosemary, thyme, fennel pollen, pepper, salt, and olive oil in a small bowl. Massage it into the belly and loin, coating every surface generously (not the skin).

Lay the loin along the length of the belly and roll the belly tightly around it. Tie it snugly with butcher's twine at 1-inch intervals. Massage the skin all over with additional salt. Place the porchetta on a rack set over a baking sheet and refrigerate, uncovered, overnight to allow the skin to dry out.

Remove the porchetta from the refrigerator at least 2 hours before you cook it to allow it to reach room temperature.

Preheat the oven to 300°F. Roast the porchetta on a rack set over a roasting pan until an instant-read thermometer inserted into the center of the loin reads 140° to 145°F, 3 to 4 hours. Increase the oven temperature to 500°F and roast until the skin is golden, puffed, and crackling (watch carefully so it doesn't burn), 15 to 25 minutes more. Let rest for at least 45 minutes before cutting into thick slices.

Serve the porchetta warm or at room temperature, on its own, stuffed into Pizza Bianca, or with Patate al Forno (page 230) on the side.

TRIPPA ALLA ROMANA

**TRIPE BRAISED
IN TOMATO SAUCE
WITH MENTUCCIA
AND PECORINO**

If you're serious about understanding Rome beyond its monuments and museums, you'll need to eat some stomach. Trippa alla romana, cow's stomach stewed in tomato sauce with local mentuccia, is a dish that weeds out the tourists from the true believers. It's silky, savory, and rich, with Pecorino Romano snowed over the top to seal the deal. Its unapologetic character even made its way into local politics: in the early 1900s, Mayor Ernesto Nathan slashed the city budget that paid for feeding stray cats with tripe, coining the phrase *non c'è trippa per gatti,* literally "there's no tripe for the cats." Today, it's a classic Roman way to say, "Forget it, there's nothing for you." Like the dish itself, the idiom is pure Roman pragmatism: blunt, unsentimental, and deeply rooted in tradition.

Tip: Most store-bought tripe is already cleaned and blanched. If yours is not, place it in a large pot and cover with cold water. Bring to a boil over high heat, then drain. Repeat this blanching process once more to help remove any impurities or odor. Drain again and proceed with the recipe..

Serves 4 to 6

1 ½ pounds honeycomb tripe
   (see Tip)
2 carrots, halved
2 celery stalks, halved
2 medium yellow onions,
   halved
¼ cup extra-virgin olive oil
Sea salt
1 (14-ounce) can whole
   peeled tomatoes, crushed
   by hand
Leaves from 4 sprigs
   mentuccia or fresh mint,
   roughly chopped
1 cup finely grated Pecorino
   Romano

Place the tripe in a large pot with cold water to cover. Bring to a rolling boil over high heat, reduce the heat to low, and simmer, skimming off any foam that rises to the top. Once the foam has subsided, add 1 each of the carrot, celery and onion. Cook until the tripe is fork tender, 2 ½ to 3 hours. Drain, rinse under cold water, then cut the tripe into ½-inch strips. Rinse out and dry the pot before continuing.

Finely chop the remaining carrot, celery, and onion. Heat the olive oil in the large pot over low heat. When the oil begins to shimmer, add the carrot, celery, and onion. Season with a heavy pinch of salt. Cook, stirring occasionally, until the vegetables are very soft, 20 to 25 minutes. Add the tomatoes, another heavy pinch of salt, and cook until they have lost their raw flavor and reduced slightly, 15 to 20 minutes. Add the tripe to the pot and simmer for 30 minutes more. Remove from the heat, then stir in the mentuccia and ¾ cup of the Pecorino Romano. Serve immediately, dusted with the remaining Pecorino Romano.

FISH, MEAT, AND OFFAL

ZUCCHINE RIPIENE ALLA ROMANA

MEAT-FILLED
ZUCCHINI

Zucchine romanesche are pale green, striated zucchini that resemble fluted columns. They're gorgeous. But this is not the recipe to make if you want to preserve and celebrate their mellow hues. In this case, the zucchini are stuffed with a meatball-like filling, then cooked in tomato sauce until they are greenish-gray and on the verge of falling apart.

If you're a Rome dweller, you can find these at butcher shops already hollowed out and filled. Otherwise, follow the tip below.

Combine the beef, breadcrumbs, egg, Pecorino Romano, and a heavy pinch of salt and pepper in a medium bowl. Set aside.

Heat the olive oil and garlic in a large pan over low heat just until the garlic starts to take on color, 5 minutes.

Salt the inside of the zucchini. Use your hands to work the meat mixture into the cored zucchini to fill them, dividing it equally.

Add the zucchini to the pan, and brown gently before adding the tomatoes. Season with salt. Increase the heat to medium-low and cook, covered, turning the zucchini occasionally, until they are very tender and the meatball mixture is cooked, 25 to 30 minutes. Add water to the pan as necessary so the zucchini have plenty of liquid to cook in and the sauce doesn't dry out. Serve warm.

Serves 4 to 6

8 ounces ground beef
½ cup coarse breadcrumbs
1 large egg, beaten
½ cup finely grated Pecorino Romano
Sea salt and freshly ground black pepper
2 tablespoons extra-virgin olive oil
1 garlic glove, smashed
8 zucchine romanesche or 6 conventional zucchini, cut crosswise into 3-inch-long pieces, and cored (see Tip)
1 (14-ounce) can whole peeled tomatoes, crushed by hand

Tip: Wash the zucchini thoroughly and pat dry. Trim off both ends, then cut each zucchini crosswise into 3-inch segments.

To core: Place a zucchini segment cut-side up on a cutting board. Using a small paring knife, insert the tip into the white interior and cut in a circular motion to remove the inner flesh, leaving about ¼ inch of flesh and skin all around the edges. Work slowly and carefully to avoid piercing the outer skin. Pull out the knife periodically to clear any buildup of pulp.

Once you've cut around the center, use the tip of the knife to scrape the inner walls and clean out the cavity. Discard any tough bits and reserve the tender flesh for Minestrone (page 144) or another dish.

ABBACCHIO ALLA ROMANA

SUCKLING LAMB
WITH HERBS,
ANCHOVIES,
AND VINEGAR

Serves 6 to 8

2 tablespoons sea salt

1 teaspoon freshly ground
black pepper

2 tablespoons extra-virgin
olive oil

2 garlic cloves, finely
chopped (see Tip on page
154)

Leaves from 3 rosemary
sprigs, finely chopped

6 fresh sage leaves, finely
chopped

3 oil-packed anchovy fillets,
drained and mashed into
a paste

1 bone-in lamb shoulder
(about 4 pounds)

2 tablespoons white wine
vinegar

1¼ cups dry white wine, plus
more for the pan sauce

Patate al Forno (page 230),
for serving

Abbacchio, a suckling lamb that is about a month old and weighs no more than fifteen pounds, is a springtime fixture on Rome's tables. In the days leading up to Easter, I place a special order with my butcher for a whole abbacchio, then marinate it and roast it the Roman way: with anchovies, garlic, herbs, and vinegar. The exquisitely tender meat is the protagonist of huge Easter feasts, which typically include no fewer than fifteen friends and family members, but I have scaled the recipe down to just the shoulder for more accessible daily use. I have also included a pan sauce, which may not be traditionally Roman but is delicious, especially with Patate al Forno on the side. Marinate the lamb overnight before roasting.

Combine the salt, pepper, olive oil, garlic, rosemary, sage, and anchovy paste in a small bowl and stir until smooth. Using your hands, massage the marinade over the lamb, distributing it evenly. Transfer to a covered container and refrigerate overnight.

Remove the lamb from the refrigerator about 90 minutes before you plan to roast it to bring it to room temperature. Transfer the meat and marinade to a roasting pan.

Preheat the oven to 325°F.

Pour the vinegar over the meat and baste with the marinade. Roast the lamb for about 3 hours covered with aluminum foil, turning it and pouring 1 cup of the wine over the meat after 1 hour. Uncover and cook 1 to 1½ hours more. The lamb is done when it is golden brown and the meat pulls away from the bone easily. Transfer the meat to a cutting board and let rest for 15 to 20 minutes.

While the lamb rests, make the sauce. Drain off the lamb fat from the roasting pan, then set the pan on the stovetop over medium-low heat, adding up to ¼ cup wine and scraping up the browned bits from the bottom of the pan with a wooden spoon. Cook until the sauce is reduced, about 5 minutes.

Cut the lamb into thick slices and drizzle with the pan sauce. Serve with roasted potatoes.

GARUM: ROME'S LIQUID GOLD

If you think anchovy paste is intense, you clearly haven't met garum, ancient Rome's go-to condiment. This fish sauce was the umami bomb of its day, a salty, savory liquid that Romans drizzled over just about everything: humble street snacks, wine, banquet dishes, even sweets. First developed during the Republic, it became a staple across the empire, revered at once for its flavor, supposed medicinal powers, and serious economic clout. Not unlike hot sauce today, garum was as much a business as it was a seasoning.

Despite the singular name, garum was a broad category of salt-cured, enzyme-liquified sauces. The most prized varieties were made by layering the guts (and sometimes whole bodies) of oily fish—typically mackerel, anchovy, or tuna—with salt in open-air vats. The mix marinated under the Mediterranean sun for weeks or months, during which natural enzymes and microbes broke the fish down into a golden, translucent elixir. The top layer was garum proper. The gritty sludge left behind, called allec, was a coarse paste more likely to show up in a plebeian's pot than on an aristocrat's plate.

Other versions circulated, too, including liquamen (a term that sometimes overlapped with, and eventually replaced, garum in later sources) and muria, the salty brine left over from preserving whole fish. These sauces weren't identical, but each had their uses in Roman kitchens and trade networks.

Garum production, which extended to coastal cities across the empire, required skill, patience, and a strong stomach. Producers kept a careful eye on temperature and smell, stirring the mixture as it ripened in the heat. The best garum was said to smell pleasant (yes, really) and fetched premium prices at market. Carthago Nova (modern-day Cartagena in Spain), the coast around Neapolis (modern-day Naples), and especially the provinces of Baetica (southern Spain) and Lusitania (modern Portugal) were famous for their sauces. Amphorae from these regions, stamped or painted with their contents, origins, weight, official seals, and even brand names, have been found from Britain to Syria.

Ancient garum factories weren't mom-and-pop operations. They were industrial-scale production sites, with rows of fermentation vats, attached workshops, and easy access to ports for export. Amphorae used for garum were even specially shaped to reduce leaks and preserve freshness on long journeys.

In the kitchen, garum did what soy sauce or Worcestershire does today: provide an instant boost of depth and umami. *De re coquinaria* includes garum in recipes ranging from pork ragouts to stuffed dormice (would try). It even turned up occasionally in sweets; who said dessert can't include fishy flavor? Modern chefs have taken note: Arcangelo Dandini prepares dishes with his homemade garum at his restaurant near the Vatican. The name of his restaurant in London's Bayswater district? Garum, of course.

FISH, MEAT, AND OFFAL

PETTO DI VITELLO ALLA FORNARA

BAKER'S-STYLE ROASTED VEAL BREAST

If Roman cooking has a protein that flies under the radar, it would be veal breast. Cheap, fatty, and full of connective tissue, this underrated cut becomes luxurious when slow-roasted until the meat nearly collapses under its own weight. The name alla fornara, literally "baker's style," hints at the dish's roots: In a city where few people historically had ovens at home, trays of food were entrusted to the neighborhood forno, which roasted them slowly in the residual heat from bread baking.

In the Roman tradition, petto di vitello alla fornara is seasoned simply, relying on time more than embellishment. It's the kind of meal that tastes like Sunday lunch at Tavernaccia Da Bruno near Stazione Trastevere. I couldn't resist sharing chef Giuseppe Ruzzettu's process (opposite page), ideal for serving 50. Start the recipe below, adapted for a smaller crowd, 12 to 24 hours ahead.

Tip: Look for veal breast with the rib bones removed and the fat cap intact. The fat provides the necessary moisture for basting the meat, which creates the flavor that defines the dish. If you can't find veal breast, use beef brisket. Expect a longer cook time and a beefier flavor.

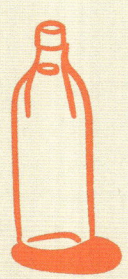

Serves 8 to 10

3 tablespoons sea salt
2 teaspoons freshly ground
  black pepper
Leaves from 5 sprigs
  rosemary
2 tablespoons extra-virgin
  olive oil
4½ pounds veal breast,
  deboned (have your
  butcher do this for you)
  and fat cap scored in a
  crisscross pattern
3 garlic cloves, smashed
½ cup dry white wine

Use a mortar and pestle or a robot coupe to blend together the salt, pepper, and rosemary. Mix in the olive oil.

Rub the meat all over with the mixture, transfer to a covered container, and refrigerate for 12 to 24 hours.

Preheat the oven to 425°F.

Let the veal sit at room temperature for about 30 minutes. Pat dry with a paper towel.

Transfer the meat to a roasting pan, fat-side up, and scatter the garlic around it. Roast, uncovered, until the surface begins to take on color, about 20 minutes. Remove the veal from the oven.

Decrease the oven temperature to 250°F. While the oven cools, pour the wine into the bottom of the pan to help keep the meat moist. Return the veal to the oven, roasting for another 3 to 3½ hours, basting every 30 minutes with pan juices, until the meat is deeply golden and fork-tender. The internal temperature should reach 185°F on an instant-read thermometer.

Remove from the oven and set aside to rest for at least 30 minutes before carving. Serve thick slices with the pan drippings spooned over.

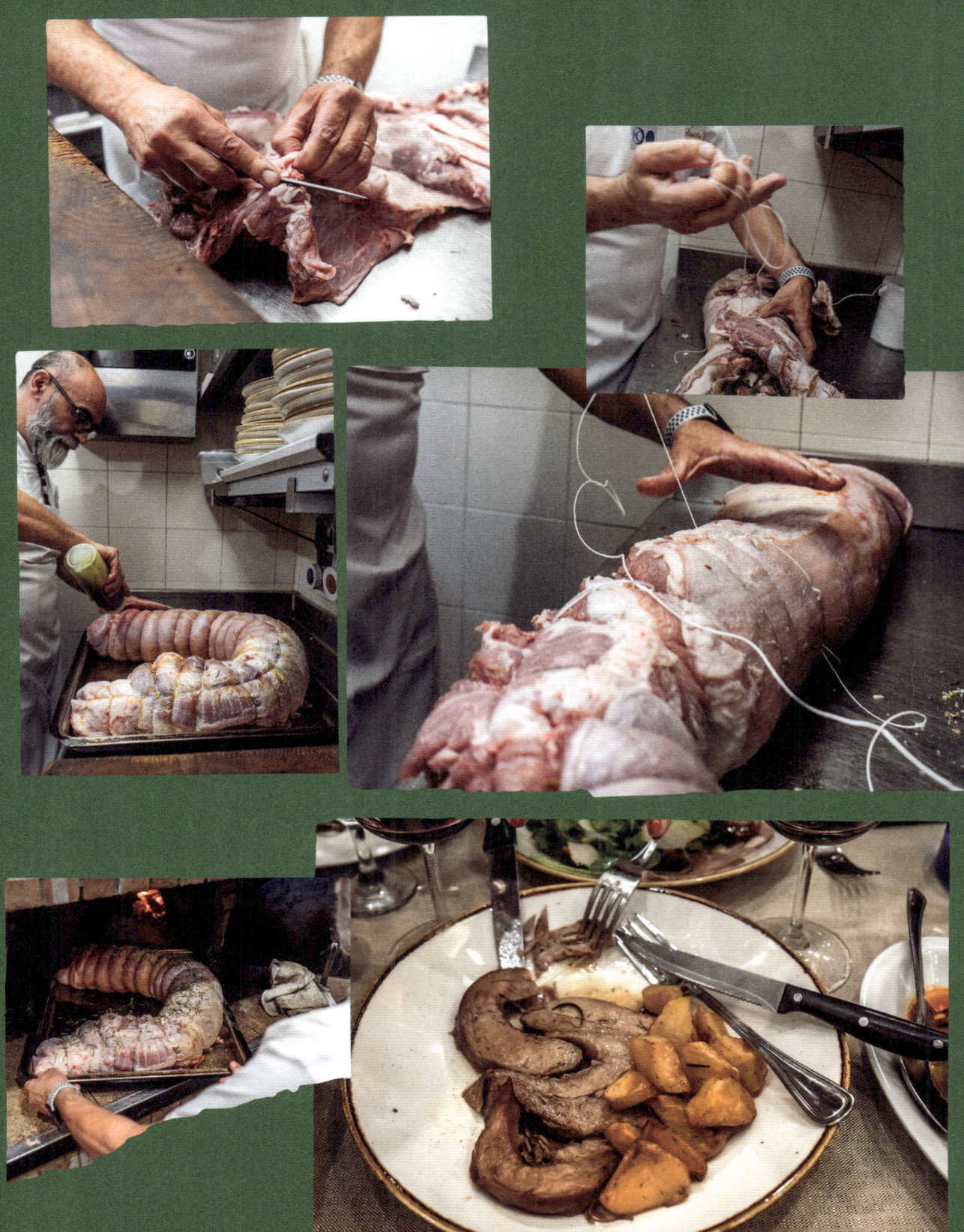

VEGETABLES, SALADS, AND SIDES

VIGNAROLA

ARTICHOKE,
PEA, AND
FAVA STEW

Serves 6

2 (½-ounce) slices guanciale
    or pancetta, finely
    chopped, or ¼ cup extra-
    virgin olive oil
4 spring onions, thinly sliced
1 garlic clove, smashed
Sea salt
3 tender young globe
    artichokes, cleaned,
    trimmed (see Tip on page
    75), then cut into eighths
1 cup dry white wine
2 cups shelled fava beans
1 cup fresh or frozen shelled
    peas
Leaves from 3 sprigs
    mentuccia or fresh mint
5 to 6 sprigs fresh flat-leaf
    parsley, roughly chopped
1 small head romaine
    lettuce, roughly chopped
    (optional)
Freshly ground black pepper
Extra-virgin olive oil, for
    serving

Spring in Rome is pure vegetable magic. Markets overflow with the tender green stars of the season, and nothing captures the spirit of this fleeting moment quite like vignarola. Traditionally, this spring stew is a humble mess of simmered greens: artichokes, peas, favas, spring onions, and, yes, lettuce. But I draw the line at hot lettuce and I omit it without remorse. My version still honors the soul of the dish as a gray-toned pulp that has never even heard the phrase al dente, with each ingredient cooked just long enough to nearly collapse. It's a dish that rewards patience and timing, and like many Roman staples, it's even better the next day, ideal for spooning over toast or folding into pasta. Or serve at a grand Easter feast alongside Abbacchio Brodettato (page 188).

Heat the guanciale in a large pan over low heat and cook until the fat starts to render, about 10 minutes, then add the spring onions and garlic with a heavy pinch of salt and cook until the spring onions soften, about 3 minutes.

Add the artichokes, season with salt, and cook in the guanciale fat for 4 to 5 minutes, then increase the heat to medium-high and add ½ cup of the wine. Once the alcohol aroma dissipates, about 1 minute, cover and cook until the artichokes are tender, about 10 minutes, adding water 2 tablespoons at a time as needed to prevent the artichokes from sticking to the pan.

Uncover the pan and add the fava beans and the remaining ½ cup wine. Cook for 5 minutes more, then add the peas, cover, and decrease the heat to medium-low. Cook the peas for 3 minutes, then uncover the pot and stir in the mentuccia, parsley, and lettuce, if using. Cook just until the herbs and lettuce are wilted, about 1 minute, then remove from the heat and set the vignarola aside to rest, covered, for 5 minutes.

Season with salt and pepper and serve drizzled with a healthy glug of olive oil.

FAGIOLI CON LE COTICHE

BEANS WITH
PORK SKIN

Serves 4 to 6

1 pound dried borlotti
   beans, soaked overnight,
   drained, and rinsed (see
   Tip on page 118)
1 sprig rosemary
6 fresh sage leaves
½ cup extra-virgin olive oil
Sea salt
8 ounces fresh pork skin
   (see Tip), cut into 1-inch
   strips
1 carrot, finely chopped
1 celery stalk, finely chopped
½ medium yellow onion,
   finely chopped
1 (14-ounce) can whole
   peeled tomatoes, crushed
   by hand
Sliced toasted bread, for
   serving

Of all the bean dishes in Rome, none is more iconic than fagioli con le cotiche (beans slow-cooked with fresh pork skin). The cotiche add richness, depth, and a silky texture that makes the beans feel indulgent. Ask your butcher for fresh pork skin. For the best marriage of pork and bean flavors, make a day ahead and reheat to serve.

Tip: To clean the fresh pork skin, use a sharp knife to carefully scrape away any remaining bristles, working in one direction.

Combine the beans, rosemary, sage, and ¼ cup of the olive oil in a large pot with enough water to cover by 2 inches. Bring to a boil over high heat, then reduce the heat to low and simmer, partially covered, until the beans are tender, about 1½ hours. Check for doneness every 30 minutes, adding hot water as needed to keep the beans covered and prevent them from getting dry.

Meanwhile, bring a small pot of water to a boil over high heat. Add salt until the water tastes like a seasoned soup. Add the pork skin and cook until fork-tender, about 1½ hours. Drain, reserving the cooking liquid, and set aside. When cool enough to handle, cut the strips into 1-inch pieces.

Heat the remaining ¼ cup olive oil in a medium pot over low heat. Add the carrots, celery, onion, and a heavy pinch of salt and cook, stirring occasionally, until the vegetables are very soft, 20 to 25 minutes. Add the tomatoes, increase the heat to medium-low, and cook until they lose their raw flavor, 20 to 25 minutes. Add the pork skin, beans, and enough reserved cooking liquid from the beans and pork skin to cover by about 1 inch. Cook until the beans are very soft but not falling apart, about 20 minutes more. Season with salt as needed. Serve with toasted bread.

THE PULSE OF ROME

If you really want to understand Rome's working-class culinary soul, forget for a moment about pasta and offal and focus instead on beans. While they rarely steal the spotlight, beans and legumes have quietly nourished Romans for millennia, fueling laborers, farmers, and monks alike with hearty, affordable sustenance that, when cooked right, becomes downright luxurious.

Long before the arrival in the sixteenth century from the Americas of *Phaseolus* (the genus of beans like borlotti and cannellini that revolutionized Roman cooking) locals relied on lentils, chickpeas, grass peas, fava beans, and black-eyed peas. These legumes symbolized renewal, connection to the dead, and ancient rituals tied to agricultural cycles. On August 15, the Feast of the Assumption, Romans honored the Virgin Mary as protector of agriculture, a tradition likely entwined with pre-Christian customs connected to female deities.

Beans and legumes were more than symbolic, though. They were essential survival food, especially during Lent, when meat was off-limits and austerity reigned. Monks and nuns of some orders embraced this simplicity year-round, subsisting on bread, legumes, and a little water for their daily diet.

When those "American beans" finally arrived from across the Atlantic, Romans quickly embraced them—so much so that borlotti and cannellini beans soon appeared on papal tables as much as they did in humble kitchen hearths. And while these particular beans became culinary stars, dishes featuring chickpeas, lentils, and fava beans instead remained central to Rome's cucina povera (see page 217).

Today, dishes like Pasta e Ceci (page 154), Fagioli con le Cotiche (page 212), and Vignarola (page 211) aren't relics; they're beloved staples that embody Rome's resourceful culinary heart. Pasta e ceci remains a comfort classic, effortlessly delicious and eternally Roman. Meanwhile, fagioli con le cotiche, with its silky pork rinds and creamy beans, perfectly encapsulates how the simplest ingredients can feel indulgent. Vignarola celebrates spring with its medley of artichokes, favas, peas, and lettuce. Lentils, often simmered into thick soups or paired with sausage for good luck on New Year's Eve, continue to echo ancient traditions.

Despite the fact that modern restaurant menus in Rome often overlook these humble ingredients, beans and other legumes remain essential flavors deeply woven into the city's cultural and culinary fabric. They're a delicious reminder that Rome's food story is as much about survival and ingenuity as it is about taste.

POMODORI RIPIENI DI RISO

RICE-FILLED
TOMATOES

Pomodori ripieni are one of Rome's definitive summertime comfort foods, a dish that appears reliably on lunch tables and beach blankets throughout the city's famously scorching months. As temperatures spike, Roman cooks strategically retreat from their hot stovetops, turning instead to seasonal produce and oven-friendly dishes. At the heart of this Roman classic are plump, ripe tomatoes stuffed with seasoned rice, then baked until soft, collapsed, and caramelized at the edges. The potatoes tucked around the tomatoes roast and soften in the bubbling pan juices. Serve it all slightly warm or, better yet, at room temperature after a few hours' rest, allowing the flavors to deepen. It's a dish that tastes best when eaten leisurely, ideally at an outdoor table with a view over Rome's terra-cotta rooftops—or at least with cold beer close at hand.

Tip: Use tomatoes with structure and medium-thick skin. It's OK if they burst open a bit while cooking, but you don't want them to explode.

Serves 3

6 ripe but firm medium
    beefsteak tomatoes or 8
    to 9 medium tomatoes on
    the vine (see Tip)
Sea salt
6 tablespoons extra-virgin
    olive oil, plus more for
    greasing
1 garlic clove, smashed
1 cup Arborio rice
6 large fresh basil leaves,
    torn
¼ cup grated Pecorino
    Romano
1 large Yukon Gold potato,
    peeled and cut into 1-inch
    pieces

Preheat the oven to 350°F.

Using a serrated knife, slice off and reserve the tops of the tomatoes. Using a serrated grapefruit spoon or melon baller, over a bowl, carefully remove and reserve the tomato pulp, taking care to leave ¼ inch of flesh next to the skin—this will help preserve the tomato's structure while baking. Season the inside of each tomato with a heavy pinch of salt.

Heat 2 tablespoons of the olive oil in a shallow, medium pan over low heat. When the oil begins to shimmer, add the garlic and cook until it begins to turn golden, 2 to 3 minutes. Add the tomato pulp, rice, 1 cup of water, and a heavy pinch of salt. Increase the heat to medium-low and cook the rice, stirring frequently until al dente, 15 to 20 minutes, adding water ¼ cup at a time to keep the mixture moist. Remove the pan from the heat and stir in the basil and Pecorino Romano. Season with salt.

Grease a medium ovenproof casserole dish with olive oil. Fill each tomato four-fifths of the way with rice, leaving room for it to expand. Place the reserved tomato tops on top of the rice. Place the tomatoes in the prepared casserole and fill in the space around them with the diced potatoes. Drizzle over the remaining 4 tablespoons olive oil and add a splash of water to the bottom of the dish. Season the potatoes with salt.

Bake until the rice is cooked through and the tomatoes are caramelizing around the cut edges, 50 to 60 minutes. Begin checking the tomatoes after 30 minutes, adding water as necessary to keep the bottom from burning. Remove from the oven and set aside to cool for at least 30 minutes before serving.

INSALATA DI RISO

RICE, HOT DOG,
AND CANNED
CORN SALAD
(SERIOUSLY)

Serves 6

Sea salt
1½ cups short-grain rice (I
like Arborio), rinsed
1 cup mixed pickled
vegetables, roughly
chopped
1 (5-ounce) can oil-packed
tuna, drained
6 ounces Emmental, cut into
¼-inch cubes
1 cup canned corn, rinsed
2 fully cooked hot dogs, cut
into ¼-inch-thick rounds
¼ cup pitted olives
Freshly ground black pepper
Extra-virgin olive oil
White wine vinegar
3 large eggs, excessively
hard-boiled (page 90),
peeled and quartered

You might think summer officially begins with the solstice in June, or when the mercury climbs above 85°F. Wrong. In Rome, the appearance of insalata di riso (rice salad) on the menu of bars, cafeterias, and takeaway joints signals the official start of the season. This mixture of cold rice with a blend of flavorings typically starts popping up in mid-May. No two insalate are the same, but they do generally draw from the following ingredients: pickled vegetables, canned tuna in oil, cubes of Swiss cheese, canned corn, würstel coins (aka hot dog rounds), and overcooked hard-boiled eggs. Sometimes there's mayo, which in Italy often comes in a tube. Calling it a "salad" is a stretch, but one I'm willing to make.

Bring a large pot of water to a rolling boil over high heat. Add salt until the water tastes like a seasoned soup. Add the rice and cook until al dente, 16 to 18 minutes. Drain the rice in a colander.

Combine the rice, pickled vegetables, tuna, Emmental, corn, hot dogs, and olives in a large bowl and stir until everything is evenly distributed. Season with salt and pepper and dress with olive oil and vinegar to taste. Serve garnished with the hard-boiled eggs.

Cucina povera is one of those terms that gets thrown around so often and so carelessly that it has lost nearly all connection to its actual historical meaning. These days, you'll find it used to describe everything from rustic pastas to elaborate offal dishes, and high-end restaurant menus use the term to justify charging twenty-four euros for a plate of cacio e pepe. If you take contemporary food journalism at face value, you'd think cucina povera was just a charming, preindustrial Italian diet built on nose-to-tail butchery and heirloom legumes. The reality is far less romantic, and far more humbling.

The phrase itself translates to "peasant cuisine," but what was actually on the plates of the poor in Italy before the economic boom of the 1950s was not a multicourse meal of simple pasta followed by a hunk of offal. It was whatever could be scraped together to provide the necessary calories to get through the day. That meant most people were eating stale bread soaked in water and vinegar to soften it, foraged greens boiled down to a bitter pulp, or maybe—on a particularly lucky day—some meat scraps simmered in a vegetable broth. In working-class Rome, meat protein was scarce, and when it did appear, it was in minuscule portions, stretched into a meal with bread or potatoes alongside to feed as many mouths as possible. Even in Testaccio, Rome's meatpacking district, residents ate only around 30 grams (1 ounce) of meat daily at the turn of the twentieth century, a paltry quantity that falls far short of the daily recommended 50 to 60 grams.

The modern fetishization of cucina povera is rooted in a profound misunderstanding of both historical poverty and the way Italians actually ate in times of economic hardship. While the quinto quarto (fifth quarter) is often cited as the epitome of cucina povera, the less desirable cuts of meat that remained after the prime cuts had been taken by the wealthy didn't always trickle down to the truly destitute. They were more likely eaten by butchers and their families, or sold at a discount to skilled home cooks who could transform them into something nourishing. The poorest Romans, meanwhile, subsisted on bread, legumes, and whatever they could scavenge.

The revisionist take on cucina povera also glosses over the immense suffering that came with true food scarcity. Take the rural laborers of the Roman countryside, where large swaths of the population spent centuries living under systems of exploitative land ownership that kept food sources scarce and inaccessible. The diet of the landless poor in those regions relied heavily on chestnuts, weeds, and wild herbs, not because they were culinary delicacies but because they were free. The idea that these ingredients were part of some idyllic, resourceful peasant cuisine is an invention of modern nostalgia.

Of course, cucina povera has evolved, and many of the dishes once born out of necessity have indeed become beloved parts of Italy's regional foodways. But when journalists and food writers treat cucina povera as little more than a synonym for "simple but delicious," they erase the desperation and ingenuity that shaped it. Real cucina povera wasn't about thrift. It was about survival.

INSALATA DI MISTICANZA CON SALSA DI ALICI E SOMMACCO

WILD GREENS SALAD
WITH ANCHOVY
SAUCE AND
SUMAC

Misticanza is the generic term for a mixture of wild greens. Produce stalls in Rome sell it from bins to be prepared all'agro (blanched, then dressed with a squeeze of lemon, page 236), ripassata in padella (sautéed with oil, garlic, and chile, page 233), or as a raw salad. Whether you can pull off a salad is up to the season. For example, when this mix of field greens features prickly nettles, you've got to cook them, but in nettle-free mixes, you might find a huge array of ready-to-eat wild weeds. The best version of this salad is at Piatto Romano in Testaccio, where owner Andrea D'Alfonsi sources his foraged mixture of more than a dozen greens from Lazio and Abruzzo. The sauce is similar to the dressing for Puntarelle alla Romana (page 226), and the whole mess is dusted with punchy dried sumac from Emporio delle Spezie, a spice shop nearby. Sumac grows wild all over Italy, yet this is the only (Italian) place in the whole country that I recall seeing it used for seasoning!

Serves 4 to 6

3 oil-packed anchovy fillets, drained, and finely chopped

1 tablespoon white wine vinegar

Sea salt and freshly ground black pepper

2 tablespoons extra-virgin olive oil

½ pound freshly picked mixed wild greens

2 teaspoons sumac

Combine the anchovies, vinegar, salt, and pepper in a small bowl and set aside to marinate for 5 to 10 minutes. Slowly whisk in the olive oil.

Place the greens in a large bowl and toss with the anchovy dressing. Serve immediately dusted with sumac.

FRIGGITELLI

PAN-FRIED
SHISHITO
PEPPERS

In the summer, market stalls display piles of friggitelli, small, mild green peppers, similar to shishitos, whose name hints at their cooking method (*friggere* means "to fry"). People always warn me that in a huge pile you might get one or two hot ones. If that's the case, only Romans can perceive this negligible Scoville scale ranking. The coarse sea salt gives the peppers a pop of salinity reminiscent of pimientos de Padrón.

Heat the olive oil and garlic in a large pan over low heat just until the garlic starts to take on color, about 5 minutes. Remove and discard the garlic. Toss in the peppers in a single layer, increase the heat to medium, and cook, stirring occasionally, until blistered and wilted, 12 to 15 minutes.

Remove from the heat. Transfer the peppers to a serving dish and serve immediately sprinkled with coarse salt.

Serves 6 to 8

¼ cup extra-virgin olive oil
1 garlic clove, smashed
1 pound shishito or Padrón
   peppers
1 tablespoon coarse sea salt

ROME THE EDIBLE CITY

Rome is edible. It goes beyond market displays heaving with violet artichokes, bitter puntarelle, and tomatoes that actually taste like something, and the fact there seem to be two gelaterie to every Roman. Rome is edible because even as it swells with traffic and tourists, nature keeps showing up. It pokes through the cracks in the pavement, creeps up the city's crumbling walls, and droops heavy from trees that dangle olives, citrus, and loquats.

This city, for all its grandeur and grit, is still rooted in the land. While emperors erected marble monuments to their own egos, fields of grain, vineyards, and grazing sheep kept Romans fed. A hundred years ago, you didn't have to leave the historic center to find farms. Grapevines covered the Janiculum Hill, draping down toward Trastevere. Until the 1720s, another vineyard spread across what's now the Spanish Steps. The valleys around the Colosseum and the Forum were once farmland, and the Forum itself—long after it stopped being Rome's political heart—was just a big pasture where cows roamed between crumbling ruins and Christian pilgrimage sites. Sure, most of that has been figuratively paved over, but the agricultural past isn't gone, it's camouflaged.

Head out to the Via Appia Antica, one of the oldest roads in Rome, and you'll pass ancient tombs, broken aqueducts, and a working sheep farm in the Parco della Caffarella. Farther out, Azienda Agricola Verdicchio plants neat rows of chard, radicchio, and broccoli rabe destined for Roman tables. In the neighborhoods of San Paolo and Monte Ciocci, community gardens thrive year-round, providing locals with tomatoes and leafy greens like their ancestors grew. Even in the middle of the city, farming survives. Behind the Basilica of Santa Croce in Gerusalemme, a monastic garden hides behind an iron gate, its rows bursting with medicinal herbs and ancient vegetables. Across town in Trastevere, the cloistered nuns of Santa Cecilia quietly grow a botanical garden and transform its bounty into teas, soaps, and preserves, living proof of a self-sufficiency that's been going strong since the Middle Ages.

And then there are the wild edibles, the things that sprout up without permission. Capers burst from cracks in the Colosseum and the Aurelian Walls like little acts of botanical rebellion. Wild arugula carpets the Circus of Maxentius with peppery leaves. In the Parco della Caffarella, prickly pears cling to cactus pads, waiting for someone with gloves and guts. Mallow grows in the shade of medieval churches. Mint perfumes the sidewalk cracks. Even the olive trees on the Palatine Hill still bear fruit, just as they did when the Barberini family planted them four hundred years ago.

Rome is a city of contradictions. It's profane and sacred, modern and ancient, urban and rural, all at once. And while it's easy to get overwhelmed by the din of motorini and construction and crowds, Rome's wild side hasn't gone anywhere.

Hecyra.

VERDURE GRATINATE

ROASTED VEGETABLES TOPPED WITH BREADCRUMBS

Serves 4 to 6

1¼ cups seasoned breadcrumbs

½ cup finely grated Pecorino Romano

1 tablespoon roughly chopped fresh flat-leaf parsley

8 tablespoons extra-virgin olive oil

Sea salt

1 zucchini, cut lengthwise into ¼-inch-thick slices

1 small eggplant, cut crosswise into ¼-inch-thick rounds

1 red bell pepper, cut into ¼-inch-thick strips

1 medium white onion, cut into ½-inch-thick rings

Verdure gratinate (soft, golden-brown vegetables generously blanketed in oil-spiked breadcrumbs) are among my favorite Roman fiber sources. You'll see trays of these savory vegetables lined up in the windows of neighborhood tavole calde, ready to be packed up in aluminum trays and spirited home for lunch or dinner. Traditionally, this dish is about simplicity: seasonal vegetables like zucchini, eggplant, peppers, and onions, sliced and layered with a generous dose of breadcrumbs, herbs, and sharp Pecorino Romano. It's a thrifty and delicious way to elevate everyday produce. In my kitchen in Monteverde Vecchio, I keep it simple, focusing on what's freshest at the market and often grabbing whatever cheese bits are lingering in the fridge. Feel free to mix and match vegetables and use this recipe as your springboard.

Preheat the oven to 375°F. Line a baking sheet with parchment paper.

Combine the breadcrumbs, Pecorino Romano, parsley, and 2 tablespoons of the olive oil in a small bowl. Season with salt and set aside.

Spread the zucchini, eggplant, pepper, and onion over the baking sheet. Season with salt, giving extra love to the egpplant. Drizzle over 4 tablespoons of olive oil.

Spoon the breadcrumb mixture evenly over the vegetables, then drizzle with the remaining 2 tablespoons olive oil.

Bake until the vegetables are tender and caramelizing around the edges, rotating the pan halfway through, 30 to 45 minutes. If the topping browns too quickly, loosely cover the pan with aluminum foil for the remaining cooking time. Serve warm or at room temperature.

FAGIOLI CORALLO AL POMODORO

**ROMANO BEANS
IN TOMATO
SAUCE**

These flat, bright-green beans, called taccole elsewhere in Italy and often Romano beans in the US, are known for their satisfying snap and subtle sweetness. Traditionally, they're cooked slowly in tomato sauce until tender and kind of gray TBH, served warm or at room temperature, and drizzled generously with extra-virgin olive oil. Romans savor this simple dish as a contorno (side dish), and it's equally satisfying spooned over crusty bread to soak up every last drop of sauce.

Serves 4 to 6

¼ cup extra-virgin olive oil

1 garlic clove, smashed

½ white onion, finely
  chopped

Sea salt

1 pound Romano beans,
  fibrous string removed

2 cups halved cherry
  tomatoes or ½ (14-ounce)
  can whole peeled
  tomatoes, crushed by
  hand

3 to 4 fresh basil leaves

Heat the olive oil, garlic, onion, and a heavy pinch of salt in a large pan over low heat just until the garlic starts to take on color, about 5 minutes. Add the Romano beans and cook for 3 minutes to infuse them with flavor. Stir in the tomatoes and basil, season with salt, increase the heat to medium, and cook until the tomatoes begin to soften, about 10 minutes. Continue cooking until the beans are very tender, 20 to 30 minutes, adding water as needed to keep the sauce loose and juicy. Serve warm or at room temperature.

VEGETABLES, SALADS, AND SIDES

PUNTA-RELLE ALLA ROMANA

CATALONIAN
CHICORY STALKS
WITH ANCHOVY-
GARLIC SAUCE

Serves 4

1 bunch puntarelle
6 oil-packed anchovy fillets,
   drained
1 garlic clove
2 tablespoons white wine
   vinegar
5 tablespoons extra-virgin
   olive oil
Sea salt and freshly ground
   black pepper

From January to March, fruttivendoli pile mountains of these alien-looking chicory shoots, their bright-green stalks curled like tight little fists, awaiting their ritualistic preparation. They are sold trimmed, a process that seems like a full-contact sport when you see it unfold in the markets, leaves discarded on the cobblestones by one member of the team while the other prunes and shreds the stalks through a makeshift screen. At home, Roman cooks wield knives adeptly, slicing puntarelle into thin, crunchy ribbons that curl in an ice-water bath, taming their bitterness. Tossed simply with garlic, salty anchovies, good olive oil, and sharp vinegar, puntarelle alla romana are a winter icon. Puntarelle and chicories in general are becoming more popular in the US, especially in the NY-NJ-PA tristate area and the Pacific Northwest. Look for them at farmers' markets attended by Pennsylvania's Campo Rosso Farm and Washington's Local Roots and Uprising Seeds.

Prepare a medium bowl with ice water.

Strip away the outer leaves of the puntarelle (you can cook these in garlic and oil later; see Verdure Ripassate in Padella, page 233). Separate the bolted stalks from their central core and use a paring knife or vegetable peeler to trim away and discard any fibrous bits or woody ends. Slice the stalks into thin strips—or pass through a Tapù (puntarelle cutter)—and drop them into the ice water. Set aside to soak for about an hour, or until they curl.

Using a mortar and pestle, mash the anchovies and garlic into a paste. Add the vinegar and set aside to marinate for 5 to 10 minutes. Slowly whisk in the olive oil to create a punchy, emulsified dressing. You may not need all the oil.

Drain and pat dry the puntarelle. Toss with the dressing until evenly coated. Season with salt and pepper and serve immediately.

CARCIOFI ALLA ROMANA

BRAISED ARTICHOKES

There's nothing that signals the arrival of spring in Rome more reliably than the scent of mint and garlic wafting from pots of carciofi alla romana simmering away in trattoria kitchens across the city. Carciofi are practically sacred here, worshipped with the kind of devotion usually reserved for soccer rivalries. Romans have perfected two preparations above all: the crispy, fried Carciofi alla Giudia (page 86) and the tender, herbaceous carciofo alla romana. For the latter, whole artichokes are meticulously trimmed, stuffed with a bit of mentuccia and parsley, then gently braised until they're so tender they practically dissolve under your fork.

Serves 6

6 tender young globe artichokes, cleaned and trimmed (see Tip on page 75)

Sea salt and freshly ground black pepper

6 sprigs fresh flat-leaf parsley, finely chopped

6 sprigs mentuccia or mint, finely chopped

¼ cup extra-virgin olive oil

2 garlic cloves, smashed

½ cup dry white wine

Drain and pat the artichokes dry. Season all over with salt and pepper. Gently loosen the leaves and work the parsley and mint into the space between them, distributing it evenly.

Heat the olive oil and garlic in a high-sided pan or pot over low heat just until the garlic starts to take on color, about 5 minutes. Fit the artichokes snugly in the pan, stem-side up. Increase the heat to medium, then add the wine and cook until the alcohol aroma evaporates, about 1 minute. Add ½ cup of water, bring to a simmer, then reduce the heat to low. Cover with a tight-fitting lid and cook until the base of the stems is fork-tender, 25 to 40 minutes. Add more water as needed to keep the pot nice and moist and to prevent the artichokes from burning.

Remove the pan from the heat and set aside to cool slightly. Serve the artichokes with the juices from the pan drizzled over.

VEGETABLES, SALADS, AND SIDES

PATATE AL FORNO

ROASTED
        POTATOES

Artichokes may be the most emblematic produce in Rome, but don't underestimate the importance of potatoes, which appear as a side dish to countless secondi, and are even wedged between rice-stuffed tomatoes (page 215). Originally from Peru, potatoes migrated to Italy via Spanish trade routes in the sixteenth century and were quickly adopted for their caloric benefits, long shelf life, and flavor. They are essential and delicious, especially when boiled and then roasted, which gives them an extra-crispy exterior. Serve these herby potatoes alongside Abbacchio a Scottadito (page 180), Petto di Vitello all Fornara (page 206), or even Porchetta (page 198).

Serves 4 to 6

Sea salt
2 pounds Yukon Gold
    potatoes, peeled and cut
    into 2-inch pieces
½ cup extra-virgin olive oil
Leaves from 2 sprigs
    rosemary, roughly
    chopped
6 to 8 fresh sage leaves,
    roughly chopped
Freshly ground black pepper

Preheat the oven to 400°F.

Bring a large pot of water to a rolling boil over high heat. Add salt until the water tastes like a seasoned soup. Carefully drop in the potatoes and cook for 8 to 10 minutes. The exterior will appear a bit velvety.

Combine the olive oil, rosemary, sage, a heavy pinch of salt, and pepper in a large bowl. Drain the potatoes and transfer them to the bowl. Stir to coat in the oil mixture.

Transfer the seasoned potatoes to a baking sheet and roast until crisp and golden, about 1½ hours, stirring every 30 minutes and checking at the 1 hour mark for doneness. Serve immediately.

THE ORIGINAL FOOD PORN: RAPHAEL'S GARDEN OF EARTHLY DELIGHTS

Lest you think the eggplant emoji is a modern invention, let me draw your attention to the unsubtle composition of an eggplant penetrating a fig on the ceiling of the Villa Farnesina's Loggia di Amore e Psiche, painted by Raphael and his workshop in the early 1500s. At first glance, it's all myth and majesty, a wedding scene between Cupid and Psyche lifted from Apuleius's *The Golden Ass*. But look a little closer, and you'll see garlands of vegetables and fruits dangling overhead: girthy squashes, swollen eggplants, ripe cantaloupes. The story might be about divine love, but the ceiling tells a steamier tale.

The villa's patron, Agostino Chigi, wasn't commissioning art for art's sake. He was trying to cement his social status—and his marriage to a Venetian courtesan who wasn't exactly blue blood. By aligning himself with myth, Chigi was casting himself as a modern-day Cupid, fighting for love against the odds. But Raphael knew better than to keep it all PG. His botanical motifs transform the space into a Renaissance garden of earthly delights, heavy with the visual language of seduction, fertility, and appetite.

Chigi could afford the best, and he got it. Raphael brought in Giovanni da Udine to create garlands so lush and vivid they practically burst from the plaster. These weren't your standard acanthus borders—they were a painted catalog of Rome's expanding food world. Many of the fruits and vegetables had just begun to arrive in Italy via Mediterranean trade routes or voyages to the Americas. What you're looking at is one of the first attempts at hyperrealistic botanical illustration in Western art, and it's gloriously extra.

Some of the most eye-catching elements are cucurbits: fat squashes, curving gourds, melons hanging like ripe promises. Others, like the eggplant, had been introduced centuries earlier by Arab agronomists but were still exotic enough to suggest rarity and power. Lemons, oranges, and citrons—originally from Asia—symbolized wealth and fertility. And the pomegranate? An ancient stand-in for passion, death, and rebirth, split open to reveal glistening seeds that practically beg to be . . . eaten. Figs, always loaded with innuendo, dangle provocatively, conjuring up Dionysian indulgence.

Raphael's genius lies in his ability to layer meanings without ever compromising beauty. Sure, the frescoes tell a mythological tale. But they also whisper about lust, power, and the delicious mess of human desire. The Villa Farnesina is a glorious Renaissance-era reminder that the line between feasting and fornication is seductively blurred. Just follow the eggplants.

VERDURE RIPASSATE IN PADELLA

SAUTÉED
GREENS

If a Roman is nasty or cranky to you, just know there is a good chance they are constipated. Vegetables, once the anchor of the local diet, have been phased out in favor of carb- and meat-heavy diets. But that's where verdure ripassate can come in.

Literally "re-passed greens," this approach is the city's canonical way of cooking leafy things. The method is simple: Blanch your chicory (or chard or broccoletti) until tender, then sauté it in olive oil with garlic and a touch of peperoncino until the greens in question are hammered and soft and unidentifiable. The double-cook is essential. It softens the greens' tough stems and coaxes out that earthy, slightly bitter flavor Romans crave. I like using wild chicory when I can get it, the kind that practically bites back, barely tamed by oil and heat. Fiber deprivation issues solved.

Tip: You can use chicory, chard, broccoli rabe, spinach, amaranth, tenerumi (tender leaves and shoots of young zucchini and squash), grattaculi (broadly, prickly greens and vines), or any green you like.

Serves 4 to 6

Sea salt
2 pounds leafy greens (see Tip)
¼ cup extra-virgin olive oil
1 garlic clove, smashed
1 peperoncino (whole dried red chile pepper) or ½ teaspoon crushed red pepper flakes

Bring a large pot of water to a boil over high heat. Add salt until the water tastes like a seasoned soup. Add the greens and cook until the stems become tender. Drain, squeezing out any excess liquid by pressing the greens against the colander over the sink.

Meanwhile, heat the olive oil and garlic in a large pan over low heat just until the garlic starts to take on color, about 5 minutes. Add the peperoncino and cook until fragrant, about 30 seconds. Transfer the greens to the pan, increase the heat to medium, and cook until they are very soft, 10 to 15 minutes. Add water to the pan as needed to prevent the greens from burning. Serve warm.

POMODORI A MEZZO

SLOW-ROASTED
TOMATOES WITH
HERBS AND
GARLIC

This classic Roman Jewish summer specialty turns ripe and juicy tomatoes into a deeply flavored, borderline caramelized side dish. Slowly roasted with olive oil, garlic, and herbs, pomodori a mezzo ("halved tomatoes") are perfect as an antipasto, a side dish, or a topping for bread.

Preheat the oven to 300°F. Line a baking sheet with parchment paper.

Arrange the tomato halves cut-side up on the prepared baking sheet. Drizzle the olive oil evenly over the tomatoes. Distribute the garlic, oregano, and thyme evenly among them, then season with salt and pepper.

Roast until the tomatoes are soft, slightly shriveled, and caramelized around the edges, about 45 minutes. Serve warm or at room temperature.

Serves 4 to 6

6 tomatoes (I like casalino),
   halved crosswise
¼ cup extra-virgin olive oil
2 garlic cloves, thinly sliced
2 teaspoons dried oregano
Leaves from a few sprigs
   thyme
Sea salt and freshly ground
   black pepper

AGRETTI ALL'AGRO

**MONK'S BEARD
WITH LEMON**

Agretti all'agro is Roman spring on a plate. These grassy, briny greens—also called barba di frate, or "monk's beard"—make a fleeting appearance at market stalls just as the city starts to shake off winter. Grown in the salty, marshy terrain near the coast, agretti are crunchy, mineral-rich, and almost absurdly good with the simplest treatment. A quick blanch preserves their electric-green hue and signature tenderness, and a squeeze of lemon juice brings enough acid to earn the dish its name (*all'agro*, meaning "on the sour side"). Hit it with a drizzle of oil and you're ready to go.

Tip: You can prepare chicory, spinach, amaranth, chard, puntarelle leaves, or any other imaginable leafy green all'agro by boiling until tender, draining, squeezing out any excess water, then seasoning with lemon, salt, and olive oil (but agretti are salty enough on their own that they don't need the extra seasoning).

Bring a large pot of water to a boil over high heat. Add salt until the water tastes like a seasoned soup. Cook the agretti until very tender, 3 to 5 minutes, skimming off any foam that rises to the top. Drain well and serve drizzled with lemon juice and olive oil.

Serves 4 to 6

Sea salt
2 bunches agretti, trimmed
Juice of 1 lemon
Extra-virgin olive oil, for
    serving

I MERCATI GENERALI: A MODERN RUIN

If you ever find yourself walking along the southern edge of Ostiense and catch a glimpse of rusted iron beams and crumbling brick warehouses flanked by wild ivy and graffiti, congratulations, you've stumbled upon the ghost of Rome's Mercati Generali. Conceived during the ultraprogressive mayoral reign of Ernesto Nathan, this massive wholesale food market built between 1913 and 1922 was supposed to be the future. Nathan, who had a thing for order and efficiency (bless him), wanted to centralize Rome's unruly food distribution system, which was then scattered chaotically across the historic center.

Architect Innocenzo Sabbatini was tapped to design the space, and he did so with a flair for the practical. Think Liberty-style flourishes layered on top of rigid logic. There were rows of warehouses, massive loading docks, refrigeration units, and offices, all neatly arranged around a wide central road. It was eighty thousand square meters (about eight hundred sixty thousand square feet) of pure function.

For decades, Mercati Generali were the belly of the beast. Trucks and trains poured in daily, hauling in crates of produce from the Roman countryside, fish from Fiumicino, grains from Italy and America. Meat, meanwhile, was processed in the nearby slaughterhouse in Testaccio. If you ate it in Rome, it had probably passed through one of these gates. The complex wasn't sexy, but it was essential, a humming machine that kept the city fed.

By the 1990s, though, the gears had begun to grind. The infrastructure aged out, bureaucracy took over, and the market was officially shut in 2002. Operations moved to a newer facility outside the city in Guidonia. Efficient, yes, but deeply soulless.

Today, what's left of the original site is a kind of industrial necropolis. The structures are imposing and empty, their once-bustling loading bays are now echo chambers for pigeons and the occasional graffiti artist. It's beautiful, in that distinctly Roman way: grand ruins, slow decay, and potential just waiting to be released.

In 2003, there was real hope for a renaissance. The starchitect Rem Koolhaas and his firm, OMA, were tapped to transform the site into a futuristic cultural district with theaters, restaurants, shops, and galleries. Romans, starved for public space that wasn't falling apart, were cautiously optimistic. And then, nothing. Bureaucracy, corruption, funding issues. In a word: Rome.

The site has since become a symbol of failed urban renewal and of Rome's constant push and pull between past and future. Still, there's something magnetic about it. The bones of the Mercati Generali are still standing. Maybe, someday, the city will let them live again.

PIZZA AND BREAD

The bread and pizza recipes in this book are designed for home cooks working with home ovens, not wood-fired setups. As romantic as cooking with fire can be, it's out of reach for most people, and unnecessary for achieving deeply flavorful, structurally sound, and beautifully baked results. These recipes have been developed and tested specifically for conventional ovens, with adjusted hydration levels and fermentation times to ensure they work reliably in a home setting.

You'll notice that nearly all the doughs here are mixed by hand, which is my preferred method. While a stand mixer can be helpful, it's not essential, and I've found that getting your hands into the dough gives you a more intuitive sense of how it's developing. Flour and water behave differently depending on environmental conditions, and yeast is very temperature sensitive. Your hands are the best tools for reading the dough.

Most of the recipes also include an autolyse, a short rest after combining flour and water. This step jump-starts gluten formation and helps the dough come together more easily. For higher-hydration doughs, some recipes also use a double hydration method, in which most of the water is added at the beginning, and the remaining water is incorporated after the autolyse. This technique improves dough structure and manageability, especially when mixing by hand. Instead of intensive kneading, I rely on stretch-and-folds, gentle, periodic folds that build strength gradually without overworking the dough. It's a method favored by professional bakers and well suited to long-fermented, high-hydration doughs.

You also won't find volume measurements here. I use grams exclusively for all dough recipes because they offer precision, consistency, and scalability. Measuring by volume (cups, tablespoons) can throw off hydration and fermentation, and in bread and pizza making, those small differences really matter. A digital kitchen scale is essential and once you start using one, you won't want to go back...promise!

One last tip: always preheat your oven for at least an hour before baking to give your steel or stone enough time to come to full temperature. And if you're baking multiple loaves or pizzas, let the baking surface recover its heat between rounds—it makes all the difference for crust development and oven spring.

PIZZA BIANCA

BAKERY-STYLE
ROMAN
FLATBREAD

Makes two 13 × 18-inch pizzas

1000 grams bread flour, plus
  more for dusting
2 grams active dry yeast
700 grams cold water
25 grams fine sea salt
Extra-virgin olive oil, for
  finishing and greasing

Pizza bianca might just be Rome's most iconic bakery snack—no small feat in a city that treats baking with religious reverence. It's deceptively simple: flour, water, yeast, salt, and a generous slick of olive oil brushed across its dimpled surface before it hits the blistering oven. But this humble snack, crisp yet chewy, airy yet substantial, is a lesson in Roman baking tradition, a bread that bakers perfect over years of repetition. Early-morning queues outside spots like Antico Forno Roscioli, Forno Campo de' Fiori, and Panificio Bonci underscore the city's eternal devotion to this salty, oily carb bomb. Eat it plain, warm from the oven, or slice it open and layer thinly shaved mortadella inside. When figs are in season, combine them with slices of prosciutto for the ultimate summer sandwich filling. Regardless of how you intend to enjoy it, mix your dough the day before you plan to bake it.

Combine the flour and yeast in a large bowl, then pour in 600 grams of the water. Stir with your fingertips or a spoon until a shaggy dough forms. Cover the bowl with plastic wrap and set aside to autolyse (see page 241) for 30 minutes.

After 30 minutes have passed, uncover the bowl, sprinkle over the salt, and pinch it in. Add the remaining 100 grams water a little bit at a time and gently knead. Once all the water is incorporated, cover the bowl again with plastic wrap and allow the dough to rest for another 30 minutes.

Uncover the bowl and do one set of stretch-and-folds to build strength (see page 246): With one wet hand, lightly grasp one edge of the dough. Pull this flap of dough upward and outward, then attach it to the top of the dough. Turn the bowl a quarter turn and repeat until you have rotated the bowl a complete revolution, or until the dough tightens up and becomes more structured.

Cover the bowl with plastic wrap again and repeat the stretching and folding once every hour for 3 more rounds, allowing it to rest between each.

After the last stretch-and-fold, place the dough in a large, lightly greased bowl. Cover it with plastic wrap, and set aside to cold-ferment in the refrigerator overnight.

The next day, remove the dough from the refrigerator and set aside until it reaches room temperature and increases in volume, about 3 hours. The dough is ready to shape and bake when a gentle poke leaves an indentation that springs back slowly.

Place a baking steel or stone in the middle rack of the oven and preheat the oven to 500°F. Grease two 13 × 18-inch baking sheets.

Dust a clean, dry work surface with a thick layer of flour. Carefully invert the bowl over the floured work surface, gently detaching the dough from the bowl.

recipe continues on next page ▶

Dust the top of the dough well with flour, then gently coax the dough into a rectangle. Halve the dough using a dough scraper or knife.

Working with one piece at a time, stretch it to the size of the baking sheet (see page 247). Begin at the top of the dough and use flattened fingertips to gently press down the sides of the dough, working top to bottom. Repeat, but this time move from the bottom edges, around the sides to the top. Next, press from the top center of the dough down to the bottom. Then press from the bottom back up toward the top. Flip the dough over and repeat the stretching process from top to bottom, then bottom to top. Shaking off any excess flour, then transfer the dough to the prepared baking sheet. Coax the dough into the corners of the pan, gently pulling from the underside of the dough over the edge of the pan. Press down the corners and edges. If the dough springs back, allow it to rest for a few minutes before trying again. Repeat with the remaining dough.

Drizzle the dough generously with olive oil. Bake the first pizza until the crust is golden with a few dark spots, 12 to 15 minutes. Transfer to a wire rack to cool for a few minutes before slicing. Repeat with the second pizza, allowing the oven to preheat once again before baking.

Serve the pizza bianca cut into strips or rectangles, either plain or drizzled with olive oil, or sliced open and filled with mortadella (recipe follows), prosciutto and figs (page 98), or other cold cuts.

Fillings and Toppings

PIZZA CON LA MORTAZZA
Pizza with Mortadella

Makes 8 sandwiches

Dough for 1 Pizza Bianca
1 pound thinly sliced mortadella

Follow the recipe above, up to and including baking and resting. Slice the pizza in half lengthwise, then use a long, serrated knife to separate the two halves into top and bottom layers. Arrange the mortadella slices evenly over the bottom, overlapping them slightly in two to three passes. Cut into individual sandwiches.

PIZZA ROSSA
Bakery-Style Roman Flatbread with Tomato Sauce

Makes two 13 × 18-inch pizzas

Dough for Pizza Bianca
2 (14-ounce) cans whole peeled tomatoes, crushed by hand
2 tablespoons extra-virgin olive oil, plus more for serving
Sea salt

Combine the tomatoes, olive oil, and salt in a medium bowl.

Follow the recipe above, up to and including stretching the dough into the baking sheets. Spoon the tomato sauce over the dough in each baking sheet in an even layer, nearly to the edge. Drizzle with olive oil.

Bake each pizza for 18 to 20 minutes, until the crust is golden and the tomato is concentrated. Transfer to a wire rack to cool. Drizzle with more olive oil. Serve in slices or slivers.

STRETCHING
AND FOLDING

When you think of Roman bakeries and pizza joints, it's easy to picture golden-crusted loaves stacked behind foggy glass or trays of pizza al taglio glistening under fluorescent lights. What you don't see is the machine behind the magic: the oven. And if that oven was made in Rome, there's a good chance it came from Castelli Forni.

Tucked behind a stretch of warehouses in Pigneto, a neighborhood better known for hipster bars and street art than for baking, Castelli Forni has been quietly fueling the city's carb culture for more than fifty years. They don't have a flashy showroom or a big PR team. What they *do* have is a reputation among Rome's bakers and pizzaioli as the people you call when you want your dough treated right.

The company was born in the 1970s when Guido Castelli—a guy with equal parts mechanical instinct and culinary appreciation—started building ovens in a modest workshop. He wasn't trying to reinvent the wheel, but rather trying to create something that worked better. And he did. Those first ovens were solid, efficient, and consistent, characteristics that bakers immediately recognized and trusted. Today, the company is still in the family, run by Elio and Emilio Castelli, who've kept their father's philosophy alive while bringing the operation into the twenty-first century.

Unlike the mass-produced models churned out by global manufacturers, Castelli ovens are made in-house from start to finish. Design and assembly all happens under one roof in eastern Rome, ensuring obsessive control over the final product. That level of attention is what makes their ovens capable of surviving the daily demands of Roman pizza joints, where a ten-hour bake isn't uncommon and failure is not an option.

Castelli makes both gas and electric models, but no matter the fuel source, performance is nonnegotiable. Heat distribution is even. Temperatures are reliable. Durability is a given. Basically, these ovens are built to work hard, last forever, and never let a pizzaiolo down.

Castelli ovens are found in some of Rome's most beloved bakeries and pizzerias—Pizzarium, Boccione, and Panificio Bonci, to name a few. The company also fabricates stainless steel kitchen equipment and complete food service systems, but at their core, they're still all about helping the dough reach its full potential. In a city that worships its bread and pizza, Castelli Forni is the unglamorous but utterly essential piece of the puzzle. They may not get a byline on the menu, but trust me, the pros know.

PIZZA TONDA ROMANA

THIN CRUSTLESS
ROMAN-STYLE
PIZZA

Makes four 12- to 13-inch pizzas

345 grams bread flour, plus
    more for dusting
40 grams semola di grano
    duro rimacinata
0.5 gram active dry yeast
230 grams cold water
10 grams fine sea salt
10 grams extra-virgin olive
    oil, plus more for greasing

Pizza tonda, Rome's beloved, wafer-thin pie, doesn't mess around. There's no puffy, pillowy crust to speak of—sorry, this isn't Naples—and definitely no stuffed edges. Instead, it's all about achieving that cracker-crisp, delicately charred crust that barely rises at the rim and acts as a sturdy canvas for simple yet perfect toppings. At legendary spots like Ai Marmi in Trastevere (lovingly nicknamed *l'obitorio*, or "the morgue," due to its cold marble tables and operating room-inspired lighting), or new wave A Rota Pizzeria in Tor Pignattara, generations of pizzaioli stretch and roll the dough thin, swiftly dressing each pizza with a light slick of tomato, a bit of mozzarella, and just enough toppings to punctuate, not overwhelm. The pies bake swiftly in a scorching wood-fired oven, emerging crispy and blistered, ready to burn the roof of your mouth immediately. This recipe is adapted to a home oven and takes one to two days to prepare and bake.

Combine the bread flour, semola, and yeast in a large bowl, then pour in the water. Stir with your fingertips or a spoon until a shaggy dough forms. Cover the bowl with plastic wrap and set aside to autolyse (see page 241) for 30 minutes.

Uncover the bowl, sprinkle over the salt, then pinch it into the dough until fully incorporated. Pour over the olive oil and work it into the dough until fully incorporated, then turn the dough out onto a work surface and knead until it is smooth and elastic, 5 to 7 minutes.

Return to the bowl, cover with plastic wrap, then set aside to rest for 30 minutes.

Grease a baking sheet. Turn the dough out onto a lightly floured surface and cut it into four (approximately 160-gram) pieces with a dough scraper or knife.

Round the dough (see page 252): Working with one piece at a time, take four edges and pull and fold them into the center. Flip the dough, seam-side down, on the work surface. Curve your hand into a loose claw, like a dome or cage, and place it over the dough. Using gentle pressure, roll the dough in small circular motions, keeping your fingertips and the heel of your hand in contact with the counter. The bottom of the dough sticks slightly as you roll, creating surface tension, pulling the dough tight into a smooth ball. When it looks taut and even, tuck any stray seams underneath. Set aside seam-side down on the prepared baking sheet. Repeat with the remaining dough.

Brush the dough lightly with olive oil and cover the whole baking sheet with plastic wrap. Transfer to the refrigerator and allow the dough to cold-ferment for 24 hours and up to 48 hours.

Three hours before baking, remove the dough from the refrigerator and allow it to come to room temperature, still covered. The dough will rise slightly as it warms.

While the dough is rising, prepare the toppings of your choice (recipes follow). Set aside.

recipe continues on next page ▶

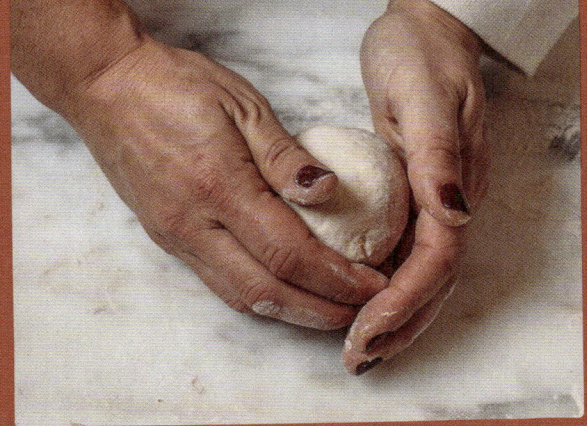

PIZZA TONDA STRETCHING

Place a baking steel or stone in the middle rack of the oven and preheat the oven to 500°F.

Shape the dough (see page 253): Place one dough ball on a well-floured surface, then sprinkle more flour on top. Use flattened fingertips to work the dough into a small disk. Continue until you have a round disk about 6 inches in diameter. Flip the disk over and move it to a lightly floured portion of the work surface. Use a rolling pin to roll out the dough. Turn a quarter turn and repeat, repositioning the dough. Continue until the disk is 12 to 13 inches in diameter and as thin as possible without tearing (see Tip).

Transfer the shaped dough to a pizza peel. Add your desired toppings, then transfer the pizza to the preheated baking steel. Bake until the crust is crisp and the toppings are cooked, 6 to 8 minutes.

Repeat with the remaining dough balls. Serve the pizzas immediately after baking.

Toppings

GRICIA
Mozzarella, Guanciale, and Pecorino Romano

Toppings for 1 pizza

2½ ounces mozzarella, torn or cut into
¼-inch pieces
1 ounce guanciale, sliced very thin and
cut into 2-inch pieces
3 tablespoons finely grated Pecorino
Romano
Freshly ground black pepper

Squeeze any excess moisture out of the mozzarella. Distribute the mozzarella, guanciale, and Pecorino Romano evenly over the shaped dough, nearly to the edge. Season with black pepper. Continue with the recipe.

Tip: Aim for paper thinness. If the dough springs back, let it rest for a few minutes before trying again. Dust with additional flour as needed to prevent sticking.

MARGHERITA
Mozzarella, Tomato, and Basil

Toppings for 1 pizza

¼ cup canned whole peeled tomatoes,
crushed by hand
2 teaspoons extra-virgin olive oil, plus
more for finishing
Sea salt
2½ ounces mozzarella, torn or cut into
¼-inch pieces
Fresh basil leaves

Combine the tomatoes, olive oil, and a heavy pinch of salt in a small bowl. Squeeze any excess moisture out of the mozzarella. Spoon the tomato mixture over the shaped dough, nearly to the edge. Distribute the mozzarella evenly over the sauce. Continue with the recipe. Garnish with basil leaves and drizzle with more olive oil after baking.

FIORI DI ZUCCA E ALICI
Mozzarella, Squash Blossoms, and Salted Anchovies

Toppings for 1 pizza

2½ ounces mozzarella, torn or cut into
¼-inch pieces
4 squash blossoms, trimmed and
opened
8 oil-packed anchovy fillets, drained

Squeeze any excess moisture out of the mozzarella. Distribute evenly over the shaped dough, nearly to the edge, followed by the squash blossoms. Continue with the recipe, then lay the anchovies evenly over the pizza after baking.

ROSSA
Tomato

Toppings for 1 pizza

¼ cup canned whole peeled tomatoes,
crushed by hand
2 teaspoons extra-virgin olive oil
Sea salt

Combine the tomatoes, olive oil, and a heavy pinch of salt in a small bowl. Spoon the mixture over the shaped dough, nearly to the edge. Continue with the recipe.

In ancient Rome, food functioned as both nourishment and as a means of power. From the crowded tenements of the capital to the wind-swept provinces, Roman leaders understood that managing the food supply meant managing the people. The grain dole, lavish banquets, and strategic manipulation of trade routes all functioned as tools of realpolitik, cleverly disguised as acts of generosity. This system of governance was summed up by the satirist Juvenal in the phrase *panem et circenses* (bread and circuses) a reference to how emperors maintained public loyalty and suppressed unrest by offering free grain and mass entertainment. Far from a throwaway slogan, it encapsulated the essence of Roman rule: combine nourishment with spectacle, and the people stay quiet.

The *cura annonae* (grain dole) was Rome's original political stunt. Launched in 123 BCE by the politically savvy tribune Gaius Gracchus, it offered subsidized grain to thousands of citizens in the city proper. Officially social welfare, unofficially a bribe to secure loyalty to political leadership and silence dissent, which was always brewing. Julius Caesar expanded the dole, and Augustus perfected it, feeding up to three hundred thousand Romans regularly and branding himself as protector of the plebs. Bread and circuses went hand in hand: while grain ensured the stomachs of the citizenry were full, public events like gladiator games, chariot races and theatrical performances kept their minds distracted and loyalty reinforced. Feeding the populace became a form of governance, as essential to Roman stability and pacification as any military campaign.

Beyond Rome's borders, food became a tool of imperial dominance. Egypt, annexed by Augustus (27 BCE–14 CE), served as a vital grain supplier to the capital; controlling its harvest meant controlling Rome. Conversely, rebellion was met with agricultural destruction—Roman legend tells of salted fields in Carthage, and in Judea, Vespasian and Titus used starvation as a tactic of war.

Food shaped political narratives, too. Augustus presented himself as *pater patriae* (father of the fatherland) minting Roman coins with cornucopias and wheat sheaves as visual shorthand for prosperity. Emperors who failed at grain logistics were publicly skewered. Tacitus roasted the short-lived emperor Vitellius (April–December 69 CE) for indulgence, which he contrasted with the leader's incompetence. Commodus (177–192 CE), unable to stave off famine, lost popular support, and citizens didn't exactly mourn when the elite finally assassinated him.

The grain dole itself was a marvel of logistics, supporting a city of over a million. Initially distributed raw from depots like the Porticus Minucia Frumentaria near today's Largo Argentina, the grain was taken to mills and bakeries to become *puls* or coarse loaves. Public bakeries produced *panis plebeius* for the masses, while the elite preferred refined *panis siligineus* made from sifted flour.

By the third century, Aurelian (270 BCE–275 CE) reformed the system by replacing raw grain with pre-baked loaves, simplifying logistics and tightening state control. Bakeries evolved into critical infrastructure, anchoring urban food security and economic activity. Grain powered both bellies and commerce, enriching provincial landowners, traders, millers, and entrepreneurs like the baker Eurysaces (see page 267). Any disruption, whether from piracy, drought, or political unrest, sent ripples through Roman society. As with so much in Rome, the real power lay not only in the sword, but in the loaf.

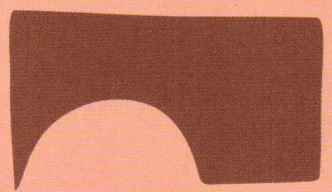

TRAPIZ-ZINI

ROMAN PIZZA POCKETS

Makes one 9 × 13-inch pizza (6 squares or 12 trapizzini)

400 grams bread flour

100 grams semola di grano duro rimacinata

350 grams cold water

100 grams Lievito Madre (100% hydration; recipe follows)

10 grams sea salt

20 grams extra-virgin olive oil, plus more for greasing

In 2008, Roman pizzaiolo Stefano Callegari took two of the city's most beloved food traditions, slow-cooked Roman stews and spongy, high-hydration pizza bianca, and merged them into one of the most recognizable street foods in the capital: the trapizzino. Named for its triangular shape similar to a tramezzino (a white bread sandwich with the crusts cut off), the format is simple but clever: a fluffy wedge of pizza dough sliced open like a pita and filled with saucy Roman classics like Pollo alla Cacciatora (page 193), Picchiapò (page 165), or Coratella (page 197). This dough, adapted for the home kitchen, mimics the structure and flavor of Callegari's bread base: tender, chewy, with a thin crust yet sturdy enough to hold a rich, moist filling. The dough undergoes a cold fermentation of 12 to 24 hours.

Combine the bread flour and semola in a large bowl, then pour in the water. Stir with fingertips or a spoon until no dry bits remain. Add the starter and mix until fully incorporated. Cover the bowl with plastic wrap and set aside to autolyse (see page 241) for 30 minutes.

Uncover the bowl, sprinkle over the salt, then pinch it into the dough. Pour over the olive oil and work it into the dough until fully incorporated, then turn the dough out onto a work surface and knead until it is smooth and elastic, 5 to 7 minutes. Return to the bowl, cover the bowl with plastic wrap, then set aside to rest at room temperature for 30 minutes.

Uncover the bowl and do the first of three stretch-and-folds to build strength (see page 246): Pull one edge of the dough up and fold it across the top of the dough, patting lightly to adhere. Turn the bowl a quarter turn and repeat until you have done a full revolution, or until the dough tightens up and becomes more structured. Cover the bowl with plastic wrap and set aside at room temperature for 30 minutes, repeating the stretch-and-fold and resting period twice more. After the final stretch-and-fold, cover the bowl with plastic wrap and transfer the dough to the refrigerator to cold-ferment for 12 to 24 hours.

Remove the dough from the refrigerator and bring to room temperature, 3 to 4 hours, allowing fermentation to resume and the dough to increase in volume.

Place a baking steel or stone on the middle rack of the oven and preheat the oven to 500°F. Oil a 9 × 13-inch pan or baking dish.

Transfer the dough to the prepared pan and use flattened fingertips to gently stretch it to fill the pan to the corners. Set the dough aside to proof, covered, for 20 minutes.

Uncover the dough and use a bench scraper or sharp knife to score the dough with deep, decisive cuts to separate it cleanly into squares: one cut along the 9-inch side of the pan, dividing it into two columns, and two cuts along the 13-inch side, dividing it into three rows. Set aside to proof again, covered, for 30 minutes more.

Bake until golden and crisp, about 20 minutes. Set aside to cool, separate the buns, then cut each diagonally to form triangular trapizzini. Use a serrated knife to carefully open each triangle along its cut side into a pocket, leaving two edges intact. Stuff with your choice of filling.

LIEVITO MADRE
Sourdough Starter

Whole wheat flour
Warm water

Combine 25 grams of flour with 25 grams of water in a small bowl or container. Stir until smooth. Set aside at room temperature, loosely covered with a lid or plastic wrap for 24 hours.

Once 24 hours have passed, discard all but 25 grams of the mixture, then add 25 grams each of flour and water. Mix thoroughly. Repeat the daily discarding and feeding process until the mixture doubles in volume within 4 hours of feeding (use a marker or rubber band to mark the container). This process may take anywhere from a week to two, depending on your environment and flour.

Once your starter is consistently rising and falling with each feeding cycle, it's ready to use. To reach the required 100 grams of starter for the recipe above, combine 20 grams of the starter (the rest can be saved and used as the base for your next feeding) with 40 grams each of flour and water 4 to 5 hours before you intend to mix your dough. Mix well. Your starter is ready to use when it is bubbly and has doubled in volume.

SCROCCHIA

SUPERTHIN,
CRISPY CRACKER-
LIKE FLATBREAD
WITH TOMATO

Makes two 13 × 18-inch pizzas

For the dough:
350 grams bread flour, plus
    more for dusting
2 grams active dry yeast
195 grams water, at room
    temperature
8 grams sea salt, plus more
    for seasoning
30 grams extra-virgin olive
    oil, plus more for greasing

For the topping:
Extra-virgin olive oil
⅔ (14-ounce) can whole
    peeled tomatoes,
    crushed by hand
2 teaspoons dried
    oregano

Named for the unmistakable crunch it makes with each bite (*scrocchiare* means "to crunch") this wafer-thin, cracker-like pizza is impossibly crispy, shatteringly thin, and deeply addictive. Sold at neighborhood bakeries, pizza-by-the-slice spots, and even some wood-fired pizzerias, scrocchia is typically brushed lightly with olive oil or tomato, then baked until blistered and golden. It's the perfect snack to munch on the go, ideally while navigating Roman cobblestones, leaving a trail of crumbs in your wake.

Make the dough: Whisk together the flour and yeast in a large bowl. Pour in the water and mix with your fingertips or a spoon until no dry bits remain. Cover the bowl with plastic wrap and set aside to allow the flour to autolyse (see page 241) for 30 minutes.

Uncover the bowl, sprinkle over the salt, then pinch it into the dough until fully incorporated. Pour over the oil and work it into the dough until fully incorporated, then turn the dough out onto a work surface and knead it just until it is smooth and elastic, 5 to 7 minutes.

Transfer the dough to a lightly oiled bowl. Cover with plastic wrap, then set aside to rise at room temperature until the dough has doubled in volume, about 2 hours.

Place a baking steel or stone on the lowest rack of the oven and preheat the oven to 450°F. Lightly oil two 13 × 18-inch baking sheets.

Uncover the bowl and turn the dough out onto a lightly floured surface. Halve the dough using a dough scraper or knife. Working with one piece of dough at a time and keeping the other piece covered, roll it out using a rolling pin, starting from the center and working outward. Adjust the dough as needed to maintain a rectangular shape, carefully turning, flipping, and dusting with additional flour to prevent sticking. Continue rolling until the dough measures about 13×18 inches and is as thin as possible without tearing. If it springs back, let it rest for a few minutes, covered, and stretch again. Transfer the dough to a prepared baking sheet and work the dough to fit all the way to the corners.

Assemble the scrocchia: Brush the dough with olive oil, then spoon half the tomatoes all the way to the edges. Sprinkle over half the oregano. Drizzle over some additional olive oil, season with salt, and bake until the pizza is very crisp and the tomato sauce starts to caramelize, 12 to 15 minutes.

Transfer the pizza to a wire rack to cool slightly, then break it into pieces and serve warm or at room temperature. Repeat with the remaining dough.

PIZZA IN TEGLIA ALLA BONCI

BONCI-STYLE
SHEET PAN PIZZA

Gabriele Bonci revolutionized Roman pizza with his high-hydration, slow-fermented dough baked in sheet pans and topped with seasonal, often unexpected ingredients. At his slice joint, Pizzarium, near the Vatican, Bonci ditched the quick-mix, short-proof doughs of old and introduced long-leavened bases made with heirloom flours, gentle folds, and a lot of patience. The result is pizza that's light, airy, and deeply flavorful, with a tender, open crumb and a crisp bottom to match his "In Crunch We Trust" merch. This recipe adapts his method for the home oven, using a high-hydration folding technique and cold fermentation to develop structure and complexity. It's not a quick project (budget 12 to 24 hours for cold fermenting), but if you want pizza with real depth, it's absolutely worth the effort.

Whisk together the einkorn and bread flours and the yeast in a large bowl, then pour in 300 grams of the water. Mix with a spoon just until no dry bits remain. Cover the bowl with plastic wrap and set aside to autolyse (see page 241) for 30 minutes.

Uncover the bowl, sprinkle over the salt, then pinch it into the dough until fully incorporated. Slowly add the remaining 100 grams water and mix until thoroughly incorporated. Mix in the olive oil. The dough will be very loose and wet at this stage and too soft to knead on a work surface. Knead in the bowl using the Rubaud method (see QR code): Use your dominant hand to scoop under the dough at the far edge of the bowl, lift it up, and stretch it in a rhythmic, circular motion. Rotate the bowl as you go, repeating this movement for 1 minute. Cover the bowl and rest the dough for 5 minutes. Repeat the Rabaud method for 1 minute followed by a 5 minute rest 2 to 3 more times, until the dough becomes elastic and cohesive. Shape the dough into a rough ball and place it in a lightly greased bowl. Cover with plastic wrap and set aside to rise in the refrigerator for 6 hours.

Uncover the bowl and do the first of three stretch-and-folds to build strength (see page 246): Pull one edge of the dough up and fold it across the top of the dough, patting lightly to adhere. Turn the bowl a quarter turn and repeat until you have done a full revolution. Cover the bowl with plastic wrap and set aside for 30 minutes, repeating the stretch-and-fold and resting period twice more. After the final stretch-and-fold, cover the bowl with plastic wrap and transfer the dough to the refrigerator to cold proof for 12 to 24 hours. If you plan to cold-ferment for the full 24 hours, give the dough another stretch-and-fold about 12 hours into the proofing time.

Remove the dough from the refrigerator and allow it to come to room temperature, about 1 hour. While the dough is resting, prepare the toppings of your choice (recipes follow) and set aside.

Makes one 13 × 18-inch pizza

400 grams einkorn or spelt flour

100 grams bread flour, plus more for dusting

1.5 grams active dry yeast

400 grams cold water

12 grams sea salt

24 grams extra-virgin olive oil, plus more for greasing

Rubaud method

recipe continues on next page ▶

Place a baking stone or steel on the middle rack of the oven and preheat the oven to 550ºF. Oil a 13 × 18-inch half baking sheet.

Cover a clean, dry work surface with a heavy layer of flour. Carefully invert the bowl over the floured surface, gently detaching the dough from the bowl with your hands or a dough scraper. Dust the top of the dough with more flour. Shape the dough to the size of the baking sheet (see page 247): Using flattened fingertips, press down around the edges of the dough, gently dimpling to create a frame and redistribute the gases toward the center. Use the same light dimpling motion to gently press down the middle. Work the dough until it is roughly the same dimensions as the pan. Gently scoop up the dough, shaking off any excess flour, and position it in the prepared pan with the side that was on the work surface facing up. Coax the dough into the corners of the pan, gently pulling from the underside of the dough over the edge of the pan. Press down the corners and edges. If the dough springs back, allow it to rest for a few minutes before trying again.

Add your toppings and set the dough aside to rise slightly for 20 minutes.

Transfer the pizza to the preheated steel and bake until the crust is golden and the undercarriage is crisp, 18 to 20 minutes.

Remove the pizza from the oven and transfer it to a rack to cool for at least 10 minutes before slicing and serving.

PIZZA MARGHERITA RIPIENA

Tomato and Mozzarella Pizza Sandwich

Fillings for 1 pizza

Dough for 2 Pizze in Teglia
2 (14-ounce) cans whole peeled tomatoes, crushed by hand
2 tablespoons extra-virgin olive oil
Sea salt
1 pound mozzarella, coarsely grated

Prepare two batches of dough according to the recipe and stretch into two baking sheets.

Combine the tomatoes, olive oil, and a heavy pinch of salt in a medium bowl. Spoon the sauce over the dough in each sheet pan, dividing it evenly. Distribute the mozzarella evenly over one of the pizzas.

Continue with the recipe, baking each pizza separately.

Invert the tomato-topped pizza over the mozzarella pizza, forming a sandwich.

PIZZA CON PATATE E MOZZARELLA

Potato and Mozzarella

Toppings for 1 pizza

2 pounds (about 4 medium) Yukon Gold potatoes
¼ cup extra-virgin olive oil, plus more for greasing
Sea salt and freshly ground black pepper
Dough for 1 Pizza in Teglia
1 pound mozzarella, coarsely grated

Place the potatoes in a medium pot with water to cover. Bring to a boil over high heat and cook until the potatoes are fork-tender, about 45 minutes. Once cool enough to handle, peel the potatoes and crumble into small pieces. Stir in the olive oil and season with salt and pepper.

Prepare one batch of dough according to the recipe until it is stretched in the baking sheet.

Distribute the potatoes and mozzarella evenly over the dough, all the way to the edge of the pan. Season with salt and drizzle over a healthy glug of olive oil. Continue with the recipe.

CROSTINO

Ham and Cheese

Toppings for 1 pizza

Dough for 1 Pizza in Teglia
1 pound mozzarella, coarsely grated
10 slices ham, torn

Prepare one batch of dough according to the recipe until it is stretched in the baking sheet.

Distribute half of the mozzarella over the dough, followed by the ham and remaining mozzarella. Continue with the recipe.

PIZZA CON RICOTTA, FICHI, E MIELE

Ricotta, Fig, and Honey

Toppings for 1 pizza

Dough for 1 Pizza in Teglia
Extra-virgin olive oil
Sea salt
1 pint whole milk ricotta, well drained
12 ripe figs, quartered
¼ cup honey, warmed

Prepare one batch of dough according to the recipe until it is stretched in the baking sheet.

Dock the dough to prevent it from rising irregularly in the oven: Use your fingertips to dimple the surface of the dough, especially the center. Drizzle with olive oil and season with salt. Continue with the recipe.

Remove the pizza from the oven and spread over the ricotta, then distribute the fig quarters evenly and season with salt. Set aside to cool on a rack for at least 10 minutes before slicing and serving with honey drizzled all over.

BREAD AND STONE: THE MONUMENTAL LIFE OF EURYSACES THE BAKER

Caught in the swirl of traffic at Porta Maggiore, the Tomb of Marcus Vergilius Eurysaces rises like a fossilized layer cake on the side of the road. Most people pass it without noticing. But look a little closer and you'll see an extraordinary narrative etched in travertine cylinders and carved reliefs: the story of a businessman who baked his way to immortality.

Eurysaces was likely a freedman—a former slave who earned his freedom and, with it, the chance to hustle. And hustle he did. The monument he commissioned for himself and (we think) his wife, Atistia, sometime around the late first century BCE, is anything but subtle. Built in concrete and faced with travertine, the tomb is crowned by three rows of round openings, interpreted either as grain-measuring vessels or dough kneading bins. A frieze wraps around the monument like an ancient instructional manual, illustrating scenes from his industrial-scale baking operation: grain milling, dough kneading, loaf shaping, and the baking itself. It's as if Eurysaces wanted to be absolutely certain that everyone knew how he made his fortune.

He had reason to brag. In a city where social status was rigidly enforced, freedmen like Eurysaces were often barred from the highest echelons of public life, but that didn't stop them from making money—and mausolea if they managed to become upwardly mobile. In fact, tradesmen often flaunted their wealth through tombs that were both declarations of financial success and architectural middle fingers to the elite. With his tomb, Eurysaces had baked himself a place in the city's urban fabric.

The tomb was a veritable billboard. It was a place of ritual, of remembrance, of feasting. Romans practiced refrigerium, a kind of memorial meal held at gravesites on certain days of the year. Picture a dusty roadside scene: friends and family gathering near the tomb, pouring wine, offering bread or cakes, sharing food in honor of the dead. These weren't quiet, solemn affairs, but rather more like picnics with the ancestors. The practice tethered the living to the dead and reinforced social bonds, especially important for someone like Eurysaces, who may have lacked an aristocratic lineage but could now anchor his memory in stone and ceremony.

The location of the tomb, right outside what was then the eastern boundary of Rome, was no accident. Roman law prohibited burials within the city, so major roads leading in and out of town became prime real estate for tombs. Eurysaces planted his right along the Via Praenestina and the Via Labicana, where thousands of travelers, merchants, and locals would pass by daily. This stone legacy of his was impossible to ignore, paving his path to immortality in the minds of Romans.

LINGUE DI PIZZA

PIZZA
"TONGUES"

Makes 6 lingue

For the dough:
350 grams bread flour
90 grams semola di grano
   duro rimacinata
2 grams instant dry yeast
300 grams water, at room
   temperature
8 grams fine sea salt
35 grams extra-virgin olive
   oil, plus more for greasing

For the topping:
1½ (14-ounce) cans tomato
   sauce (passata)
1 tablespoon extra-virgin
   olive oil, plus more for
   serving
Sea salt

Lingue di pizza, literally "pizza tongues," are long, flat, paddle-shaped stretches of dough. Despite the name, these bakery staples aren't made with offal, but are assembled from an olive oil-enriched dough and dressed with a bit of tomato sauce. Making lingue is a relatively fast process, and any bubbles formed during proofing are mostly pressed out when the dough is stretched into its signature elongated oval shape, creating its classic thin, crisp structure with just a bit of chew.

Make the dough: Whisk together the bread flour, semola, and yeast in a large bowl, then pour in 250 grams of the water. Mix with your fingertips or a spoon until no dry bits remain. Cover the bowl with plastic wrap and set aside to autolyse (see page 241) for 30 minutes.

Uncover the bowl, sprinkle over the salt, then pinch it into the dough. Slowly add the remaining 50 grams of water until fully incorporated, then mix in the olive oil. Turn the dough out onto a work surface and knead until it is smooth and elastic, 5 to 7 minutes. Shape the dough into a rough ball and place it in a lightly greased bowl. Cover with plastic wrap and set aside to rise at room temperature for 1 hour.

Uncover the bowl and do one set of stretch-and-folds to build strength (see page 246): Pull one edge of the dough up and fold it across the top of the dough, patting lightly to adhere. Turn the bowl a quarter turn and repeat until you have done a full revolution. Cover the bowl with plastic wrap and set aside until the dough has doubled in volume, 1½ to 2 hours more.

Place a baking steel or stone on the middle rack of the oven and preheat the oven to 475°F.

Turn the dough out onto a lightly oiled surface and gently stretch it into a rough rectangle. Using a bench scraper or knife, slice the dough once lengthwise and twice crosswise to create six rectangular portions, each weighing approximately 130 grams. Cover loosely with plastic wrap and set aside to allow the gluten to rest for 10 minutes before shaping.

Prepare the topping: Combine the tomato sauce, olive oil, and a heavy pinch of salt in a small bowl and set aside.

Assemble the lingue: Lightly grease two 13 × 18-inch baking sheets. Working with one piece of dough at a time, grip it firmly at one end, lift it off the work surface, and let the rest hang down so gravity stretches it gently. Once it elongates under its own weight, lay it down on the tray. Repeat with the remaining dough. Drizzle each piece with olive oil then, using flattened fingertips, stretch into an elongated oval of uniform thickness measuring around 3 inches wide by 12 inches long.

Spoon 3 heaped tablespoons of sauce over each lingua, nearly to the edge.

Transfer the first tray to the preheated steel and bake until the edges are crisp and the crust is golden, 16 to 18 minutes.

Remove the tray from the oven and transfer the lingue to a rack to cool for at least 10 minutes before serving. Finish with a drizzle of olive oil, then serve warm or room temperature. Repeat with the second tray of lingue.

PANE CASERECCIO

**ROMAN-STYLE
COUNTRY BREAD**

This rustic loaf is a staple in Roman bakeries and on trattoria tables—an un-fussy, crackly-crusted bread with a chewy, open crumb and mild, slightly tangy flavor. It's made from a simple mix of flour, water, salt, and biga (a typical Roman pre-ferment), shaped into a free-form oval, and baked directly on a steel or stone for maximum crunch. Serve it alongside Roman stews, dunk it in extra-virgin olive oil, or use it to do a scarpetta in the last bits of pasta sauce. Prepare the biga the night before you intend to mix and bake.

Makes 1 loaf

500 grams bread flour, plus
    more for dusting
350 grams lukewarm water
Biga (recipe follows)
12 grams fine sea salt

Combine the flour and water in a large bowl. Mix with your fingertips or a spoon until no dry bits of flour remain. Set aside, covered with plastic wrap, to autolyse (see page 241) for 30 minutes.

Uncover the bowl. Add the biga and mix until incorporated, then pinch in the salt. Turn the dough out onto a clean, dry work surface. Knead until the dough is smooth and elastic, 5 to 7 minutes. Return the dough to the bowl, cover with plastic wrap, and set aside to rise until it has doubled in volume, about 1 hour.

Uncover the bowl and do the first of two stretch-and-folds to build strength (see page 246): Pull one edge of the dough up and fold it across the top of the dough, patting lightly to adhere. Turn the bowl a quarter turn and repeat until you have done a full revolution. Cover the bowl with plastic wrap and set aside for 30 minutes, repeating the stretch-and-fold once more. After the final stretch-and-fold, cover the bowl with plastic wrap and set aside to rise at room temperature until doubled in volume, about 1½ hours.

Gently turn the dough out onto a lightly floured surface. With floured hands, gently coax the dough into an elongated oval shape, taking care not to deflate it.

Fold the top third down toward the center, then fold the bottom third up over it, like folding a letter. This creates internal structure and starts to build surface tension. Flip the dough seam-side down and use your hands to gently roll and elongate it into a log, tapering the ends slightly while keeping the middle full and rounded. The goal is a relaxed, torpedo-shaped loaf with a smooth, taut surface that will hold its shape during the final rise and bake.

Transfer the dough to a floured couche or parchment paper–lined baking sheet, cover with a damp cloth, and set aside to rise at room temperature until puffy but not collapsed, 1 to 1½ hours.

BIGA
Yeasted Pre-Ferment

Biga is a stiff Italian pre-ferment made from flour, water, and a small amount of yeast. It's mixed the day before baking to develop flavor, improve structure, and create a light, airy crumb in breads.

100 grams water
200 grams bread flour
Pinch of active dry yeast
Extra-virgin olive oil, for
    greasing

In the bowl of a stand mixer fitted with the dough hook, combine the water, flour, and yeast. Mix on medium speed for 5 minutes. Transfer the biga to an oiled bowl, cover with plastic wrap, and set aside to ferment at room temperature until it doubles in volume, 10 to 12 hours.

Place a baking steel or stone on the middle rack of the oven and a cast-iron skillet or oven-safe pan on the bottom rack to create steam. Preheat the oven to 450°F.

Score the loaf with a razor or sharp knife. Slide it onto the steel and pour a cup of hot water into the skillet to create steam. Bake until deep golden brown and hollow-sounding when tapped, 35 to 40 minutes.

Set aside to cool completely on a wire rack before slicing.

PIZZETTE DI SFOGLIA

LITTLE PUFF PASTRY PIZZAS

Roman bakeries or forni are known for turning the humblest ingredients into addictive snacks, and pizzette di sfoglia are the perfect example. These little puff pastry rounds are topped with tomato sauce and baked until sticky, tempting you from behind the glass alongside trays of rustic pizza bianca and golden supplì. The magic here happens as the sauce bubbles down, dripping off the edges, creating crisp, savory caramelization that seasons the flaky pastry beneath. Pizzette are best enjoyed slightly warm, straight out of a paper bag on the cobblestone streets outside the bakery, as generations of Romans have done on their way home from school or work.

Makes 32 pizzette

⅓ cup tomato sauce
(passata)
2 teaspoons extra-virgin
olive oil
Sea salt
1 teaspoon dried oregano
All-purpose flour, for dusting
1 pound very cold store-
bought puff pastry

Preheat the oven to 400°F. Line two 13 × 18-inch baking sheets with parchment paper.

Combine the tomato sauce, olive oil, a heavy pinch of salt, and oregano in a small bowl.

Dust your work surface with flour. Dust the surface of the puff pastry and roll into a rectangle that is approximately 10 × 20 inches and ⅛ inch thick. Using a 2-inch round cookie cutter, cut out thirty-two pizzette. Place on the prepared baking sheets, leaving about ¼ inch between each. Transfer the trays to the refrigerator to allow the dough to chill for 15 to 20 minutes. Remove the first tray from the refrigerator and brush the center of each pizzetta with the tomato sauce, leaving a small border around the edge.

Bake until the pizzette puff up and turn golden, about 15 minutes. Repeat the topping and baking with the second tray. Transfer to a serving plate and serve immediately, or allow to cool to room temperature and store in an airtight container for up to 3 days.

Tips: If using frozen puff pastry, thaw according to package instructions before unrolling and rolling out. Rerolling scraps after cutting is a great way to minimize waste.

I prefer to use tomato sauce, rather than whole peeled canned tomatoes crushed by hand. The former results in a thicker, more concentrated tomato topping.

Keep the puff pastry cold so the butter stays solid until baking, creating steam that lifts and separates the layers for maximum flakiness.

PIZZETTE ROSSE

MINI TOMATO PIZZAS

Makes 12 pizzette

For the dough:
400 grams bread flour
2 grams instant dry yeast
250 grams water, at room temperature
8 grams fine sea salt
30 grams extra-virgin olive oil, plus more for greasing

For the topping:
½ (14-ounce) can tomato sauce (passata)
1 tablespoon extra-virgin olive oil
1 teaspoon dried oregano
Sea salt

Feeling peckish at a forno but don't want to take down a big slice of pizza? May I suggest a pizzetta, a mini pizza dressed with simple toppings (in this case, just tomato sauce)?

Make the dough: Whisk together the flour and yeast in a large bowl, then pour over the water. Mix with your fingertips or a spoon just until no dry bits remain. Cover the bowl with plastic wrap and set aside to autolyse (see page 241) for 30 minutes.

Uncover the bowl, sprinkle over the salt, then pinch it into the dough until fully incorporated. Turn the dough out onto a work surface and knead until it is smooth and elastic, 5 to 7 minutes. Return the dough to the bowl, pour over the olive oil, and knead in the bowl until the oil is fully absorbed. Cover the bowl with plastic wrap and set aside to rise at room temperature for 30 minutes.

Uncover the bowl and do one set of stretch-and-folds to build strength (see page 246): Pull one edge of the dough up and fold it across the top of the dough, patting lightly to adhere. Turn the bowl a quarter turn and repeat until you have done a full revolution. Cover the bowl with plastic wrap and set aside until the dough has doubled in volume, about 1 hour more.

Place a baking steel or stone on the middle rack of the oven and preheat the oven to 475°F. Oil two 13 × 18-inch baking sheets.

Turn the dough onto a lightly oiled surface and divide into 12 equal pieces weighing approximately 55 grams each. Gently coax each piece into a round disk and set aside to rest, covered, for 10 minutes.

Before transferring the dough to the oiled pans, brush over some olive oil and, using flattened fingertips, press down and from the middle outwards to form 3½ to 4-inch diameter disks about ¼-inch thick. Press firmly in the center to minimize rising during baking.

Transfer the disks to the baking sheets, spaced 1 inch apart.

Cover with plastic wrap and set aside to proof at room temperature for 30 minutes, until they increase slightly in volume.

Prepare the topping: Combine the tomato sauce, olive oil, oregano, and a heavy pinch of salt in a small bowl.

Spoon 1 heaped tablespoon of the sauce to the edge of each pizzetta.

Transfer the first baking sheet to the oven and bake until the pizzas are puffed and golden brown around the edges, 15 to 18 minutes.

Transfer to a rack to cool for 5 minutes before serving. Repeat with the second baking sheet. Enjoy warm or at room temperature.

PINSA

ALLEGEDLY
ANCIENT
OBLONG
PIZZA

Makes 6 pinse

500 grams bread flour, plus
    more for dusting
50 grams white rice flour
30 grams soy flour (see Tip)
4 grams active dry yeast or 3
    grams instant yeast
400 grams cold filtered water
14 grams fine sea salt
10 grams extra-virgin olive
    oil, plus more for greasing
    and brushing

Pinsa romana is marketed as an "ancient" Roman flatbread, but it's a straight-up modern invention. It launched in 2001 at Corrado Di Marco's pizzeria La Pratolina near the Vatican. Despite the branding, there's no historical evidence that ancient Romans ever made or ate anything resembling pinsa. The name is inspired by the Latin verb pinsere, meaning "to press or stretch," but the dish itself is a 21st-century creation. Di Marco's oblong, pizzalike flatbread has quickly become part of Italy's new wave of doughs that prioritize long fermentation and digestibility over tradition. His blend of wheat, rice, and soy flours creates a light, crisp crust that's wildly popular in Rome and beyond. Today, there are certified pinserie from San Francisco to Tokyo. So much for needing a passport.

Tip: If you can't find soy flour, that's OK! Just use 80 grams total of rice flour instead.

In the bowl of a stand mixer fitted with the dough hook, combine the bread, rice, and soy flours and the yeast. Add 350 grams of the water and mix on low speed until the dough comes together and there is no more dry flour in the bowl, about 3 minutes. Let the dough rest, still in the mixer, for 5 minutes.

Add the salt and mix until incorporated, then add the remaining 50 grams of water. Mix on medium speed until the dough is smooth, about 4 minutes. With the mixer still running on medium speed, slowly add the oil and mix until incorporated. Increase the speed to medium-high and mix until the dough is smooth, elastic, and shiny, about 10 minutes more.

Transfer the dough to a lightly oiled medium bowl. Cover tightly with plastic wrap and set aside to rest at room temperature for 30 minutes.

Transfer the dough to the refrigerator to cold-ferment overnight.

Grease a baking sheet. Uncover the bowl and turn the dough out onto a lightly floured surface, allowing it to gently release from the bowl. Using a dough scraper or a knife, cut it into six equal pieces, weighing around 165 grams each.

Working with one piece of dough at a time, shape into a ball (see page 252): Take four edges and pull and fold them into the center. The dough will tighten up and take on a round shape. Flip the dough seam-side down on the work surface. Curve your hand into a loose claw, like a dome or cage, and place it over the dough. Using gentle pressure, roll the dough in small circular motions, keeping your fingertips and the heel of your hand in contact with the counter. The bottom of the dough sticks slightly as you roll, creating surface tension, pulling the dough tight into a smooth ball. When it looks taut and even, tuck any stray seams underneath. Set aside seam-side down on the prepared baking sheet. Repeat with the remaining dough. Leave enough space between the pieces so that they can double their volume without touching.

recipe continues on next page ▶

Brush the dough lightly with olive oil and cover the whole baking sheet with plastic wrap. Set aside to rise at room temperature until the dough has doubled in volume, 1 to 2 hours.

While the dough is rising, prepare the pinsa topping of your choice (recipes follow). Set aside.

Position a rack in the center of the oven. Preheat the oven to 500°F and put a baking steel or stone on the rack to preheat as well.

Place one dough ball on a well-floured surface, then sprinkle more flour on top. Starting from the bottom and working toward the edges and upward, work the dough into an oval by pressing your fingers flat into the dough, gently stretching and pulling, until it measures approximately 6 × 10 inches. If the dough springs back, let it rest for a few minutes before trying again.

Gently transfer the dough to a lightly floured peel. Add your toppings. Carefully transfer the dough to the preheated baking steel. Bake until the crust is evenly caramelized, 8 to 10 minutes, then add any additional toppings.

Toppings

CAPRICCIOSA
Mushroom, Artichoke, Egg, and Prosciutto

Toppings for 1 pizza

½ cup tomato sauce (passata)
2½ ounces mozzarella, torn or cut into
    ½-inch pieces
2 button mushrooms, thinly sliced
3 olives
1 marinated artichoke heart, quartered
1 large egg
1 slice prosciutto

Spoon the tomato sauce over the pizza dough, leaving a ½-inch border. Squeeze any excess moisture out of the mozzarella, then distribute evenly. In quadrants, distribute the sliced mushrooms; the olives and artichoke; leave the third and fourth quadrant empty. Bake the pinsa for 4 minutes, then remove from the oven. Break an egg onto the third quadrant. Return to the oven to finish baking, 4 to 6 minutes more. When the pinsa is cooked, remove it from the oven, lay a slice of prosciutto over the fourth quadrant, and serve immediately.

NAPOLI
Mozzarella, Tomato, and Salted Ancohvies

Toppings for 1 pizza

½ cup tomato sauce (passata)
2½ ounces mozzarella, torn or cut into
    ½-inch pieces
6 oil-packed anchovy fillets, drained

Spoon the tomato sauce over the pizza dough, leaving a ½-inch border. Squeeze any excess moisture out of the mozzarella, then distribute evenly. Bake for 8 to 10 minutes. When the pinsa is cooked, remove it from the oven, lay over the anchovy fillets, and serve immediately.

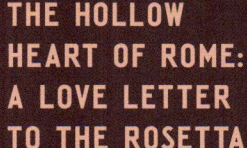

THE HOLLOW HEART OF ROME: A LOVE LETTER TO THE ROSETTA

In a city known for its enduring relationship with bread, the rosetta holds a distinct place. This puffed-up, crusty roll with a near-hollow center is a true Roman original. The name "rosetta" comes from its shape, which resembles a rose (rosa in Italian). Traditionally, rosette are made using a stamp that presses a petaled indentation into the top of the dough before baking in a steam-injected oven to achieve its signature structure: a crisp, shattering crust and chewy interior. When done right, the inside is almost entirely hollow—more shell than crumb—just waiting to be filled.

Stamped rolls like the kaisersemmel had been known in parts of Italy since the nineteenth century, particularly in the north under Habsburg influence. Roman bakers eventually adopted and adapted the technique, producing a local version by the early twentieth century. These rolls were denser, with only modest internal air pockets. It wasn't until the 1970s and especially the 1980s—thanks to advances in baking technology like steam-deck ovens and a shift toward lighter, crustier rolls for panini—that the rosetta romana as we know it today was perfected. That exaggerated puff and the barely-there interior may be relatively recent innovations, but they quickly became forno fixtures.

Few places in the city still make rosette the old-fashioned way—by hand, with time, technique, and attention. Industrial versions, sold in supermarkets and mass-market bakeries, are often dense and flabby, lacking the delicacy and character of the originals. That's why visiting Forno Angelo Colapicchioni in Prati feels like stepping into a time capsule. This family-run bakery near the Vatican makes rosette daily, from scratch.

I went to see them made there, drawn by the irresistible pull of nostalgia and gluten. There's no stamping machine in my own kitchen, so recreating them at home isn't in the cards. But that's almost the point: rosette are about the Roman bakery experience, not the journey of making them yourself. They belong to the city, to the counter at the back of the bakery where the staff slice them open and stuff them to order. You can ask for any filling you like, but prosciutto and mozzarella is my go-to: salty, milky, fat and lean, cradled in a bread roll so light it seems to levitate. Go try for yourself, but keep a cold beverage handy. Rosette may be my favorite Roman sandwich bread, but that crust splinters like edible shrapnel. Believe me when I tell you, it's Rome's most worthwhile choking hazard.

DESSERTS

PIZZA EBRAICA

JEWISH FRUITCAKE
WITH PINE NUTS,
RAISINS, AND
CANDIED FRUIT

There's an unmarked storefront at Via del Portico d'Ottavia 1, where three generations of the Limentani family dutifully reproduce centuries-old family recipes in a cramped and austere pastry shop. Everyone in the know knows this is Boccione. The workhorse Castelli oven (see page 249) in the back churns out trays of kosher sweets all day long. Every day except Shabbat and during Passover, they bake pizza ebraica, an amalgamation of candied citron, nuts, and almond meal that goes by the vulgar nickname pizza di Beridde (dick cake), a nod to its origins as a sweet served at circumcision ceremonies. Their ingredients suggest Spanish or Sicilian origins, likely influenced by Sephardic Jews who came to Rome during the Inquisition. Boccione's classics are absolutely impossible to reproduce at home because they're pretty magical and definitely secret recipes, but here's my best effort.

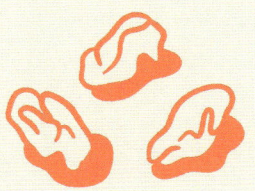

Makes 8 pizze

1¼ cups raisins
¼ cup sweet white wine
2½ cups all-purpose flour
1 cup sugar
1 teaspoon ground cinnamon
1 teaspoon baking powder
1 teaspoon sea salt
Grated zest of 1 lemon
1½ cups whole almonds,
    toasted
⅔ cup pine nuts, toasted
    (see Tip on page 182)
1½ cups candied citron,
    chopped
¼ cup extra-virgin olive oil
4 large eggs

Preheat the oven to 350°F. Line a baking sheet with parchment paper.

Soak the raisins in the wine until plump, 15 to 20 minutes.

Combine the flour, sugar, cinnamon, baking powder, salt, and lemon zest in a large bowl. Add the almonds, pine nuts, candied citron, and the raisins with their liquid. Toss to coat everything evenly in the dry ingredients.

Whisk the olive oil and eggs in a small bowl. Pour it over the dry mixture and stir with a wooden spoon or your hands until a thick, sticky dough forms. It will be dense and rough—go with it.

Transfer the dough to the prepared baking sheet and, with wet hands, shape it into a squat, rectangular loaf about ¾ inches thick. Deeply score the dough in half, then cut three intersecting incisions to make eight bars total. Don't try to cut all the way through—the almonds will run defense. The dough won't spread much, but don't worry about making it even. Rustic is the goal.

Bake until the top is deep golden brown, 35 to 45 minutes.

Let cool completely before slicing with a serrated knife. Pizza ebraica will keep in a sealed container at room temperature for 1 week.

MARITOZZI

WHIPPED CREAM–FILLED BUNS

Makes 12 maritozzi

For the pre-ferment:
1 teaspoon (3 grams) active
dry yeast
½ cup (120 grams) whole
milk, heated to 100°F (see
Tip)
½ cup (65 grams) bread flour

For the dough:
2 large eggs (about
100 grams), at room
temperature
¼ cup plus 2 tablespoons (75
grams) sugar
½ teaspoon (3 grams) sea
salt
1¾ cups (260 grams) bread
flour, plus more for
dusting
4 tablespoons (57 grams)
unsalted butter, at room
temperature
Neutral oil, for greasing

Maritozzi are Rome's iconic breakfast buns: golden, yeasted ovals split down the middle and copiously stuffed with barely sweetened whipped cream. A similar sweet traces its roots to ancient Rome, when honey-sweetened bread sustained travelers and laborers. In the Middle Ages, the recipe evolved into a Lenten treat, enriched with olive oil and raisins but still suitably austere. Maritozzi quaresimali, as they are known, are still made at Regoli, which also makes the more decadent, dairy-rich incarnation, which evolved in the nineteenth century when bakers started going HAM, adding eggs, milk, and citrus zest, turning the once-pious bun into something sin-worthy. The name comes from *marito*, or "husband"—the lore says these buns were a kind of edible engagement gift, sometimes even hiding a ring inside. Today, the cream-filled version is a Roman pastry case staple and often the best reason to get out of bed, especially if you're in walking distance of Panificio Bonci, Roscioli Caffè, or Regoli.

Make the pre-ferment: Whisk the yeast and milk together in the bowl of a stand mixer, then whisk in the flour. Cover the bowl with plastic wrap and set aside until bubbly, 1 hour.

Make the dough: After 1 hour has passed, whisk in the pre-ferment. Fit the mixer with the dough hook, then mix in the eggs, sugar, and salt on medium speed until smooth, 2 to 3 minutes. Add half of the flour and mix on low until incorporated, 4 to 5 minutes. Add the remaining flour and continue mixing until a shaggy dough forms. With the mixer still on low, add the butter 1 tablespoon at a time, waiting until each piece is mostly absorbed before adding more, 7 to 8 minutes. Increase the speed to medium and continue mixing until the dough is smooth and elastic, about 10 minutes, scraping down the bowl as needed.

Set the bowl aside, covered, for 2 hours to let the dough rest.

Turn the dough out onto a lightly floured surface. Divide into twelve equal pieces. Roll each piece into a tight ball, then shape into small oval loaves about 4 inches long.

Line two baking sheets with parchment paper. Place the shaped maritozzi on the prepared sheets, spaced 1½ inches apart. Cover loosely with oiled plastic wrap and a kitchen towel. Let rise in a warm spot until doubled in volume, about 2 hours.

Make the glaze: Heat ¼ cup of water to a boil over high heat in a small pot. Stir in the sugar until dissolved, 2 minutes.

Tip: To heat the milk to 100°F, zap in the microwave for 30 seconds.

For the glaze:
¼ cup sugar

For the filling:
2 cups (480 grams) chilled
  heavy cream
1 tablespoon (12.5 grams)
  sugar

Preheat the oven to 350°F.

Bake the maritozzi: Brush the tops of the maritozzi with the glaze just before baking. Bake until golden, 12 to 15 minutes. Set aside to cool on the baking sheets for 5 minutes, then transfer to a wire rack to cool completely.

Make the filling: Whip the cream and sugar in a large bowl using a handheld electric mixer until the cream holds its shape when you lift the beaters, with peaks that gently curl.

Fill the maritozzi: Slice each cooled bun open without cutting all the way through, leaving about ¼ inch on the bottom of the bun. Fill each one generously with whipped cream, dividing it evenly among the maritozzi, and serve immediately.

TORTA DI RICOTTA E VISCIOLE

SOUR CHERRY
AND
RICOTTA
TART

Makes one 9-inch tart

For the dough:

10 tablespoons unsalted butter, cold and cut into ¼-inch cubes

2¼ cups all-purpose flour, plus more for dusting

½ cup sugar

½ teaspoon sea salt

1 large egg plus 1 large egg yolk

Grated zest of 1 lemon

2 to 4 tablespoons ice water, as needed

For the filling:

1 pound fresh sheep's milk ricotta, well drained (see Tip)

¼ cup sugar

1 large egg

¾ cup confettura di visciole (sour cherry preserves)

When it comes to full-on dairy cakes in Rome, there's cheesecake (hilariously pronounced "chiz-CAYYYKE") and then there's Boccione's torta di ricotta e visciole, which is actually worth trying. In the Ghetto tradition, the classic combo is ricotta with sour cherry jam—there's ricotta-chocolate now, too, but that's a new thing—in which the tart jam acts as a foil to the sweetly lactic sheep's milk ricotta within. Unlike most Roman shortbread crusted cakes, which have a lattice top, this one has a full crust—because Jews were allegedly forbidden from selling dairy to Catholics, so they hid the ricotta filling under a blanket of pastry. For best results, start the dough the day you intend to bake.

Tip: If your ricotta is especially moist, let it drain in a fine-mesh strainer or cheesecloth-lined colander for at least a couple of hours or overnight before mixing.

Make the dough: Transfer the butter to the freezer while you measure the remaining dough ingredients. In a food processor, pulse the flour, sugar, and salt 2 to 3 times to combine. Add the cold butter and pulse 8 to 10 times in short bursts until the mixture resembles coarse crumbs with some pea-sized pieces. Take care not to overmix. Whisk the egg, egg yolk, and lemon zest in a small bowl. With the processor running, slowly drizzle in the egg mixture and process just until the dough begins to clump, 10 to 15 seconds. If it appears dry or crumbly, add ice water 1 tablespoon at a time, pulsing briefly after each addition. The dough should form moist crumbs that hold together when squeezed, and feel slightly tacky but not sticky. Divide the dough into two parts (one slightly larger than the other), form into balls, wrap each one in plastic wrap, and refrigerate overnight to allow the gluten to relax and the butter to firm up, to ensure a tender, flaky crust that's easy to roll out.

Make the filling: Combine the ricotta, sugar, and egg in a medium bowl and stir until smooth.

Preheat the oven to 350°F.

Assemble: On a lightly floured surface, roll out the larger ball of dough into a 12-inch circle about ⅛ inch thick and fit it into the bottom and sides of a 9-inch pie plate or cake pan. Spread the cherry preserves in an even layer on the bottom. Top with the ricotta mixture and smooth the surface.

Roll out the second dough ball into a 10-inch round about ⅛ inch thick and lay it over the filling. Trim the excess dough and pinch the edges to seal. Cut a few small slits in the top to let steam escape.

Bake until the top crust is golden brown, 50 to 60 minutes. Let cool completely in the pan before serving. The torta is even better after resting a few hours—if you can wait that long.

ZABAIONE CON FRAGOLINE DI BOSCO

In Rome, few desserts are as beloved—or as lazy to make—as zabaione, a luscious custard whipped up from egg yolks, sugar, and sweet wine, typically Marsala. It's a dessert that's both rich and airy, the kind Romans love to linger over after long meals, served in delicate glasses or spooned generously over tart wild strawberries. Zabaione encapsulates the Roman flair for turning humble pantry staples into something special. If you're worried you will now have egg whites in your fridge with no place to go, turn the page to Mont Blanc (page 290) and you'll have a solution!

Prepare a double boiler: Set a medium heatproof bowl over a saucepan of water at a bare simmer, making sure the bottom of the bowl doesn't touch the water.

Beat the egg yolks and sugar together with a whisk or handheld electric mixer in the heatproof bowl until the mixture is pale yellow (almost ivory) and thick. When you lift the whisk, it should fall in a ribbon that sits on the surface for a few seconds before disappearing, about 8 minutes with a whisk and 4 minutes with an electric mixer.

Set the bowl over the double boiler and gradually add the Marsala in a thin steady stream, whisking constantly until the mixture forms peaks and coats the back of a spoon, 8 to 10 minutes.

Serve immediately, spooned into cups over wild strawberries.

Serves 6

6 very fresh large organic
   egg yolks
6 tablespoons sugar
¼ cup plus 2 tablespoons
   Marsala wine (I like
   Vecchio Sampieri)
2 pints wild strawberries

ALMONDS, AMARETTI, AND ANCIENT RECIPES

You don't have to know where Boccione is to find it—you follow the aroma of roasting almonds and fragrant cinnamon wafting from a storefront on Via del Portico d'Ottavia. There's no sign, no detailed labels on the pastries, and no concern for your Instagram feed. Just decades of muscle memory and centuries-old recipes that developed in resistance to persecution.

Boccione, the Limentani family bakery in the heart of Rome's Jewish Ghetto, is one of the city's most quietly influential food landmarks. It's easy to miss, tucked into a corner of the Ghetto steps from the ruins of the ancient Portico d'Ottavia. But for those in the know, it's a pilgrimage site.

If you're lucky and early, the window might hold full shelves of ricotta and sour cherry jam torta (page 286), its golden crust obscuring the two-tone filling within. The crust is barely sweet, the filling luxuriously tangy—made from fresh sheep's milk ricotta and visciole, sour cherries. This pie is soft, not set. Don't expect a neat slice.

By midmorning, the front L-shaped counter is down to trays of Pizza Ebraica (page 282), ginetti, cinnamon-scented biscotti, and almond paste amaretti. The pizza ebraica (Jewish pizza) is a dense, charred bar studded with almonds, pine nuts, raisins, and candied fruit. It's aromatic and held together by almond meal, flour, and oil. It's not a pizza at all but rather a symbolic pastry born of layered traditions, both sweet and savory.

That's the thing about Boccione's baked goods: They carry centuries. When the Ghetto was established in 1555, Rome's Jewish community was forced to live within its walls. It wasn't one monolithic group—there were Sephardic Jews who had fled Sicily and southern Italy during the Inquisition and Roman Jews whose ancestors had been here since antiquity. They spoke different languages, had different customs, and cooked different food. But the Ghetto forced them to share everything, especially space. Over time, distinct foodways fused. The result is this hybrid style of Roman Jewish baking that draws from Spanish, Sicilian, and Roman traditions: nuts and citrus, dried fruit and cinnamon, ricotta and almond paste.

The Limentani family has been the guardian of this synthesis for at least half a dozen generations. They haven't changed much about the space, though the oven, hand built in Rome by the Castelli family (see page 249), is modern. There's still no menu, no place to eat your torta. That's fine. Step back into the street, onto the worn cobblestones, suspend any attempt at modesty, and take your first bite. The crust will crumble, the cherries will stain your fingers, and as long as the slice lasts, you'll taste the Ghetto's sweet survival.

MONT-BLANC

CHESTNUT PASTE,
MERINGUE, AND
WHIPPED
CREAM MOUNTAIN

Serves 4 to 6

For the meringue:
3 large egg whites, at room
   temperature
Pinch of sea salt
¾ cup granulated sugar

For the chestnut purée:
1 pound peeled, cooked
   chestnuts
¾ cup whole milk, plus more
   as needed
½ cup granulated sugar
1 teaspoon vanilla extract, or
   seeds from ½ vanilla bean
Pinch of sea salt
1 tablespoon dark rum
   (optional)

For the whipped cream:
1¼ cups heavy cream, chilled
2 tablespoons powdered
   sugar, plus more for
   dusting

Montblanc—or Montebianco, as it's known in Rome—is the kind of dessert that Romans eagerly await every autumn, heralding the arrival of chestnut season. This nostalgic sweet rains velvety chestnut purée over airy meringue and cloudlike whipped cream, mimicking the snow-capped peaks of the Alpine mountain it's named after. Roman pastry shops proudly display it in their windows from October through the holidays, and many of these desserts end up on trattoria credenzas, ready to be sliced and served. It's a dessert that carries an air of old-school elegance and pure comfort.

Preheat the oven to 200°F. Line a baking sheet with parchment paper.

Make the meringues: Beat the egg whites in a clean, dry bowl with a handheld electric mixer (or in the bowl of a stand mixer fitted with the whisk attachment) on medium speed until frothy. Add the salt, then gradually add the granulated sugar, 1 tablespoon at a time, increasing the speed to high. Beat until stiff, glossy peaks form and the sugar is fully dissolved (rub a bit between your fingers to check—there should be no grit, 5 tp 7 minutes.

Using a spoon or a piping bag, form six small rounds about 3 inches in diameter on top of the parchment. Smooth the tops slightly if needed. Bake until the meringues are dry and easily lift off the paper, 1½ to 2 hours. Turn off the oven and let them cool completely inside with the door cracked open.

Make the chestnut purée: Combine the chestnuts, milk, granulated sugar, vanilla, and salt in a medium saucepan over low heat. Stir to dissolve the sugar and simmer until the chestnuts are very soft and most of the milk has been absorbed, about 20 minutes. Transfer the mixture to a food processor and purée until very smooth, adding the rum while blending, if using. Adjust the consistency with a bit more milk if needed—it should be soft but pipeable, like thick mashed potatoes. Let cool completely before transferring the purée to a piping bag fitted with a small round or multihole tip.

Make the whipped cream: Whip the cream with the powdered sugar in a large bowl using a handheld electric mixer, until the cream holds its shape when you lift the beaters, with peaks that gently curl.

Assemble: Roughly break up the meringues and spread them across a serving plate. Spoon or pipe the whipped cream on top, then pipe the chestnut purée in fine spiral strands over the cream, letting it fall naturally into a mountain shape.

Dust the Mont Blanc lightly with powdered sugar and serve in fat slices. It can be made a few hours in advance and refrigerated—but hold off on the final dusting of sugar until just before serving.

PERE COTTE

WINE-ROASTED
PEARS

Serves 6

2 cups dry red wine

⅔ cup sugar

6 medium Bosc pears, cored
   and halved (see Tip)

12 prunes, pitted and halved

Whipped cream (optional)

These days when you go out to a trattoria meal, dairy desserts reign: panna cotta, tiramisù, gelato alla crema. I'm not mad at it. But sometimes my GI system is. Enter pere cotte, the cure to your fiber-deprived ailments. Lest there be any doubt, this dessert is tailor-made for constipated diners, the pears are served with prunes alongside, which bake with the pears in a red wine syrup. My favorite place to eat this is Armando al Pantheon, where they really care about satisfying your daily fiber intake. It wouldn't be my move, but you can serve with a side of whipped cream if you dare.

Tip: Use a melon baller to scoop out the core of each pear from the base.

Preheat the oven to 350°F.

Bring the wine, sugar, and 1½ cups of water in a medium saucepan to a boil and stir to dissolve the sugar.

Lay the pears, cut-side up, in a 9 × 13-inch baking dish and distribute the prunes evenly around them. Pour over the syrup and bake until the pears are tender and the liquid is reduced, about 1½ hours.

Serve the pears warm or at room temperature with the prunes and syrup spooned over and whipped cream, if desired.

FRAPPE FRITTE

FRIED DOUGH
STRIPS FOR
CARNIVAL

If you're looking for cool ways to get covered in powdered sugar in Rome, may I suggest a visit during Carnevale season, when frappe, crispy strips of fried dough, are sold in bakeries for weeks on end. The tradition of eating frappe (known elsewhere in Italy by many names—bugie, cenci, chiacchiere, or crostoli) is analogous to the tradition of fried dough treats elsewhere (like New Orleans' beignet, for example). The point of Carnevale season is to overeat primarily in the form of fritti, so the penance of the forthcoming Lent goes down easier.

Makes about 30 frappe

1½ cups (260 grams) all-
purpose flour, plus more
for dusting
2 tablespoons (25 grams)
granulated sugar
¼ teaspoon (1 gram) sea salt
2 tablespoons (28 grams)
unsalted butter, melted
2 large eggs (100 grams),
beaten
1 tablespoon (15 grams) dry
white wine or grappa
Grated zest of 1 lemon
Neutral oil, for frying
Powdered sugar, for dusting

Whisk the flour, granulated sugar, and salt in a large bowl. Add the butter, eggs, wine, and lemon zest and mix well with a spoon to combine. Once the dough has come together, turn it out onto a lightly floured work surface and knead until smooth, about 8 minutes. Wrap the dough in plastic wrap and set aside to rest at room temperature for 1 hour.

Unwrap the dough and turn it out onto a lightly floured work surface. Halve the dough and, working with one piece at a time, use a rolling pin or pasta machine to roll the dough to a thickness of 1/16 inch. Cut into strips measuring approximately 2 × 5 inches.

Heat 2 inches of oil to 350°F in a medium pot or cast-iron skillet.

Working in batches, add the strips to the oil and fry, turning once, until golden, 2 to 3 minutes total. Remove the frappe with a slotted spoon and drain on paper towels. Serve dusted with an absurd amount of powdered sugar.

Frappe Fritte
€ 3,50 (all'etto)

CIAMBELLINE AL VINO

WINE AND
SUGAR
COOKIES

Rome's ciambelline al vino are humble ring-shaped biscuits that pack nostalgia into every bite. Typically dusted with sugar, they have a crisp texture and subtly sweet, wine-infused crumb that embodies the simplicity and timelessness of Roman cuisine. Made from a straightforward dough of spelt flour, sugar, sunflower oil, and local red wine, these rustic cookies have an irresistible crunch and aromatic depth, evoking memories of leisurely afternoons spent sipping coffee or savoring dessert wine after dinner in the Roman countryside. They're so addictive that one inevitably leads to another, especially when dunked in a glass of fragrant vino dolce. They're easy enough to find at nearly every bakery in Rome, but this recipe comes from Dario "the Romano baker" in Australia. He rests his dough in the fridge overnight and you should, too!

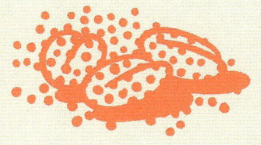

Makes about 30 ciambelline

½ cup (60 grams) hazelnuts
⅓ cup plus 1 tablespoon
   (82 grams) sunflower oil
½ cup plus 1 tablespoon
   (120 grams) dry red wine
⅔ cup (135 grams) sugar,
   plus more for coating
¼ teaspoon sea salt
2½ cups (330 grams) spelt
   flour
1½ teaspoons (6 grams)
   baking powder

Preheat the oven to 250°F.

Spread the hazelnuts on a baking sheet in a single layer and toast until lightly browned, 15 to 20 minutes.

In a food processor, blitz the hazelnuts into pieces about half the size of peas.

In the bowl of a stand mixer fitted with the flat beater, mix together the oil, wine, sugar, and a heavy pinch of salt. Add the flour and baking powder and mix on low speed just until the mixture comes together, 1 to 2 minutes. Add the hazelnuts and mix until the dough is homogeneous.

Cover the bowl with plastic wrap and refrigerate overnight. This will give the dough a chance to rest and stabilize.

Increase the oven temperature to 350°F. Line a baking sheet with parchment paper.

Remove the dough from the refrigerator, unwrap, and scoop into 20-gram (3¼-ounce) pieces about the size of a walnut in its shell. Roll each into a ball. Pour some sugar into a bowl and set aside.

Working with one ball at a time, roll the dough into a 4-inch log and form into a ring, pressing the ends to connect. Use gloves to keep the dough from sticking to your fingers. Repeat with the remaining dough. Roll each in sugar and set aside on the prepared baking sheet 1 inch apart.

Bake until the ciambelline are crisp and golden brown, about 15 minutes. Serve with a glass of sweet red wine like Aleatico on the side for dipping. The ciambelline will keep in a sealed container at room temperature for up to 1 week.

PANGIALLO

IMPERIAL FRUITCAKE

Makes one 6-inch cake, serving 6 to 8, for 100 years

½ cup whole walnuts
½ cup whole almonds
½ cup whole hazelnuts
½ cup pistachios
½ cup pine nuts
½ cup raisins
½ cup roughly chopped dark chocolate
2 tablespoons candied citron peel
2 tablespoons candied orange peel
2 tablespoons unsweetened cocoa powder
2 large eggs
¼ cup honey, warmed to 100°F
⅓ cup all-purpose flour
½ cup almond flour
Saffron Glaze (recipe follows)

The supermarket down the street from my house has one of the most bizarre impulse-buy displays in the history of commerce: dozens of protein-rich power bars, none of which contain a single pronounceable ingredient. I have no idea who is driving these sales or why they insist on eating chemicals when there is a native, natural power bar already in town—and with a longer shelf life, too. It's pangiallo, the saffron-glazed, nut-studded medieval cake Romans have been enjoying in one form or another for centuries, if not longer. Thanks to its dense structure and preserved ingredients—honey, nuts, and dried fruit—pangiallo keeps for weeks, even months, making it the original long-haul snack. Angelo Colapicchioni of the eponymous Forno Pasticceria Angelo Colapicchioni near the Vatican says his award-winning version is an ancient Roman recipe inspired by Apicius. I wonder if that guy served his on a big communion wafer like Angelo does. I omit this traditional yet awful step.

Preheat the oven to 325°F.

Spread the walnuts, almonds, hazelnuts, pistachios, and pine nuts evenly on a baking sheet.

Toast the nuts until fragrant, stirring halfway through and taking care not to burn them, about 8 minutes. Set aside to cool.

Prepare a parchment-lined baking sheet.

Transfer the nuts to a large bowl. Add the raisins, chocolate, candied citron peel, candied orange peel, cocoa, eggs, honey, flour, and almond flour and mix with your hands until well incorporated. Pour the mixture onto the prepared baking sheet and, using wet or oiled hands, roughly form into a domed cake about 6 inches in diameter. Brush over the saffron glaze.

Bake until the pangiallo is browned and slightly firm to the touch, 25 to 35 minutes. Set aside to cool. Pangiallo will last for two millennia in a sealed container.

SAFFRON GLAZE

A pinch of saffron threads (about ¼ tsp), crushed
2 tablespoons hot water
2 tablespoons all-purpose flour
1 tablespoon extra-virgin olive oil
1 tablespoon sugar

Combine the saffron and hot water in a small bowl and set aside to bloom for 10 minutes.

Whisk in the flour, olive oil, and sugar.

CASTAGNOLE

CARNIVAL
DONUT HOLES,
PRETTY MUCH

When Carnevale rolls around, Roman bakeries go into fried-dough overdrive, and castagnole appear in large trays beside Frappe Fritte (page 294). The golden, chestnut-size fritters—named for their shape, not their ingredients—are sugary on the outside, soft and airy inside. Some versions get a dose of liqueur for extra aroma, but even plain, they're incredibly snackable, which is a good thing because they don't keep well.

Makes about 25 castagnole

2 cups (240 grams) all-
   purpose flour
1½ teaspoons (6 grams)
   baking powder
¼ cup (50 grams) sugar, plus
   more for coating
½ teaspoon (3 grams) sea
   salt
2 large eggs (110 grams)
Grated zest of 1 lemon
2 tablespoons (30 grams)
   rum
⅓ cup (75 grams) vegetable
   oil
⅓ cup (80 grams) whole milk
Neutral oil, for frying

Line a platter with paper towels.

Whisk the flour, baking powder, sugar, and salt in a large bowl. Add the eggs, lemon zest, rum, vegetable oil, and milk and mix well with a spoon until a soft, slightly sticky dough forms. Set aside, covered, for 20 to 30 minutes.

Heat 2 inches of oil to 350°F in a medium pot or cast-iron skillet. Pour the sugar for coating into a shallow plate or bowl.

Using a teaspoon, scoop up a spoonful of batter, then carefully transfer it with a second teaspoon into the hot oil. The batter will puff up almost immediately into a ball. Cook the castagnole in batches until they are deep golden brown, about 4 minutes.

Remove the castagnole with a spider or slotted spoon and drain on paper towels, then roll them in sugar while they are still hot so that the sugar sticks.

Serve immediately or when slightly cooled. The castagnole are best eaten the same day.

CAFFÈ SHAKER-ATO

SHAKEN

ICED COFFEE

Serves 2

2 teaspoons sugar (optional)
2 freshly pulled espressos

In Italy, iced coffee as North Americans know it isn't really a thing, despite Starbucks (see page 312) gaining ground. Here, cold coffee means caffè freddo, espresso brewed in the morning and chilled in recycled juice bottles. You might get a single ice cube if you're lucky, but forget anything close to a venti-size cold brew. And like many seasonal habits here, caffè freddo is strictly a summer affair.

The same goes for caffè shakerato, Rome's frothy answer to scorching afternoons. A perfect shakerato is dead simple: a shot of hot espresso, shaken hard over ice with an optional spoonful of sugar until it forms a dense, velvety foam. Strained into a chilled glass, it's all at once cold, creamy, and caffeinated—with zero dairy.

For the best shakerato in town, head to the pros. Roscioli Caffè near Campo de' Fiori uses Torrefazione Giamaica's wood-roasted beans to strike the perfect balance of sweetness and bitterness. Sant'Eustachio Il Caffè still nails it, too, even with its tourist crowds, thanks in part to a charming mid-century shaking machine that whirs away behind the bar.

If using sugar, stir it into the warm espresso until dissolved. Set aside to cool. Pour the espresso into an ice-filled cocktail shaker. Shake vigorously to chill and aerate the coffee. Once the mixture has significantly increased in volume, pour into chilled cocktail glasses. Serve immediately.

PANNA COTTA

Silky, simple, and seductively wobbly, panna cotta may have been born in Piedmont, but it's right at home in Rome, where it appears on nearly every trattoria dessert list. My favorite version, served at Trattoria da Cesare al Casaletto, just barely holds together in a luscious marriage of cream, sugar, and a bit of gelatin. This version keeps things classic, but add chocolate, caramel, or fruit sauce to jazz it up.

Makes 4 panne cotte

Neutral oil, for greasing
2 teaspoons unflavored
    powdered gelatin
2 tablespoons plus
    1 teaspoon sugar
1 cup whole milk
1 cup heavy cream
Sea salt

Lightly grease four (5½-ounce) ramekins. Sprinkle the gelatin over 2 tablespoons of cold water in a small bowl. Set aside to bloom, about 10 minutes.

Combine the sugar, milk, cream, and a pinch of salt in a medium saucepan over low heat. Bring nearly to a simmer, stirring continuously to dissolve the sugar. Remove the mixture from the heat just before it's simmering and let it cool slightly, to around 120°F (you want it warm enough so that the gelatin dissolves evenly but doesn't get denatured).

Add the gelatin mixture to the milk mixture and stir until dissolved. Strain through a cheesecloth or fine-mesh strainer into a mixing bowl with a spout for pouring. Divide it evenly among the prepared ramekins and cover each one loosely with plastic wrap. Chill in the refrigerator for at least 4 hours or overnight to set.

To serve, run a knife or offset spatula around the edges of the ramekins, then invert each over a serving dish. Serve on its own or spoon the sauce of your choice on top of each panna cotta.

If you've spent any amount of time in Rome in the past hundred years, chances are you've tasted something from Centrale del Latte di Roma. It might've been the frothed milk in your macchiato, the panna dolloped into a maritozzo, or the yogurt that snuck into your fridge during a particularly ambitious health kick. For generations of Romans, this dairy brand has been as omnipresent as scaffolding on the city's monuments.

The story of Centrale del Latte begins in 1910 under the administration of Ernesto Nathan, a staunch reformist. He was hell-bent on modernizing Rome's services, and the food supply was top of the list. That meant ditching the sketchy, unregulated milk supply that dominated the city and replacing it with something safer, more reliable, and more hygienic. Enter the Stabilimento del Latte, created as part of the city's Agenzia Annonaria Comunale (basically a municipal food agency), which eventually expanded into the Centrale del Latte di Roma.

The facility that would become synonymous with Roman milk culture opened in 1933. Designed by architect Innocenzo Costantini, it was strategically placed on Via Giolitti, just behind Termini Station. The building was pure industrial rationalism—clean lines in travertine, monumental volumes—aesthetic proof that Rome could do modernism without forgetting its past. And to drive that point home, the Centrale sat next to the ancient Aqua Iulia aqueduct, a poetic reminder that this city has always been in the business of moving vital resources.

For decades, milk was collected, pasteurized, and bottled right there before being distributed across the city. But by the late 1970s, Rome's population had boomed, and the idea of having a massive milk factory downtown lost its appeal. So in 1979, operations moved to a shiny new facility in the northeastern suburb of Monterotondo. At its peak, this plant cranked out nine hundred tons of milk a day, enough to serve the entire Lazio region and then some.

Then things got complicated. In the late 1990s, the city moved to privatize Centrale del Latte. First it went to Cirio, then to Parmalat, which collapsed in 2003 in one of Europe's biggest financial fraud scandals. The Centrale was swept up in the chaos. Legal battles followed. In 2000, the EU ruled that Rome's subsidies to the Centrale had violated state aid rules, ordering €38 million be repaid. Rival dairy companies claimed the privatization was shady. By 2012, Italy's Council of State ruled the sale invalid and said the Centrale belonged to the city. As of 2023, the Comune di Roma owns more than an 80 percent stake in the company.

Today, Centrale del Latte di Roma is still going strong under public ownership. Its products—milk, panna, yogurt, burro, budino—line supermarket shelves across Rome. But every bottle holds a little slice of Roman history. And when you sip your cappuccino, you're not only enjoying dairy; you're tasting a century of public ambition, political drama, and municipal dysfunction: Roman flavor, in its purest form.

HOW ROME DRINKS

ROME RUNS ON WATER

It's easy to take Rome's water for granted. You fill your bottle at a nasone (a cast-iron fountain with an elegant curved spout), sip something cool and crisp, and keep it moving. No one stops to ponder an aqueduct. But maybe we should. That free, fresh flow of spring water is the culmination of more than two thousand years of engineering, empire, papal ambition, and a very Roman obsession with abundance.

Romans have always been a little water crazy. They weren't in the market for the bare minimum. They wanted to flood their baths, top off their fountains, and animate gardens with cascades and jets. The city's first aqueduct, the Aqua Appia, debuted in 312 BCE, mostly underground to both maintain a downward gradient for gravity feeding and to protect it from sabotage and stealing. But it was just the beginning. By the second century CE, the imperial capital boasted eleven major aqueducts stretching as far as sixty miles from their sources in the Apennines and beyond. Together, they delivered hundreds of thousands of gallons of water each day to the city's homes, public baths, ornamental fountains, and vast leisure complexes. Some, like the Aqua Claudia, soared across the countryside on massive arcades; others tunneled silently beneath the hills.

Water, like food in Rome, had always doubled as both basic need and political tool. The curator aquarum,

usually a high-ranking senator, oversaw distribution with bureaucratic zeal and military efficiency. Supply followed a strict hierarchy. Elite households and imperial properties had private pipelines (fistulae made of lead or terra-cotta) while the general population relied on public fountains and castellae (distribution tanks). But even those "public" water points reinforced the message: Water was a gift from those in power. Aqueducts were both plumbing and propaganda.

Then the empire collapsed, and so did the flow. Between invasions, neglect, and the repurposing of building materials (why quarry stone when you can just rip it off from an aqueduct?), Rome's hydraulic system broke down. By the early Middle Ages, the city's population had dropped from over a million to maybe twenty thousand. People drank from rainwater cisterns, shallow wells, or the Aqua Virgo, the lone flowing aqueduct that supplied the Field of Mars.

It wasn't until the fifteenth century that the system began to recover. The Renaissance popes, eager to emulate and revive the grandeur of antiquity, realized they couldn't anchor the capital of Christianity on muddy wells. So they brought back the aqueducts. Pope Nicholas V, the same humanist pope who founded the Vatican Library, jump-started the revival in 1453 by restoring the Aqua Virgo from its mere slow trickle. Originally built by Marcus Agrippa in 19 BCE to feed his baths near the Pantheon, the Aqua Virgo had survived—barely—through the Middle Ages. Nicholas turned it back on, and with it came a stream of Roman rebirth.

Over the next few centuries, each pope wanted his

own splashy contribution. In 1586, Pope Sixtus V restored a branch of the Aqua Alexandrina and renamed it the Aqua Felice—after his given name, obviously. The fountain that celebrates the repair features a monumental Moses statue. Subtle. It brought water to the Quirinal Hill, then being redeveloped as a center of papal and aristocratic power. In 1612, Pope Paul V restored the Aqua Traiana and called it the Acqua Paola (again: after himself), culminating in the bombastic Fontanone that still rushes over the Janiculum with theatrical flair. These infrastructure upgrades were ideological monuments, liquid proof of papal dominance, architectural prowess, and access to divine abundance.

And then came the fountains. If ancient aqueducts were wonders of engineering, the fountains of Baroque Rome were feats of drama. The Trevi, built in the eighteenth century, is a marble riot of sea gods, horses, and roaring water. It may be the most famous, but it's hardly alone. There are more than fifteen hundred fountains in Rome today, many with roots in restored ancient water sources.

By the time Italy unified in 1870 and Rome was declared the capital, the water system was again central to its identity. In 1874, the nasoni were introduced as part of a modern public health push. They've been flowing and growing in number ever since, dispensing free spring water across the city. Locals know the trick: Cover the spout's bottom opening with your finger and a small arc of water spurts upward, letting you drink, no bottle needed.

Today, Rome still draws about 97 percent of its drinking water from natural springs in Lazio, including ancient sources like the Aqua Marcia. The Aqua Virgo feeds the Trevi. The Acqua Paola pours down the Janiculum. And the water, remarkably, still flows without chlorination; it's filtered naturally through volcanic rock before it even reaches the city.

But the system isn't flawless. Nearly 40 percent of the water is lost through leaks, thanks to aging infrastructure and decades of deferred maintenance. Climate change isn't helping either. Hotter, drier summers and snowless winters put pressure on supplies and make

Nasoni map

Rome's aqueduct network more vulnerable than ever. And yet, it endures: Fountains still gurgle, nasoni still drip under the umbrella pines, and deep underground, stone channels carved by hand two millennia ago still carry water into the heart of the city.

COFFEE CULTURE

Walk into any Roman bar at 9:00 a.m. and you'll witness the city's most practiced ritual: the morning caffè. Elbows out. Eyes sharp. Regulars bypass the register and head straight for the counter, where they order with confidence. While seasoned locals might seem to breeze straight to the counter, most bars actually prefer you pay first, especially during the morning rush. The standard protocol is to go to the register, pay, and bring your scontrino (receipt) to the counter to place your order. It keeps the chaos in check and the espresso flowing. Even in today's tap-and-go economy, some of us still slap a coin on top of our scontrino to signal we're ready. The key is moving with purpose: if in doubt, pay first and follow the rhythm of the room.

You'd be forgiven for thinking Rome's relationship with coffee dates back to antiquity, but the bean didn't even arrive in Italy until the sixteenth century, when it landed in Venice via Ottoman trade routes. By the time

To reach the Egeria Spring, head southeast from Rome's historic center along the Appia Nuova, a modern road that echoes the ancient Via Appia Antica's trajectory. Just past the built-up stretch of the Tuscolano district, turn onto Via dell'Almone and pull into the unassuming parking lot, where, on weekends, a small farmers' market pops up with crates of seasonal produce and foraged greens. From there, descend the stone steps tucked behind a low wall. You'll likely be following in the footsteps of locals clutching empty glass bottles or repurposed plastic jugs, ready to fill up on still or sparkling water for a nominal fee—only a few cents per liter.

This is the Fontana Egeria, a natural spring within the Caffarella Park, part of the Parco Regionale dell'Appia Antica. The spring feels like a secret, even if it's hiding in plain sight. No grand Baroque sculptures, no tour groups. Just cool, mineral-rich water flowing from deep underground, as it has for thousands of years.

The name and myth of Egeria are rooted in Rome's earliest days. She was no ordinary nymph; Egeria was a divine counselor, as well as the lover and adviser to Numa Pompilius, Rome's purported second king and the architect of much of the city's early religious life. According to legend, the pair would meet in the sacred groves near this very spring, where Egeria whispered the will of the gods into Numa's ear. After his death, grief overwhelmed her, and she dissolved into tears, giving birth to the spring itself.

The spring became somewhat of a pilgrimage site. Ancient Romans believed its waters possessed healing properties and made regular trips here for rituals, reflection, and refreshment. The surrounding area, dotted with tombs and shrines, served as a place of reverence, memory, and natural beauty.

Like many ancient water sources in Rome, the Egeria Spring was eventually tapped for more pragmatic uses. During the imperial period, its flow was channeled into the Almone River, a tributary of the Tiber, and incorporated into the local hydraulic system. But even as aqueducts rose and fell and Rome's water infrastructure evolved, this spring remained a constant.

Today, the Egeria Spring is still a source of daily sustenance. It sits within one of Rome's most bucolic parks, a semiwild space where sheep graze among Roman ruins and joggers dart between crumbling cisterns and potholes. Its water is bottled and sold under the name Acqua Santa di Egeria, but the most authentic way to taste it is straight from the tap, bottle in hand.

In a city defined by continuity, Egeria flows through centuries unchanged—myth, utility, and ritual all bottled into a single sip.

HOW TO ORDER COFFEE IN ROME WITHOUT GETTING YELLED AT

Roman coffee culture is all about rhythm and observation. Yes, you can order a cappuccino after 11:00 a.m. at the bar—don't believe TikTok. *She lies.* Just don't try it in Naples. That said, it's never acceptable to order one at a restaurant or trattoria, or generally consume one immediately after a meal.

Most bars (aka cafés) operate on a pretty standard system: Head to the register if there is one, pay, and bring your receipt (scontrino) to the bar. Or, if it's a pay-after place, go straight to the counter, place your order, then settle up before you leave. In either case, making eye contact with the barista is the Roman equivalent of taking a number. Some people still leave a coin on their receipt to signal they're ready. It's a sweet old-school move, but not mandatory.

And yes, there *is* table service at most Roman bars—but it usually costs more. Some spots will let you carry your caffè to a table at the same price, but most tack on a service charge. There's no hard rule, so watch what the regulars do. Is everyone lingering at tables with waiter service? Cool. Is the vibe all standing-room speed drinkers? Probably not the spot to spread out with a newspaper.

When in doubt: Pause, scan the room, and read the bar like a menu.

Antico Caffè Greco, Rome's first proper café, opened near the Spanish Steps in 1760, Venice already had more than two hundred. Greco quickly became a haven for artists, expats, poets, and intellectuals, many of whom wrote manifestos while drinking near-lethal quantities of coffee. It's still there, gilded and theatrical, with padded benches and steep prices to match.

Back then, coffee was a luxury, an aristocratic affectation served in porcelain cups in palatial salons and elite cafés, where it was typically brewed by boiling the grounds with water, a method that predated modern espresso technology. Rural folk and the urban poor made do with substitutes: chicory root or toasted barley, simmered into bitter brews that mimicked the taste of the real thing. The democratization of coffee didn't begin until the early twentieth century, thanks in part to technological leaps like Milanese inventor Luigi Bezzera's espresso machine, which debuted in 1901. His invention forced hot water through ground beans under pressure, producing a concentrated shot in seconds and setting the stage for the stand-at-the-bar culture that would come to define Italy.

Still, widespread coffee drinking didn't take hold in Rome until the Fascist era. Mussolini's push for national self-sufficiency led to rationing and propaganda campaigns that celebrated barley-based caffè d'orzo as a patriotic substitute. Real coffee, being imported, was both scarce and politically fraught. Yet paradoxically, the regime leveraged espresso during wartime—it was a stimulant, an appetite suppressant, and a convenient way to placate the hungry working classes. Mussolini even exploited Ethiopia's status as the birthplace of coffee to rationalize the brutal colonial occupation in the 1930s. Tellingly, Rome's most famous coffee shop, Sant'Eustachio near the Pantheon, didn't open until 1938, when Italy was reeling from sanctions and cafés delivered a subsidized distraction in the form of espresso. A cup of coffee, like so many things in Fascist Italy, was political.

Coffee remained a rare treat into the postwar years, but by the time the economic miracle of the 1960s rolled around, Rome was awash in espresso. Homegrown companies like Danesi, Trombetta, and Palombini signed exclusive deals with bars, flooding the city with bitter blends and darker roasts that were more about consistency than origin. For home use, the moka pot, invented by Alfonso Bialetti in 1933, became a mid-century staple, bringing strong, espresso-adjacent coffee into Italian kitchens and further embedding the ritual into daily life. Rome stuck with this flavor profile for decades, even as places like Melbourne and Berlin led a third-wave coffee revolution. In 2006, the Nespresso boutique opened in Piazza San Lorenzo in Lucina,

DECODING THE ROMAN COFFEE MENU

Ordering coffee in Rome can feel like navigating an insider club. Here's how to use the lingo like you've been doing it your whole life:

Caffè—This is a single espresso. It's the default. No need to specify espresso. Just caffè. One word, one shot.

Caffè al vetro—Same espresso, but served in a small glass instead of ceramic. Some people swear it tastes better; others are into the aesthetics. Either way, it feels fancy.

Caffè lungo—Pulled longer than usual, with more water. Slightly less strong, more volume.

Caffè ristretto—Super-short shot. Tiny but intense.

Caffè macchiato—Espresso "stained" with a touch of milk. Ask for macchiato caldo (hot milk) or macchiato freddo (cold milk) if you've got a preference.

Cappuccino—A classic: espresso, steamed milk, and foam. Totally fine to order after breakfast hours—but only at the bar, never at a restaurant—but know it's not standard Roman behavior.

Caffè latte—Milk-forward, espresso-light. If you ask for just a latte, you'll get a glass of cold milk. Ask properly.

Caffè shakerato—Espresso shaken with ice, often served in a martini glass and sweetened with sugar. Chic and summery. Ask for it from October to May and you'll be reprimanded. Follow the recipe on page 303 to make your own.

Marocchino—A layer of cocoa powder, a shot of espresso, and foamed milk on top. Served in a glass, perfect for a midmorning buzz.

Caffè d'orzo—Caffeine-free barley brew. Popular with the caffeine averse, pregnant women, and people still living in the shadow of wartime rationing.

Caffè corretto—Literally a "corrected" coffee, spiked with a shot of booze like grappa, sambuca, or brandy. Popular in the morning among men of a certain age and people already having a *day*.

Granita di caffè—More of a Sicilian import, but you'll find it in Roman bars with southern roots. Strong coffee frozen into icy shards, usually layered with sweetened whipped cream (panna). A full meal if you do it right.

a capsule-powered Trojan horse of the specialty coffee world. George Clooney's smirk on ads did more for espresso branding than a thousand baristi ever could.

But change was brewing. In the 2010s, young Romans who had worked abroad in the wake of the 2008 financial crisis came home, bringing with them a new vocabulary: *single-origin, light roast, pour-over*. When Faro opened near Piazza Fiume in 2016, it kicked off a wave of specialty cafés that now dot the city, many roasting their own beans. Starbucks arrived in Italy in 2018 and Rome in 2023, cautiously and controversially, but Roman coffee culture didn't blink. It's still standing at the bar, sipping fast, and savoring slow.

ROME DRINKS (LOCAL) WINE

Romans have been drinking wine for millennia, and yet the local vino from Lazio has never gotten the respect it deserves. In antiquity, when Rome was the center of an empire and its emperors drank deeply from goblets of local wine, the most sought-after bottles came from Campania. These days, Tuscany to the north remains a marketing juggernaut that outshines Lazio's sensational wines. But things are changing slowly and deliciously. A quiet revolution is fermenting in the hills, cellars, and

#PARLAPICKS: COFFEE

Barnum
Café Merenda
Casa Manfredi Teatro
Faro
Fax Factory
Fischio
Luna
Mostro
Origine
Otaleg Monteverde
Sciascia Caffè 1919

No one comes to Italy for bad coffee. When you're posted up at a bar knocking back an espresso in three seconds flat, the ritual is sacred, efficient, and blissfully unadulterated. So when Starbucks announced plans to open in Italy, the collective response was a mix of horror, confusion, and begrudging curiosity. Did Italians really need a grande no-whip white chocolate mocha with five pumps and an extra shot?

If you wanted to convince Italians to drink Starbucks, you weren't going to start with the skeptical nonni in their neighborhood café. You were going to ease it into the ecosystem, testing it on young Italian mall rats with TikTok accounts. It was a carefully curated rollout, one that allowed Starbucks to test the waters without diving straight into the deep end of Italy's notoriously opinionated coffee culture.

The first Starbucks in Italy opened in central Milan in September 2018, and it wasn't just any store. It was a twenty-five-thousand-square-foot Reserve Roastery in a historic post office near the Duomo. A gilded temple to coffee with gleaming brass machinery and a menu more third-wave than drive-thru, the Milan Roastery generated massive international press. That attention helped demystify the brand and introduced it to an Italian public that had only ever encountered Starbucks abroad. The store was more spectacle than shop, a strategic move to build buzz without alienating traditionalists outright.

Once awareness was in place, the real expansion began. Starbucks moved into outlet malls and shopping centers, safe zones where global brands already thrived and where foot traffic skewed younger and more open to international chains. These locations quietly did the heavy lifting, getting Frappuccinos into the hands of Gen Z Italians before the brand inched its way into city centers.

Behind Starbucks' Italian debut was Antonio Percassi, a former professional footballer turned retail magnate known for bringing global names like Zara, Victoria's Secret, and The North Face to Italy. He understood the psychology of Italian consumers and the importance of timing and context when introducing a new brand to a deeply traditional market.

By May 2023, Starbucks had made its way into the heart of Rome, opening a location next to Parliament, followed by another in Piazza San Silvestro, and eventually three in Termini Station. And the brand is still growing. The strategy is simple: Don't try to compete with Italian espresso. Instead, offer something entirely different: sweet, dairy-laden drinks treated like desserts, sold at a premium. It's working.

These days, Rome's Starbucks locations host a mix of local students on laptops, tourists refueling between museum visits, and yes, even some older Romans, tentatively cupping their caramel lattes, testing the waters. But the apocalypse has not come. The city's beloved bars still thrive. The reality is this: Italians don't live in a vacuum. They travel, they evolve, and sometimes, they want a milkshake-inspired coffee in a giant to-go cup.

trattoria wine lists of the capital, one that's challenging old assumptions and reshaping Lazio's place on Italy's wine map. The shift has been decades in the making, fueled by a handful of visionary producers who have rejected Lazio's bulk-wine reputation and embraced organic viticulture, native grapes, and low-intervention cellar practices. For curious drinkers, the city's wine bars have become portals to a region rediscovering its soul, one bottle at a time.

The best place to start is the Castelli Romani, the hill towns southeast of Rome—Frascati, Monte Porzio Catone, Grottaferrata, Genzano di Roma—where wines have flowed since the Republic. This is Malvasia and Trebbiano territory, grapes that too often have been treated like workhorses, vinified into watery whites that were cheap, forgettable, and ubiquitous in Roman trattorias. But producers like Ribelà and Icaro are flipping the script, bottling structured, mineral-forward whites, reds, and rosati with real verve and character. Their projects are focused on native grapes and volcanic soils, and are some of the most exciting things happening in Castelli right now.

To the south, Marco Carpineti, based in Cori, has been one of Lazio's most committed advocates for native varietals and biodynamic farming. His revival of Bellone, a juicy, golden grape once used almost exclusively in blends, has been revelatory. Treated with care, Bellone delivers notes of wild herbs, citrus, and crushed stone.

Head southeast to Olevano Romano. This is Cesanese country, home to a peppery, herbaceous red with just enough wildness to remind you you're in the Italian countryside. For years, Cesanese was sidelined as rustic fare, poured in carafes at countryside sagre, or seasonal festivals. But producers like Damiano Ciolli and Riccardi Reale are rewriting its story. Ciolli's wines lean toward elegance and freshness, while Riccardi e Reale, an energetic natural wine project, embraces Cesanese's full untamed soul.

Further southeast in the Ciociaria, a sub-region bordering Abruzzo and Molise, the wines reflect the rugged terrain and deep agricultural traditions of this underexplored area. A growing number of natural winemakers like Palazzo Tronconi, Il Vecchio Poggio, and I Ciacca are reclaiming forgotten vineyards and indigenous grapes such as Maturano, Lecinaro, and Pampanaro, working with minimal intervention to produce expressive, soulful

wines. Carlo Noro and La Visciola craft exceptional Cesanese-based vino. These bottles are alive with the energy of sandstone soils and mountain air, often unfiltered and full of character.

Up in northern Lazio, near Bracciano and Viterbo, the wine scene is getting a jolt from a new generation of winemakers working in tune with nature. La Villana, run by American Joy Kull, is a standout. Her wines, made from Procanico (aka Trebbiano Toscano), Malvasia, and other local grapes, are unfiltered, unpretentious, and fun to drink. They reflect the volcanic soils and untamed beauty of the landscape. And around here, there's also Aleatico, a fragrant red grape with a rose-and-berry perfume that gets a bad rap for being too sweet or old-fashioned. In the hands of Andrea Occhipinti, it's anything but. His dry versions are luminous, balanced, and full of personality, a perfect pairing for sunset over the lake.

Along the coast, in the ancient Etruscan heartlands of Cerveteri and Tarquinia, vines have been cultivated since long before Rome was even a village. Whites from these zones are typically built on Trebbiano with Malvasia playing a key supporting role; in Tarquinia, Giallo also enters the picture, adding citrusy lift. Reds are anchored by Sangiovese and Montepulciano, occasionally softened with a splash of Merlot or lifted with a bit of Cesanese. These coastal wines rarely get much airtime, but the potential is there, especially as more growers embrace low-intervention farming and focus on quality over quantity.

No conversation about Lazio wine would be complete without mentioning Fiorano, the estate that launched a thousand myths. Prince Alberico Boncompagni Ludovisi's vineyard near Ciampino, 10 miles from central Rome, became a legend in the twentieth century—less for its accessibility (the wine was barely distributed) and more for the prince's eccentric commitment to organic farming and long aging. His Semillon and Malvasia bottlings were years, sometimes decades, in the making, and the wines (when you could get them) were like time capsules. Fiorano's legacy remains a symbol of what Lazio can achieve when vision meets patience.

Of course, Lazio still faces challenges. Its name doesn't carry the same weight in Italy nor abroad as Tuscany or Piedmont. The market is crowded. And the shadow of past mediocrity lingers. But there's real momentum here, powered by producers who believe in their land, their grapes, and the stories they tell in every glass.

Bacchus is one of those gods who's so deeply embedded in Roman culture it's easy to forget he wasn't Roman to begin with. As with so many other things—architecture, olive trees, organized chaos—the Romans borrowed him from the Greeks, who called him Dionysus, then made him their own. In typical Roman fashion, they didn't simply adopt him, they absorbed him, rebranded him, and built him into their mythology, religion, art, and even city planning. Bacchus shows up everywhere: in crumbling temple ruins, in marble reliefs of boozy banquets, in frescoes of dining rooms where Roman elites reclined and drank under his vine-draped gaze.

The Greeks had already imagined Dionysus as a god of contradictions: He's the ruler of wine and ecstasy, yes, but also of disorder, boundary-blurring, and wildness. When his cult traveled west, hitching a ride through Etruria and Magna Graecia, regions with long-standing Greek ties, Rome wasn't quite ready for the vibe shift. By the time the Romans got their hands on Bacchus, his image was loaded with even more meaning. He wasn't just the god of getting drunk. He embodied transformation, liberation, and everything that scared the pants off the Roman elite.

In 186 BCE, Bacchus's followers, who were into secret, all-night rites called Bacchanalia, set off one of the biggest religious freak-outs in Roman history. The Senate panicked and issued the Senatus Consultum de Bacchanalibus, an official decree aimed at tamping down the madness. The powers that be were terrified by what Bacchic gatherings represented: people of different classes and genders mixing freely, dancing and drinking and worshipping outside the control of the state. In a society obsessed with hierarchy and public order, that was radical and dangerous.

But Bacchus worship didn't disappear; it just evolved. The wildest parts of the rites were toned down (at least officially), and his public image shifted to emphasize agricultural abundance and seasonal renewal. He became less of a rule-breaker and more of a divine drinking buddy, still powerful, still unpredictable, but a little more socially acceptable. In art, he shows up in multiple guises: sometimes a soft, youthful figure wreathed in vine leaves, other times a heavy-lidded reveler surrounded by satyrs, maenads, and a whole entourage of grape-related accessories.

His presence saturated daily life in Rome. You'd find his image on drinking vessels, carved into furniture, painted onto walls. The triclinium (dining room) of the Roman houses on the Celio portray Bacchic rites as pudgy Cupids harvest grapes. His mythology straddled the line between sacred and profane, pleasure and power.

Even after the fall of the Roman Empire, Bacchus stuck around. Early Christians tried to scrub pagan gods from the public imagination, but Bacchus was slippery. His association with wine, rebirth, and transcendence made him surprisingly hard to kill off. Some of his symbols and energy echoed in early Christian imagery. And one could argue that Bacchus's spirit lingers in modern rituals like ottobrate romane, informal wine festivals of the eighteenth and nineteenth centuries where revelers overindulged just as they did in the past.

#PARLAPICKS: LAZIO PRODUCERS TO SEEK OUT AND TO VISIT

Castelli Romani and Roman Suburbs

Colleformica (Velletri)—colleformica.it

Icaro (Genzano di Roma)—icarovino.it

La Torretta (Grottaferrata)—latorretta.bio

Ribelà (Monte Porzio Catone)—cantinaribela.it

Terracanta (Ardea)—cantinaterracanta.it

Southern Lazio (Cori and Surroundings)

Damiano Ciolli (Olevano Romano)—damianociolli.it

Marco Carpineti (Cori)—carpinetiterrae.com

Riccardi Reale (Bellegra)—cantinericcardireale.it

Sete (Priverno)—progettosete.it

Ciociaria

Abbia Nòva (Piglio)—instagram.com/abbia_nova

Carlo Noro (Labico)—biodinamicanoro.net

Fra i Monti (Terelle)—fraimonti.it

Il Vecchio Poggio (Isola del Liri)—ilvecchiopoggio.it

La Visciola (Piglio)—instagram.com/azienda_agricola_la_visciola

Macciocca (Piglio)—agricolamacciocca.com

Palazzo Tronconi (Arce)—palazzotronconi.com

Bracciano, Viterbo, and Northern Lazio

Andrea Occhipinti (Gradoli)—occhipintiandrea.it

La Villana (Gradoli)—lavillanavino.com

Podere Orto (Trevinano)—podereorto.it

Poggio Bbaranello (Montefiascone)—poggiobbaranello.it

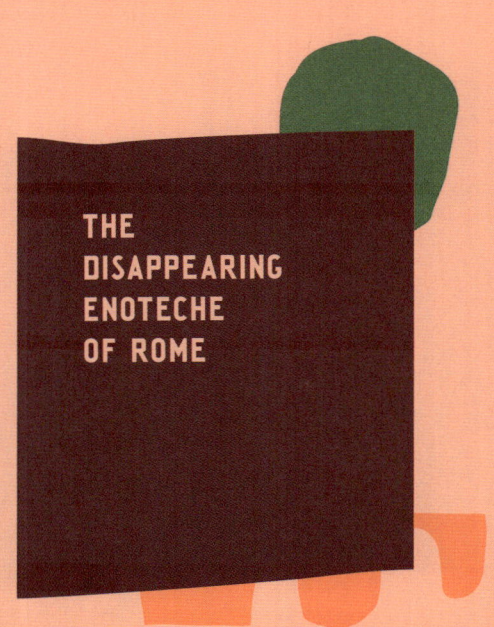

THE DISAPPEARING ENOTECHE OF ROME

Rome's old-school enoteche are extinct. Wander through the centro storico today and you'll see plenty of places calling themselves enoteche—wine bars with minimalist lighting, curated selections of vino, and cold cuts plated artfully. But the modern enoteca bears little resemblance to its predecessor. Wine was a daily staple, and enoteche were neighborhood fixtures where you'd get your vino frequently, casually, and in volume.

Up until the 1990s, places in central Rome like Il Vinaietto and L'Angolo Divino near Campo de' Fiori, Il Goccetto on Via dei Banchi Vecchi, and Il Piccolo in the shadow of Piazza Navona functioned as bulk wine shops. You'd show up with your own bottle and get it filled straight from the cask, shell out a few lire, and be on your way. No pretense, no wine flights, no sommelier hovering nearby to talk about maceration.

These spots were part of a larger system, one rooted in a centuries-old Roman wine culture shaped by state regulation and practicality. For generations, wine and olive oil were sold sfuso (in bulk, by volume) and prices were regulated by municipal authorities to ensure affordability. Romans treated wine as fuel: something that accompanied every meal, not a luxury. In the city, the enoteca was the go-to for topping off your household's supply. Out in the Castelli Romani, the country-side just southeast of the capital, the fraschette served the same function, pouring young local wines from Marino or Frascati to thirsty city dwellers who'd bring their own food to pair with it.

The wines weren't meant to be profound. They were usually local: light Lazio whites or off-dry reds, often rustic and unstable, and frequently oxidized by the time they hit the glass. Sold by volume, the wine was measured out in government-issued glass vessels, each marked with a metal stamp to certify its authenticity.

But in the 1990s, things started to change. Rome's historic center was gentrified. Italy's wine industry underwent a quiet revolution with a greater focus on quality, less on quantity. Winemakers started bottling instead of selling in bulk. Rome's food scene became more in-

ternational, tourism exploded, and suddenly, the humble neighborhood enoteca had no choice but to evolve. Slowly, shelves filled with labeled bottles from Lazio and beyond. Il Vinaietto is one that remained closest to the spirit of its original incarnation. Though they don't pour vino sfuso these days, they do serve hard-boiled eggs, once an enoteca staple (page 90), from a tower on the counter.

There's nothing wrong with this evolution. In fact, it's led to a wine renaissance in Rome, better wine, and new businesses. Today, it's possible to be in some of Rome's most popular areas and drink small-batch, low-intervention wines from across Italy, poured by people who know what they're talking about, and, in the case of Rocco Caroselli at Il Vinaietto, actually make them (he's part of the quartet behind Icaro). That's a good thing. But something was lost in the transition. The enoteca used to be for everyone. Now, many are a destination, a curated experience.

That said, vino sfuso hasn't disappeared entirely. You'll still find it flowing from the taps in neighborhood markets in Testaccio and Trionfale, among other places, where it's sold by the litre to loyal locals, often older Romans who bring their own bottles. In these corners of Rome, wine remains a humble staple; elsewhere, it's a lifestyle signifier.

This shift in Rome's enoteca culture reflects more than just changing tastes. It mirrors the city's broader transformation in the face of gentrification and globalization. As in so many capitals, wine has become an identity marker, shaped by global influences and guided by new standards of taste and presentation. The same forces reshaping Rome's drinking scene are part of a wider move away from quantity to quality. That's not necessarily a loss, but it is a realignment.

#PARLAPICKS: WINE BARS

Avanvera	L'Andtidoto
Bar Bozza	Latteria
Beppe e I Suoi Formaggi	Machiavelli 64
Bulzoni	Mostò
Da Corrado	L'Angolo Divino
Enoteca il Piccolo	Piano C
Fischio	SO2
Il Goccetto	Solovino
Il Vinaietto	Sorso
La Mescita	Vigneto

HOW ROME DRINKS

ROME'S COCKTAIL CULTURE

When I first arrived in Rome more than two decades ago, craft cocktail culture was barely a blip on the city's drinking radar. If you wanted a proper mixed drink, your best bet was one of the grand hotel bars—places like the Hassler, the St. Regis, or Hotel de Russie. These old-school watering holes came with gilded mirrors, velvet armchairs, bartenders in pressed jackets, and prices that were way out of reach for my budget.

Fortunately, the early aughts also offered extremely cheap cocktails in student districts like San Lorenzo and Piazza Bologna. Pigneto, believe it or not, wasn't yet a thing. Neither were spritzes, which didn't reach critical mass in Rome until around 2009.

At those student bars, seven euros could get you an aggressively sweet mojito, a caipirinha, or a tequila sunrise—and access to a carb-heavy buffet you could pile onto a plate. The drinks weren't balanced, but they signaled a shift: Young Romans were ready for something other than industrial lagers and house wine. Piazza Trilussa and Campo de' Fiori turned into open-air clubs,

packed with students and tourists waving plastic cups of syrupy cocktails. It wasn't refined, but it was cheap. And that counted for something.

Toward the end of that decade, the Aperol spritz arrived. After Campari acquired Aperol, it launched a national marketing campaign, transforming a low-ABV aperitivo once limited to the Veneto—especially Padova—into a drink beloved across Italy and eventually around the world.

Around the same time, a few Romans began taking cocktails seriously. In 2010, the Jerry Thomas Project (now called Jerry Thomas Speakeasy) changed everything. Tucked behind an unmarked door near Campo de' Fiori, it was the city's first proper cocktail bar in the international sense. Founders Leonardo Leuci, Roberto Artusio, Antonio Parlapiano, and Alessandro Procoli were reviving forgotten recipes and importing the philosophy of American craft mixology. (Jerry Thomas, after all, was the US's first celebrity bartender.) Rome, a city rooted in wine and spritz culture, suddenly had a speakeasy. And not just any speakeasy, but one that became a pilgrimage site for mixologists from around the world.

Its influence was immediate. Craft cocktail bars began popping up around the city: Banana Republic in Prati, Co.So. in Pigneto (back when that neighborhood was still a frontier), and Barnum Café, which has since transitioned to specialty coffee. The Jerry Thomas team expanded their reach with a spirits brand, educational initiatives, and a growing list of ventures. Roberto Artusio opened La Punta in Trastevere, home to one of Europe's largest collections of agave-based spirits. His partner in the project, Cristian Bugiada, runs Freni e Frizioni—once a chaotic spritz spot, now one of the city's most fun bars for creative cocktails. Alessandro

#PARLAPICKS: COCKTAIL BARS
Bar Locarno
Drink Kong
Freni e Frizioni
Jerry Thomas Bar Room
Jerry Thomas Speakeasy
La Punta Expendio de Agave
Latta Fermenti e Miscele

HOW ROME DRINKS

Procoli, meanwhile, leads Latta near Ponte di Ferro, a hybrid space for drinking, dining, and fermentation projects, including the brand's line of canned cocktails.

Patrick Pistolesi picked up that thread and ran with it. After getting his start at Barnum, he opened Drink Kong, a sleek, neon-lit temple to cocktail futurism near Piazza Vittorio, in 2018. With its Japanese-inspired minimalism, cinematic vibe, and perfectly calibrated drinks, Drink Kong feels more Tokyo than Trastevere. And that's the point. Within a year, it landed on the World's 50 Best Bars list, cementing Rome's place on the global cocktail map.

Today, the scene is expansive and eclectic. The classic hotel bars are still delivering old-school glamour, but now some, like the Bulgari and The Rome EDITION's cocktail bars, are embracing innovation and stepping outside the Negroni-and-martini comfort zone. Across the city, a new generation of bartenders is blending Roman irreverence with global technique. The best bars feel confident, curious, and rooted in place, even as they pull inspiration from abroad.

Rome may have been late to the cocktail party, but it's more than caught up. The scene now spans the elegant and the experimental, the historic and the futuristic. It's a city that's finally found its rhythm—shaken and stirred.

HOP(E) SPRINGS ETERNAL: CRAFT BEER AND BREWING IN ROME

Rome has always been a wine city, hydrating itself on wines blending local Malvasia and Trebbiano grapes, but in the past couple of decades, beer has become more than just an afterthought. Industrial lagers still dominate, of course, and locals have long washed down pizza with a cold Peroni; a Peroni plant in the Salario district is now home to the MACRO, Rome's contemporary art museum, a fitting reimagining of a space once dedicated to thirst and now devoted to culture.

But something changed in the early 2000s. Rome's beer awakening began not in a brewery but in a tiny bar on a cobbled Trastevere alley. When Ma Che Siete Venuti a Fà (roughly "What Did You Even Come Here For?" in Roman dialect) opened in 2001, the city's beer culture was nearly nonexistent, save for a bunch of faux Irish pubs. Romans were suspicious of anything other than the usual lager-and-pizza combo, and the idea of ordering a small-batch Belgian sour or obscure Franconian lager was laughable. But the bar's mission—to serve the best beer in the world—slowly won people over. It became a haven for beer nerds, curious tourists, and eventually, skeptical locals who started to believe beer could be interesting.

By the early 2010s, craft beer had taken root in Italy. National pioneers like Baladin (from Piedmont), Birra del Borgo (from Lazio), and Toccalmatto (from Emilia-Romagna) helped redefine what beer could be, and Rome, ever the consumer capital, was suddenly pouring more of it than any other city in the country. That energy gave rise to a homegrown brewing scene, and soon, Romans were drinking good beer and making it, too.

Ritual Lab, founded in 2015 in Formello, 30 kilometers northwest of the city, quickly earned a reputation for precision and polish. Their beers are thoughtful and technically dialed-in, with stouts, pale ales, and pilsners that demonstrate both restraint and creativity. You're as

likely to find their cans at a Roman bottle shop as you are at a beer competition abroad, where they regularly pick up awards for flavor and balance.

In 2016, Jungle Juice took things in a louder direction. Tucked into Mandrione, a postindustrial pocket among the aqueducts, this brewery is all haze and hops, churning out juicy New England–style IPAs (called NEIPAs), sours, IPAs, and crowd-pleasing experimental beers from a garage-like warehouse. Their look is punk, their beer is playful, and their ethos is pure Roman DIY. From 6:00 p.m. nightly, their taproom serves hopheads gathering over glasses of whatever new batch just dropped.

A year later, Rebel's emerged on the Via Ardeatina, throwing itself into the scene with bold, expressive beers and irreverent design. Their IPAs and pale ales hit hard and fast, winning over a young crowd hungry for something fresher, cooler, more international. Rebel's helped cement Rome's place as a hub for modern beer culture—one where American influences are filtered through a Roman lens and poured with swagger.

Today, Rome's craft beer establishments stretch across the city, from serious beer bars like Artisan in San Lorenzo and Birra Più in Pigneto to bottle shops like Johnny's Off License in San Giovanni and Centro. What started as a niche obsession has turned into a legitimate drinking culture. Sure, wine will always reign supreme at the trattoria, but these days, it's not unheard of to find a Rome-brewed saison or sour alongside the Cesanese.

And maybe that's what makes Rome's beer scene so compelling. It's not trying to replace tradition, its adding to it. In a city known for clinging to the past, these brewers are building something new: a fresh layer of drinking culture that sits comfortably alongside aperitivo hour and bottles of Lazio wine.

#PARLA PICKS: CRAFT BEER BARS

Artisan	Ma Che Siete Venuti a Fà
Be.Re.	Mashroom
Birra Più	Nettare
Johnny's Off License	Open Baladin
Jungle Juice	Pork 'n' Roll
Luppolo Station	Rebel's

#PARLAPICKS: HOW AND WHERE TO EAT AND SHOP FOR FOOD IN ROME

HOW TO TRATTORIA

When I moved to Rome in 2003, the trattoria was the dominant form of local, seated dining. These casual, often family-run spots serve straightforward food rooted in regional traditions. A trattoria isn't fancy or formal. It offers a menu of Roman dishes prepared without fuss, delivered in an unpretentious setting, often by the people who have cooked the meal themselves. Trattorie are where Romans go to eat comforting, familiar food. They aren't trying to be anything other than what they are.

Back then, most trattorie focused on Roman classics. You'd find the same greatest hits across the city. A few trattorie stood out for showcasing regional cuisines from outside Lazio. Colline Emiliane brought Bolognese food to the capital and still makes some of the best fresh egg pasta in town. Trattoria Monti focused on the food of Le Marche, introducing Romans to dishes from the Italian northeast. Both places are still going strong.

The trattoria experience looked different then. Before the economic crisis, it was common for diners to order a full meal (antipasto, primo, secondo, contorno, and dolce) and to linger at the table for hours. There was no need to turn tables. A single seating could sustain a business, because the average check was high enough to make it work. But that began to change in the early 2000s. The arrival of the euro brought price hikes that didn't match stagnant wages. Labor reforms shifted much of the young workforce into precarious freelance contracts with fewer protections. Youth unemployment soared. Many Roman families had to divert disposable income to support their adult children. When the 2008 financial crisis hit, already strained household budgets were stretched even thinner. Eating out became less frequent and more strategic. Diners started ordering fewer courses. Trattorie could no longer rely on one generous seating to break even. Turning tables became the new norm, even for businesses that had never structured service that way before.

Despite all this, trattorie haven't disappeared. They've adapted quietly, adjusting portion sizes and pacing, streamlining menus, and in some cases leaning into nostalgia to bring people back. At their best, they still offer a taste of how Romans used to eat, and how some still do. Even as the city's dining scene has exploded with wine bars, bistros, fast casual concepts, burger joints, steakhouses, and gourmet pizzerias, the trattoria endures. And for good reason. When done right, it captures something essential about Roman life that no other format quite can.

When visiting yourself, you don't need to order every course, but it's polite to choose at least two or three, like an antipasto with a secondo and contorno or a primo followed by a secondo, so the kitchen isn't firing a single plate per table.

Keep reading for a guide to my perennial favorite trattorie. I write endless guides for online and print publications that are constantly revised and reshuffled, but this list reflects the spots that get it right every time. No trends. No editorial mandates. Just the best of the best.

CUCINA ROMANA

The cucina romana is built on bold flavors, minimal ingredients, and precise technique, shaped by centuries of poverty, papal opulence, and working-class ingenuity. But its most profound transformations came in the twentieth century, when waves of internal migration, the postwar economic boom, and mass urbanization redrew the city and its appetite. Regional ingredients became staples, new cooking methods entered home kitchens, and trattorie adapted to feed a broader, faster-moving clientele. Still, its identity remains inseparable from the city itself. Basically, it's the collection of recipes in this book, each of which tells the story of Rome through the way people cook and eat.

Armando al Pantheon (Centro Storico)

Just steps from the Pantheon, Armando al Pantheon is one of the few central Roman trattorias that actually deserves the hype. The Gargioli family has been serving Roman comfort food here since 1961 with a steady hand. The menu sticks to the hits: fettuccine with chicken innards, slow-cooked tripe, and seasonal sides like braised artichokes and puntarelle with anchovy dressing. Finish with the torta antica Roma, a ricotta and strawberry jam pie. The wine list is tightly curated and always evolving thanks to the dedication of Armando's granddaughter Fabiana.

Cesare al Casaletto (Gianicolense)

When Leonardo Vignoli and Maria Pia Cicconi took over Trattoria da Cesare al Casaletto in 2009, they brought sharp technique to a beloved Monteverde spot without messing with its soul. Leonardo applied his fine dining chops to Roman classics, while Maria Pia kept things running smoothly and won over regulars. The trattoria dates to the 1950s, when it opened as Trattoria della Palma. The owners' son Cesare changed the name when he took over and ran the place for decades before the handoff. Today, the food is tight and satisfying. Fried gnocchi with cacio e pepe sauce are crisp and creamy. The gricia is spot-on. Lamb dishes hit all the right notes. The three hundred-label wine list leans natural, with affordable bottles from Italy, France, and Slovenia. It feels like a neighborhood place because it is, but the cooking hits harder than most.

Cesare al Pellegrino (Centro Storico)

When Settimio al Pellegrino, the cult trattoria made famous by Anthony Bourdain's Parts Unknown, closed in 2022, it felt like the end of an era. Owners Mario Zazza and Teresa Luciani had run the place for more than half a century, but their children, a surgeon and a lawyer, had no interest in taking it over. Their favorite spot across town was Cesare al Casaletto (relatable!), so they turned to its owners, Leonardo and Maria Pia, and asked them to carry the torch. The couple agreed and preserved the details that made Settimio iconic: the tiled floors, midcentury tables, and marble accents. The menu is focused and deliberate, with dishes like minestra con broccoli e arzilla, a romanesco and skate soup, and Teresa's legendary pan-fried meatballs, which still taste exactly how they should.

Hosteria Grappolo d'Oro (Centro Storico)

Hosteria Grappolo d'Oro feels like a Roman trattoria from a friendlier dimension. The staff is genuinely welcoming, a rarity in a city where brusque service is part of the brand. Beneath the wood-beamed ceilings, they turn out faithful renditions of the Roman canon. Tonnarelli cacio e pepe comes perfectly toothsome with a glossy sauce that actually clings, and the roasted suckling lamb is so tender it barely needs a knife.

Osteria Bonelli (Tor Pignattara)

Patrizio Bonelli was my fruttivendolo di fiducia when I lived in Monti years ago. When his shop closed, I didn't expect to see him again, much less running a place in Tor Pignattara, one of Rome's most diverse and down-to-earth neighborhoods. The opposite of Monti, basically. The vibe at Osteria Bonelli is unfussy, the portions are generous, and the kitchen leans into bold flavors and off-the-beaten-path cuts. Look for roasted lamb or horse skirt steak alongside an unusually deep bench of vegetable contorni, a nod to Patrizio's days in the veggie biz.

Piatto Romano (Testaccio)

In the heart of Testaccio, Piatto Romano keeps the quinto quarto tradition alive with dishes like rigatoni con la pajata and fettuccine con le rigaglie di pollo. The offal is excellent, but the menu isn't just for carnivores. Baccalà baked with onions, pine nuts, apricots, and prunes is a standout, and the vinegar-spiked anchovies with chile bring the heat. The vegetables are some of the best in the city, treated with the same care as the mains. Owner Andrea D'Alfonsi sources obscure greens and herbs from across the region and is one of the few restaurateurs you'll see shopping at the Mercato di Testaccio.

Tavernaccia da Bruno (Porta Portese)

Bruno Persiani opened La Tavernaccia in 1968 after moving from Umbria to Rome, bringing with him a love for slow-cooked meats and regional comfort food. His daughters, grandchildren, and Sardinian son-in-law now run the place, keeping his Umbrian and Roman roots alive while adding dishes from chef Giuseppe Ruzzettu's own island tradition, including wood oven-roasted suckling pig. The pastas are dreamy, especially the Sunday lasagna, which disappears early. Don't sleep on the veal breast either. The wine list favors small producers from Italy, and the warm, generous service feels like a revelation in a city that's not exactly known for coddling diners.

Trecca (San Paolo)

Trecca is a new-school trattoria that nails the old-school essentials. Run by brothers Manuel and Nicolò Trecastelli, this offal-loving spot serves Roman comfort food with precision and personality. The carbonara and amatriciana are bold, unapologetically rich, and packed with guanciale. Tomato and vinegar keep the meaty mains from tipping into heaviness, and the natural wine list hits all the right notes. It's casual, seasonal, and deeply Roman.

CUCINE REGIONALI

Everyone in Rome loves to tell you they're seventh-generation Roman. That "sette generazioni" line is the gold standard for claiming true Roman status. But peel back the myth and you'll find most folks here descend from waves of internal migration. Between the post-Unification staffing of ministries, the fascist-era population reshuffling, and the economic booms of the 1960s, Rome became a magnet for workers from all over Italy. And while plenty of these modern Rome dwellers eat amatriciana like it's their birthright, their nonni, or even their parents, were born in Calabria or Abruzzo. Consequently, you'll find some stellar Italian regional cuisine options in town. Here are the standouts.

Colline Emiliane (Centro Storico)

Just a few minutes walking from the Trevi Fountain, this welcoming trattoria has been dishing out Emilia-Romagna classics since 1931, with the current family running the show since 1967. The menu leans into the region's egg-rich, house-made pastas, including tortelli di zucca tossed in butter and sage, and tagliatelle alla bolognese layered with deeply flavored meat sauce. Be sure to leave space for secondi like bollito misto or pan-fried liver.

Tram Tram (San Lorenzo)

At Tram Tram in San Lorenzo, Rosanna Di Vittorio serves the kind of food that tells you exactly where she's from and where she's been. Born to a Pugliese mother, she opened the place two decades ago with her daughters, transforming a shuttered tavern into a Roman-Pugliese trattoria with zero pretense and total sincerity. The menu blends the comforts of two regions: gnocchi with mutton ragù, tiella with mussels, orecchiette with broccoli and clams, dishes that once felt whimsical in a Roman context, but now read as classics. The space rumbles every time the tram rolls past, which is exactly how it got its name.

Trattoria Monti (Esquilino)

The Camerucci family's well-loved trattoria is not actually in Monti, but rather the adjacent multicultural Esquilino district near Stazione Termini. The cuisine is heavily Marchigiano (from the Italian region of Le Marche) so expect lots of game like braised rabbit and roasted duck, meat-filled fried olives, and fresh pasta like the legendary raviolo filled with a runny egg yolk and dressed with butter and sage.

NEW CLASSICS

Even though they turn out some of the city's best versions of Roman classics, these places don't really fit the trattoria mold. Call them neo-trattorie, neo-bistros, or whatever label you like, but the point is they feel contemporary. The menus balance expertly executed cucina romana icons such as carbonara, amatriciana, and coda alla vaccinara with dishes that are entirely their own, often seasonal, sometimes experimental, always thoughtful. What they share is a modern sensibility and a dining experience that is rooted in tradition but not confined by it.

Baccano (Centro Storico)

The décor channels a French bistro and the location near the Trevi Fountain does not inspire confidence, but none of that matters once you sit down. There is no better place in Rome to walk in, grab a seat at the bar (a rarity in Rome), and eat a plate of pasta. Chef Nabil Hadj Hassen, who ran the kitchen at Salumeria Roscioli for 18 years, turns out perfectly executed cacio e pepe, carbonara, and amatriciana.

Mazzo (San Lorenzo)

Francesca Barreca and Marco Baccannelli have reinvented Mazzo, moving it from Centocelle to an easy-to-reach spot in San Lorenzo. While it's not a trattoria in the traditional sense, Francesca and Marco have been riffing on Roman classics for their two-decade career, and their flavors are firmly rooted in Roman nostalgia. What was once a twelve-seat communal dining room in Rome's periphery has grown into a full restaurant with a wine bar at the entrance. True to their roots, a communal table now sits in front of a giant porthole framing the kitchen. The menu channels their signature style, so order the cult-favorite fried tripe with tomato sauce and Pecorino Romano and the wagon wheel pasta tangled with oniony braised beef.

Salumeria Roscioli (Centro Storico)

Salumeria Roscioli is a deli, wine bar, and restaurant all crammed into one chaotic, irresistible space. The shelves are stacked with wheels of cheese, legs of prosciutto, jars of preserves, and tins of anchovies, while tables are wedged between the displays and deli counter. It can feel hectic, even overwhelming, but that is part of the charm (for me, at least). The food more than justifies the squeeze, as long as you stick to the starters and pastas. My order? Mortadella with Parmigiano-Reggiano, butter and anchovies on toast from their bakery Antico Forno Roscioli, and gnocchi all'amatriciana. The wine list is vast, the service brisk, and the atmosphere charged. Love it or hate it, Roscioli is essential.

Santo Palato (Appio-Latino)

Chef Sarah Cicolini has made Santo Palato one of the most compelling restaurants in Rome by putting offal and cucina romana back at the center of the conversation. Since opening in 2017, she has served dishes like trippa alla romana in a minty tomato sauce that is both faithful to tradition and sharper than any version you will find elsewhere. Her cooking draws on her Abruzzese roots and a deep respect for whole animal butchery, yet everything feels current and precise. In 2025, she moved into a larger space with an aquarium kitchen that gives diners a front row seat to the action. The room is lively and colorful, the service is relaxed, and the food delivers big flavors. It is the sort of place where a classic becomes new again, and where Roman cooking feels very much alive.

RISTORANTI DI PESCE

Rome sits a dozen miles from the sea and straddles the Tiber, but seafood has never been the backbone of the city's cuisine. The old-school rhythm of fish on Fridays still holds in some homes, but until refrigeration and a steady economy came into play a few decades ago, the fish trade wasn't exactly thriving. These days, you'll spot baccalà or a steaming bowl of minestra broccoli e arzilla on a trattoria menu, and most markets have at least one fish stall. But finding truly great seafood in Rome still takes effort. That's where my go-to spots come in.

Da Michele (San Paolo)

Da Michele in San Paolo has been quietly turning out some of Rome's best seafood since 1991. Run by two generations of the Pignotta family, this neighborhood favorite keeps things low-key while delivering pristine fish and a seriously deep wine list. Think linguine with tiny telline clams, expertly fried catch from Fiumicino, and white wines with real age and structure. It's refined without being fussy, and totally worth the detour.

Tempio di Iside (Colosseo)

Just a few blocks from the Colosseum, Tempio di Iside serves some of the freshest fish in town in a setting that feels more like a celebration than a casual neighborhood joint. Crudi are the star here with sea urchin, oysters, and shrimp leading the way. The pasta dishes are just as memorable. The spaghetti with clams and the pecorino-laced shrimp pasta (seafood and cheese *do* go together!) both defy expectations in the best way. Reserve ahead and brace for the bill. It is absolutely worth it.

CUCINE INTERNAZIONALI

Even in a place often caricatured as spice and seasoning averse, immigrant cooks and second-generation Romans are serving bold, uncompromising flavors from Ethiopia, Venezuela, Mexico, Korea, Yemen, and beyond. These spots are not pandering to Roman palates or watering things down for tourists. They are cooking with pride, drawing on traditions and ingredients that bring new life to the city's dining landscape.

Aqla (Monteverde Vecchio)

Opened in Monteverde in spring 2023, Aqla brings Yemeni and Ethiopian cooking to a quiet street just off Viale dei Quattro Venti. The project is run by Samantha, Nada, and their mother Aqla, who cooks exactly as she would at home. The menu includes sambusa filled with meat or spiced lentils, and mutabbaq, a savory Yemeni pastry stuffed with beef, scallions, and coriander. There are half a dozen sandwiches made with Antico Forno Roscioli bread, each named for a member of the family and filled with marinated chicken, lentils with feta and eggs, or zighinì.

El Jalapeño (Aurelia)

El Jalapeño is a no-frills Mexican spot inside Mercato Irnerio in northwest Rome, where a pair of adjacent stalls serve food and groceries to a mostly Latin American crowd. Orders are placed by filling out a paper slip, tables are plastic, and traditional music plays throughout the market. The kitchen delivers bold, carefully made dishes that stand out in a city where Mexican food is often watered down to appease Rome's spice terror. Tacos are filled with cochinita pibil, carnitas, or suadero, all layered with fresh herbs, pickled onions, and lime. Tortillas are soft and deeply corn-flavored, and the tostada with chicken tinga and crema is rich and balanced. El Jalapeño serves real Mexican cooking at fair prices.

El Maíz (Prati)

El Maíz is a Venezuelan street food shop in Prati serving some of the city's best arepas and cachapas without compromise. The small space functions more like a counter-service bakery than a restaurant, but the food has serious depth. Arepas are split and stuffed generously with slow-cooked meats like shredded beef or chicken in tomato and spices, then layered with beans, cheese, or avocado, depending on the filling. The cachapa, a sweet corn pancake folded around soft cheese, is crisp at the edges and molten in the center. Tostones round out the menu, and everything is made with care using imported ingredients where it counts.

Enquatatash (Villa Gordiani)

Enquatatash serves deeply flavored Ethiopian and Eritrean dishes in a low-key space off the Via Prenestina.

The injera is made in-house and has the right balance of tang and bounce to anchor classics like doro wat, lentil misir, and beef kitfo. Platters come loaded with slow-cooked vegetables, spiced pulses, and tender meat, all seasoned with berbere or niter kibbeh. Portions are generous and everything is meant to be shared.

IGIO (Trastevere)

Opened in 2005, IGIO was one of the first restaurants to bring Korean cooking to central Rome. The menu covers the basics with confidence. There's house-made kimchi, grilled pork belly, and marinated beef cooked tableside. There are soups, braised short ribs, and bibimbap served in hot stone bowls.

Mrgda (Pigneto)

Via Prenestina has long been home to Rome's Ethiopian and Eritrean communities, and Mrgda, located on the border of Pigneto, is easily one of the best spots to experience these vibrant cuisines. Honey-fermented tej flows generously, ideal alongside gently spiced legumes, fragrant vegetables, tender braised chicken, and impeccably seasoned raw beef. Everything is served with naturally leavened injera, perfectly tangy and light.

Sinosteria (Marconi)

After nearly 30 years at the helm of Rome's first Thai restaurant, Beijing-born chef Ge Jing Hua opened Sinosteria in 2020 to serve a blend of Chinese regional cuisines featuring dishes like Beijing-style tripe with chile oil and cilantro, and Shandong-inspired squid with peppers, ginger, and bamboo. There are also signature creations like basmati rice with coconut milk, shrimp, capers, and oregano from Pantelleria. The front-of-house is expertly managed by the chef's gregarious sommelier son Jun, whose natural wine list and coffee and tea menus are outstanding.

MORE GLOBAL BITES

Chef Pum Thai Street Food (Trionfale)
Jiamo Lab (Porta Pia)
Gainn (Termini)
Himalaya Palace (Gianicolense)

PIZZERIE

Rome might not have Naples' centuries-old pizza pedigree, but what it lacks in tradition, it makes up for in sheer range, creativity, and straight-up deliciousness. The capital has carved out its own pizza identity, shaped mostly in the twentieth century, and it's anything but monolithic.

Here, you'll find two major styles of pizza al taglio (pizza by the slice): pizza in teglia, baked in rectangular pans and served in neighborhood joints, and pizza alla pala, baked directly on the oven floor and usually sold from forni (more on where to try that style in the next section). In Rome, pizza al taglio is sold by weight, not by the slice, and it's generally a lunch or snack thing, not a sit-down dinner. Whether you're at a slice shop or a bakery, hang back and see how ordering works before jumping in. Some places have a number system, others are a full-on rugby scrum. When it's your turn, point to the tray you want and show with your hands how much. Specify if you're eating in or taking away. The pizzaiolo will cut it (often with scissors), weigh it, and hand you a receipt. Take that to the register to pay, then dig in or head out.

Then there's pizza tonda romana, the round, thin-crust pie with a barely-there cornicione, always served whole with a knife and fork. It's wood fired, but at a lower temperature and for longer than Neapolitan pizzas, giving it that signature crisp snap. This style dominates the dinner scene, though some spots open for lunch. Add to that the Neapolitan-style pizzerias in town with their soft, puffed-up rims, plus a growing crop of hybrids blending Roman snap with Neapolitan chew, and you've got a city that's doing its own thing, loud and proud.

However you slice it, no Roman pizza session is complete without fritti: crisp, golden starters like supplì, crocchette di patate, and fiori di zucca. In Rome, fried things aren't merely snacks—they're the preamble to any great pizza experience.

Ai Marmi (Trastevere)

Locals call Ai Marmi l'obitorio ("the morgue") for its cold marble tables and fluorescent lighting, but that hasn't stopped this Trastevere institution from slinging some of the city's most iconic pizza tonda for nearly a century. The name on the oven says "pizza napoletana" in retro '60s script, but ignore that—these are textbook Roman pies: thin, crisp, and so wide they spill over the plate. Start with the fritti, listed on the glowing lightbox above the bar: filetti di baccalà and supplì al telefono with that perfect, stretchy mozzarella center. It's old-school, fast-paced, and exactly what a Roman pizzeria should be.

A Rota (Tor Pignattara)

Pizzaiolo Sami El Sabawy got his start slinging slices at teglia-style Pizzarium, but it is his paper-thin, wood-fired personal pizzas that now draw crowds to A Rota in Tor Pignattara. The name, Roman slang for doing something nonstop, is fitting. Once you taste his crisp pies and golden fried snacks like supplì and fiori di zucca, you will probably want to go back again and again. El Sabawy uses a low-hydration dough that he rolls out with a pin, creating a shatteringly crisp crust that holds up to both classic and creative toppings. The margherita, with its vibrant tomato sauce, fior di latte, and fresh basil, is beautifully balanced. Do not miss the rotating specials, like a stuffed pizza packed with chard, potato, ham, and Parmigiano-Reggiano.

Frumentario (Re di Roma)

Alessandro Santilli, a former fine-dining chef with a passion for baking, opened Frumentario in 2023, just off Piazza Re di Roma. His Roman pizza al taglio is shaped by both restaurant rigor and deep respect for dough. Each slice is finished to order at the counter, with toppings added like a chef plating at the pass. Expect long-fermented, high-hydration doughs and sharp attention to detail. The setup is small, with just a counter and a few places to perch, and the vibe is more chef's table than classic pizza shop. Santilli sources vegetables from small farms and meats from expert butchers. Nothing goes out without intention.

I Quintili (Tuscolano, EUR)

Marco Quintili opened his first (now shuttered) pizzeria on the outskirts of Rome in 2017, bringing serious technical skill and a modern approach to the city's Neapolitan-style pizza scene. The second location, near the Via Tuscolana, followed in July 2020 and the third, near EUR, two years later. Quintili's pies merge Neapolitan dough with Roman flavor logic. The bases are long-fermented and baked long enough to hold their structure. The carbonara pizza is finished with grated cured egg yolk. The frittatine are filled with cacio e pepe or amatriciana. The menu is clever without being showy, and the crust holds up every time.

La Gatta Mangiona (Monteverde)

At his Monteverde pizzeria and trattoria, Giancarlo Casa balances Roman and Neapolitan techniques to create thick-rimmed pies with crusts that are tender, chewy, and crisp. The broccoli rabe and sausage pizza with smoked provolone leans southern. The capricciosa is a Roman staple, topped with artichokes, olives, prosciutto, and a hard-boiled egg. The fried starters are essential, especially the seasonal carciofi infarinati and the well-executed supplì. The drinks list covers craft beer, wine, grappa, and whiskey. At this point, La Gatta Mangiona is an institution.

L'Elementare (Trastevere)

Mirko Rizzo made a name for himself slinging top-tier pizza in teglia at Pommidoro in Centocelle, and with L'Elementare in Trastevere, he's taken on pizza tonda with the same irreverent, full-flavored approach. His pies don't hold back—toppings like the Porco Blu (chicory, capocollo, and a punchy blue cheese cream) lean rich and bold. But it's the fritti that really double down on indulgence: deep-fried tortellini swimming in cream and golden bricks of lasagna turned into crispy snacks. The beer list is stacked, so grab a cold one to balance it all out.

Lievito (EUR)

On a quiet street in the EUR district, Rome's marble-clad Fascist-era suburb, Lievito turns out some of the city's best pizza in teglia. Francesco Arnesano opened the place in 2022 and quickly earned a reputation for his light, deeply fermented dough and sharp flavor combinations. The toppings shift with the seasons and might include porcini with smoked provola and potatoes, stracciatella with coppa, and long-aged Prosciutto di Parma with cantaloupe. The fritti are listed on a chalkboard and often draw from Roman pasta traditions. Look out for carbonara fritters and cacio e pepe potato croquettes. Arnesano also bakes exceptional sourdough loaves year-round using heritage grains and panettone at Christmas.

Piccolo Buco (Centro Storico)

Few places near the Trevi Fountain care about sourcing, and frankly, most visitors don't expect them to. But at Piccolo Buco, pizzaiolo Luca Issa is doing something different. He works exclusively with local organic ingredients, partnering with small producers committed to traditional methods. His dough is mixed by hand and shaped into thick-rimmed rounds, then topped with things like sweet yellow tomatoes, buffalo mozzarella, anchovies, and a dusting of olive powder and capers. Every pie is finished with a carefully chosen olive oil that enhances the flavors without overwhelming them. It's thoughtful pizza in a part of town where that's anything but guaranteed.

Pizzarium (Cipro)

Roughly two decades ago, Gabriele Bonci flipped the script on Roman pizza al taglio with Pizzarium, pioneering a new-school take on pizza in teglia that leaned hard into artisanal breadmaking, impeccable sourcing, and wild topping combos. His high-hydration,

PIATTI DEL BUON RICORDO: ITALY'S EDIBLE SOUVENIRS

Some people collect "popeners" (Pope-themed bottle openers), or ill-advised bottles of limoncello as souvenirs from their travels in Italy. But for those in the know, the real prize is a Piatto del Buon Ricordo—a hand-painted ceramic plate that's both a piece of art and a passport to regional Italian cuisine. These plates aren't sold new in stores, though you can find them in thrift shops and on eBay for anywhere from €10 for 150 to €1,200 for a single plate (wild range, I know). Instead, they are earned, one meal at a time, at select restaurants across Italy that belong to the Unione Ristoranti del Buon Ricordo (Union of Restaurants of Good Remembrance).

The concept was cooked up in 1964 as a way to celebrate and safeguard regional Italian dishes. Each restaurant in the association chooses a signature dish that represents local traditions and ingredients. Diners who order the designated meal receive a Piatto del Buon Ricordo to take home, essentially a plate-sized certificate of gastronomic achievement. Painted by hand at Ceramiche Artistiche Solimene in Vietri sul Mare, these vibrant plates depict the restaurant's name, location, and often the dish itself in an unmistakable, slightly naive artistic style that oozes mid-century charm. The plates can change every five years, ensur-

ing that each restaurant can continue to evolve while still staying true to its roots.

Since their inception, Piatti del Buon Ricordo have inspired a dedicated following, and in 1977, an association of collectors was formed. Some people travel the length and breadth of Italy in search of new plates to add to their collection. Others stumble upon them by accident, perhaps lured into a trattoria in Mantova for tortelli di zucca or enticed by  a perfect cacciucco in Livorno and leave with more than just a full stomach.

At its core, the Piatto del Buon Ricordo initiative is a way of preserving Italy's culinary heritage, ensuring that traditional dishes don't get lost in the shuffle of fleeting food trends. Each plate tells a story of a dish, a place, a trattoria, and the people who keep these food traditions alive. It's also a way of encouraging food lovers to explore beyond the usual tourist circuits and dive into Italy's regional diversity, one meal (and one plate) at a time.

Romanè, near the Vatican Museums, is a contemporary trattoria in Rome participating in the tradition. Another Roman member, Checchino dal 1887, serves up a plate that has more appeal as a collectible than the food does as a meal these days, but the restaurant still pulls diners curious to eat inside Monte Testaccio's ancient amphora dump (see page 91). So next time you are in Roma, skip the kitschy Colosseum keychains and hit up a thrift shop in search of a Piatto del Buon Ricordo. A memorable meal beats a cheap souvenir every time.

long-fermented, and deeply flavorful dough is baked in rectangular pans and cut to order. You'll find everything from seasonal artichokes stewed until tender, to curls of guanciale under snowy heaps of pecorino. The classics like rossa and patate e mozzarella still hit every time. But don't stop at the pizza. The fried stuff here is next level: think polpette di bollito (croquettes made with shredded boiled beef), supplì alla carbonara (yes, deep-fried spaghetti with guanciale and egg), and lasagna fritta (exactly what it sounds like). Pizzarium pulls crowds from all over the world, so expect a wait, especially since it's just a stone's throw from the Vatican.

Ruver Teglia Frazionata (Aventino)

Alessandro Ruver opened this compact shop on Viale Aventino in late 2023, offering a personal take on Roman pizza al taglio shaped by years working alongside Gabriele Bonci. His dough is thinner and less airy than Bonci's signature style, a deliberate nod to old-school teglia traditions. Each base is made with organic flour from Mulino Belotti, hydrated heavily, and fermented for up to 36 hours. Vegetables come from a trusted farm in Ladispoli, mozzarella is delivered fresh daily, and every cooked topping goes through the electric oven, including slow-cooked rabbit and Chianina beef ragù. The pizza reflects both precision and personal style. You might find a margherita alongside a more composed option like the Ruver Rabbit, layered with potato, carrot cream, lemon oil, and braised rabbit finished with its own jus. This is pizza that respects tradition without replicating it and invites repeat visits from anyone who values careful sourcing and honest technique.

VICO Pizza & Wine (Centro Storico)

Enzo Coccia, the Neapolitan pizzaiolo behind La Notizia, opened VICO Pizza & Wine in 2023 in a former Renaissance palazzo near the Pantheon. VICO brings refined Neapolitan pizza to Rome in an elegant, almost baroque setting. Ciro De Vincenzo, Coccia's protege, runs the oven with precision: dough is long-fermented and baked into light, aromatic crusts. The menu bridges classic Margherita and Marinara with more inventive pies like Nerano and Genovese with tuna alongside street-food bites like Montanarine. The drinks list is curated by Salotto 42, and the whole atmosphere manages upscale warmth without pretension. For anyone craving standout Neapolitan pizza in Rome, VICO delivers.

MORE PIZZERIAS WORTH YOUR DOUGH

AmaRAnto (Salario)
Casa Manco (Testaccio)
Emma Pizzeria con Cucina (Centro Storico)
Eroi della Pizza (Trionfale)
Fratelli Trecca (Circo Massimo)
La Pratolina (Prati)
Pizza Chef (Tusculano)
Seu Pizza Illuminati (Trastevere)

FORNI

In Italian, "forno" translates to "oven," but in Rome, it also refers to bread bakeries, known elsewhere as "panifici" or "panetterie." While bread has been baked in Rome for millennia, the modern Roman forno emerged in the mid-twentieth century. Up until the 1970s, many Roman bakeries operated with coal-fired ovens and offered a limited selection of breads. After the day's bread baking concluded, locals would often bring their own dishes to cook using the ovens' residual heat.

During this period, new items like pizza bianca and pizza rossa were introduced to the forno repertoire, often baked "alla pala," referring to the wooden peel (pala) used to launch the uncooked dough onto the oven deck for baking. Some bakers claim this method originated as a way to test the oven's stone consistency, while others believe it was a clever means to feed many people using the ovens' downtime. Regardless of origins, pizza alla pala is typically as long as the oven is deep. That means up to five feet in some places.

Over the following decades, forni expanded their offerings beyond bread and pizza alla pala to include pizzette (small pizzas) made from puff pastry or over-proofed bread dough, as well as pastries and cookies. Today, stepping into most forni, you'll encounter a wide array of Roman sweets, from jam tarts to biscotti. During Carnevale, counters are heaped with fried dough in various forms.

All these forno goods have been joined by more elaborate meals, establishing cafeteria-like dining options featuring rotisserie chickens, roasted vegetables, pasta salads, and other roasted and baked specialties sold in aluminum containers for takeaway.

In a city where food traditions remain largely intact, the forno persists as a cultural anchor. Even with modern trends in sourdough and specialty flours, the Roman bakery continues to embody simplicity, quality, and the daily ritual of stopping in for something freshly made.

The best approach to navigating a Roman bakery is to start just by hanging back and seeing how the flow works. Often there are separate sections divided by an imaginary line only regulars know. At Antico Forno Roscioli, for example, the counter on the right is for placing bread, cake, and made-to-order sandwich orders while the attached counter is for pizza, supplì, and pre-made pizza sandwiches. If you mess up, no one behind the counter is shy about letting you know.

honey and nuts, and excellent rosette (see page 279), the hollow Roman sandwich rolls that can be filled to order at the deli counter in the back. With its old-school feel and loyal following, Colapicchioni continues to serve real Roman bakery culture without the spectacle.

Antico Forno Roscioli (Centro Storico)

Founded in 1972 by Marco Roscioli, Antico Forno Roscioli might not qualify as truly "antico," but that doesn't stop Romans from lining up for its pizza alla pala, pane casereccio, and crunchy tozzetti. Today Marco's kids run the place, keeping those deep bread ovens working overtime in the back. Service can be brusque and the lines painfully long (go in the morning to beat them). The real reason to join the crowd lined up under the glowing neon sign is the pizza alla pala. In the morning, the offerings are stripped back to essentials like rossa with bright tomato sauce, bianca with olive oil and salt, and patate with thin slices of potato. Around lunch, the place shifts into high gear as the counter fills with elaborate toppings. The best bet is always one of the classics. The dough has structure and depth, with a crispy base and a bit of chew that nails the Roman standard.

Forno Angelo Colapicchioni (Prati)

Forno Angelo Colapicchioni in the Prati neighborhood has been baking Roman breads and sweets since 1934, when Nunziatella Colapicchioni brought her Umbrian know-how to the capital. Today, the shop is run by Angelo Colapicchioni and remains a local favorite for its seasonal sweets like Pangiallo, a golden cake packed with

Forno Campo de' Fiori (Centro Storico)

Despite the linen curtains suggesting an 1888 foundation, Forno Campo de' Fiori actually opened in 1970 and has been feeding locals and tourists from its corner spot in the bustling piazza ever since. Now run by Fabrizio Roscioli, cousin and competitor to the family behind Antico Forno Roscioli nearby, the bakery turns out Roman staples, both sweet and savory. Pizza alla pala, baked directly on the oven floor, is sold by weight. Go straight for the pizza con i fiori di zucca if it's out. You can watch the pizzaiolo stretch out the next batch through the side window while you eat yours standing on the cobblestones. During the afternoon break, when the main shop closes, the annex across the alley stays open. That's where you get the pizza con mortadella: pizza bianca split and stuffed with mortadella. No frills. Just salt, fat, and carbs in the best possible combination.

Panificio Bonci (Trionfale)

Panificio Bonci, a short walk from Gabriele Bonci's famed Pizzarium near the Cipro metro stop, is a compact bakery that delivers big on flavor and technique. Known for its deeply fermented doughs and use of heirloom stone-milled flours, the shop turns out exceptional pizza bianca, rustic loaves, cookies, and pastries. Sandwiches stuffed with porchetta or mortadella draw steady crowds, and regulars know to order a few pizzette di sfoglia for the road. While Pizzarium is the better-known destination for creative pizza al taglio, the panificio shows off Bonci's obsessive attention to bread and grain, offering a different but equally essential taste of his approach to Roman baking.

Triticum Micropanificio Agricolo (Marconi)

Triticum in the Marconi district keeps things simple, directing all attention to the glass case packed with sweet and savory baked goods. The offerings rotate but often include soft focaccia topped with tomatoes or olives, crisp slices of pizza alla pala, buttery laminated pastries, and tightly wound cinnamon rolls. Behind the counter, shelves are lined with crusty sourdough loaves inspired by French and Italian baking traditions (the pane multicereale is a showstopper). These breads are sold alongside a curated selection of condiments, including preserves from Marco Colzani and honey from Miele Thun, chosen to complement the bakery's precise, grain-forward work.

Pizza Nader (Roma 70)

Pizza Nader sits in Roma 70, a suburban pocket in the city's south that once stored grain for Emperor Nerva's Rome. The place might look like your run-of-the-mill pizza al taglio joint, but Nader Abdelkader is doing something else entirely. Stone-milled flours from Campania, Le Marche, and Sicily are stacked near the door like a quiet flex. Nader talks about flour the way some people talk about wine, crediting farmers and millers for the complexity of his crust and the depth of his naturally leavened breads. His kebab, made with house-made flatbread and carefully seasoned meat, is one of the best in town. The breads alone are worth the trip, each one showing the same obsessive attention to grain, fermentation, and technique, but stick around for the supplì and pizza, too.

STREET FOOD AND CAFETERIAS

Romans eat a lot of fast food on the go. And not just McDonald's (see page 191), KFC, and the other global chains planted around town. Plenty of people need a quick and cheap lunch. Forget the fantasy that everyone is sitting down to five courses with a carafe of wine. Traffic makes going home impossible, and time is short. That is where fast food joints, cafeteria counters, and what locals call "strit fud" come in. But we are not talking about food trucks or mobile carts. These are brick-and-mortar spots with a couple of stools at most, a short menu, and cooking that gets straight to the point. You eat standing, leaning, or perched for a minute before moving on. This is Rome's real fast food: a hot supplì still steaming from the fryer, a sandwich stuffed with braised off-cuts, pizza baked in a tiny pan, or a trapizzino filling oozing sauce down your wrist. This is the fuel that keeps the city running.

Amerina (Centro Storico)

Amerina La Piazzetta, tucked into Largo dei Librari just off Campo de' Fiori, nails the balance between neighborhood vibes and contemporary drinking culture. Named for proprietor Paolo Angelucci's Abruzzese grandma, supplì are textbook (crisp shell, molten rice and mozzarella inside) and the pizza in padellino comes out light, airy, and perfectly charred in its little pan. What sets the place apart, though, is the beverage list: natural wines from thoughtful producers and a rotation of Italian craft beers that actually match the food's quality. It's casual, lively, and one of the few spots in the historic center where you can snack like a local and drink like you're in on the secret.

C'è Pasta e Pasta (Trastevere)

A short stroll from Trastevere Station lands you at this kosher counter-service spot, a favorite for Roman Jewish staples. At C'è Pasta e Pasta, the menu spans crowd-pleasers like crispy carciofi alla giudia, golden fried cod fillets, and alicitti con l'indivia, a comforting baked dish of anchovies and escarole. Zucchini concia, fried and marinated, is essential. True to its name, there's no shortage of pasta: some ready to eat, others to take home and cook later.

Mordi e Vai (Testaccio)

Mordi e Vai is the Testaccio Market stall that distills Rome's working-class cooking into a sandwich. It was founded by the late Sergio Esposito, a former butcher who turned his skills to stuffing ciabatta rolls with slow-cooked Roman mains like braised brisket and simmered artichokes. The recipes were developed alongside Sergio's wife Mara, whose cooking channels pure Roman comfort. After Sergio's passing, their son Giuliano took the reins, keeping the family tradition alive.

Supplizio (Centro Storico)

Supplizio is Arcangelo Dandini's love letter to Rome's most iconic fried snack. The chef behind L'Arcangelo serves supplì in a range of flavors—classic meat sauce with mozzarella, carbonara, cacio e pepe, amatriciana—each one fried in small batches (hence the lines). The space feels deliberately unfussy, with mismatched chairs and a retro vibe, which keeps the focus exactly where it belongs: on the city's ultimate comfort food, elevated but still faithful to its roots.

Trapizzino (Testaccio, Trastevere, Ponte Milvio, Prati, Esquilino)

A trapizzino is not a pizza in the traditional sense, but something that Trapizzino owner Stefano Callegari invented in 2008 in Testaccio at his (now closed) slice joint 00100. The clever fast food concept became so popular that he converted the place into a dedicated fast-ca-

sual spot. A trapizzino is a triangular piece of spongy, naturally leavened pizza dough baked in a sheet pan. One side is sliced open and filled like a pita with your choice of a savory dish, which could be chicken cacciatore, burrata and salted anchovies, a single meatball, or eggplant parmigiana. The trapizzino, so-called because it is made from pizza dough but resembles the tri-cornered tramezzino sandwich, is served in a paper cone to capture any juices as you eat it on the street or perched at one of Trapizzino's high-top tables. What began as a way to deliver hearty food in an affordable, portable form to local Romans during an era of financial crisis completely took off in the years that followed, and now there are Trapizzino locations all over town (and indeed all over the world) serving this delectable street food.

MORE QUICK BITES

Becco (Trionfale)
Da Corrado (Testacio)
Dar Filettaro (Centro Storico)
I Supplì (Trastevere)
Pandalì (Centro Storico)
Rotolo (Cipro)
SiCCHè Roba Toscana (Testaccio)

PASTICCERIE AND CIOCCOLATERIE

Romans have a sweet tooth that keeps the city's pastry and chocolate shops buzzing from dawn to dusk. In the morning, cornetti and maritozzi are the go-to breakfast, washed down with a caffè or cappuccino at the bar. Later in the day, locals might swing by a pasticceria for a sugar hit or to pick up a tray of pasticcini (those glossy bite-sized pastries that make the perfect gift when you're invited to someone's home for dinner). Here's where I get my sugar rush.

Boccione (Ghetto)

Il Boccione, the tiny kosher bakery in Rome's Jewish Ghetto (see page 40), has been turning out pastries since the nineteenth century from its unmarked storefront on Via del Portico d'Ottavia. It is best known for its torched-looking ricotta and sour cherry tart, whose nearly burnt crust hides a rich, sweet filling. Another standout is the dense, chewy pizza ebraica, packed with almonds, raisins, pine nuts, and candied fruit. The shop is run by generations of the Limentani family, a small group of formidable women who keep the pace brisk and the quality high. Lines form early and the goods often sell out by early afternoon, so plan accordingly if you want a true taste of Roman Jewish baking tradition.

Cafè Merenda (Ostiense)

Caffè Merenda in Ostiense is a pastry-focused café that takes its baking seriously without ever feeling precious. Everything is made on-site, from the delicate cornetti to cakes and tarts that change with the seasons. The coffee program is strong, with specialty coffee served alongside espresso and cappuccino. The vibe is calm and unforced, and regulars come for quality without the usual fuss.

Casa Manfredi (Aventino)

Casa Manfredi is a sleek pasticceria and café near the FAO (see page 58), where precision meets indulgence. Run by Giorgia Proia and Daniele Antonelli, it's known for buttery viennoiserie, polished pastries, and composed cakes. The maritozzi are airy and not too sweet, filled with gently whipped cream. Their modern takes on classic Italian desserts show serious technique without losing soul. It's a favorite among locals for a quiet breakfast or afternoon pick-me-up, served with style but never stiff.

Moriondo e Gariglio (Centro Storico)

Moriondo e Gariglio is Rome's most storied chocolate shop, founded in the late nineteenth century as the official supplier to the House of Savoy and still going strong in its discreet location just off Via del Corso. Inside, you won't find trendy branding or flashy displays. Instead, there are glass cases filled with hand-molded pralines, boozy cremini, candied orange peels dipped in dark chocolate, and old-school gianduja squares wrapped in metallic paper. The atmosphere is austere, almost monastic, and the service is formal and unfussy. This is a place where time stands still and chocolate is treated with quiet reverence.

Regoli (Esquilino)

The Regoli family were originally charcoal makers

from Tuscany when they came to Rome in 1916. In the mid-twentieth century, they shifted the family business to pastry making. Since then, they have transformed their small operation into one of the city's most beloved pastry shops. The display cases are packed with cakes, maritozzi, and seasonal treats like bignè in March, colombe at Easter, and pandoro at Christmas. Get your pastries packaged to take away, or order at the counter and the kitchen will send the items to your table at the neighboring Caffé Regoli, which also serves coffee.

WORTH A DETOUR FOR A SWEET TREAT

Andreotti (Ostiense)
Barnum (Centro Storico)
Casa Manfredi Teatro (Ostiense)
Gastromario (San Giovanni)
Gruè (Nomentano)
Libera (Appio-Latino)
Luna (Centro Storico)
Nero Vaniglia (Garbatella)
Roscioli Caffè (Centro Storico)
SAID dal 1923 (San Lorenzo)

GELATO

Gelato is one of Italy's great culinary contributions, but the truth is, much of what's out there in Rome is industrial garbagio churned from oil, emulsifiers, and artificial colors and flavors. Don't buy it? Just check the ingredient lists, which have to be posted or produced upon request. You'd be surprised how much olio vegetale and codes for additives make an appearance. You can hardly blame spots for giving up as the cost of natural ingredients has soared. That's left locals guessing and tourists totally adrift when it comes to spotting the real stuff. TikTok might try to help, but the aesthetic cues it pushes, like gelato hidden under metal lids is superior, are just wrong. You can't rely on a gelato's container alone to determine quality.

It is a pretty safe bet, however, that if the tubs are piled high with fluffy, overflowing heaps, it's not artisan. It's chemistry. That volume comes from stabilizers and powders that whip air into the base, not from skill or quality ingredients. Neon green mint? That's dye. Real mint gelato is white, or at most a pale sage if it's leaf-infused. If the ingredient list is littered with items starting with "E," you're eating coded additives, and many of them are totally unnecessary. While some, like carob bean flour (E410), are harmless and natural, others are better suited to a lab than a cone. Steer clear of shops with giant plastic gelato cones out front or that sling bizarre flavors like Puffo (bubble gum, and yes, named after the Smurfs). And don't be fooled by buzzwords like "artigianale" or "produzione propria." Those terms suggesting artisanship are slapped on anything, even if it's made from industrial powder and paste.

Now for the basics: gelato is not ice cream. It contains less air, which gives it a dense, smooth texture. It's served slightly warmer than ice cream, so it melts more evenly and delivers flavor more immediately. It also tends to have less fat because it's made with milk (or milk and cream) instead of just cream. Another key difference is the base. While American ice cream is typically custard-based with eggs, most traditional Italian gelato is not. Flavors like crema and zabaione are the exceptions—they're egg-enriched by design.

Rome has its own classics when it comes to gelato. Riso (rice) is surprisingly hard to find outside the capital. The aforementioned crema and zabaione are staples. Stracciatella, nocciola, cioccolato fondente, and pistachio are everywhere, but the real test is how natural and balanced those familiar flavors taste. If the pistachio is neon, run away.

Sorbetto has always cohabited with gelato in Roman shops, giving dairy-free eaters a seat at the table and offering everyone else a tart, refreshing foil to creamier scoops. Lemon and strawberry are the classic Roman flavors, and when done well, their flavors remind you that the best sorbetti taste exactly like ripe fruit and nothing else.

Rome eats a shocking amount of gelato and sorbetto, and not just in summer. This is a year-round ritual. The standard used to be two flavors even for the smallest cup or cone. These days, you can ask for just one scoop, which honestly feels like the end of an era. Maybe it's a sign of restraint, or maybe people just want to enjoy one thing done right. Whatever the reason, the gelato obsession isn't going anywhere. And if you're in Rome, here's a local tip: ask for doppia panna, a generous dollop of barely sweetened whipped cream in the cone and again on top. Now let's get into it.

Al Settimo Gelo (Prati)

An OG in the natural gelato movement, Al Settimo Gelo has been quietly turning out meticulously crafted, all-natural gelato since the late '90s. The commitment to quality is absolute: organic milk, fresh eggs, raw cane sugar, no dyes, no additives, ever. Their Sicilian pistachio—intensely nutty, creamy, and unapologetically savory—is one of Rome's finest. Equally noteworthy are their Persian-inspired flavors like saffron and rosewater, which offer a subtle, elegant departure from the usual Italian standards. Many of the fruit sorbets are made with produce gelataia Mirella Fiumanó cultivates herself, giving seasonal flavors like fig, apricot, and pear extraordinary freshness and character. It's a place for purists and curious palates alike.

Fatamorgana (Centro Storico, Monti, Trastevere)

Fatamorgana is a small chain founded by Maria Agnese Spagnuolo, a student of the Claudio Torcè gelato school (see page 339). Each flavor is made from all-natural ingredients, without chemical additives or artificial flavors, and all are gluten free. Spagnuolo's whimsical creations are often seasonal and always draw on quality produce, spices, nuts, and herbs. In the summer, try Panacea (ginseng, almond milk, and mint) with Punch Paradise (strawberries and wine). There are a number of chocolate variations ideal for winter, including Kentucky (dark chocolate and tobacco).

Fior di Luna (Trastevere)

Only fair trade and high quality ingredients go into Fior di Luna's seasonally driven gelato. Look for strawberry in the spring and persimmon in the fall, as well as year-round classics like hazelnut and pistachio. In the winter, Fior di Luna produces chocolate and serves thick, rich hot chocolate of their own production.

Formaessenza (Marconi)

Stefano Ferrara's Formaessenza opened in 2024 and ditches cones and cups altogether. Everything is served in jars, a format that gives him full control over texture, temperature, and layering. The lineup includes Lovers (gelato cakes), Spiritoso (boozy flavors), Quintessenza (his signatures, like salted peanut with caramel and chocolate crumble), Must Have (classics done his way), Gelaveg (fully vegan), and Kelato (sugar-free, keto-friendly, and developed with a nutritionist). Ferrara also reinvents industrial formats: I-Conico, a nod to the Cornetto; Diametro 7, a customizable ice cream sandwich; and bonbons, which deliver big flavor in a single bite. It's all made in-house, using cutting-edge equipment and a sharp eye for detail that favors taste over tradition.

Gelateria dei Gracchi (Prati, Centro Storico, Nomentano)

I'm obsessed with the Zibibbo (zabaione spiked with Sicilian sweet wine) and pistachio at this beloved artisanal gelato shop. Beyond the classic flavors, there is also apple-cinnamon and meringue with pistachios. If you're not in the market for a whole scoop, they are famous for their bonbons.

Gelateria del Teatro (Centro Storico)

Lemons from Amalfi, pistachios from Sicily, and hazelnuts from Piedmont are transformed into creamy gelato at Gelateria del Teatro's two central locations. There are really rare and surprising flavors like dark chocolate with Nero d'Avola wine and raspberry with sage.

Gelateria Gori (Piazza Sempione)

The Gori siblings studied the art of gelato making with the master Claudio Torcè and have brought his approach to natural, creative, quality production to their own shop near Piazza Sempione in northern Rome. Try unusual flavors like buckwheat, whortleberry, and pumpkin seed, or go for the equally impressive classics.

La Gourmandise (Monteverde Vecchio)

La Gourmandise sits on a quiet street in Monteverde Vecchio, far from the city's tourist churn, and turns out some of the most thoughtful gelato in town. The focus is on technique and clarity, with a commitment to seasonal and often organic ingredients. Flavors like marron glacé and rose are calibrated for depth. The pistachio, made from slow-roasted Sicilian nuts, is rich without being heavy. But the real reason to keep coming back is the rotating lineup of lesser-known seasonal flavors that hit with precision.

Neve di Latte (Centro Storico, Flaminio, Prati)

Originally opened by gelato pioneer Ermano di Pomponio behind the MAXXI in 2011, Neve di Latte was the fruit of maniacal sourcing and expert churning. Though the maestro left his shop (you can find him in Civitavecchia at Gelateria Ingredienti Nobili), his sensibilities have generally been preserved by new ownership, which has also expanded the brand. Expect gelato made with rich Bavarian milk and cream, Amedei chocolate from Tuscany, certified organic pistachios, and seasonal fruits.

Otaleg! (Trastevere, Monteverde Vecchio)

The name of Torcè alum Marco Radicioni's gelateria is simply "gelato" spelled backwards. Marco hand crafts gelato daily in his laboratorio in Monteverde Vecchio (where he also offers classes), relying on exceptional ingredients churned in a vertical Cattabriga machine. He has a knack for sorbetti, especially stone fruit flavors, and the salted pistachio is stunning. The location in

Trastevere only serves scoops, while up in Monteverde there is a specialty coffee corner and a selection of sweet and savory pastries.

Torcè (Aventino, EUR)

If there is one person responsible for the relatively recent and completely dramatic improvement of Rome's gelato culture, it is Claudio Torcè. He trained some of Rome's premier gelatai (Maria Spagnuolo of Fatamorgana, Marco Radicioni of Otaleg, and the Gori siblings, to name a few) and prided himself on producing more than 100 all-natural gelato flavors without compromising quality. In 2018, Juraj Detvaj purchased Claudio's gelato chain and continues the tradition. Options range from the classics chocolate and strawberry to unique flavors such as Sichuan pepper, habanero, cacio e pepe, and black sesame.

SHOPPING

Shopping for food in Rome is woven into the rhythm of daily life. Meals are often built around what looks good that day, rather than planned in advance. Small refrigerators mean people shop more often, and seasonality still matters to many. Most Romans buy their groceries at supermarkets, and Italy has nearly as many per capita as the United States. Yet many, especially older generations, continue to visit markets, butchers, fishmongers, and gastronomie on a regular basis. These small, specialized shops are in constant competition with supermarket chains, whose convenience and low prices threaten their survival. This section is not about supermercati. It is about the markets, butchers, and cheese mongers that prioritize quality and keep Rome's food culture grounded.

MERCATI

When Italy was unified in 1870, King Victor Emanuele II's new government was tasked with whipping Rome into shape. After centuries of papal neglect, the city of more than one hundred fifty thousand people was hardly ready to act like a European capital. Poverty was widespread, market hygiene was dire, food prices soared, and poor infrastructure made it difficult to get provisions into the city. The government set about modernizing daily life, and food was part of the agenda. New municipal markets were constructed across the growing metropolis, and the Mercati Generali (see page 237) were created as a central hub where vendors could buy directly from the state before reselling at their stalls.

It has been roughly one hundred fifty years since most produce in Rome has had any real farm-to-table identity. A few farmers' markets exist, and some stalls in Testaccio or Trionfale are run by farmers themselves, but the norm is the fruttivendolo: the produce vendor who buys wholesale and sells retail. This is not a criticism, just the reality of eating in Rome. Which is why having a fruttivendolo di fiducia (a trusted greengrocer) is essential if you care about provenance. I do not need to visit every farm myself; I rely on my vendors to do the vetting. That trust is sacred, and it extends well beyond produce to fishmongers, butchers, salumerie, and cheese shops.

Markets in Rome reflect the city's layered history. Some are open-air, with stalls dismantled by early afternoon. Others are semi-enclosed, offering partial shelter. A few occupy nineteenth-century iron and glass pavilions, while others sit in modern structures with cold storage and parking. The typical mercato rionale, or neighborhood market, is about utility: locals buying raw ingredients for home cooking. You may find a bar tucked inside for a quick espresso, but otherwise these are not places to linger.

Farmers' markets are different. They are rarer, more curated, and usually convene weekly. The Mercato di Campagna Amica near the Circus Maximus runs most weekends, the Biomercato della Città dell'Altra Economia takes place some Sundays in Testaccio's former slaughterhouse, and Terra Terra bounces between Centocelle and San Paolo.

Some municipal markets have evolved. Trionfale, near the Vatican, and Testaccio, in the repurposed slaughterhouse district, now host vendors serving cooked food: Roman street snacks, Thai noodles, made-to-order salads. These are designed for workers on lunch break, not home cooks, but the markets still identify primarily as places to buy ingredients. And plenty of those ingredients come prepped: artichokes trimmed, puntarelle shredded, peas shelled, chicory cleaned, minestrone mixes bagged up from vegetables too tired to sell whole.

The truth is most Romans shop at supermarkets, and very few use markets regularly. The convenience and pricing of the chains have won out, and neighborhood markets tend to survive in districts with aging populations. They are open Monday through Saturday from about 8 a.m. to 1 p.m. Most fishmongers and many produce stalls keep Tuesday through Saturday hours. The clientele skews heavily toward women over sixty who came of age just as supermarkets were spreading, and who still devote the time to market shopping two or three times a week.

Do not underestimate them. On a Friday or Saturday morning these women will elbow you out of the way at the butcher or plow through with a trolley on their way to the fishmonger. Stay alert. Vendors generally do not mind you looking or taking photos, but block a paying customer and that's a problem.

You don't need fluent Italian to shop in Rome's markets, but you do need basic manners. Say "*buongiorno*" when you walk up, and "*grazie, arrivederci*" when you leave. That's the bare minimum, and no one's mad if that's all you've got. Between the greetings, pointing and gestures work well, especially if you're smiling. Nothing disarms a Roman like a grinning foreigner.

The two most important phrases when it comes to shopping in markets are "*posso?*" (may I?) and "*ci provano sempre*" (they'll always try to get one over on you). Let's start with the first. When you're at a produce stall, it is not only polite—it is borderline the law—that, unless you are a seasoned regular, you ask permission to select your produce before jumping in and manhandling it. Sometimes your "posso" will be met with a stern "no," especially if you're ordering figs, persimmons, or another delicate fruit. Other times, the response will be to simply throw a paper bag in your direction as an invitation to start selecting. Use one bag per type. Most produce is sold by weight rather than by the item (artichokes are an exception), so items need to be separated for proper tabulation. If you are not granted permission to select on your own, the vendor will take your order, filling bags with your requested items.

This is where the second phrase comes in. If you're not a regular, if you are young, and even if you speak flawless Italian, the vendor will try to sneak in bruised or blemished things. This is part furbizia (cunning) and

part hazing. If you call them out, they will know that you know your stuff, and if you become a regular, they won't try the funny business again. The good news: It doesn't take long for vendors to recognize you. Here's where to start.

Campo de' Fiori (Centro Storico)

Now more tourist trap than traditional market, Campo de' Fiori is worth a pass-by for the few remaining produce stalls, but skip the sad vendors selling rancid oil, industrial salumi, and phallic-shaped pasta and limoncello bottles.

Mercato di Campagna Amica del Circo Massimo (Circo Massimo)

Every weekend a building near the Circus Maximus turns into one of the city's few true farmers' markets. Organized by Coldiretti, Italy's national agricultural association, the Mercato di Campagna Amica brings in producers from Lazio and beyond who sell directly to consumers. Stalls are piled with seasonal fruit and vegetables, olive oil, wine, honey, cured meats, cheeses, and breads, much of it organic and all of it traceable to the farm. I'm a devotee of dairy farmers and cheesemakers Casa Lawrence and Az. Ag. Valleluterana. Go see them and buy their cheeses!

Mercato di San Giovanni di Dio (Monteverde)

This neighborhood market in Monteverde is super local, with friendly vendors selling seasonal fruit, vegetables, and pantry staples to longtime residents who still shop daily.

Mercato Nomentano (Nomentano)

Housed in a beautiful 1920s building, this market has a vintage vibe and a strong core of traditional vendors.

Mercato di Piazza Epiro (Appio-Latino)

In a quiet pocket of the Appio-Latino district, Piazza Epiro hosts one of Rome's most overlooked neighborhood markets. It's home to La Formaggeria, Francesco Loreti's exceptional cheese shop packed with regional Italian wheels, raw milk specialties, and rare finds you won't see in tourist-heavy areas. Just steps away, Bottega delle Carni – Fratelli Papalotti delivers top-quality cuts with old-school Roman precision.

Mercato Trionfale (Trionfale)

Mercato Trionfale, just north of the Vatican on Via Andrea Doria, is Rome's largest covered food market, with over two hundred seventy stalls dedicated to fresh ingredients. The red-coded meat section features butchers. In the blue-coded aisles, you'll find the city's highest concentration of fishmongers offering pristine seafood: whole fish, filets, and shellfish so fresh they look just pulled from the sea. The pale green stalls sell farm-direct produce.

Mercato Campo Marzio (Centro Storico)

This tiny, open-air market in the heart of the historic center is low-key but high-quality, drawing locals for its excellent produce, fresh herbs, and small-town vibe just steps from the tourist crush.

Nuovo Mercato di Testaccio (Testaccio)

Anchored by decades-old produce stalls and legendary butchers, this modern glass-and-steel market is where Testaccio's soul lives on. Look for simmered veal brisket at Mordi e Vai, a huge selection of meat and offal at Sartor, and vibrant Roman greens stacked high at Giancarlo il Velletrano.

Nuovo Mercato Esquilino (Esquilino)

Rome's most international market bursts with Chinese, Bangladeshi, and North African ingredients you won't find elsewhere, alongside some of the city's best-priced fish and imported produce.

MACELLAI

Butcher stalls in Rome's markets and brick-and-mortar shops reflect both deep traditions and the city's shifting demographics. Some are old-school, selling the fifth quarter that defines cucina romana. Others cater to newer tastes, specializing in dry-aged beef, which has gone from luxury to standard fare. At a typical macelleria you will find veal, pork, chicken, lamb, and, more and more, refrigerated cases devoted to steaks resting on the bone and darkened with age. You might also see whole rabbits or deboned chicken thighs already seasoned and ready to cook.

Roman butchers are indispensable for ingredients that don't get play at supermarkets but remain staples at home. Coratella, a mix of lamb lungs, heart, and liver, is especially popular. Pajata, the intenstines of milk-fed veal, can be found whole or tied into rings. Vegetables like zucchini or peppers may be hollowed out and ready to stuff with ground meat. These butchers serve cooks who still work with time and technique.

The multicultural layers of the city are visible here, too. Halal butchers cluster at Mercato Esquilino and on the city's eastern edge. Kosher butchers, like Pascarella in Trastevere, supply Rome's Jewish community. Filipino-run stalls at Trionfale are heavy on pork cuts and seasoned sausages. Eastern European butchers favor smoked meats and pork cuts unfamiliar to most Italians. Equine butchers remain common across neighborhoods, selling steaks, ground meat, sausages, and lean roasts.

Shopping at a Roman butcher requires some vocabulary and a bit of trust. Cuts do not always correspond to what Anglophones know, and the simplest way to order is to tell the vendor what you plan to cook and for how many people. Clarity counts more than charm. Regulars tend to get better treatment, and with time a good butcher will remember your preferences and set aside what you want without needing to be asked.

MACELLAI DI FIDUCIA

Antica Macelleria Annibale (Centro Storico)
Bioenomacelleria Novecentosedici (Colosseo)
Bottega delle Carni-Fratelli Papalotti
   (Appio-Latino)
Bottega Liberati (Don Bosco)
Feroci (Centro Storico)
Mariani (Monteverde Vecchio)
Pascarella (Trastevere)
Sartor (Testaccio)
The Butcher (Trionfale)

PESCIVENDOLI

Pescivendoli, or fishmongers, are a fixture of most markets. The largest cluster is at Trionfale, where the southern side is devoted entirely to seafood from across the Mediterranean. Deliveries usually arrive Tuesday and Friday. Look for clear eyes, shiny skin, and red, moist gills. Avoid dull eyes, slimy texture, or a strong odor. Shellfish should be tightly closed or react to touch. Labels can be inconsistent, but vendors are supposed to identify fish as wild, farmed, or frozen. Ask to have it scaled, cleaned, or cut however you want. Some of my favorite fishmongers also have brick-and-mortar shops around town, which means you can count on them for consistent quality even outside the market setting.

PESCIVENDOLI DI FIDUCIA

Da Olaf il Vichingo (Trionfale)
Famiglia Galluzzi – Pescheria dal 1894 (Gregorio VII)
Sor Duilio (Pietralata)

CHEESE, CURED MEATS, AND PANTRY ITEMS

Rome is full of gourmet food shops that specialize in cheeses, cured meats, and pantry staples. These shops range from market counters run by cheese enthusiasts to sleek addresses where natural wine flows alongside cheese boards. They are the places Romans turn to for everyday provisions and special-occasion splurges, and most will happily vacuum-pack things to survive the trip home. Whether you are after a wedge of raw milk cheese, a hunk of aged prosciutto, or jars of marinated vegetables, these counters deliver a crash course in the city's dairy and salumi obsessions.

Beppe e I Suoi Formaggi (Centro Storico)

After more than a decade of selling Italian and French cheeses and wine at the edge of the historic Ghetto, Beppe e I Suoi Formaggi renovated and considerably downsized its space and menu. Now the single dining room is mostly occupied by an incredible array of chees-

DECODING FOOD LABELS

Understanding how to decode the labels and signage in Roman markets can give you a major edge when it comes to buying food that's local, fresh, and responsibly sourced. While not every vendor will offer complete transparency, especially in the busiest markets, there are standard codes and designations that can help you assess provenance, quality, and in some cases, how a product was handled before reaching the stall.

Let's start with fruits and vegetables. EU regulations require fresh produce to be labeled by category and origin. Category I (Cat. I) means the produce is visually uniform: smooth peppers, blemish-free apples, photogenic zucchine. Cat. II products may be smaller or more irregular in shape but are often just as flavorful, sometimes more so. Don't assume the prettier tomato is the better one. Many seasoned Roman shoppers prefer Cat. II when buying for flavor and value.

Origin labels tell you where something was grown.

"Origine Italia" means it was produced somewhere in the country, but more specific regional markers like "Lazio", "Sicilia," or "Puglia" are especially helpful if you're shopping seasonally. Produce marked "extracomunitario" comes from outside the EU and usually involves longer transport and more storage time. Some market stalls will mark items as "produzione propria", indicating the goods were grown on their farm. Those are your best bet for freshness.

When it comes to seafood, the most important code is the FAO zone, a designation from the UN's Food and Agriculture Organization that tells you where the fish was caught. The most relevant one for Rome is FAO 37, which refers to the Mediterranean Sea. FAO 37.1.1, in particular, covers the western Mediterranean and the Tyrrhenian Sea—coastal waters that include most of Italy's western seaboard. Fish labeled FAO 27 (North-East Atlantic) or FAO 34 and FAO 51 (off the coast of Africa or in the Indian Ocean) generally traveled farther and may have been frozen.

You'll also see additional terms at fish stalls. "Pescato" means wild-caught. "Allevato" means farmed. "Decongelato" means previously frozen. This last one is especially important; some vendors will try to pass off

es made by, among others, owner Beppe Giovale. The menu is predictably dairy focused with cheese plates, as well as butter and ricotta, which are paired with salted anchovies and honey, respectively, alongside natural vino. There's a second location in the Mercato Trionfale

Forme Dispensa a Ripa (Trastevere)

After a career working in Roman gourmet temples like Salumeria Roscioli, Pasquale Borriello struck out on his own in 2022. His small shop in Trastevere near the church of San Francesco a Ripa has a few high-top tables where you can sip natural wine or craft beer alongside Italy's greatest cheeses. All the big names are on the menu– Parmigiano-Reggiano, gorgonzola, and mozzarella di bufala among them–but Borriello favors the smallest and most artisanal producers of these famous styles. In addition to formaggio, Forme sells cured meats, sandwiches, and pantry items like jars of obscure marinated vegetables.

La Formaggeria (Appio-Latino)

At his stall in Mercato di Piazza Epiro, Francesco Loreti sells more than 100 cheeses from Italy, France, and the UK, including raw milk cheddars and funky Stilton. A second-generation vendor with roots in Umbria, Loreti built La Formaggeria on pure love of dairy. He'll spend an hour curating a tasting and send you off with some of the best cheeses available anywhere.

MORE ESSENTIAL COUNTERS
DOL - Di Origine Laziale (Centocelle)
La Differenza (Appio-Latino)
La Tradizione (Cipro)
Salumeria Roscioli (Centro Storico)
Taste'Accio (Testaccio)
Va Sano (Salario)

defrosted shrimp or calamari as fresh. They're required to disclose it, but the signage can be easy to miss. If in doubt, ask. The answer may determine whether you're sautéing a local catch or something that's been shipped halfway across the world and thawed that morning.

Meat and eggs come with a different set of identifiers. Eggs in Italy are stamped with a number that tells you everything from farming conditions to country of origin. The first digit ranges from 0 to 3, and it matters: 0 is organic, 1 is free-range, 2 is barn-raised, and 3 is caged. Most market vendors and small grocers sell eggs in categories 0 and 1.

Following the initial number is a country code (IT for Italy) followed by a sequence that identifies the farm. For example, 0IT12345 means the egg is organic and produced in Italy. This code might seem bureaucratic, but it's a reliable way to spot better-quality eggs, especially when cartons look similar but the pricing varies.

For meat and dairy, particularly cheeses and cured meats, look for EU designations like DOP (Denominazione di Origine Protetta) and IGP (Indicazione Geografica Protetta). DOP means the item was produced entirely in a specific area using local ingredients and traditional methods. Think Parmigiano-Reggiano or Pecorino Romano. IGP is slightly broader. It means that at least one stage of the production process is tied to a specific region. You might also encounter STG (Specialità Tradizionale Garantita), which recognizes traditional recipes even if they're not tied to a particular place, and PAT (Prodotto Agroalimentare Tradizionale), a designation from the Italian government for regionally significant products.

These labels aren't guarantees of quality, but they do indicate traceability and compliance with production standards. If you're deciding between two wheels of cheese or two varieties of salami, a DOP or IGP seal can help narrow the field, especially if you're not yet familiar with the producers or vendors.

Learning to read the codes and labels in Roman markets won't turn you into an expert overnight, but it will give you a much better sense of what you're buying and where it comes from. Combine that knowledge with a little curiosity and a few good questions, and you'll start to earn the trust of vendors, who, over time, will begin steering you toward their best goods without you having to ask.

RESOURCES

Ingredients

Buon'Italia
buonitalia.com
For flours, pasta, salted anchovies, cheese, and assorted Italian specialties.

Caputo Brothers Creamery
caputobrotherscreamery.com
For mozzarella, ricotta, provolone, and ricotta salata made in southwestern Pennsylvania.

Di Bruno Brothers
dibruno.com
For Pecorino Romano, Parmigiano-Reggiano, sheep's-milk ricotta, mozzarella, and other Italian cheese.

Formaggio Kitchen
formaggiokitchen.com
For cheeses, pastas, olive oils, and other specialty products.

Fra' Mani
framani.com
Paul Bertolli's stellar salumi company for guanciale.

Gustiamo
gustiamo.com
Bronx-based importer of real Italian ingredients made ethically. It's my go-to for excellent pantry items.

King Arthur Flour
kingarthurflour.com
For quality flours.

La Salumina
lasaluminany.com
All-natural, artisan guanciale and other cured meats and sausages.

Pastaio Via Corta
pastaioviacorta.com
Glouchester, MA-based fresh and dried pasta maker selling exquisite Italian pantry items and wines from Lazio.

Rancho Gordo
ranchogordo.com
For borlotti (cranberry beans).

Zingerman's
zingermans.com
For a huge variety of Italian specialty products.

Tools

Cambro
cambro.com
For dough proofing containers.

Baking Steel
bakingsteel.com
For baking steels and pizza tools.

Davide Occhi
davide.occhi@tin.it
For handmade rolling pins.

Fantes
fantes.com
For pasta and pizza tools.

QB Cucina
qbcucina.com
For pasta tools.

PARLA TOURS
Want to get even deeper into the history and food of Rome? Join me for a tour! On my site you'll find a range of experiences led by me and my team of incredible guides, each with at least a decade of work in food and beverage. We offer private culinary walking tours through Rome's neighborhoods, wine tastings that highlight both classic and natural producers, hands-on cooking classes, and excursions to vineyards and cheesemakers just outside the city. These are not off-the-shelf tours. They are designed to immerse you in Rome's food culture and to connect you to the people who make our food. Browse the full lineup and book directly through my website katieparla.com.

ACKNOWLEDGMENTS

This book is dedicated to my mom, Joj, who scrimped and saved to send me to Italy for that first trip back in the '90s, and who only panicked a little when I announced my move to Italy as a high school sophomore.

This book was absolutely a team effort. Ed Anderson's photographs bring Rome's grit and beauty into focus. Ian Dingman's design raises the bar yet again for what's possible when the publisher lets creative genius run wild. Heather Rodino's edits kept the prose sharp, and Ken DellaPenta's meticulous index makes the whole thing navigable.

None of this would exist without the generosity of the people who welcomed me into their kitchens, bakeries, enoteche, dining rooms, and cocktail bars. Rome is endlessly complicated and always changing, and having the chance to cook, eat, and talk with those who keep its food culture alive was a gift. I am especially grateful to the Gargioli family of Armando al Pantheon; Leonardo Vignoli and Maria Pia Cicconi at Cesare al Casaletto; the Roscioli family; Sarah Cicolini at Santo Palato; chef Nabil Hadj Hassen at Baccano; Andrea D'Alfonsi, Umberto Mussato, and everyone at Piatto Romano; Gabriele Bonci and the crews at Panificio Bonci and Pizzarium; Antonio Cossu of Latteria; Patrizia and Paola Persiani and Giuseppe Ruzzettu of Tavernaccia da Bruno; Stefano Callegari of Trapizzino and Romanè; Fabrizio Roscioli and the whole Forno Campo de' Fiori team; Francesca Barreca and Marco Baccanelli of Mazzo; Il Vinaietto; Massimo Crippa at L'Angolo Divino; Sora Lella; Da Corrado; Tram Tram; Pastificio Mauro Secondi; Trecca; Al Moro; The Jerry Thomas Bar Room; Sami El Sabawy at A Rota; Ale Ruver of Ruver Taglia Frazionata; Forno Colapicchioni; Eroi della Pizza; Artenio; Boccione; the winemakers of Icaro; Matteo Zed and the crew at The Court; and Pizzeria Ostiense. Your time, trust, and generosity made this project possible.

The wardrobe was by Jessica Harris, whom I first met as a student in Rome back in college. She dreamed up Leopardessa originals and paired them with loaned and gifted pieces from Repe, Ioselliani, AS Roma, and Miss Sunshine, making me look like an extremely fashionable adult human for once. Additional wardrobe came from Pezzi Roma.

Dario Polani, aka the Roman Baker, generously shared his ciambelline al vino recipe. *Daje.*

Thanks also to Mattia Gandini for support during the shoot, Lydia O'Brien for a first read, and to the Parla Tours guides for pressing pause on their jobs as the city's finest culinary ambassadors to show up and eat and drink for the camera.

Grazie to Roberto, who endures my endless editing agita without a single complaint.

Finally, thank you to you, the reader. This is something like my fortieth book, but the third to be published under Parla Publishing, a project I founded to create books on food and culture outside the limits of traditional publishing. Your support makes it possible for me to share Rome in my own way, on my own terms, with a book that was independently financed, published, and 100% made in Italy.

A

abbacchio. *See* lamb
Abdelkader, Nader, 334
Agretti all'Agro, 236
Agrippa, Marcus, 307
Ai Marmi, 251, 329
Ajo, Ojo, e Peperoncino, 159
Alaric, 29
Alfredo alla Scrofa, 60, 134, 160
almonds
    Pangiallo, 299
    Pizza Ebraica, 283
Al Moro, 93, 107, 131
Al Settimo Gelo, 337
Amerina, 334–35
anchovies, 14
    Abbacchio alla Romana, 204
    Fiori di Zucca, 74
    Insalata di Misticanza con Salsa
       di Alici e Sommacco, 218
    Lingua in Salsa Verde, 179
    Lumache alla Romana, 93
    Mozzarella in Carrozza, 88–89
    Pinsa, 277–78
    Pizza Tonda Romana, 251–54
    Puntarelle alla Romana, 226
    Spaghettoni Burro e Alici, 152
    Vitello Tonnato, 94
Angelucci, Paolo, 334
L'Angolo Divino, 316, 317
Antico Caffè Greco, 44, 310
Antico Forno Roscioli, 8, 242, 328,
    333
Antonelli, Daniele, 336
Apicius, 27, 37, 299
Apuleius, 231
Aqia, 328
aqueducts, 42, 307–8
Armando al Pantheon, 131, 139, 159,
    293, 324
Armando's, 57
Armellini, Carlo, 47
Arnesano, Francesco, 330
A Rota, 78, 251, 329
artichokes, 15
    Carciofi alla Giudia, 86
    Carciofi alla Romana, 229
    cleaning and trimming, 75, 76–77
    Frittata ai Carciofi, 75

    Pinsa, 277–78
    Vignarola, 211
Artisan, 321
Artusi, Pellegrino, 52
Artusio, Roberto, 319
Augustus, Emperor, 21, 27, 36, 59,
    187, 255
Aurelian, Emperor, 255

B

Baccalà alla Romana, 182
Baccannelli, Marco, 326
Baccano, 107, 121, 326
Bacchus, 314
bakeries, 66, 332–34
Barreca, Francesca, 326
Bastianich, Joe, 191
beans, 16, 213. *See also* chickpeas
    Fagioli con le Cotiche, 212
    Fagioli Corallo al Pomodoro, 225
    Pasta e Fagioli, 118
    Vignarola, 211
beef. *See also* oxtail
    Cannelloni di Carne, 147–48
    Garofolato, 173
    Gnocchi al Ragù, 137
    Involtini alla Romana, 194
    Lasagna della Domenica, 149–51
    Lingua in Salsa Verde, 179
    Picchiapò, 165
    Polpette di Bollito, 73
    Ragù di Carne, 151
    Straccetti con le Zucchine, 186
    Supplì al Telefono, 80–81
    Trippa alla Romana, 201
    Zucchine Ripiene alla Romana,
       202
beer, 321
Belli, Giuseppe Gioacchino, 45
Beppe e I Suoi Formaggi, 343
Bernabei, Vitaliano, 198
Besciamella, 148
Bezzera, Luigi, 310
Bialetti, Alfonso, 310
Biga, 271
Birgitta, Saint, 34
Birra Più, 321
Boccione, 249, 283, 287, 289,
    335–36
bombolotti, 105
Bonci, Gabriele, 66, 68, 156, 263,
    330, 333, 334
Bonelli, Patrizio, 325
Boni, Ada, 52–53, 80, 107

Bonilli, Stefano, 64
Borghese, Camillo, 46
Borriello, Pasquale, 343
Bottega Liberati, 68, 183, 342
Bourdain, Anthony, 324
Bramante, 37
bread. *See also* pizza; sandwiches
    bakeries, 66, 332–34
    Pane Casereccio, 270
    rosette, 279
    tips for, 241
Bronté, Patricia, 57
bucatini, 105
Bugiada, Cristian, 319
Burghy, 191
butchers, 183, 341–42

C

cafeterias, 334–35
Caffè Merenda, 336
Caffè Shakerato, 303, 311
Calapicchioni, Angelo, 299
Callegari, Stefano, 65, 68, 156, 193,
    256, 335
Callixtus III, Pope, 35
Camerucci family, 326
camion bars, 99
Campo de' Fiori, 35, 340
Cannelloni di Carne, 147–48
cannolicchi, 105
    Pasta e Ceci, 154
    Pasta e Fagioli, 118
    Pasta e Lenticchie, 136
Canova, Antonio, 46
carbonara, 57
    Spaghetti alla Carbonara, 107
    Supplì alla Carbonara, 96
Carciofi alla Giudia, 86
Carciofi alla Romana, 229
Caroselli, Rocco, 317
Carpineti, Marco, 313, 315
Casa Manfredi, 336
Castagnole, 300
Castelli family, 249, 289
Castelli Forni, 249
Cato the Elder, 21
Cavour, Count, 47
Centrale del Latte di Roma, 305
C'è Pasta e Pasta, 335
Cernilli, Daniele, 64
Cesare al Casaletto, 78, 112, 114,
    165, 190, 304, 324
Cesare al Pellegrino, 324
Charles V, Emperor, 37

Checchino dal 1887, 173, 331
cheese, 342–43. *See also
  individual cheeses*
cherries
  Torta di Ricotta e Visciole, 287
chestnuts
  Montblanc, 290
chicken
  Fettuccine con le Rigaglie di
    Pollo, 139
  Pollo alla Cacciatora, 193
chickpeas, 16, 154
  Pasta e Ceci, 154
chicories, 15, 226
Chigi, Agostino, 35, 231
chocolate, 335–36
  Pangiallo, 299
I Ciacca, 313
Ciambelline al Vino, 297
Cicconi, Maria Pia, 324
Cicolini, Sarah, 121, 327
cioccolaterie, 335–36
Ciolli, Damiano, 313, 315
Claudius, Emperor, 26
Clement VII, Pope, 37
Cleopatra, 21
Clooney, George, 311
Coccia, Enzo, 332
cocktail bars, 66, 319–20
Coda alla Vaccinara, 169–70
coffee, 66, 308, 310–12
  Caffè Shakerato, 303, 311
Colapicchioni, Angelo, 333
Colline Emiliane, 323, 326
Columella, 27
Commodus, Emperor, 255
Concia, 84
Constantine, Emperor, 31
cookies
  Ciambelline al Vino, 297
Coratella, 197
corn
  Insalata di Riso, 216
Costantini, Innocenzo, 305
Cracco, Carlo, 121
Cremonini family, 191
Crostino, 265
cucina povera, 217
cuttlefish
  Seppie con Piselli in Umido, 174

D

Da Corrado, 136, 317, 335
D'Alfonsi, Andrea, 218, 325

Da Michele, 327
Dandini, Arcangelo, 80, 205, 335
Dar Filettaro di Santa Barbara, 78
da Sangallo, Antonio, the Younger,
  39
De Sica, Vittorio, 60
desserts
  Castagnole, 300
  Ciambelline al Vino, 297
  Frappe Fritte, 294
  Maritozzi, 284–85
  Montblanc, 290
  Pangiallo, 299
  Panna Cotta, 304
  Pere Cotte, 293
  Pizza Ebraica, 283
  Torta di Ricotta e Visciole, 287
  Zabaione con Fragoline di Bosco,
    288
Detvaj, Juraj, 339
diaconia, 33
Di Lelio, Alfredo, 160
Di Marco, Corrado, 277
di Pomponio, Ermano, 338
ditalini
  Pasta e Fagioli, 118
Di Vittorio, Rosanna, 326
Domitian, Emperor, 27, 36
Dressel, Heinrich, 91
Drink Kong, 319, 320

E

East African communities, 55
Eataly, 49, 68
Egeria Spring, 309
eggplant
  Parmigiana di Melanzane, 100
eggs, 16, 343
  Abbacchio Brodettato, 188
  Frittata ai Carciofi, 75
  Insalata di Riso, 216
  in pasta, 110
  Spaghetti alla Carbonara, 107
  Stracciatella, 131
  Supplì alla Carbonara, 96
  Uova Sode, 90
L'Elementare, 330
Emporio delle Spezie, 218
enoteche, 316–17
Enquatatash, 328
equipment, 12, 344
Ersoch, Gioacchino, 183
Esposito family, 73, 335
Eurysaces, Marcus Vergilius, 255, 267

F

Fagioli con le Cotiche, 212
Fagioli Corallo al Pomodoro, 225
Fairbanks, Douglas, 160
Farinetti, Oscar, 68
farmers' markets, 339, 340
Faro, 66, 311
Fatamorgana, 337
Fegatelli di Maiale, 190
Ferrara, Stefano, 338
fettuccine, 105
  Fettuccine al Sugo di Coda, 132
  Fettuccine Burro e Parmigiano,
    160
  Fettuccine con le Rigaglie di
    Pollo, 139
  Fresh Fettuccine, 134
  Pasta con Broccoli, 140
figs
  Pizza con Ricotta, Fichi, e Miele,
    265
  Prosciutto e Fichi, 98
Filetti di Baccalà, 78
Fiorano, 313
Fior di Luna, 337–38
Fiori di Zucca, 74
fish, 187, 327, 342–43
  Baccalà alla Romana, 182
  Filetti di Baccalà, 78
  Minestra di Broccoli e Arzilla, 125
  -mongers, 342
  restaurants, 327–28
  Vitello Tonnato, 94
Fiumanó, Mirella, 337
flour
  measuring, 17, 241
  for pasta, 111
Food and Agriculture Organization
  (FAO), 56, 58–59, 342
food labels, decoding, 342–43
Formaessenza, 338
La Formaggeria, 343
Forme, 343
forni, 332–34
Forno Angelo Colapicchioni, 279,
  299, 333
Forno Campo de' Fiori, 242, 333
Forum Boarium, 22, 23
Forum Holitorium, 23
Frappe Fritte, 294
Freni e Frizioni, 319
Friggitelli, 220
Frittata ai Carciofi, 75
Frumentario, 330

G

Gambero Rosso, 62, 64
Gargioli family, 324
Garibaldi, Giuseppe, 47
garlic, 13
Garofolato, 173
garum, 205
La Gatta Mangiona, 330
Gelateria dei Gracchi, 338
Gelateria del Teatro, 338
Gelateria Gori, 338
gelato, 336–39
Giovale, Beppe, 343
Giovanni da Udine, 231
gnocchi, 105
    Fresh Gnocchi di Patate, 122
    Gnocchi all'Amatriciana, 120–21
    Gnocchi al Ragù, 137
    Gnocchi Fritti Cacio e Pepe, 114
Il Goccetto, 90, 316, 317
Gori family, 338, 339
La Gourmandise, 338
Gracchus, Gaius and Tiberius, 21, 255
grain dole, 29, 255
Greco, Emanuele, 91
greens. *See also individual greens*
    Agretti all'Agro, 236
    Insalata di Misticanza con Salsa di Alici e Sommacco, 218
    Verdure Ripassate in Padella, 233
Gregory the Great, Pope, 32
Gregory VII, Pope, 34
guanciale, 14
    Gnocchi all'Amatriciana, 120–21
    Mezze Maniche alla Gricia con Zucchine, 128
    Pasta e Fagioli, 118
    Pizza Tonda Romana, 251–54
    Spaghetti alla Carbonara, 107
    Spaghetti alla Gricia, 128
    Vignarola, 211
guilds, 38

H

ham. *See* prosciutto and ham
hardware stores, 155
Hassen, Nabil Hadj, 121, 326
hazelnuts
    Ciambelline al Vino, 297
herbs, 13
Horace, 154
Horrea Piperataria, 31
Hosteria Grappolo d'Oro, 324–25

hot dogs
    Insalata di Riso, 216
Hua, Ge Jing, 328

I

IGIO, 328
Imperial Fora, 36
Insalata di Misticanza con Salsa di Alici e Sommacco, 218
Insalata di Riso, 216
International Fund for Agricultural Development (IFAD), 59
Involtini alla Romana, 194
Issa, Luca, 330

J

El Jalapeño, 328
Jerry Thomas Speakeasy (Jerry Thomas Project), 66, 319
Jewish Ghetto, 39, 40–41, 187, 289
Johnny's Off License, 321
Julius Caesar, 21, 36, 255
Jungle Juice, 321
Justinian, Emperor, 32
Juvenal, 255

K

Keys, Ancel, 56
Koolhaas, Rem, 237
Kull, Joy, 313

L

lamb
    abbacchio, 16
    Abbacchio alla Romana, 204
    Abbacchio a Scottadito, 180
    Abbacchio Brodettato, 188
    Abbacchio Panato, 166
    Coratella, 197
lasagna, 105, 149
    Lasagna della Domenica, 149–51
    Mattonelle di Lasagna, 96
Latta, 319, 320
legumes, 16, 213. *See also individual legumes*
lentils, 16, 136
    Pasta e Lenticchie, 136
Leo X, Pope, 35
Leuci, Leonardo, 319
Liberati, Roberto, 68
Lievito Madre, 257
Lievito Pizza e Pane, 330
Limentani family, 283, 289, 336
Lingua in Salsa Verde, 179

Lingue di Pizza, 268–69
Loreti, Francesco, 343
Luciani, Teresa, 324
Ludovisi, Prince Alberico Boncompagni, 313
Lumache alla Romana, 93
Luther, Martin, 37

M

macellai, 341–42
Ma Che Siete Venuti a Fà, 321
El Maíz, 328
Maltagliati, 134
    Pasta e Ceci, 154
    Pasta e Fagioli, 118
    Pasta e Lenticchie, 136
Maoloni, Piergiorgio, 64
Marchesi, Gualtiero, 191
Mariani, Elio, 173
Maritozzi, 284–85
Mark Antony, 21
Martial, 154
Martino, Maestro, 37
Martin V, Pope, 34
Mattonelle di Lasagna, 96
Maxentius, Emperor, 31
Mazzini, Giuseppe, 47
Mazzo, 326
McDonald's, 62, 191
measuring, 17
mercati, 339–41
Mercati Generali, 49, 237, 339
Mercato Campo Marzio, 341
Mercato Centrale, 68
Mercato di Campagna Amica del Circo Massimo, 339, 340
Mercato di Piazza Epiro, 340–41
Mercato di San Giovanni di Dio, 340
Mercato Nomentano, 340
Mercato San Cosimato, 341
Mercato Trionfale, 339, 341
mezze maniche, 105
    Mezze Maniche alla Gricia con Zucchine, 128
Michelangelo, 37, 39
Minestra di Broccoli e Arzilla, 125
Minestrone, 144
mint, 13
Montano, Umberto, 68
Montblanc, 290
Monte dei Cocci (Monte Testaccio), 91, 183, 33130
Mordi e Vai, 335
Moriondo e Gariglio, 336

mortadella
  Pizza con la Mortazza, 244
mozzarella
  Crostino, 265
  Fiori di Zucca, 74
  Mozzarella in Carrozza, 88–89
  Parmigiana di Melanzane, 100
  Parmigiana di Zucchine, 100
  Pinsa, 277–78
  Pizza con Patate e Mozzarella, 265
  Pizza Margherita Ripiena, 265
  Pizza Tonda Romana, 251–54
  Supplì al Telefono, 80–81
Mrgda, 328
mushrooms
  Pinsa, 277–78
  Tagliolini ai Funghi Porcini, 143
Mussolini, Benito, 22, 47, 48, 50–51, 53, 54, 59, 310

N

Napoleon, 45–46, 47
Nathan, Ernesto, 201, 237, 305
Nero, Emperor, 27
Nerva, Emperor, 36, 334
Nespresso, 310
Neve di Latte, 338
Nicholas V, Pope, 307
Norcino Bernabei, 198
Noro, Carlo, 313, 315
Numa Pompilius, 309
Nuovo Mercato di Testaccio, 339, 341
Nuovo Mercato Esquilino, 341

O

Occhipinti, Andrea, 313, 315
Odoacer, 32
offal, 16
olive oil, 14–15
Osteria Bonelli, 325
osterie, 63
Ostia Antica, 26
Otaleg!, 338–39
ovens, 249
oxtail, 16
  Coda alla Vaccinara, 169–70
  Fettuccine al Sugo di Coda, 132

P

Palazzo Tronconi, 313, 315
pancetta
  Vignarola, 211

Pane Casereccio, 270
Pangiallo, 299
Panificio Bonci, 66, 68, 198, 242, 249, 284, 333–34
Panna Cotta, 304
Pantanella, Michelangelo, 123
Parlapiano, Antonio, 319
Parmigiana di Melanzane, 100
Parmigiana di Zucchine, 100
Parmigiano-Reggiano, 14
  Cannelloni di Carne, 147–48
  Fettuccine Burro e Parmigiano, 160
  Gnocchi a Ragù, 137
  Lasagna della Domenica, 149–51
  Parmigiana di Melanzane, 100
  Parmigiana di Zucchine, 100
  Stracciatella, 131
  Supplì al Telefono, 80–81
  Tonnarelli Cacio e Pepe, 112
Pasolini, Pier Paolo, 62
pasta. See also individual pastas
  cook times, 17
  dried, 15–16, 105
  eggs in, 110
  flour for, 111
  fresh, 105, 110–11
  portions, 17
  salting water for, 17
Pasta con Broccoli, 140
Pasta e Ceci, 154
Pasta e Fagioli, 118
Pasta e Lenticchie, 136
pasticcerie, 335–36
Patate al Forno, 230
Paul III, Pope, 39
Paul IV, Pope, 39, 40, 187
Paul V, Pope, 308
pears
  Pere Cotte, 293
peas
  Seppie con Piselli in Umido, 174
  Vignarola, 211
Pecorino Romano, 14
  Abbacchio Panato, 166
  Fettuccine al Sugo di Coda, 132
  Fettuccine con le Rigaglie di Pollo, 139
  Gnocchi all'Amatriciana, 120–21
  Gnocchi Fritti Cacio e Pepe, 114
  Mezze Maniche alla Gricia con Zucchine, 128
  Pasta con Broccoli, 140
  Pizza Tonda Romana, 251–54

Polpette di Bollito, 73
Pomodori Ripieni di Riso, 215
Ravioli Cacio e Pepe, 156–57
Rigatoni con la Pajata, 108
Spaghetti alla Carbonara, 107
Spaghetti alla Gricia, 128
Tonnarelli Cacio e Pepe, 112
Trippa alla Romana, 201
Verdure Gratinate, 224
Zucchine Ripiene alla Romana, 202
pepper, black, 13, 27, 29, 31
peppers
  Ajo, Ojo, e Peperoncino, 159
  Friggitelli, 220
  peperoncini, 15
Percassi, Antonio, 312
Pere Cotte, 293
Persiani, Bruno, 325
Petrini, Carlo, 64, 191
Petronius, 27
Petto di Vitello alla Fornara, 206
Piatti del Buon Ricordo, 331
Piatto Romano, 143, 197, 218, 325
Picchiapò, 165
Il Piccolo, 316, 317
Piccolo Buco, 330
Pickford, Mary, 160
Pignotta family, 327
pine nuts
  Baccalà alla Romana, 182
  Coda alla Vaccinara, 169–70
  Pangiallo, 299
  Pizza Ebraica, 283
  toasting, 182
Pinsa, 277–78
Pipero, 107
pistachios
  Pangiallo, 299
Pistolesi, Patrick, 320
Pius V, Pope, 39
Pius VI, Pope, 45
Pius IX, Pope, 47
pizza, 329
  Crostino, 265
  Lingue di Pizza, 268–69
  Pinsa, 277–78
  Pizza Bianca, 242–47
  Pizza con la Mortazza, 244
  Pizza con Patate e Mozzarella, 265
  Pizza con Ricotta, Fichi, e Miele, 265
  Pizza Ebraica, 283

Pizza in Teglia alla Bonci, 263–65
Pizza Margherita Ripiena, 265
Pizza Rossa, 244
Pizza Tonda Romana, 251–54
Pizzette di Sfoglia, 273
Pizzette Rosse, 274
Scrocchia, 258
tips for, 241
Trapizzini, 256–57
Pizza Nader, 334
Pizzarium, 66, 94, 249, 263, 329, 330, 332, 333
pizzerie, 329–30, 332
Pliny the Elder, 13, 27, 154
Pollo alla Cacciatora, 193
Polpette di Bollito, 73
Pomodori a Mezzo, 234
Pomodori Ripieni di Riso, 215
Porchetta, 198
pork. See also pancetta; prosciutto and ham
Fagioli con le Cotiche, 212
Fegatelli di Maiale, 190
Porchetta, 198
Portico d'Ottavia, 187
Porto Fluviale, 48–49
potatoes, 230
Fresh Gnocchi di Patate, 122
Patate al Forno, 230
Pizza con Patate e Mozzarella, 265
Pomodori Ripieni di Riso, 215
La Pratolina, 277
Procoli, Alessandro, 319–20
Proia, Giorgia, 336
prosciutto and ham
Abbacchio Brodettato, 188
Crostino, 265
Involtini alla Romana, 194
Pinsa, 277–78
Prosciutto e Fichi, 98
Saltimbocca alla Romana, 185
prunes
Pere Cotte, 293
puff pastry
Pizzette di Sfoglia, 273
La Punta, 319
puntarelle, 15
preparing, 227
Puntarelle alla Romana, 226

Q

Querini, Pietro, 182
Quintili, Marco, 330

I Quintili, 330
quinto quarto, 16, 217

R

Radicioni, Marco, 338–39
Ragù di Carne, 151
raisins
Baccalà alla Romana, 182
Coda alla Vaccinara, 169–70
Pangiallo, 299
Pizza Ebraica, 283
Raphael, 37, 231
ravioli, 105
Ravioli Cacio e Pepe, 156–57
Reale, Riccardi, 313, 315
Rebel's, 321
Regoli, 284, 336
rice
Insalata di Riso, 216
Pomodori Ripieni di Riso, 215
Supplì al Telefono, 80–81
ricotta, 14
Pizza con Ricotta, Fichi, e Miele, 265
Ravioli Cacio e Pepe, 156–57
Torta di Ricotta e Isciole, 287
rigatoni, 105
Pasta con Broccoli, 140
Rigatoni con la Pajata, 108
ristoranti, 63
Ritual Lab, 321
Rizzo, Mirko, 330
Rodríguez, José Remesal, 91
Romanè, 331
romanesco, 140
Minestra di Broccoli e Arzilla, 125
Pasta con Broccoli, 140
Roman history
Iron Age (1200–509 BCE), 19–20
Republic (509–27 BCE), 20–21
Empire (27 BCE–476 CE), 27, 29–31, 36
Middle Ages (476–1420), 32–34
Renaissance (1420–1527), 34–35, 37, 38
Counter-Reformation (1527–1700), 37, 39, 42
eighteenth century (1700–1798), 44–45
Napoleon (1798–1814), 45–46
Republic to Risorgimento (1814–1922), 47, 50
Fascism (1922–1943), 50–51, 54
postwar (1944–1960), 54, 56, 60, 62

mid-century to modern (1960–2000), 62, 65
contemporary (2000–present), 65–66
Romulus Augustulus, Emperor, 29
Roscioli, Fabrizio, 333
Roscioli, Marco, 333
Roscioli Caffè, 284, 303
rosette, 279
Rossellini, Roberto, 56, 60
Ruver, Alessandro, 332
Ruver Teglia Frazionata, 332
Ruzzettu, Giuseppe, 206, 325

S

Sabawy, Sami El, 329
Sabbatini, Innocenzo, 237
Saffi, Aurelio, 47
salads
Insalata di Misticanza con Salsa di Alici e Sommacco, 218
Insalata di Riso, 216
salt, 13, 17, 61
salt cod
Baccalà alla Romana, 182
Filetti di Baccalà, 78
Saltimbocca alla Romana, 185
Salumeria Roscioli, 107, 326, 327
Salvi, Nicola, 44
sandwiches
Mozzarella in Carrozza, 88–89
Pizza con la Mortazza, 244
Sant'Eustachi, 46, 303, 310
Santilli, Alessandro, 330
Santo Palato, 107, 121, 188, 327
sauces
Besciamella, 148
Ragù di Carne, 151
scamorza
Parmigiana di Melanzane, 100
Parmigiana di Zucchine, 100
Scappi, Bartolomeo, 37, 43
Scrocchia, 258
Secondi, Mauro, 156
Seppie con Piselli in Umido, 174
serrande, painted, 135
Settimio al Pellegrino, 324
shopping, 339–43
Sinosteria, 328
Sixtus IV, Pope, 35, 37
Sixtus V, Pope, 39, 42, 308
skate
Minestra di Broccoli e Arzilla, 125
Slow Food movement, 62, 64, 191

snails
    Lumache alla Romana, 93
Sora Lella, 188
soups
    Minestra di Broccoli e Arzilla, 125
    Minestrone, 144
    Stracciatella, 131
spaghetti, 105
    Ajo, Ojo, e Peperoncino, 159
    Minestra di Broccoli e Arzilla, 125
    Spaghetti alla Carbonara, 107
    Spaghetti alla Gricia, 128
    Supplì alla Carbonara, 96
spaghettoni, 105
    Spaghettoni Burro e Alici, 152
Spagnuolo, Maria Agnese, 337, 339
spices, 27, 31
squash. *See* squash blossoms;
    zucchini
squash blossoms
    Fiori di Zucca, 74
    Pizza Tonda Romana, 251–54
Stadio Olimpico, 99
Starbucks, 311, 312
Straccetti con le Zucchine, 186
Stracciatella, 131
strawberries
    Zabaione con Fragoline di Bosco,
      288
street food, 65–66, 334–35
Suetonious, 27
Supplì (shop), 80
Supplì alla Carbonara, 96
Supplì al Telefono, 80–81
Supplizio, 80, 335

T

Tacitus, 255
Tagliolini, 134
    Tagliolini ai Funghi Porcini, 143
Tavernaccia da Bruno, 206, 325
Tempio di Iside, 327
Terra Terra, 339, 341
Theodoric, 32
Thomas, Jerry, 319
Tiber River, 48
tips, 17
tomatoes
    Baccalà alla Romana, 182
    canned, 15
    Cannelloni di Carne, 147–48
    Coda alla Vaccinara, 169–70
    Fagioli con le Cotiche, 212
    Fagioli Corallo al Pomodoro, 225

Fettuccine al Sugo di Coda, 132
Fettuccine con le Rigaglie di
    Pollo, 139
Garofolato, 173
Gnocchi all'Amatriciana, 120–21
Gnocchi al Ragù, 137
Involtini alla Romana, 194
Lasagna della Domenica, 149–51
Lingue di Pizza, 268–69
Lumache alla Romana, 93
Parmigiana di Melanzane, 100
Parmigiana di Zucchine, 100
Picchiapò, 165
Pinsa, 277–78
Pizza Margherita Ripiena, 265
Pizza Rossa, 244
Pizza Tonda Romana, 251–54
Pizzette di Sfoglia, 273
Pizzette Rosse, 274
Pomodori a Mezzo, 234
Pomodori Ripieni di Riso, 215
Ragù di Carne, 151
Rigatoni con la Pajata, 108
Scrocchia, 258
Seppie con Piselli in Umido, 174
Supplì al Telefono, 80–81
Trippa alla Romana, 201
Zucchine Ripiene alla Romana,
    202
tonnarelli, 105
    Fresh Tonnarelli, 115–17
    Tonnarelli Cacio e Pepe, 112
tools, 12, 344
Torcè, 339
Torcè, Claudio, 337, 338, 339
Torrefazione Giamaica, 303
Torta di Ricotta e Visciole, 287
tours, 344
Trajan, Emperor, 36
Trajan's Markets, 36
Tram Tram, 326
Trapizzini, 256–57
Trapizzino, 68, 193, 335
Trattoria Monti, 323, 326
trattorie, 63, 65, 323–28
Trecastelli, Manuel and Nicolò, 325
Trecca, 325
tripe, 16
Trippa alla Romana, 201
Triticum Micropanificio, 334
tuna
    Vitello Tonnato, 94

U

Uova Sode, 90

V

Varro, 21
veal
    Petto di Vitello alla Fornara, 206
    Rigatoni con la Pajata, 108
    Saltimbocca alla Romana, 185
    Vitello Tonnato, 94
Il Vecchio Poggio, 313, 315
vegetables, 342. *See also*
    individual vegetables
    Minestrone, 144
    Verdure Gratinate, 224
Verdure Gratinate, 224
Verdure Ripassate in Padella, 233
Il Vero Alfredo, 134, 160
Vespasian, Emperor, 36
VICO Pizza & Vino, 332
Victor Emanuele II, King, 47, 50,
    339
Vignarola, 211
Vignoli, Leonardo, 112, 324
Villa Farnesina, 35, 37, 231
La Villana, 313, 315
Il Vinaietto, 90, 316, 317
vinegar, 16
La Visciola, 313, 315
Vitellius, Emperor, 255
Vitello Tonnato, 94

W

walnuts
    Pangiallo, 299
water, 307–8, 309
wine, 311, 313–15
    Ciambelline al Vino, 297
    Pere Cotte, 293
wine bars, 316–17
World Food Programme (WFP), 59

Z

Zabaione con Fragoline di Bosco,
    288
Zazza, Mario, 324
zozzoni, 99
zucchini
    Concia, 84
    Mezze Maniche alla Gricia con
      Zucchine, 128
    Parmigiana di Zucchine, 100
    Straccetti con le Zucchine, 186
    Zucchine Ripiene alla Romana, 202

Library of Congress Control Number: 2025917829
ISBN: 9798986997650

Printed in Italy

Cover and book design by Ian Dingman

Photographs on pages 31, 52, 55, 57, 154, and 205 by
Katie Parla

Photograph on page 54 Italian children eating breakfast
at a Red Cross orphanage in Monte Mario, Rome,
2 July 1945. Gift of Dylan Utley, The National WWII
Museum, 2012.019.248.

Photograph on page 60 Bernardo Bertolucci (left) and
Pier Paolo Pasolini (center) on the set of Accattone,
spring 1961 / Wikimedia Commons / Public Domain

Photograph on page 304 by Ines Glaser

First edition

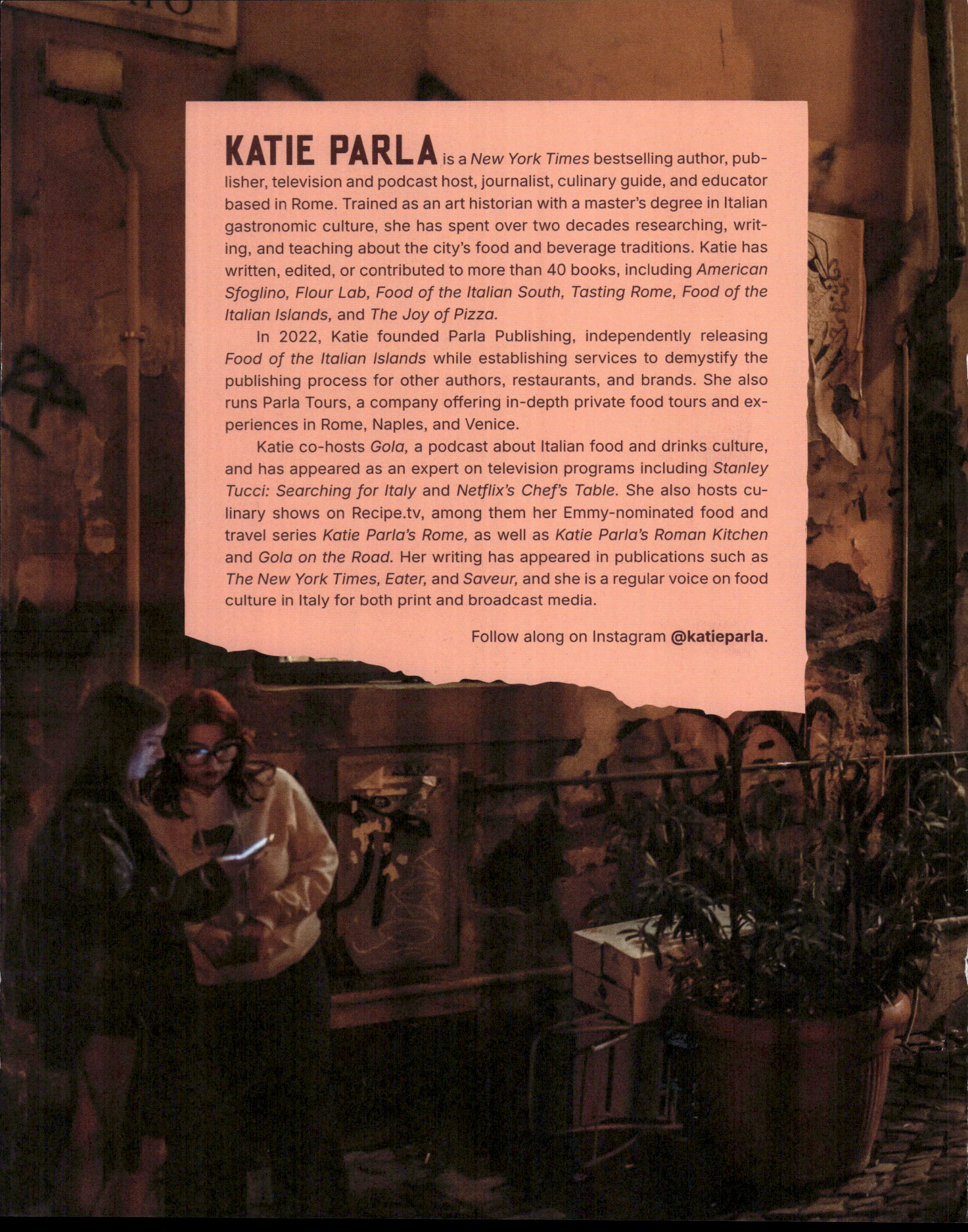

KATIE PARLA is a *New York Times* bestselling author, publisher, television and podcast host, journalist, culinary guide, and educator based in Rome. Trained as an art historian with a master's degree in Italian gastronomic culture, she has spent over two decades researching, writing, and teaching about the city's food and beverage traditions. Katie has written, edited, or contributed to more than 40 books, including *American Sfoglino, Flour Lab, Food of the Italian South, Tasting Rome, Food of the Italian Islands,* and *The Joy of Pizza.*

In 2022, Katie founded Parla Publishing, independently releasing *Food of the Italian Islands* while establishing services to demystify the publishing process for other authors, restaurants, and brands. She also runs Parla Tours, a company offering in-depth private food tours and experiences in Rome, Naples, and Venice.

Katie co-hosts *Gola,* a podcast about Italian food and drinks culture, and has appeared as an expert on television programs including *Stanley Tucci: Searching for Italy* and *Netflix's Chef's Table.* She also hosts culinary shows on Recipe.tv, among them her Emmy-nominated food and travel series *Katie Parla's Rome,* as well as *Katie Parla's Roman Kitchen* and *Gola on the Road.* Her writing has appeared in publications such as *The New York Times, Eater,* and *Saveur,* and she is a regular voice on food culture in Italy for both print and broadcast media.

Follow along on Instagram **@katieparla**.